DOROTHY AND THE WIZARD IN OZ

OZ: DOROTHY & THE WIZARD IN OZ. Contains material originally published in magazine form as DOROTHY & THE WIZARD IN OZ #1-8. First printing 2012. ISBN# 978-0-7851-5554-6. Published by MARVEL WORLDWIDE, INC., a subsidiary of MARVEL ENTERTAINMENT, LLC. OFFICE OF PUBLICATION: 135 West 50th Street, New York, NY 10020. Copyright © 2011 and 2012 Marvel Characters, Inc. All rights reserved. $29.99 per copy in the U.S. and $32.99 in Canada (GST #R127032852); Canadian Agreement #40668537. All characters featured in this issue and the distinctive names and likenesses thereof, and all related indicia are trademarks of Marvel Characters, Inc. No similarity between any of the names, characters, persons, and/or institutions in this magazine with those of any living or dead person or institution is intended, and any such similarity which may exist is purely coincidental. **Printed in the U.S.A.** ALAN FINE, EVP - Office of the President, Marvel Worldwide, Inc. and EVP & CMO Marvel Characters B.V.; DAN BUCKLEY, Publisher & President - Print, Animation & Digital Divisions; JOE QUESADA, Chief Creative Officer; TOM BREVOORT, SVP of Publishing; DAVID BOGART, SVP of Operations & Procurement, Publishing; RUWAN JAYATILLEKE, SVP & Associate Publisher, Publishing; C.B. CEBULSKI, SVP of Creator & Content Development; DAVID GABRIEL, SVP of Publishing Sales & Circulation; MICHAEL PASCIULLO, SVP of Brand Planning & Communications; JIM O'KEEFE, VP of Operations & Logistics; DAN CARR, Executive Director of Publishing Technology; SUSAN CRESPI, Editorial Operations Manager; ALEX MORALES, Publishing Operations Manager; STAN LEE, Chairman Emeritus. For information regarding advertising in Marvel Comics or on Marvel.com, please contact Niza Disla, Director of Marvel Partnerships, at ndisla@marvel.com. For Marvel subscription inquiries, please call 800-217-9158. **Manufactured between 7/16/2012 and 8/27/2012 by R.R. DONNELLEY, INC., SALEM, VA, USA.**

10 9 8 7 6 5 4 3 2 1

DOROTHY AND THE WIZARD IN OZ

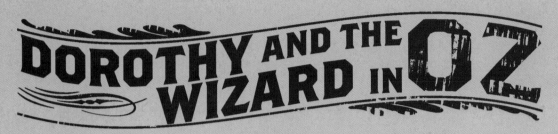

ADAPTED FROM
THE BOOK BY
L. FRANK BAUM

Writer: ERIC SHANOWER
Artist: SKOTTIE YOUNG
Colorist: JEAN-FRANCOIS BEAULIEU
Letterer: JEFF ECKLEBERRY

Assistant Editors: RACHEL PINNELAS & JON MOISAN
Editor: SANA AMANAT

Collection Editor: MARK D. BEAZLEY
Assistant Editors: NELSON RIBEIRO & ALEX STARBUCK
Editor, Special Projects: JENNIFER GRÜNWALD
Senior Editor, Special Projects: JEFF YOUNGQUIST
Senior Vice President of Sales: DAVID GABRIEL
SVP of Brand Planning & Communications: MICHAEL PASCIULLO

Editor in Chief: AXEL ALONSO
Chief Creative Officer: JOE QUESADA
Publisher: DAN BUCKLEY
Executive Producer: ALAN FINE

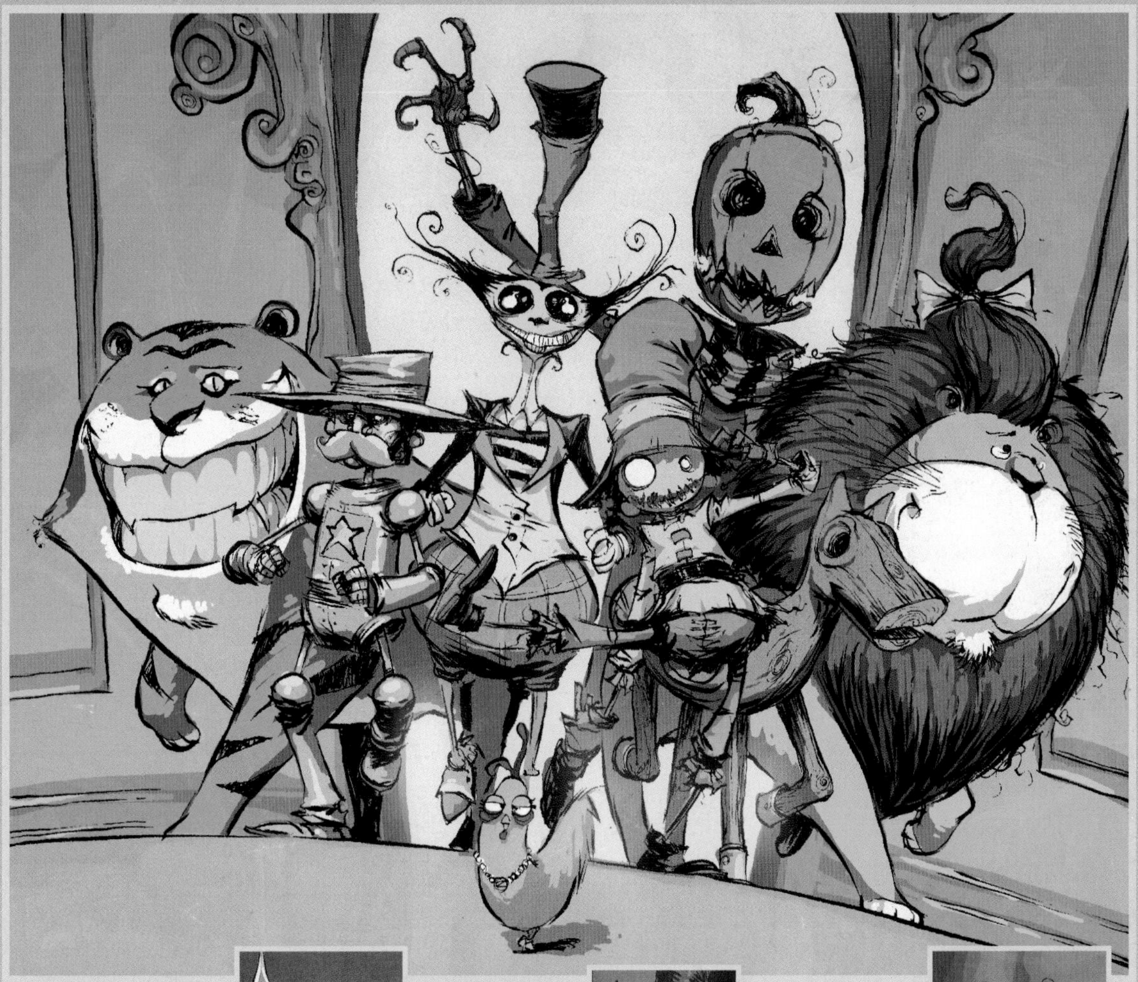
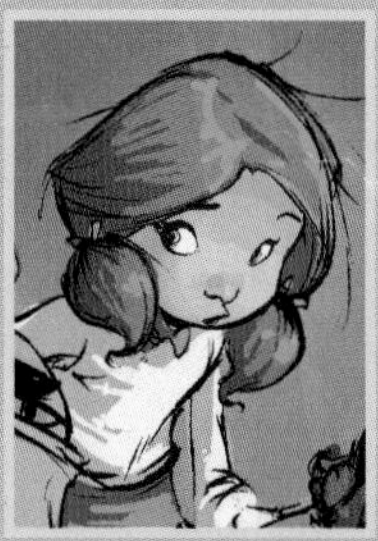
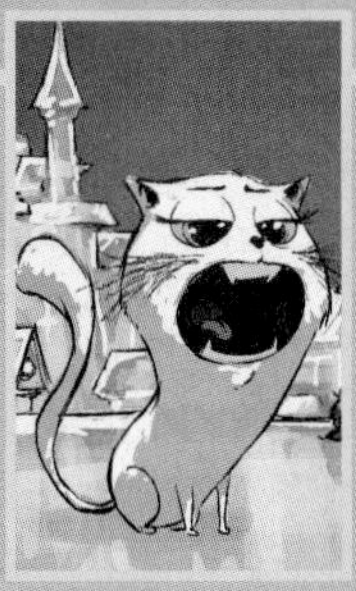
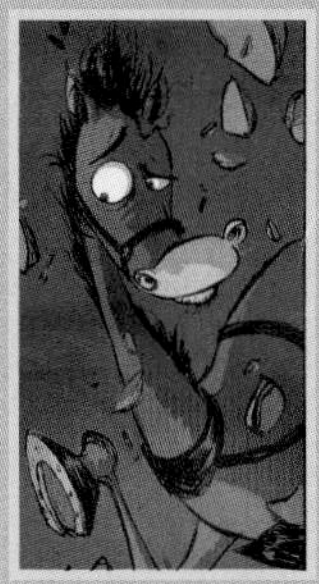
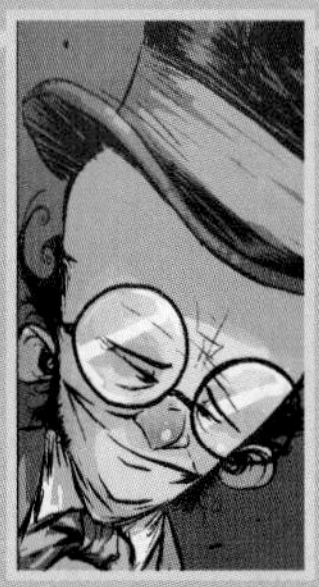
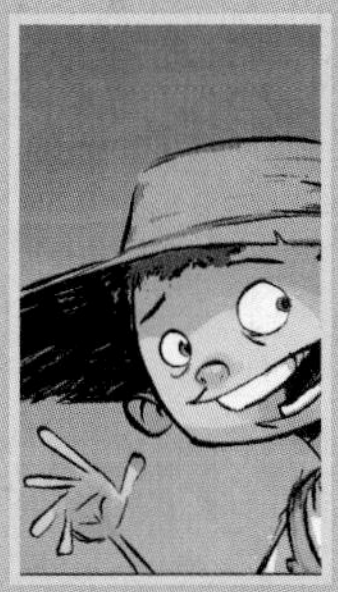
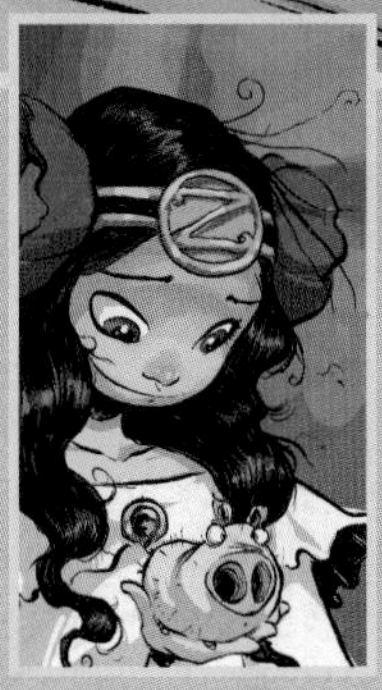

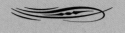

Shake It Up!

The San Francisco earthquake of Wednesday, April 18, 1906, was one of the greatest disasters in U.S. history, shaking California's then-most populous city at an estimated 7.9 on the Richter scale and spawning a massive fire. Thousands of lives were lost and thousands more thrown into disarray. Newspaper headlines of the day trumpeted the news across the globe.

Half a world away on a European tour, Oz author L. Frank Baum must have been aware of news of the earthquake. Using his imaginative powers he was able to find in this great disaster fodder for his 1908 Oz book. Violent acts of nature had been starting points for Dorothy Gale's trips to Oz in his earlier Oz books. *The Wonderful Wizard of Oz* started with a cyclone. Ozma of Oz began with a storm at sea. Why not start the next Oz adventure with an earthquake? So Baum incorporated features of the great San Francisco quake into *Dorothy and the Wizard in Oz*.

As the story begins, Dorothy and her Uncle Henry have returned to the USA after visiting Australia in the previous book in the series, *Ozma of Oz*. On their way home to Kansas, they intend to visit their California relatives, the Hugsons. Uncle Henry has traveled on ahead to Hugson's Ranch, leaving Dorothy in San Francisco to follow later. In the opening scene Dorothy is riding the train from San Francisco to join Uncle Henry.

Baum's story diverges from the actual 1906 earthquake. He writes of tremors all along the train line from San Francisco, tremors that occur throughout the night before the quake. The real 1906 San Francisco earthquake, however, was more localized and there were no tremors to herald its approach. But Baum reproduced one aspect of the quake quite exactly. It struck San Francisco at 5:12 a.m. Baum carefully worked that timing into his story. Dorothy, her cousin Zeb, and their animals are caught in a terrible earthquake shortly after five o'clock in the morning.

(An aside to readers interested in variations on a theme: Gregory Maguire's recent fourth entry in his best-selling Wicked Years series, the excellent *Out of Oz*, begins with another version of Dorothy experiencing the 1906 San Francisco earthquake.)

This massive earthquake is just the beginning of one of the most thrilling of Baum's Oz books. Strange new beings and alarming situations threaten Dorothy and her friends at every turn. They're in almost constant fear for their lives. Small wonder that readers of the Oz series have called *Dorothy and the Wizard in Oz* one of Baum's darkest works.

By this fourth book in the series, Baum had brought back most of the major characters from his first Oz book, *The Wonderful Wizard of Oz*. But two significant omissions remained. One of them reappears in this story. His identity should be no surprise, since he's mentioned in the title—the Wizard of Oz himself. (The other major character who hasn't been back is Toto, Dorothy's dog. But don't worry. We'll see Toto's return in the next book, *The Road to Oz*.)

The last time we saw the Wizard, Dorothy had penetrated his disguise as the great and terrible ruler of Oz and seen him for what he was, a circus performer whose vaunted magical powers consisted merely of ventriloquism, stage illusion, and sleight-of-hand tricks. The Wizard insisted to Dorothy that although he was "a very bad Wizard, I must admit," he was "really a very good man." He promised to transport Dorothy out of the Land of Oz by means of hot air balloon. But Dorothy missed the balloon, and the Wizard sailed off without her.

The Wizard's past didn't sail off with him, however. In the second Oz book, *The Marvelous Land of*

Oz, the great sorceress Glinda discovered information to indicate that the Wizard wasn't as much of "a very good man" as he claimed to be. Soon after his arrival in Oz, the Wizard had delivered Ozma, infant daughter of the King of Oz, to old Mombi the witch. Mombi agreed to hide Ozma, leaving the path clear for the Wizard to claim the crown.

After the Wizard's balloon-borne departure from Oz, Ozma was restored to her rightful place on the throne. In the volume you hold, the Wizard returns to Oz and meets Ozma, the former baby he once betrayed. Their conversation about the past is as intriguing for what it reveals—more of the political history of Oz—as it is for what it avoids—that the Wizard turned Ozma over to a witch. I suspect that Baum, who was never particularly finicky about minor inconsistencies among his Oz books, simply hoped readers would forget the darkest aspects of the Wizard's past.

Whatever the Wizard's past failings may have been, he acts bravely and cleverly throughout the present story, ready to fight to the death to save his life and the lives of his friends. Just as in *The Wonderful Wizard of Oz*, he's quick to fool people and to hide behind illusions. He employs stage trickery as a defense against the heartless Mangaboos and through misguided compassion he perpetrates fraud to protect Dorothy's pet kitten, Eureka. But his use of such humbug is no longer cast in a negative light.

Whatever Baum's intentions may have been in glossing over the Wizard's past, I couldn't ignore that past in adapting this story for the comics medium. During the Wizard's first meeting with post-infant Ozma I made no major changes to Baum's original words, but I chose with care which of his words to use, and I suggested to Skottie Young what to emphasize in his artwork. My intention was to leave the subject of the Wizard's past actions as the elephant in the room. I hope that any reader who cares to listen can hear the elephant's trumpeting.

I did make one significant change to *Dorothy and the Wizard in Oz* in an effort to mitigate a perceived plot weakness that troubles many readers of the book, i. e. Dorothy suddenly remembering that she can contact Ozma for convenient rescue from a tight spot. I introduced this awareness of rescue into the story earlier than Baum introduced it in the original book, and I tried to weave it through the story in a natural manner. I thank J. L. Bell and the contributors to The Ozzy Digest e-mail list for the basic idea. This change also allowed me to reconcile Baum's inconsistencies in Ozma's schedule of watching Dorothy in the Magic Picture.

I know many readers will join me in being overjoyed that the singular and fascinating art of Skottie Young continues to grace the pages of this fourth Oz book from Marvel Comics, along with Jean-Francois Beaulieu's rich coloring and Jeff Eckleberry's efficient lettering. I'm grateful to be part of this creative team and hope for a long association yet to come.

Now hold on to your hats for one wild ride of an Oz story, full of man-eating dragonettes, weird wooden gargoyles, invisible killer bears, and vegetable people who can walk on air. So sit tight, fasten your seatbelts, and try not to get too shaken up.

Eric Shanower
July 2012

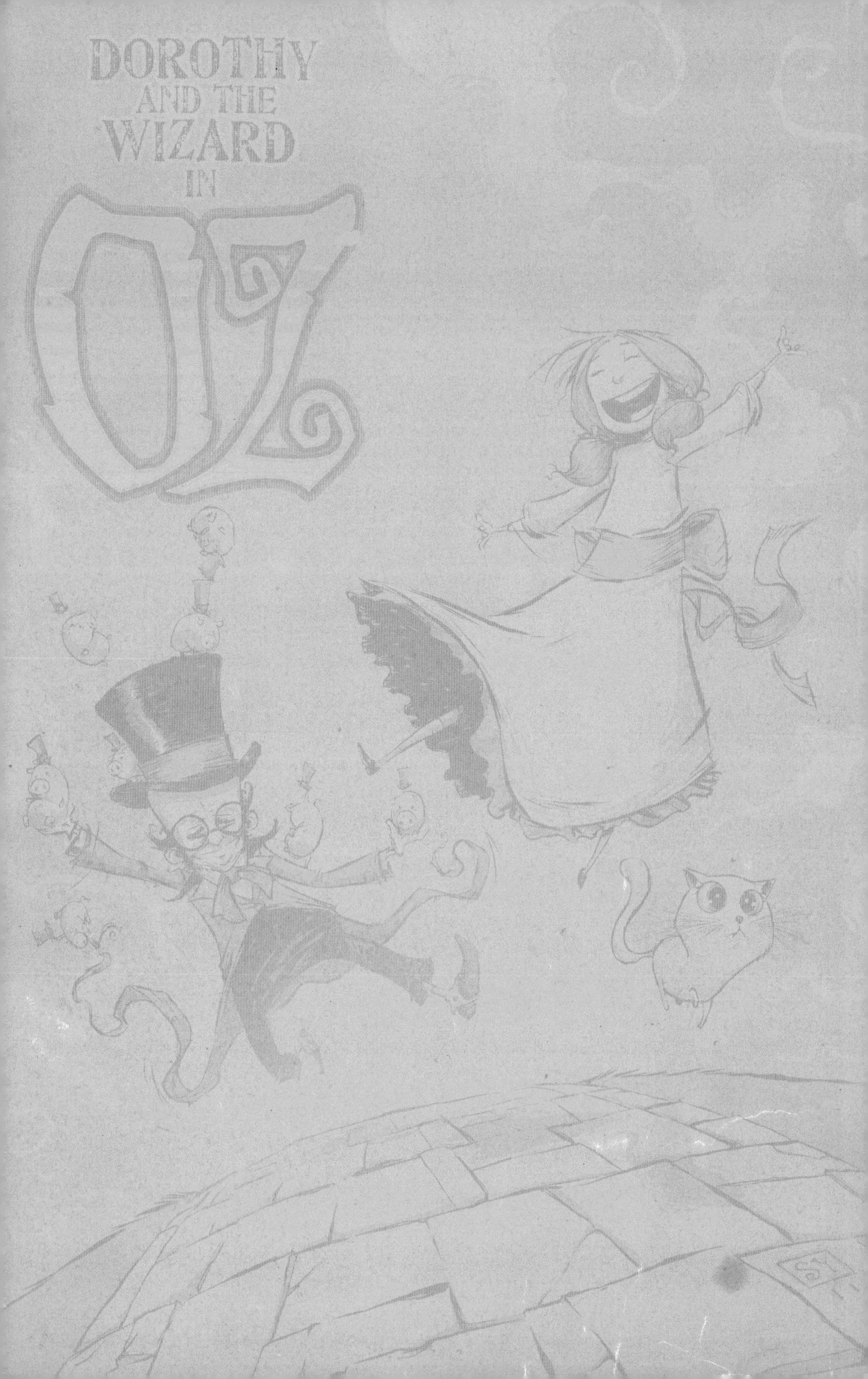
DOROTHY AND THE WIZARD IN OZ

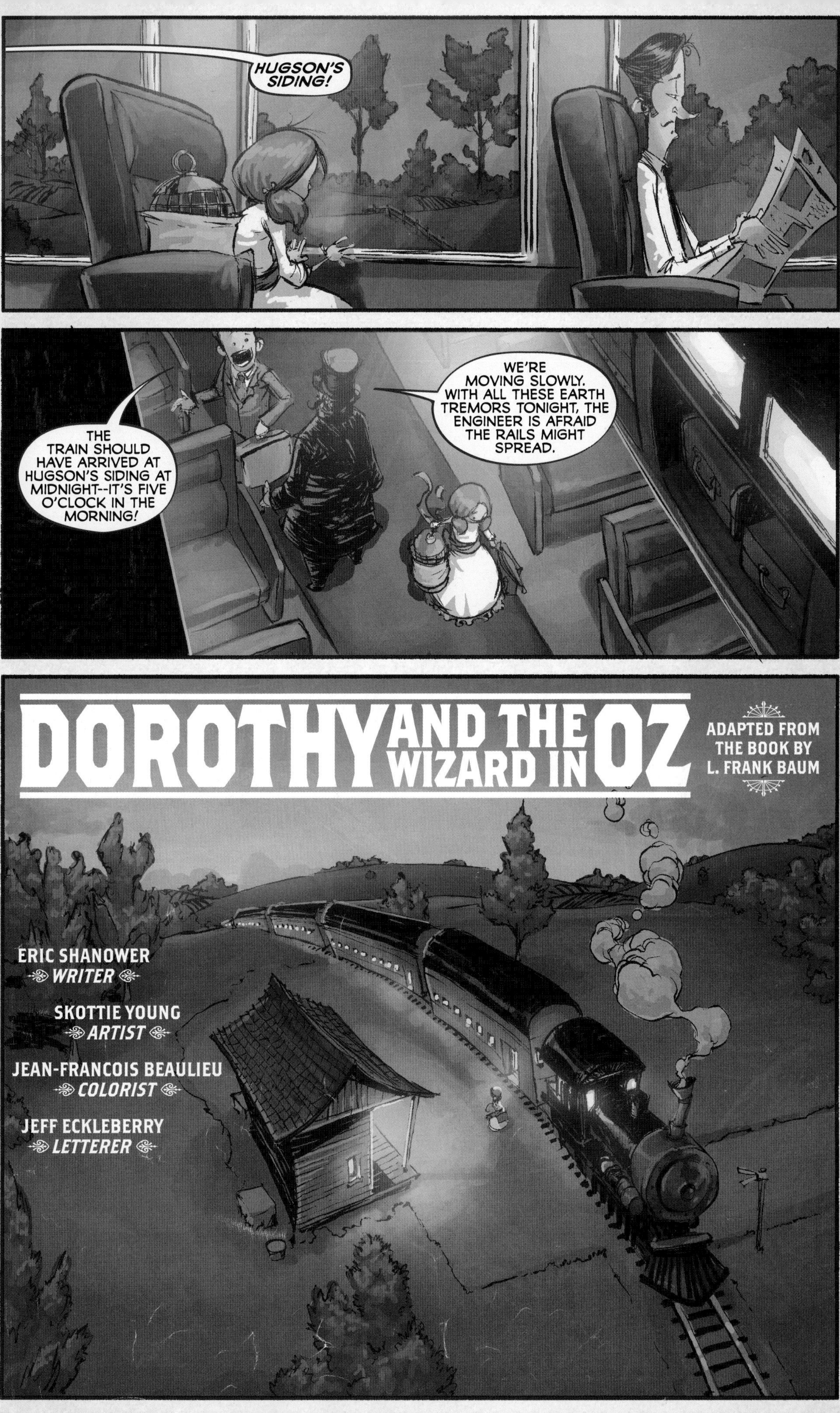
HUGSON'S SIDING!
THE TRAIN SHOULD HAVE ARRIVED AT HUGSON'S SIDING AT MIDNIGHT--IT'S FIVE O'CLOCK IN THE MORNING!
WE'RE MOVING SLOWLY. WITH ALL THESE EARTH TREMORS TONIGHT, THE ENGINEER IS AFRAID THE RAILS MIGHT SPREAD.
DOROTHY AND THE WIZARD IN OZ
ADAPTED FROM THE BOOK BY L. FRANK BAUM
ERIC SHANOWER WRITER
SKOTTIE YOUNG ARTIST
JEAN-FRANCOIS BEAULIEU COLORIST
JEFF ECKLEBERRY LETTERER

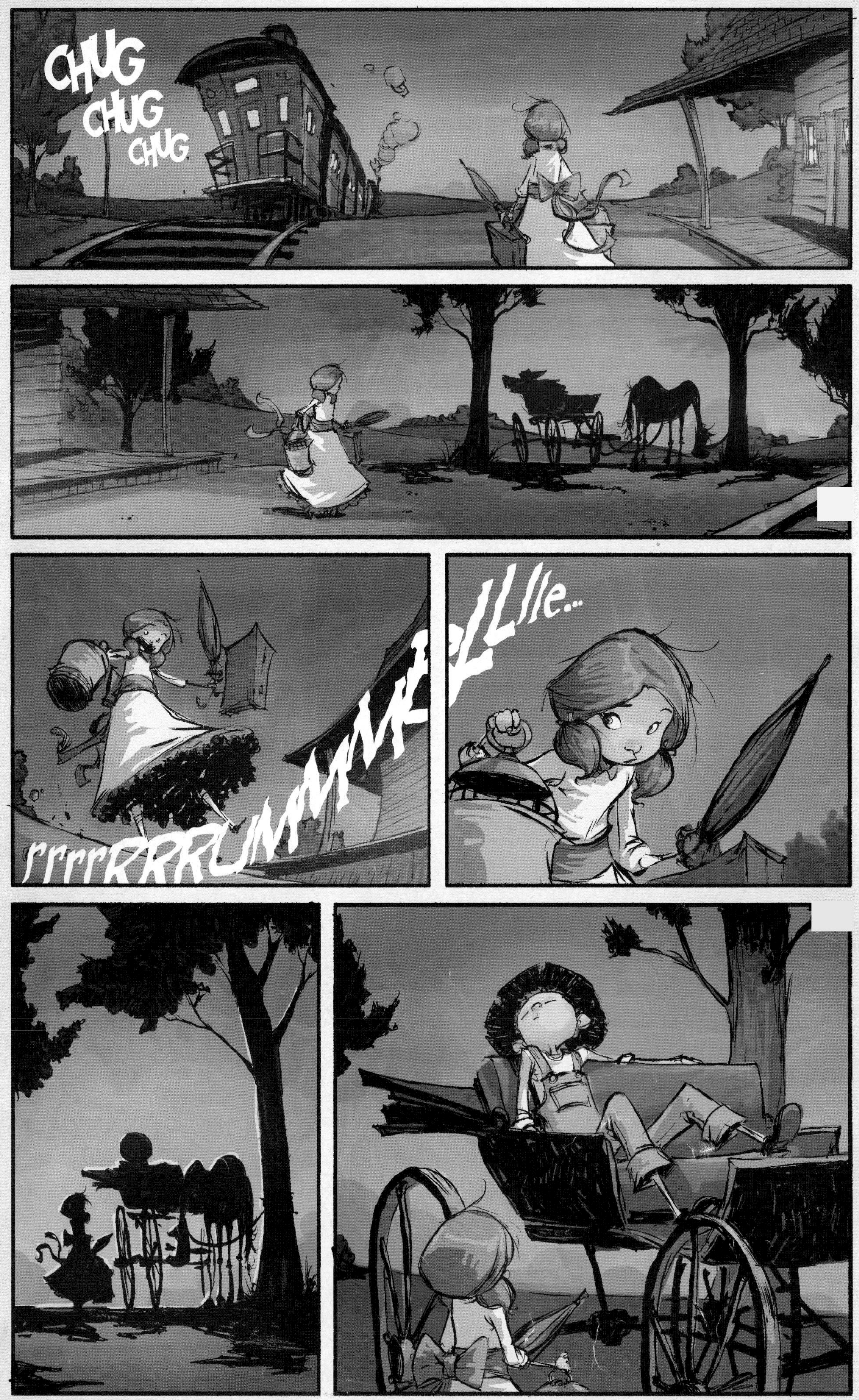
CHUG
CHUG
CHUG
rrrrRRRUMMMMBBLLlle...

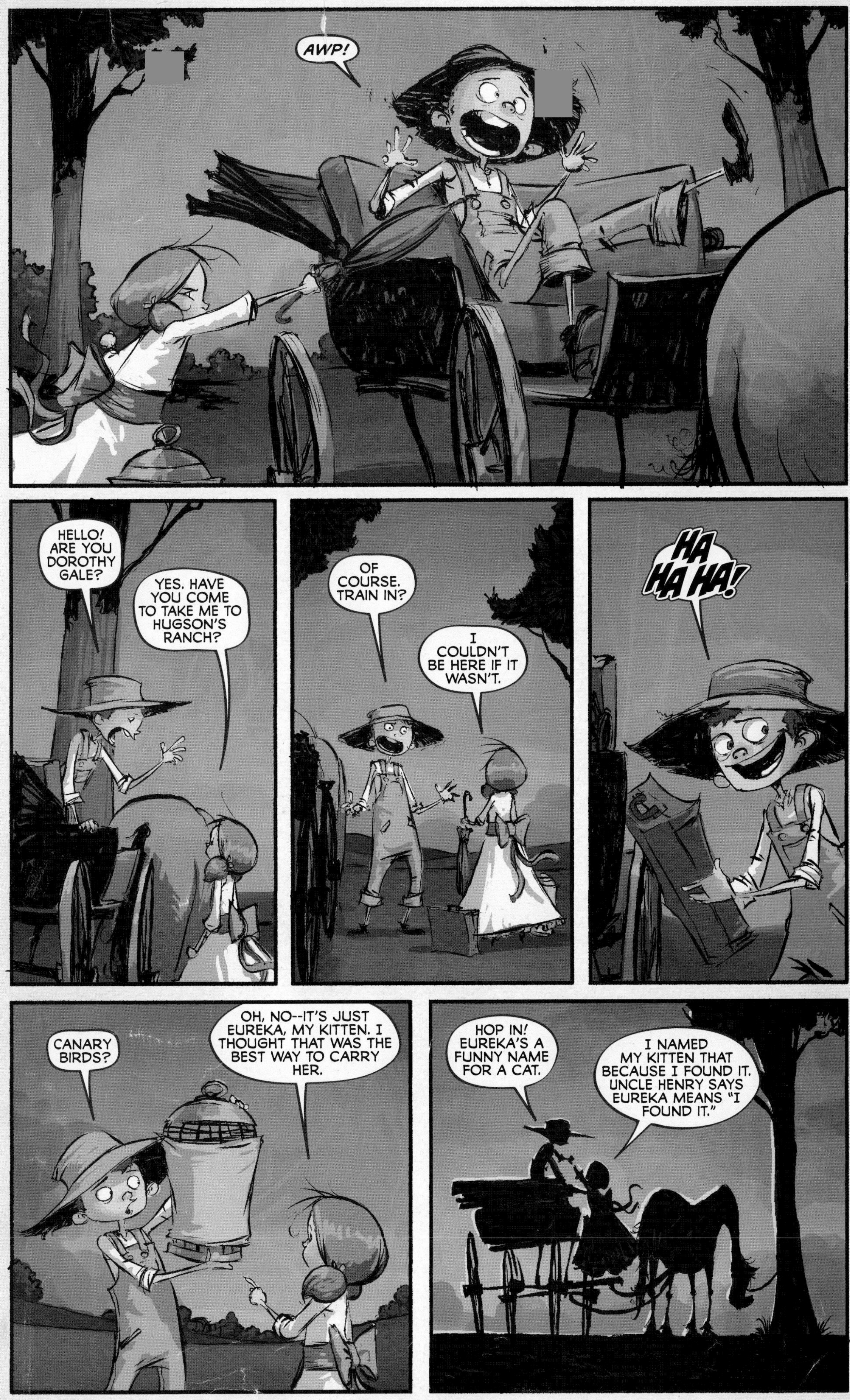
AWP!
HELLO! ARE YOU DOROTHY GALE?
YES. HAVE YOU COME TO TAKE ME TO HUGSON'S RANCH?
OF COURSE. TRAIN IN?
I COULDN'T BE HERE IF IT WASN'T.
HA HA HA!
CANARY BIRDS?
OH, NO--IT'S JUST EUREKA, MY KITTEN. I THOUGHT THAT WAS THE BEST WAY TO CARRY HER.
HOP IN! EUREKA'S A FUNNY NAME FOR A CAT.
I NAMED MY KITTEN THAT BECAUSE I FOUND IT. UNCLE HENRY SAYS EUREKA MEANS "I FOUND IT."

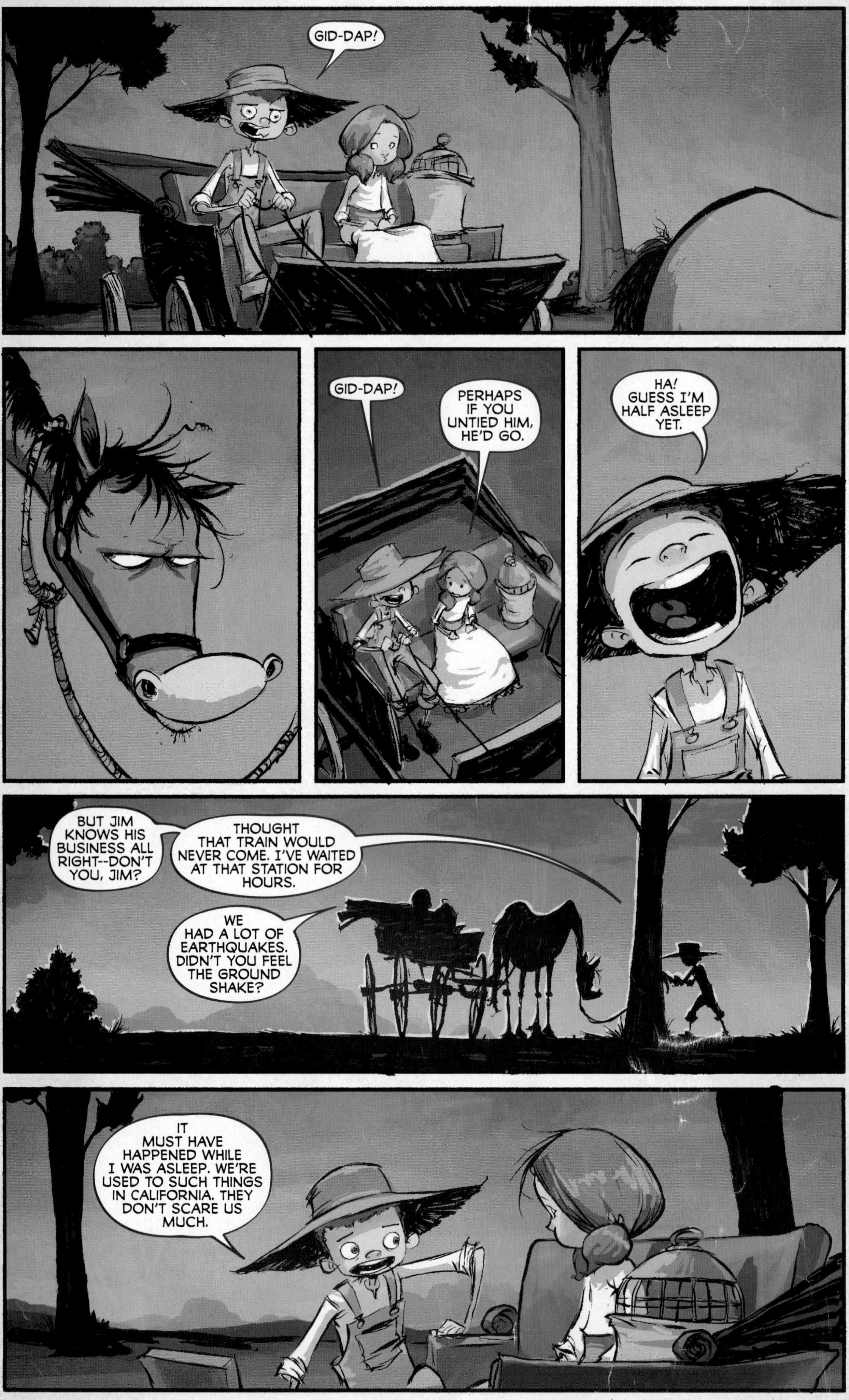
GID-DAP!
GID-DAP!
PERHAPS IF YOU UNTIED HIM, HE'D GO.
HA! GUESS I'M HALF ASLEEP YET.
THOUGHT THAT TRAIN WOULD NEVER COME. I'VE WAITED AT THAT STATION FOR HOURS.
BUT JIM KNOWS HIS BUSINESS ALL RIGHT--DON'T YOU, JIM?
WE HAD A LOT OF EARTHQUAKES. DIDN'T YOU FEEL THE GROUND SHAKE?
IT MUST HAVE HAPPENED WHILE I WAS ASLEEP. WE'RE USED TO SUCH THINGS IN CALIFORNIA. THEY DON'T SCARE US MUCH.

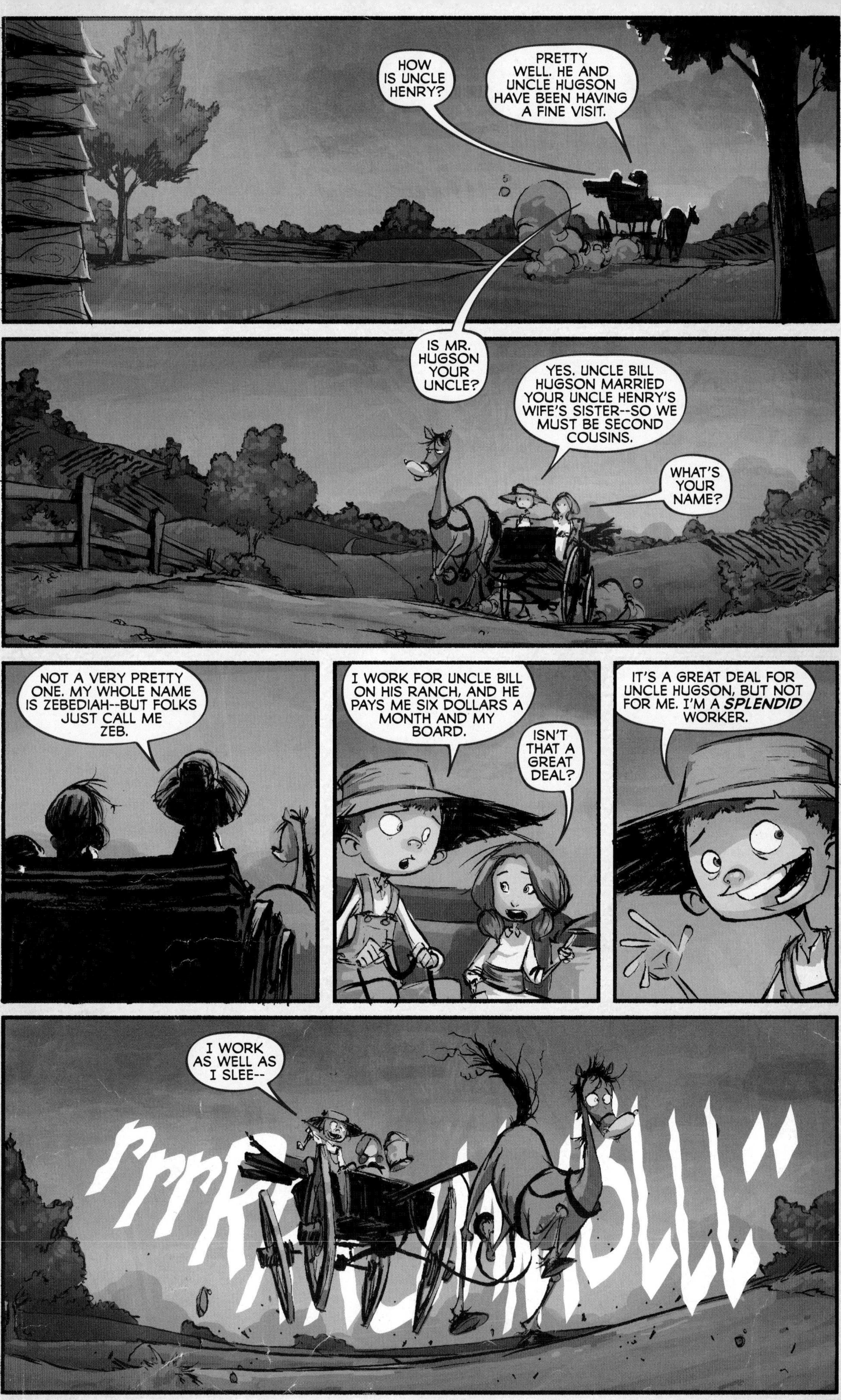
HOW IS UNCLE HENRY?
PRETTY WELL. HE AND UNCLE HUGSON HAVE BEEN HAVING A FINE VISIT.
IS MR. HUGSON YOUR UNCLE?
YES. UNCLE BILL HUGSON MARRIED YOUR UNCLE HENRY'S WIFE'S SISTER--SO WE MUST BE SECOND COUSINS.
WHAT'S YOUR NAME?
NOT A VERY PRETTY ONE. MY WHOLE NAME IS ZEBEDIAH--BUT FOLKS JUST CALL ME ZEB.
I WORK FOR UNCLE BILL ON HIS RANCH, AND HE PAYS ME SIX DOLLARS A MONTH AND MY BOARD.
ISN'T THAT A GREAT DEAL?
IT'S A GREAT DEAL FOR UNCLE HUGSON, BUT NOT FOR ME. I'M A *SPLENDID* WORKER.
I WORK AS WELL AS I SLEE--

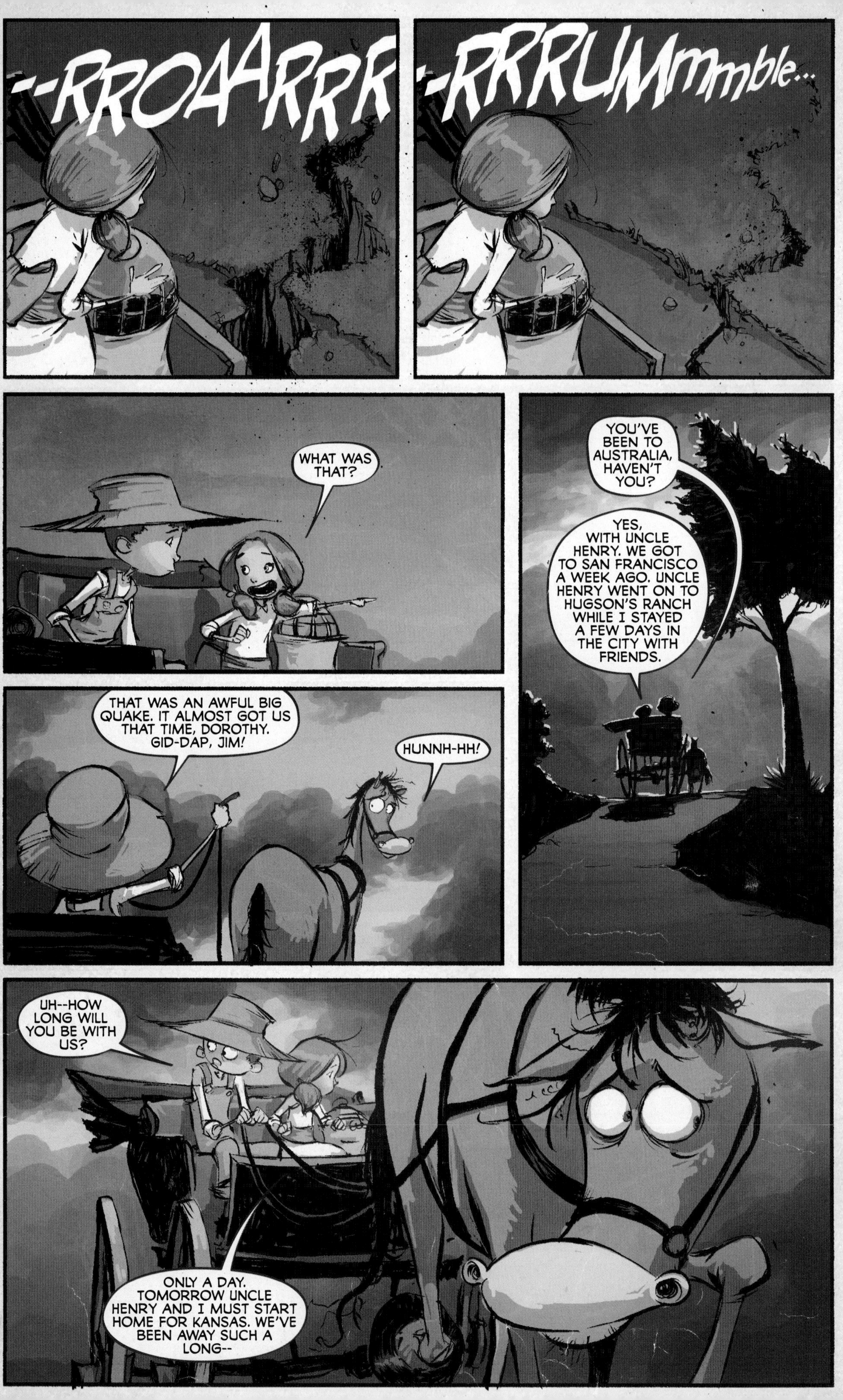
--RROAARRR
--RRRUMmmble...
WHAT WAS THAT?
YOU'VE BEEN TO AUSTRALIA, HAVEN'T YOU?
YES, WITH UNCLE HENRY. WE GOT TO SAN FRANCISCO A WEEK AGO. UNCLE HENRY WENT ON TO HUGSON'S RANCH WHILE I STAYED A FEW DAYS IN THE CITY WITH FRIENDS.
THAT WAS AN AWFUL BIG QUAKE. IT ALMOST GOT US THAT TIME, DOROTHY. GID-DAP, JIM!
HUNNH-HH!
UH--HOW LONG WILL YOU BE WITH US?
ONLY A DAY. TOMORROW UNCLE HENRY AND I MUST START HOME FOR KANSAS. WE'VE BEEN AWAY SUCH A LONG--

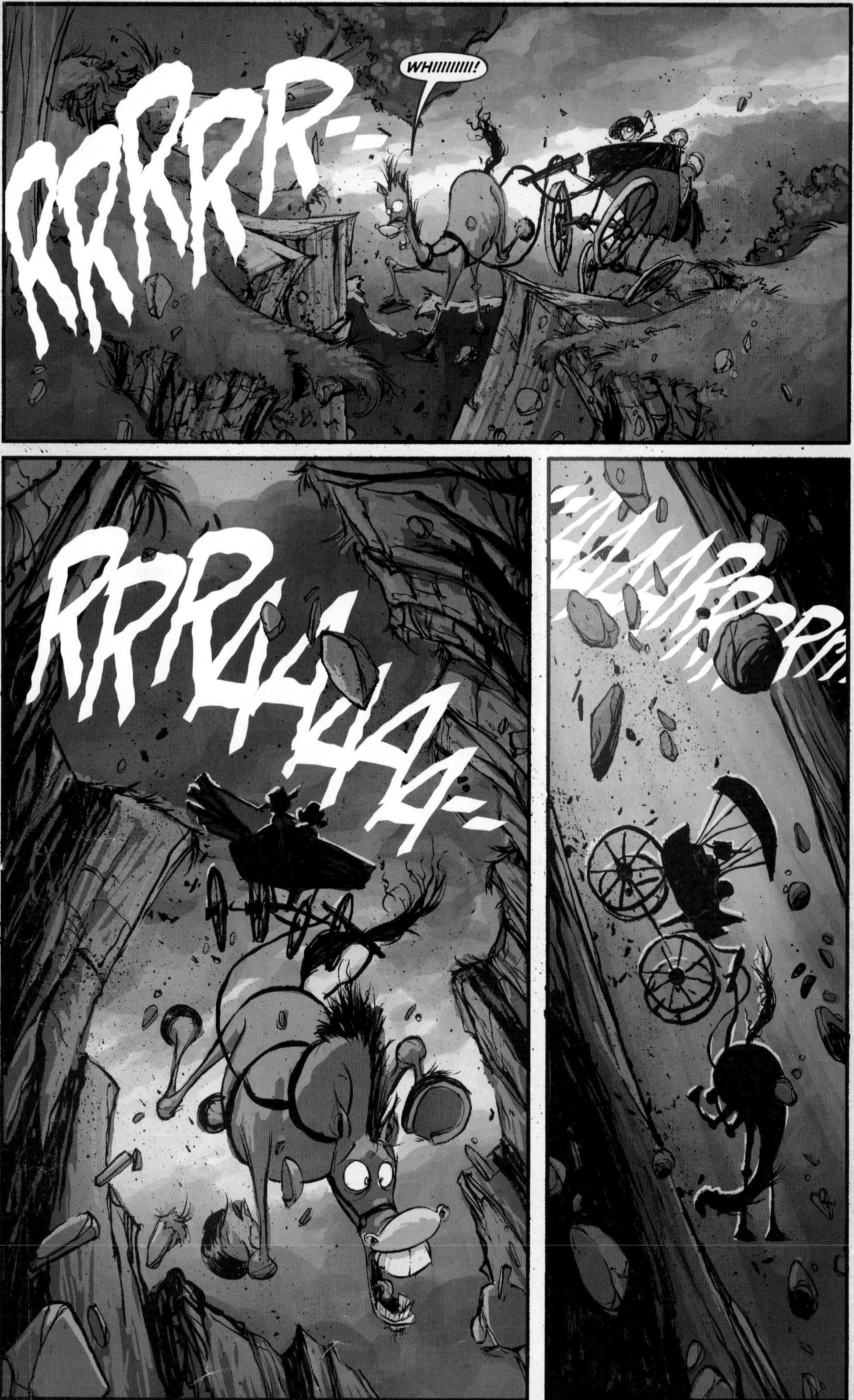
RRRRR-
WHIIIIIIIIII!
RRRAAAA-

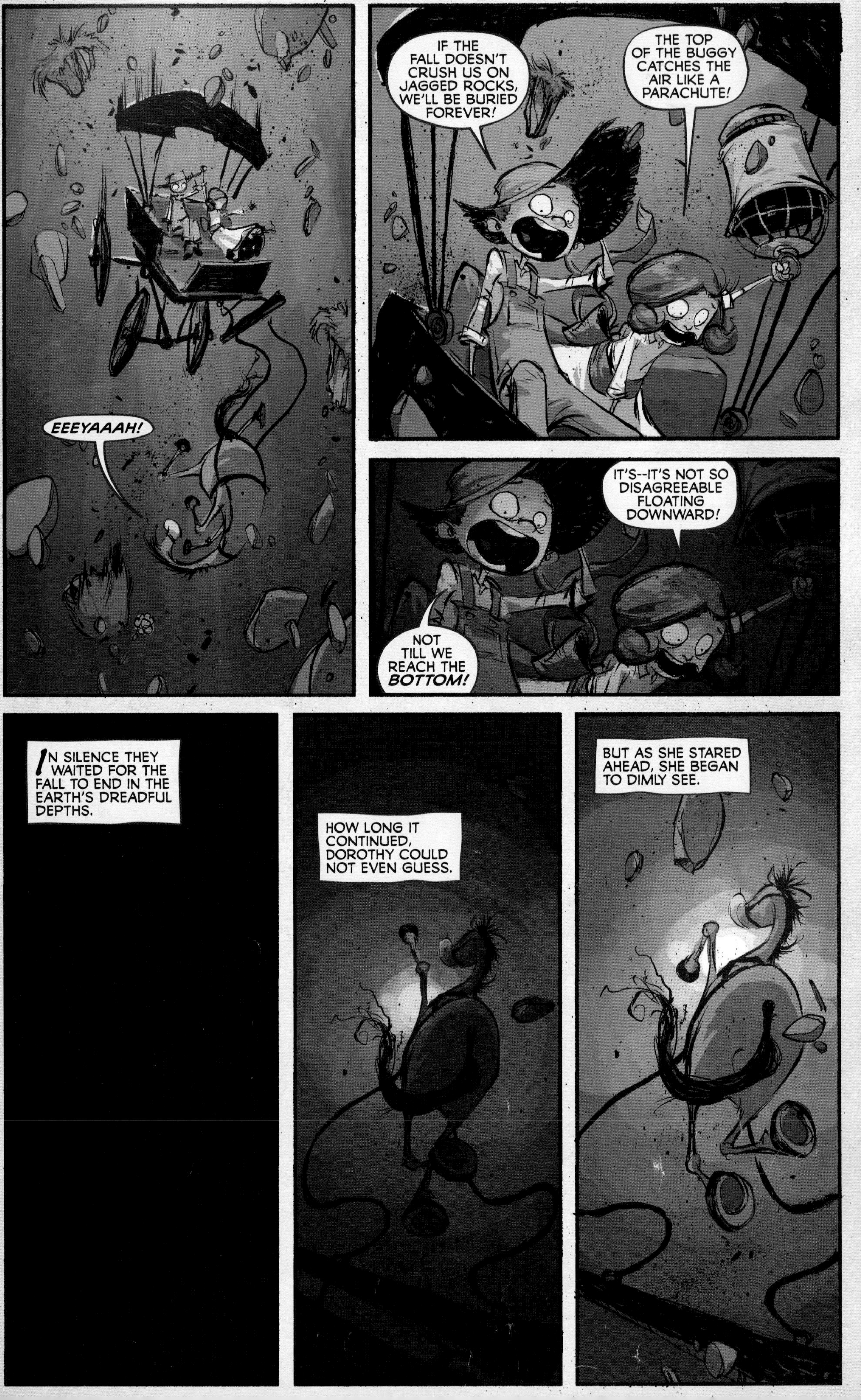
EEEYAAAH!
IF THE FALL DOESN'T CRUSH US ON JAGGED ROCKS, WE'LL BE BURIED FOREVER!
THE TOP OF THE BUGGY CATCHES THE AIR LIKE A PARACHUTE!
IT'S--IT'S NOT SO DISAGREEABLE FLOATING DOWNWARD!
NOT TILL WE REACH THE BOTTOM!
IN SILENCE THEY WAITED FOR THE FALL TO END IN THE EARTH'S DREADFUL DEPTHS.
HOW LONG IT CONTINUED, DOROTHY COULD NOT EVEN GUESS.
BUT AS SHE STARED AHEAD, SHE BEGAN TO DIMLY SEE.

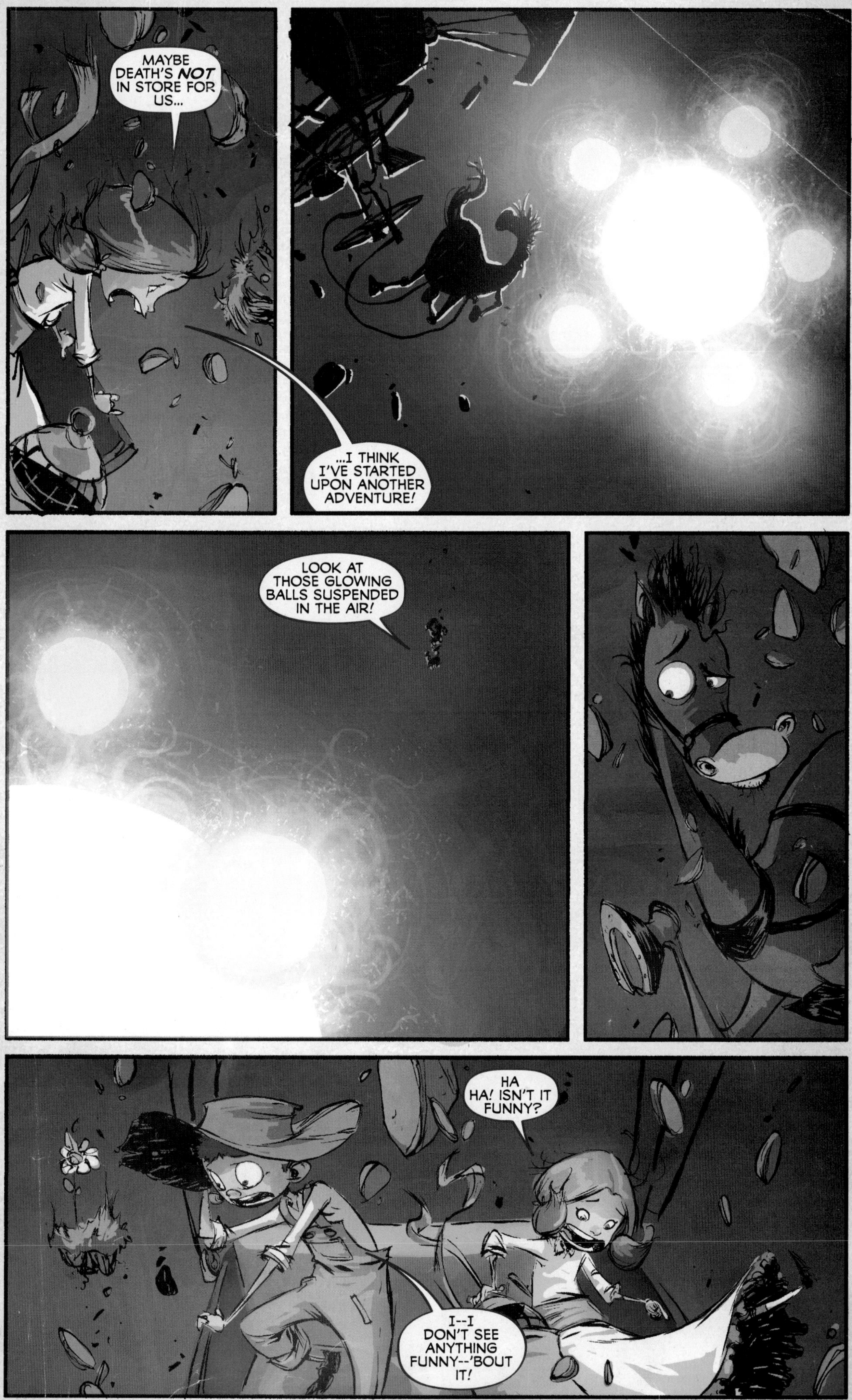
MAYBE DEATH'S ***NOT*** IN STORE FOR US...
...I THINK I'VE STARTED UPON ANOTHER ADVENTURE!
LOOK AT THOSE GLOWING BALLS SUSPENDED IN THE AIR!
HA HA! ISN'T IT FUNNY?
I--I DON'T SEE ANYTHING FUNNY--'BOUT IT!

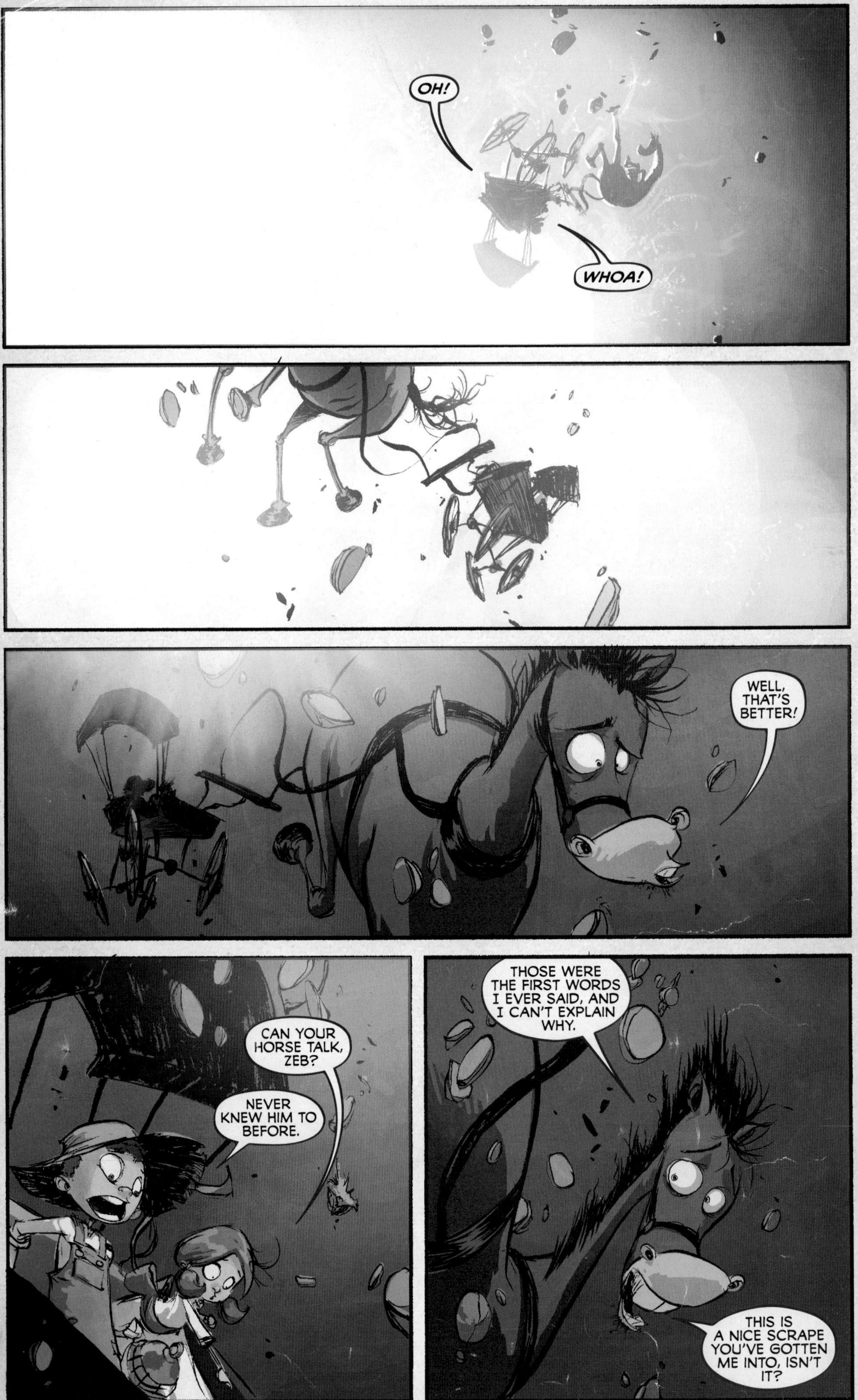
OH!
WHOA!
WELL, THAT'S BETTER!
CAN YOUR HORSE TALK, ZEB?
NEVER KNEW HIM TO BEFORE.
THOSE WERE THE FIRST WORDS I EVER SAID, AND I CAN'T EXPLAIN WHY.
THIS IS A NICE SCRAPE YOU'VE GOTTEN ME INTO, ISN'T IT?

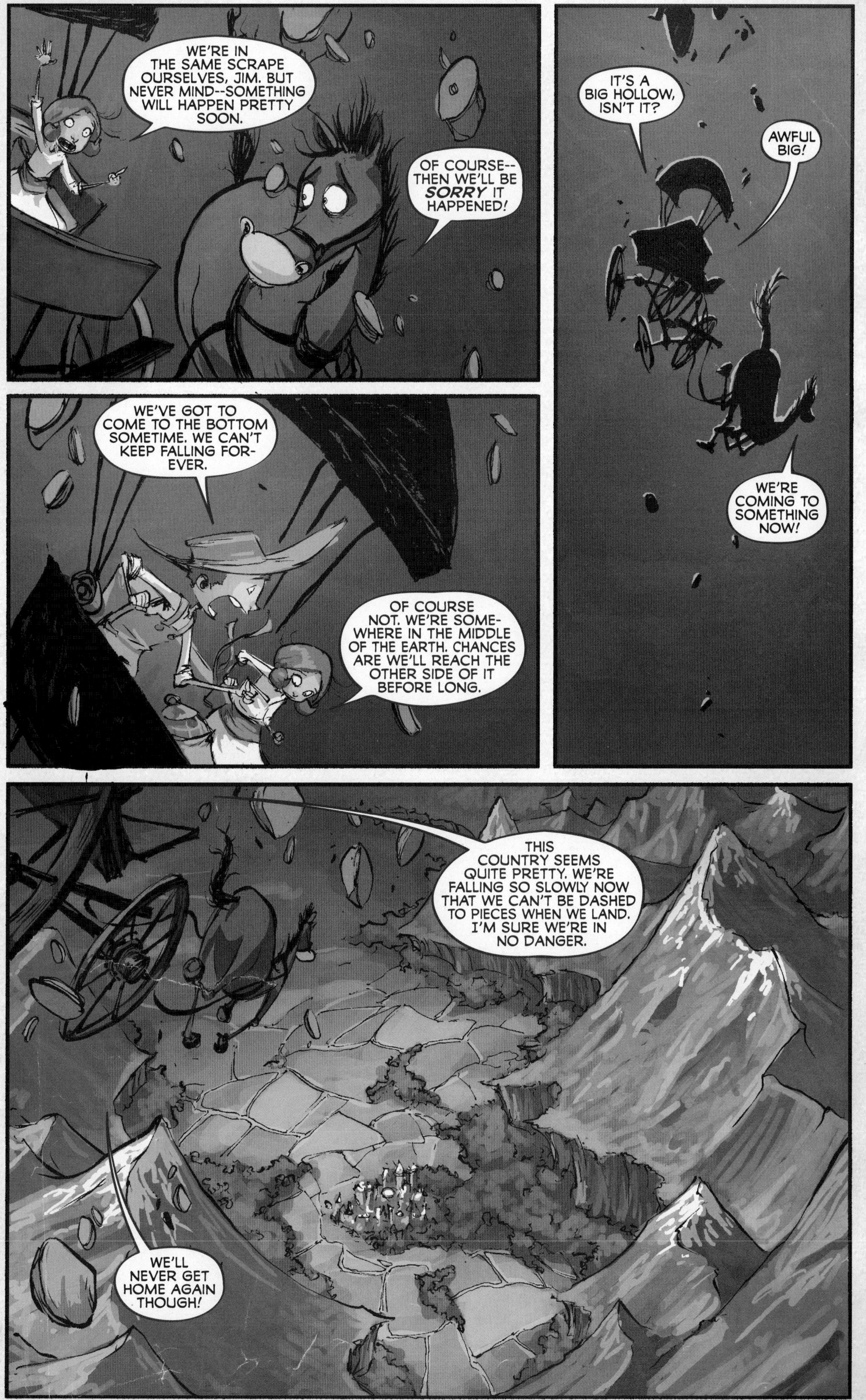
WE'RE IN THE SAME SCRAPE OURSELVES, JIM. BUT NEVER MIND--SOMETHING WILL HAPPEN PRETTY SOON.
OF COURSE-- THEN WE'LL BE *SORRY* IT HAPPENED!
IT'S A BIG HOLLOW, ISN'T IT?
AWFUL BIG!
WE'RE COMING TO SOMETHING NOW!
WE'VE GOT TO COME TO THE BOTTOM SOMETIME. WE CAN'T KEEP FALLING FOR-EVER.
OF COURSE NOT. WE'RE SOME-WHERE IN THE MIDDLE OF THE EARTH. CHANCES ARE WE'LL REACH THE OTHER SIDE OF IT BEFORE LONG.
THIS COUNTRY SEEMS QUITE PRETTY. WE'RE FALLING SO SLOWLY NOW THAT WE CAN'T BE DASHED TO PIECES WHEN WE LAND. I'M SURE WE'RE IN NO DANGER.
WE'LL NEVER GET HOME AGAIN THOUGH!

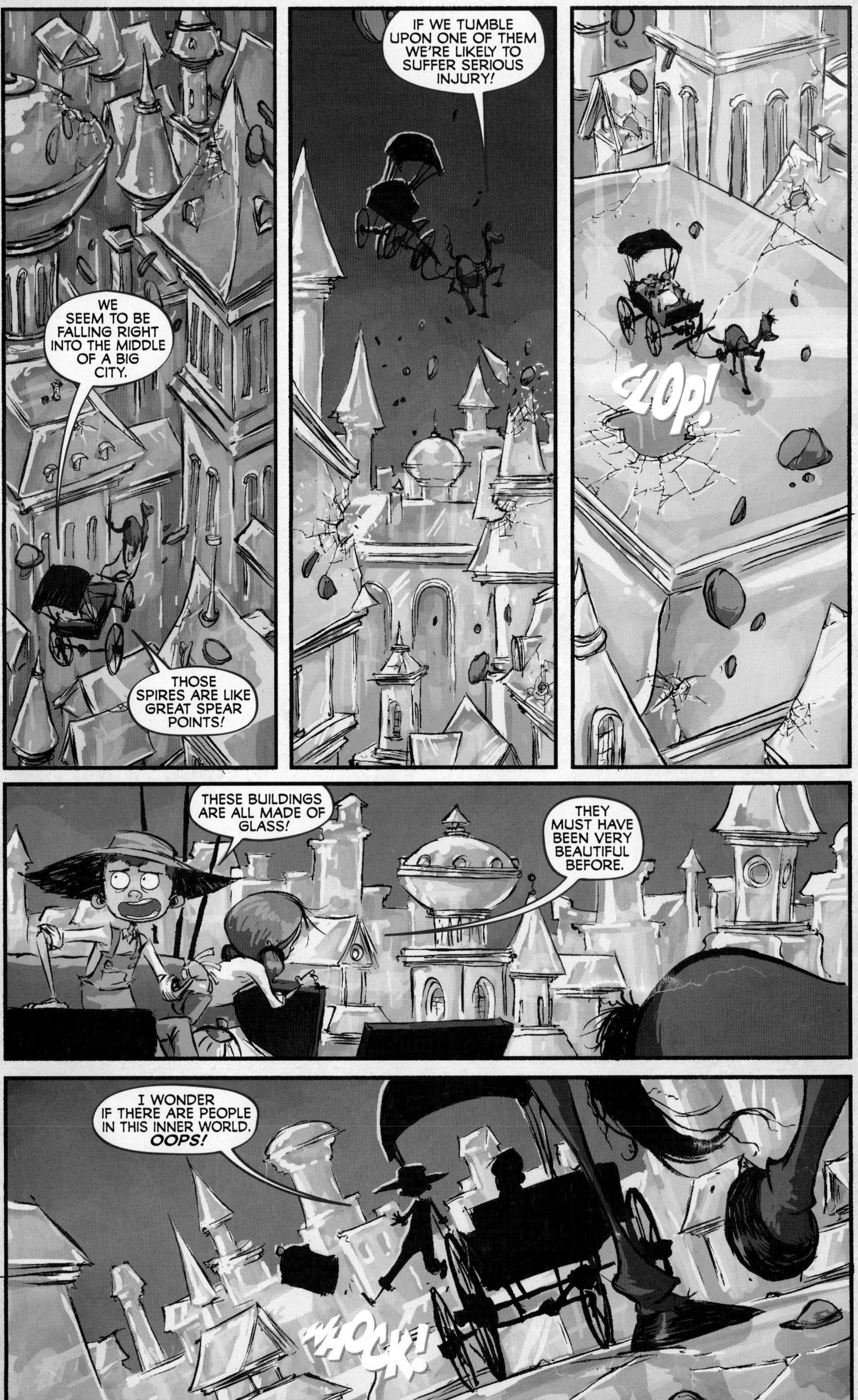
WE SEEM TO BE FALLING RIGHT INTO THE MIDDLE OF A BIG CITY.
THOSE SPIRES ARE LIKE GREAT SPEAR POINTS!
IF WE TUMBLE UPON ONE OF THEM WE'RE LIKELY TO SUFFER SERIOUS INJURY!
CLOP!
THESE BUILDINGS ARE ALL MADE OF GLASS!
THEY MUST HAVE BEEN VERY BEAUTIFUL BEFORE.
I WONDER IF THERE ARE PEOPLE IN THIS INNER WORLD. OOPS!
WHOCK!

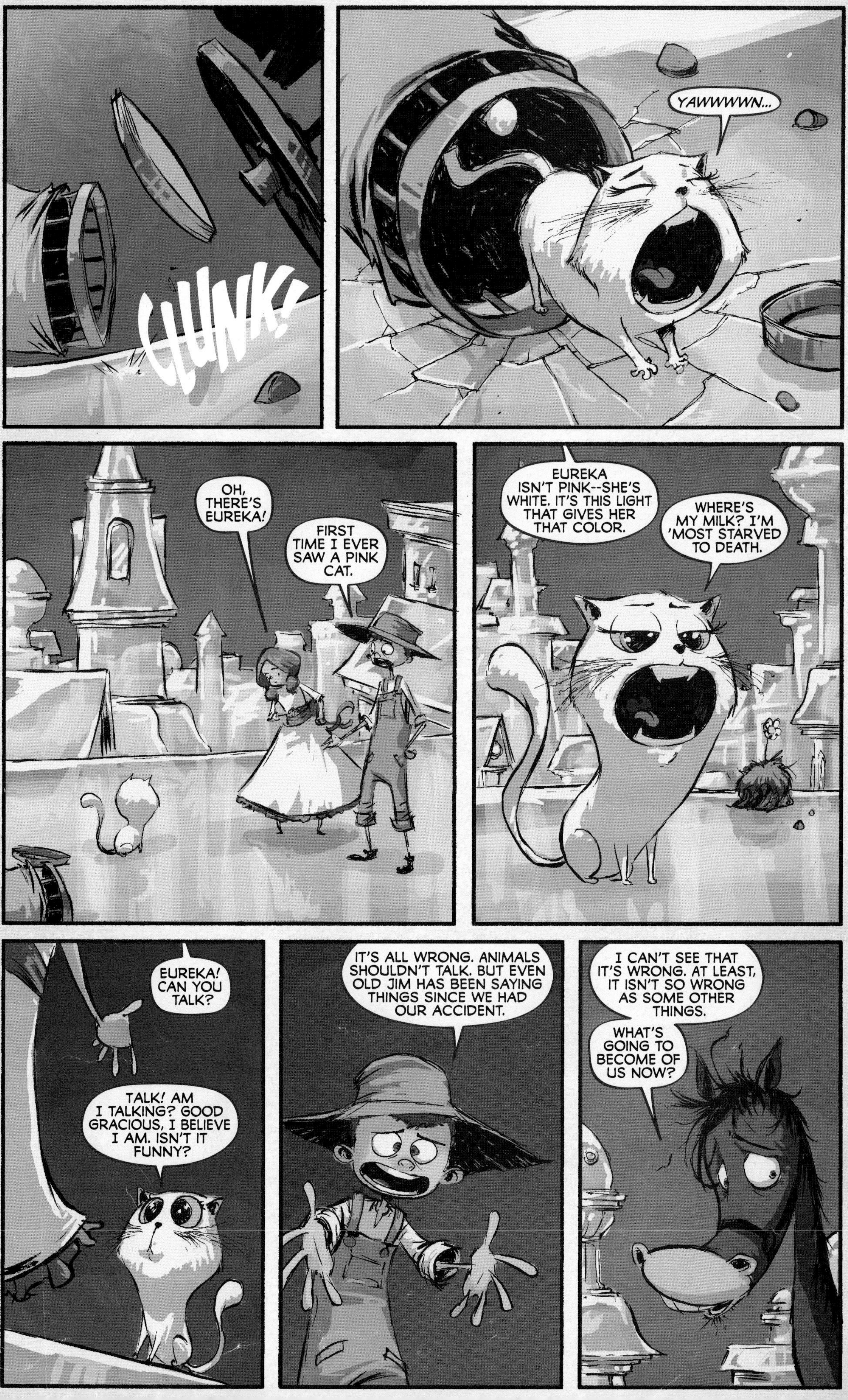
CLUNK!
YAWWWWN...
OH, THERE'S EUREKA!
FIRST TIME I EVER SAW A PINK CAT.
EUREKA ISN'T PINK--SHE'S WHITE. IT'S THIS LIGHT THAT GIVES HER THAT COLOR.
WHERE'S MY MILK? I'M 'MOST STARVED TO DEATH.
EUREKA! CAN YOU TALK?
TALK! AM I TALKING? GOOD GRACIOUS, I BELIEVE I AM. ISN'T IT FUNNY?
IT'S ALL WRONG. ANIMALS SHOULDN'T TALK. BUT EVEN OLD JIM HAS BEEN SAYING THINGS SINCE WE HAD OUR ACCIDENT.
I CAN'T SEE THAT IT'S WRONG. AT LEAST, IT ISN'T SO WRONG AS SOME OTHER THINGS.
WHAT'S GOING TO BECOME OF US NOW?

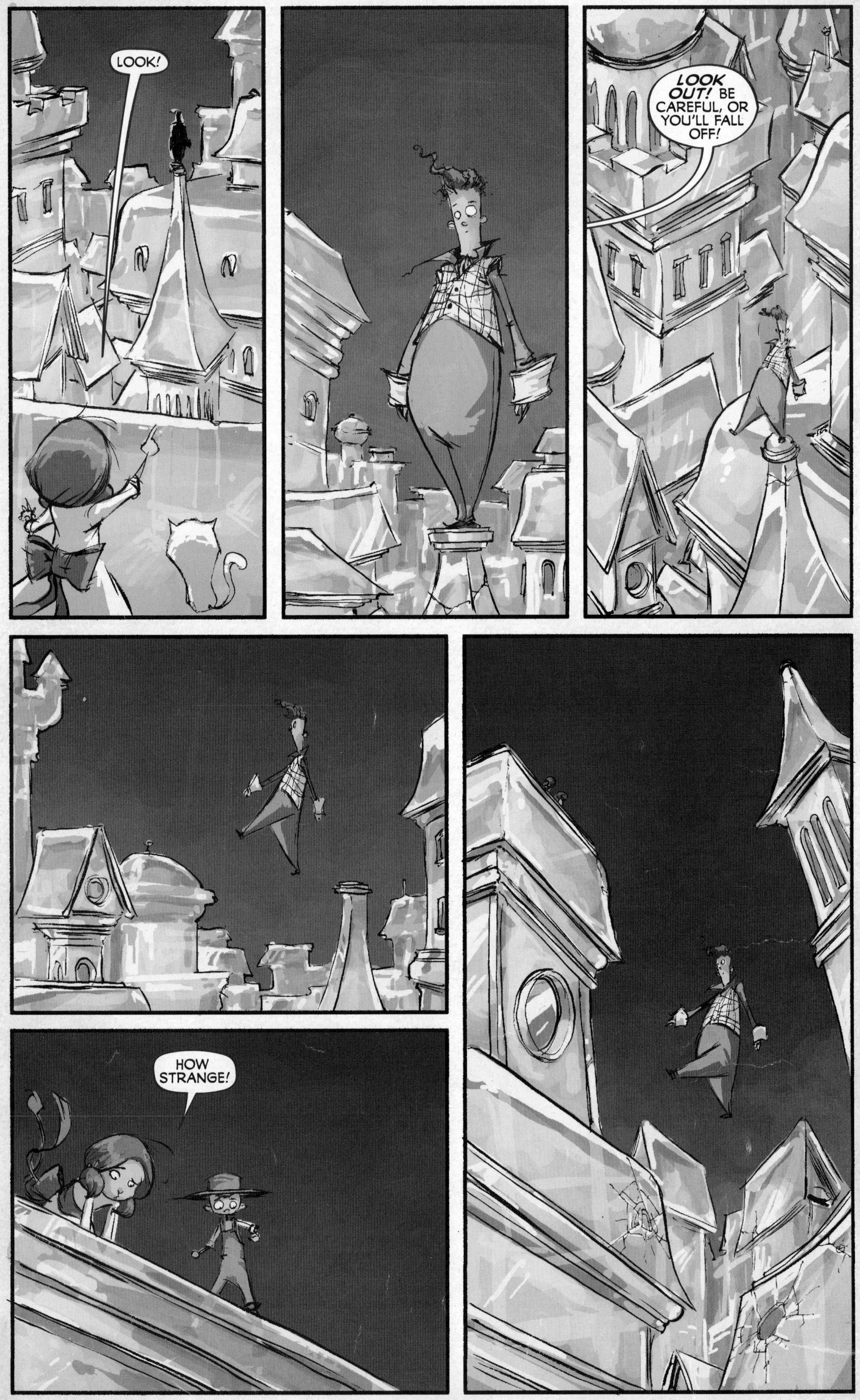
LOOK!
LOOK OUT! BE CAREFUL, OR YOU'LL FALL OFF!
HOW STRANGE!

YES, BUT IT'S LOTS OF FUN--IF IT *IS* STRANGE!

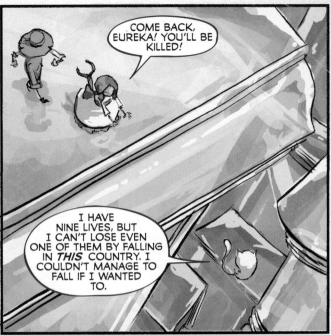

COME BACK, EUREKA! YOU'LL BE KILLED!

I HAVE NINE LIVES, BUT I CAN'T LOSE EVEN ONE OF THEM BY FALLING IN *THIS* COUNTRY. I COULDN'T MANAGE TO FALL IF I WANTED TO.

SUPPOSE WE LET EUREKA GO DOWN TO THE STREET AND GET SOMEONE TO HELP US?

DOES THE AIR BEAR UP YOUR WEIGHT?

OF *COURSE*-- CAN'T YOU SEE?

PERHAPS WE CAN WALK ON THE AIR OUR-SELVES.

I WOULDN'T DARE TRY!

MAYBE JIM WILL GO.

AND MAYBE HE *WON'T!*

BY THE TIME WE REACHED THE ROOF WE WERE FLOATING VERY SLOWLY. I'M ALMOST SURE WE COULD FLOAT DOWN TO THE STREET WITHOUT GETTING HURT.

EUREKA WALKS ON THE AIR ALL RIGHT.

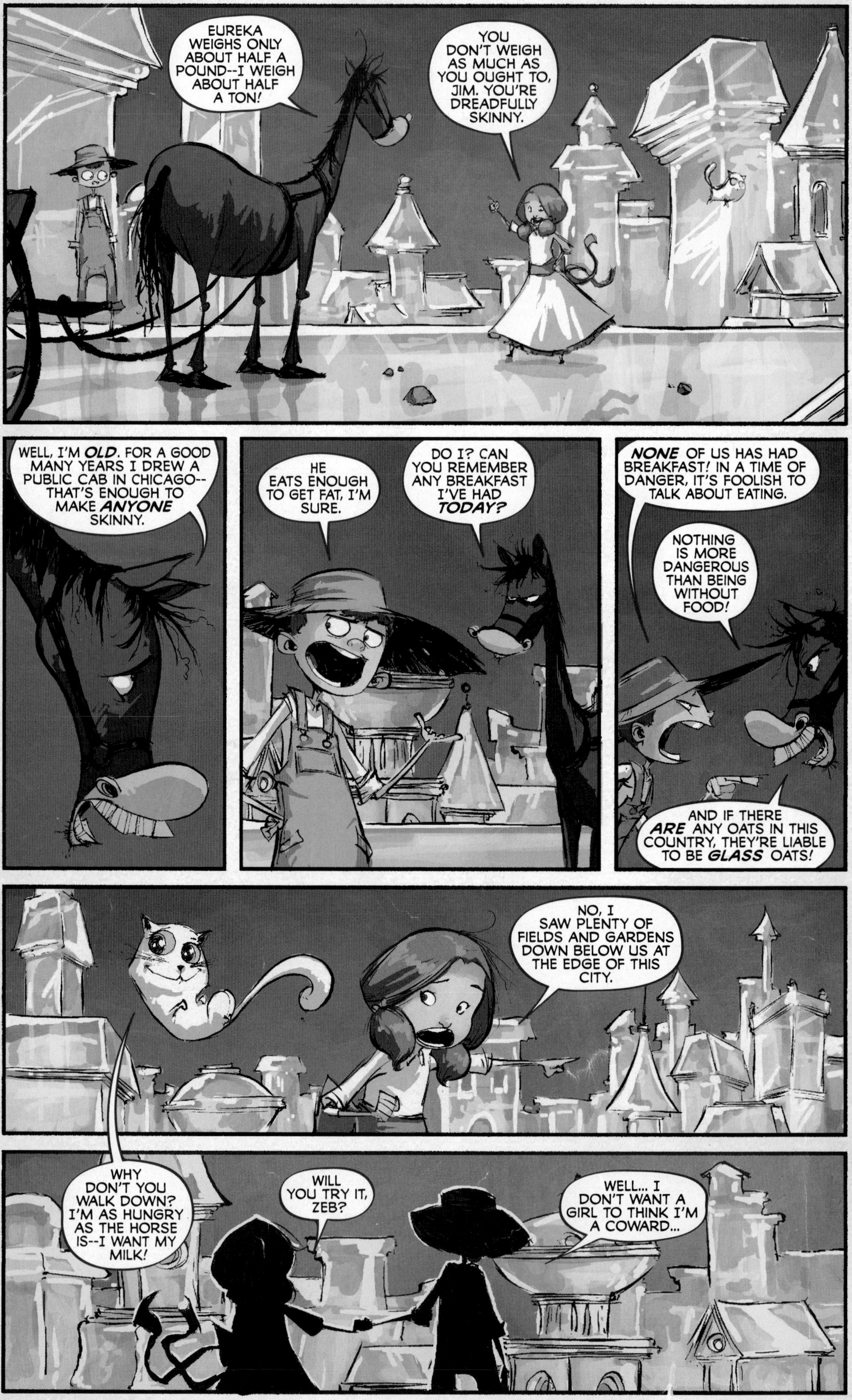
EUREKA WEIGHS ONLY ABOUT HALF A POUND--I WEIGH ABOUT HALF A TON!
YOU DON'T WEIGH AS MUCH AS YOU OUGHT TO, JIM. YOU'RE DREADFULLY SKINNY.
WELL, I'M **OLD**. FOR A GOOD MANY YEARS I DREW A PUBLIC CAB IN CHICAGO-- THAT'S ENOUGH TO MAKE **ANYONE** SKINNY.
HE EATS ENOUGH TO GET FAT, I'M SURE.
DO I? CAN YOU REMEMBER ANY BREAKFAST I'VE HAD **TODAY?**
NONE OF US HAS HAD BREAKFAST! IN A TIME OF DANGER, IT'S FOOLISH TO TALK ABOUT EATING.
NOTHING IS MORE DANGEROUS THAN BEING WITHOUT FOOD!
AND IF THERE **ARE** ANY OATS IN THIS COUNTRY, THEY'RE LIABLE TO BE **GLASS** OATS!
NO, I SAW PLENTY OF FIELDS AND GARDENS DOWN BELOW US AT THE EDGE OF THIS CITY.
WHY DON'T YOU WALK DOWN? I'M AS HUNGRY AS THE HORSE IS--I WANT MY MILK!
WILL YOU TRY IT, ZEB?
WELL... I DON'T WANT A GIRL TO THINK I'M A COWARD...

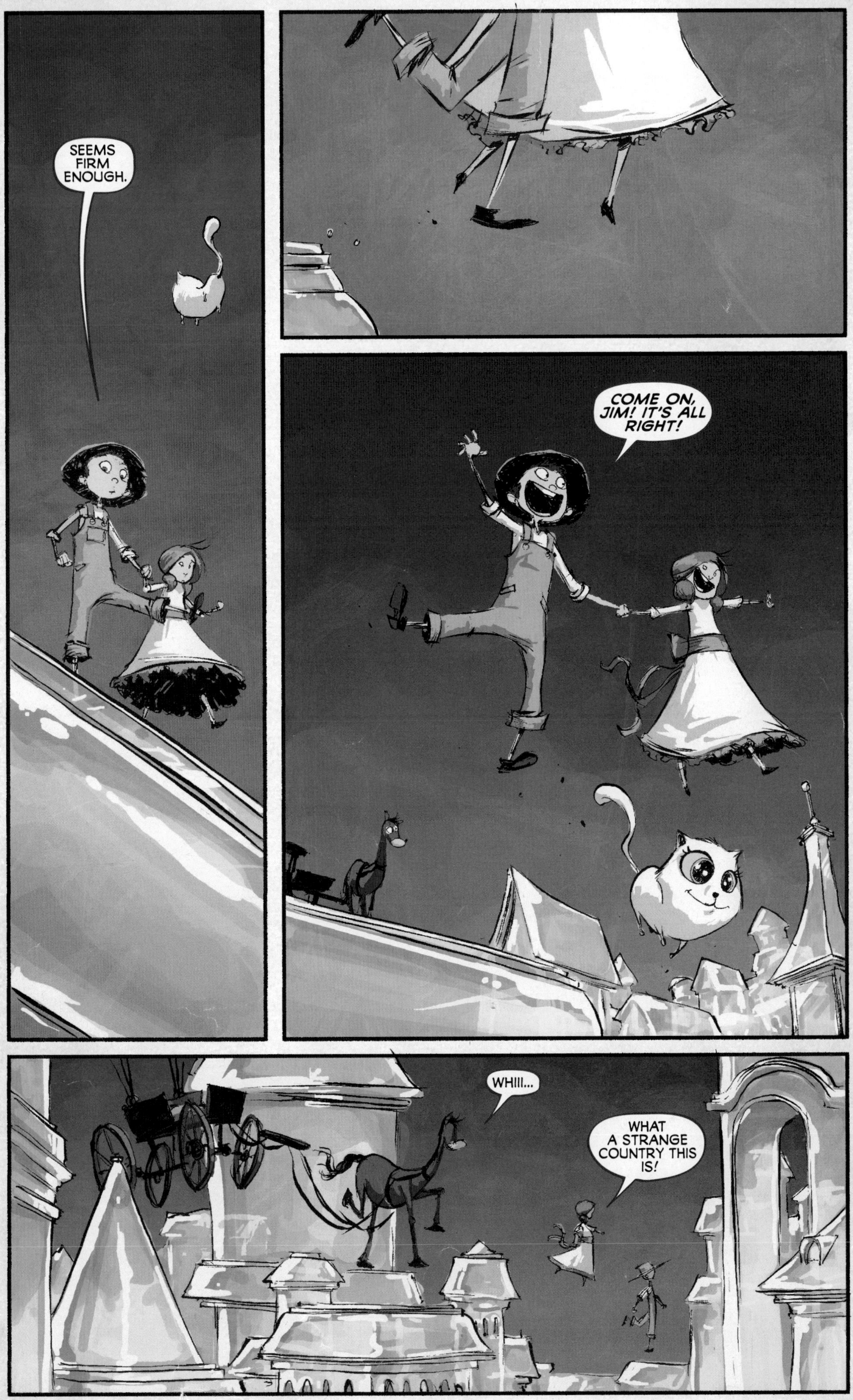
SEEMS FIRM ENOUGH.
COME ON, JIM! IT'S ALL RIGHT!
WHIII...
WHAT A STRANGE COUNTRY THIS IS!

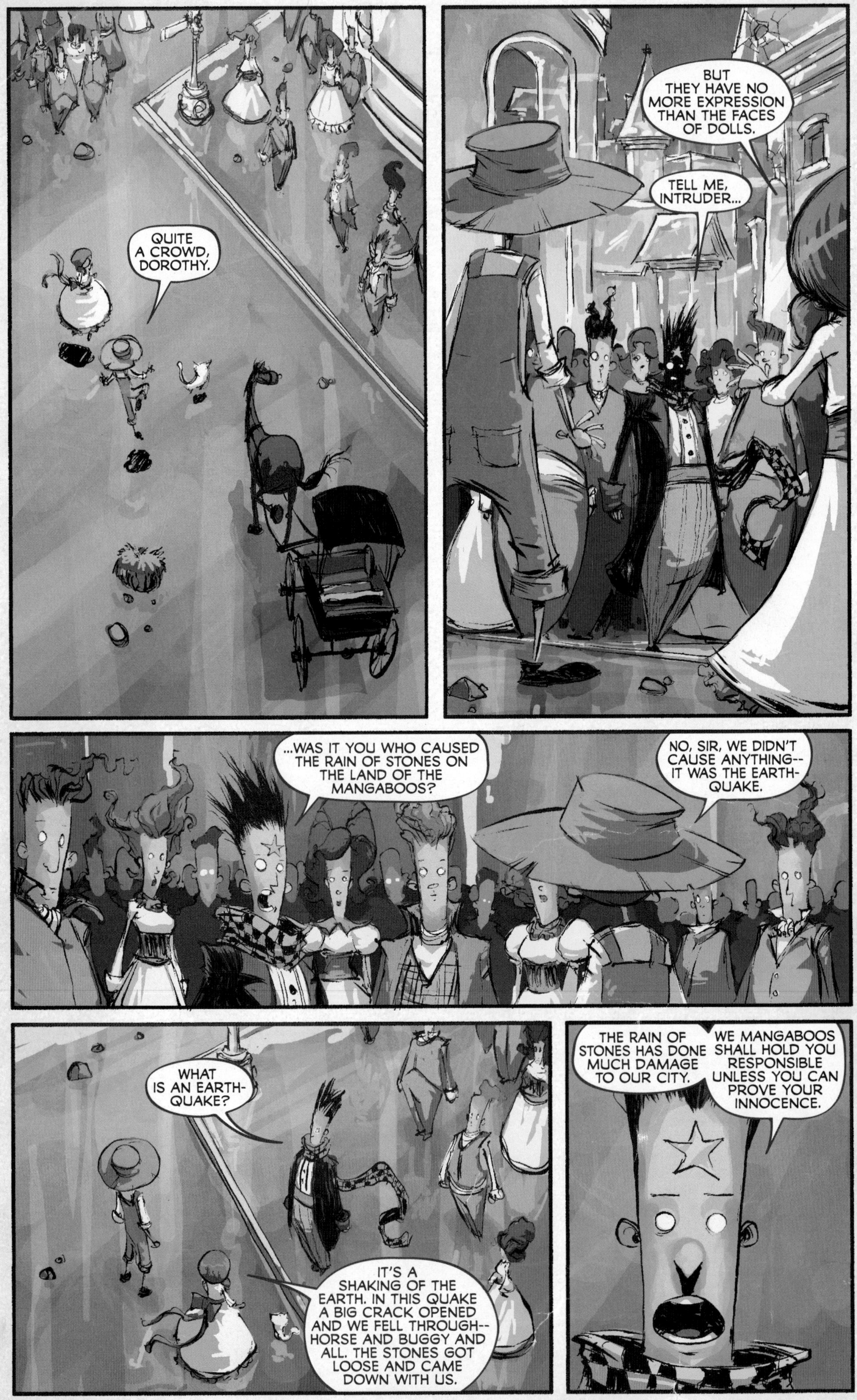
QUITE A CROWD, DOROTHY.
BUT THEY HAVE NO MORE EXPRESSION THAN THE FACES OF DOLLS.
TELL ME, INTRUDER...
...WAS IT YOU WHO CAUSED THE RAIN OF STONES ON THE LAND OF THE MANGABOOS?
NO, SIR, WE DIDN'T CAUSE ANYTHING-- IT WAS THE EARTH-QUAKE.
WHAT IS AN EARTH-QUAKE?
IT'S A SHAKING OF THE EARTH. IN THIS QUAKE A BIG CRACK OPENED AND WE FELL THROUGH-- HORSE AND BUGGY AND ALL. THE STONES GOT LOOSE AND CAME DOWN WITH US.
THE RAIN OF STONES HAS DONE MUCH DAMAGE TO OUR CITY.
WE MANGABOOS SHALL HOLD YOU RESPONSIBLE UNLESS YOU CAN PROVE YOUR INNOCENCE.

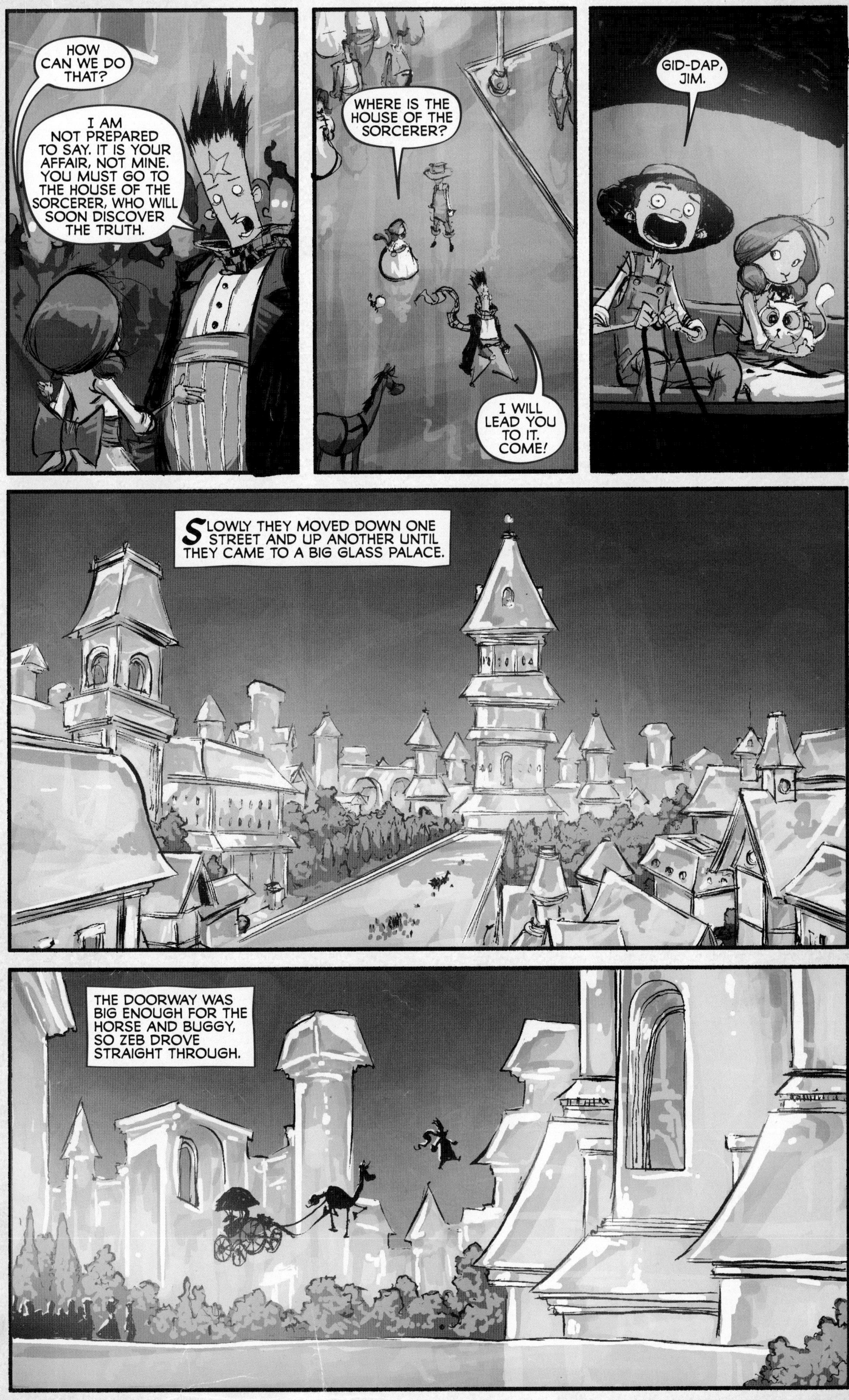
HOW CAN WE DO THAT?
I AM NOT PREPARED TO SAY. IT IS YOUR AFFAIR, NOT MINE. YOU MUST GO TO THE HOUSE OF THE SORCERER, WHO WILL SOON DISCOVER THE TRUTH.
WHERE IS THE HOUSE OF THE SORCERER?
I WILL LEAD YOU TO IT. COME!
GID-DAP, JIM.
SLOWLY THEY MOVED DOWN ONE STREET AND UP ANOTHER UNTIL THEY CAME TO A BIG GLASS PALACE.
THE DOORWAY WAS BIG ENOUGH FOR THE HORSE AND BUGGY, SO ZEB DROVE STRAIGHT THROUGH.

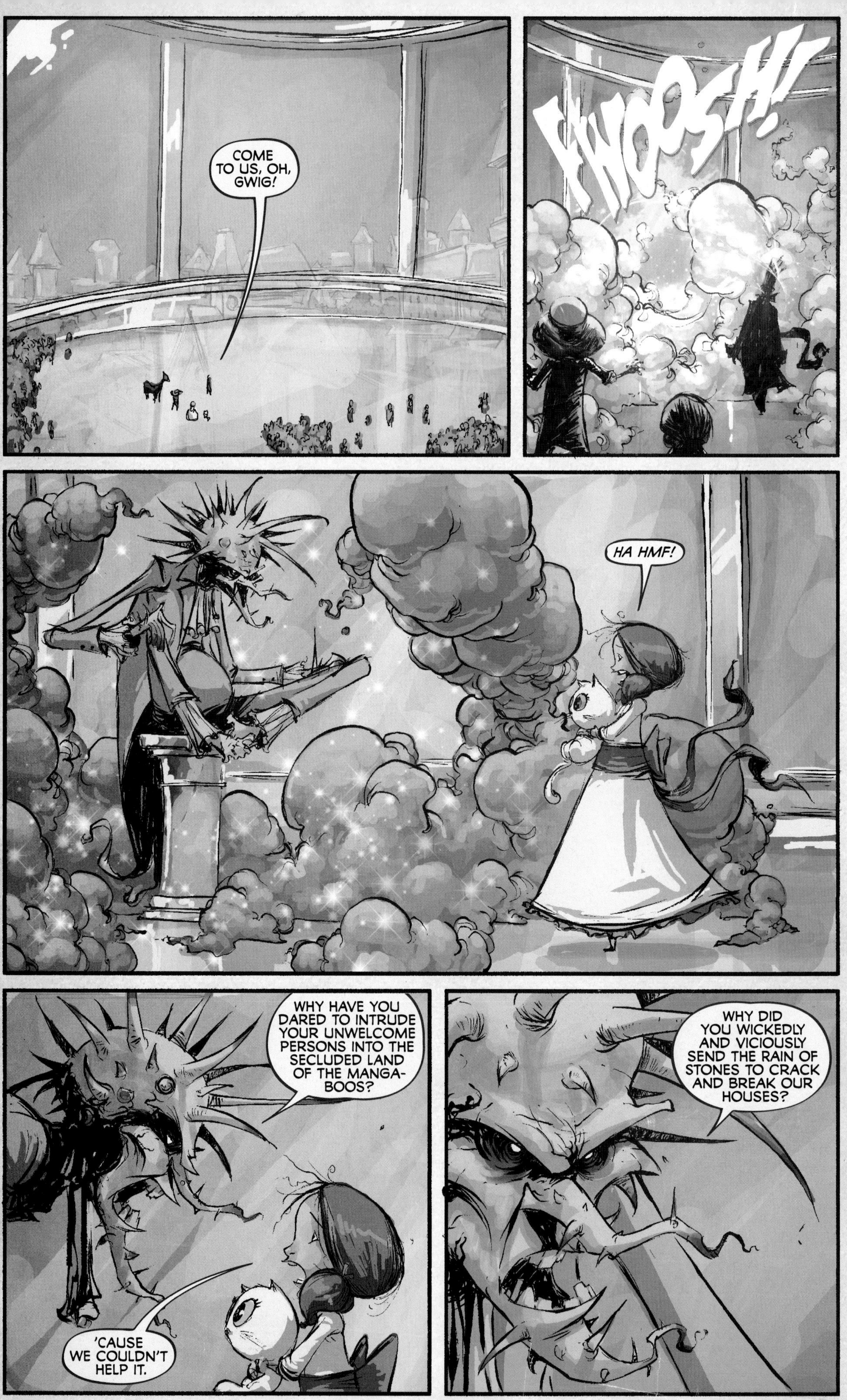
COME TO US, OH, GWIG!
FWOOSH!
HA HMF!
WHY HAVE YOU DARED TO INTRUDE YOUR UNWELCOME PERSONS INTO THE SECLUDED LAND OF THE MANGA-BOOS?
'CAUSE WE COULDN'T HELP IT.
WHY DID YOU WICKEDLY AND VICIOUSLY SEND THE RAIN OF STONES TO CRACK AND BREAK OUR HOUSES?

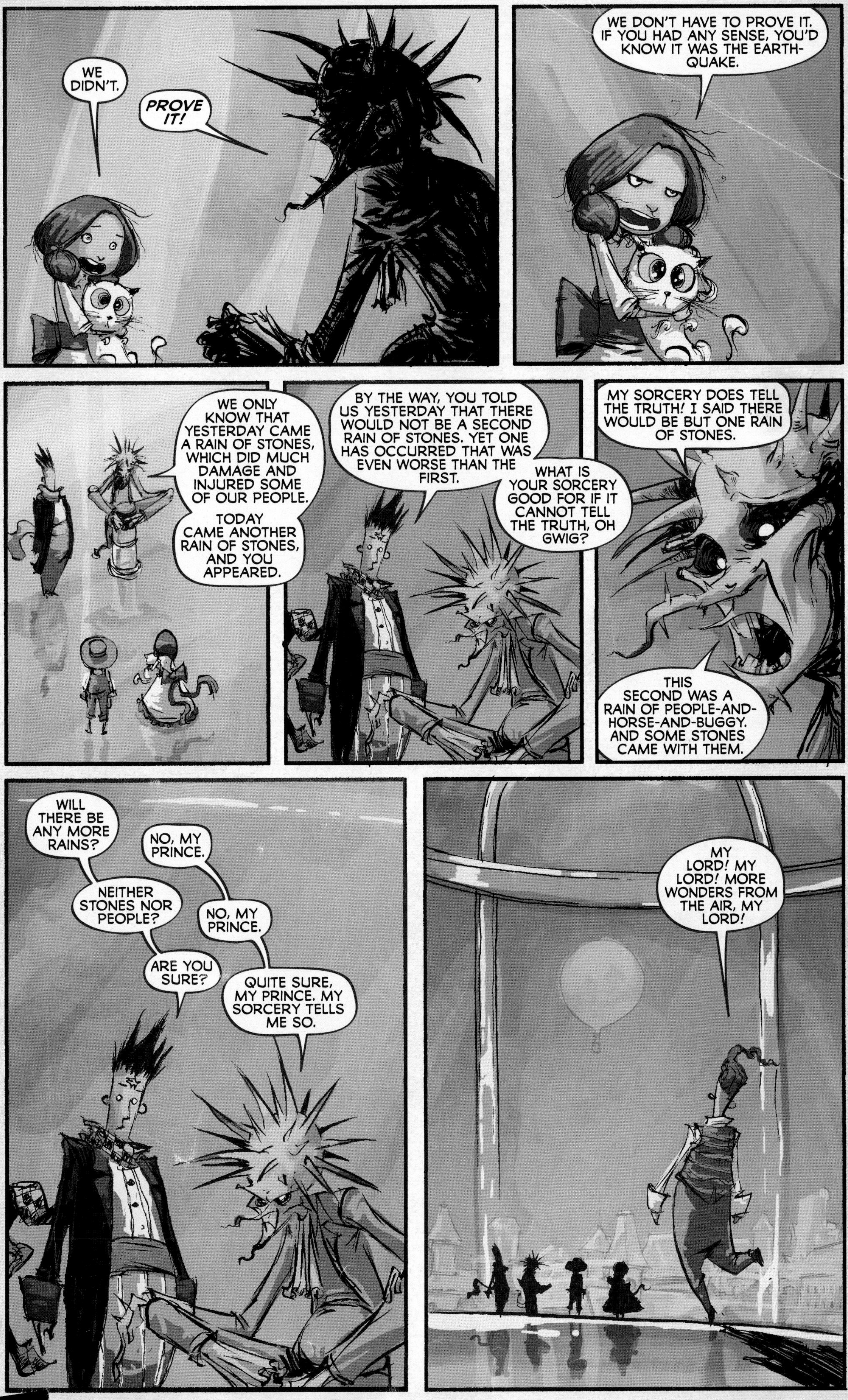
WE DIDN'T.
PROVE IT!
WE DON'T HAVE TO PROVE IT. IF YOU HAD ANY SENSE, YOU'D KNOW IT WAS THE EARTH-QUAKE.
WE ONLY KNOW THAT YESTERDAY CAME A RAIN OF STONES, WHICH DID MUCH DAMAGE AND INJURED SOME OF OUR PEOPLE.
TODAY CAME ANOTHER RAIN OF STONES, AND YOU APPEARED.
BY THE WAY, YOU TOLD US YESTERDAY THAT THERE WOULD NOT BE A SECOND RAIN OF STONES. YET ONE HAS OCCURRED THAT WAS EVEN WORSE THAN THE FIRST.
WHAT IS YOUR SORCERY GOOD FOR IF IT CANNOT TELL THE TRUTH, OH GWIG?
MY SORCERY DOES TELL THE TRUTH! I SAID THERE WOULD BE BUT ONE RAIN OF STONES.
THIS SECOND WAS A RAIN OF PEOPLE-AND-HORSE-AND-BUGGY. AND SOME STONES CAME WITH THEM.
WILL THERE BE ANY MORE RAINS?
NO, MY PRINCE.
NEITHER STONES NOR PEOPLE?
NO, MY PRINCE.
ARE YOU SURE?
QUITE SURE, MY PRINCE. MY SORCERY TELLS ME SO.
MY LORD! MY LORD! MORE WONDERS FROM THE AIR, MY LORD!

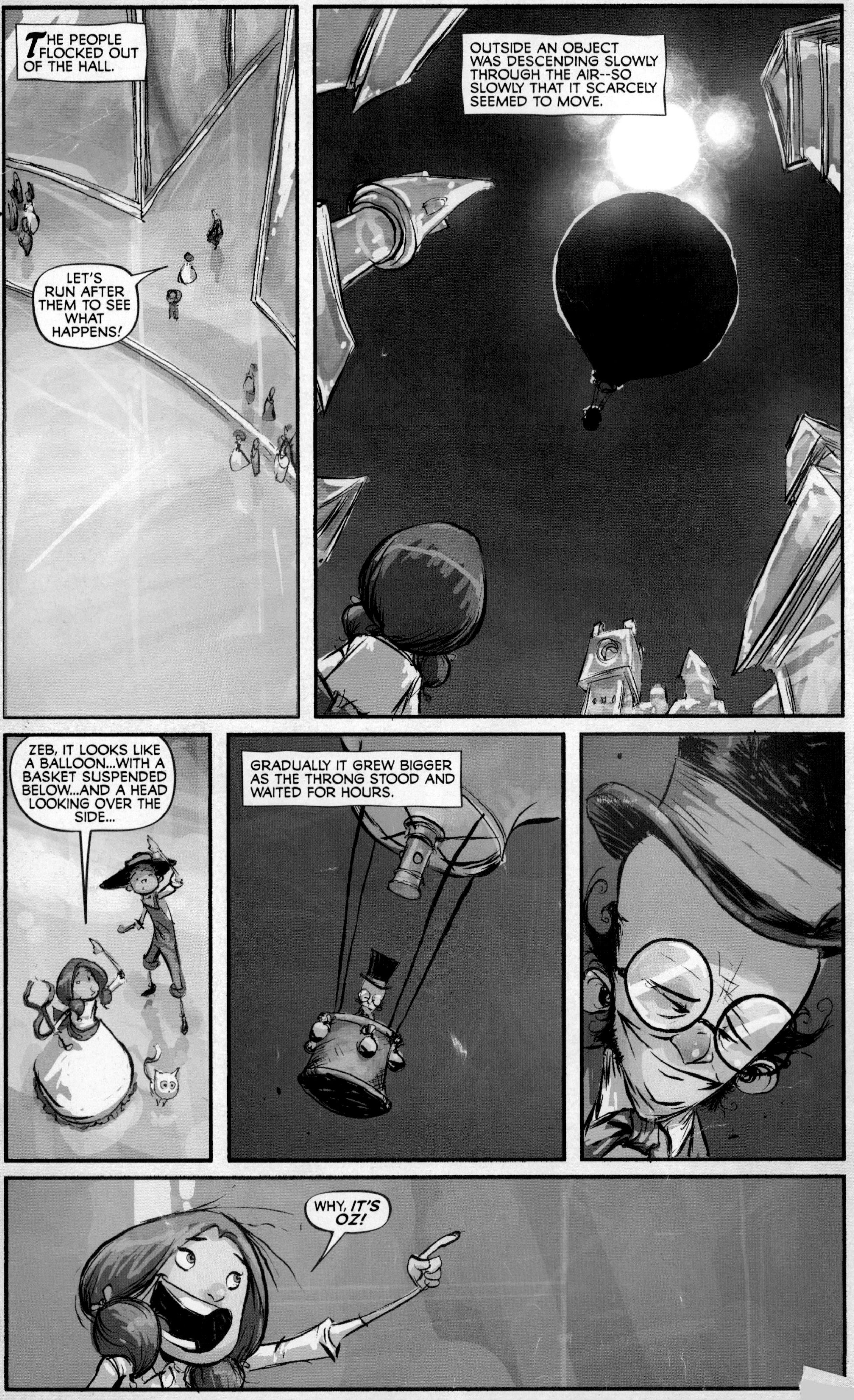
THE PEOPLE FLOCKED OUT OF THE HALL.
LET'S RUN AFTER THEM TO SEE WHAT HAPPENS!
OUTSIDE AN OBJECT WAS DESCENDING SLOWLY THROUGH THE AIR--SO SLOWLY THAT IT SCARCELY SEEMED TO MOVE.
ZEB, IT LOOKS LIKE A BALLOON...WITH A BASKET SUSPENDED BELOW...AND A HEAD LOOKING OVER THE SIDE...
GRADUALLY IT GREW BIGGER AS THE THRONG STOOD AND WAITED FOR HOURS.
WHY, *IT'S OZ!*

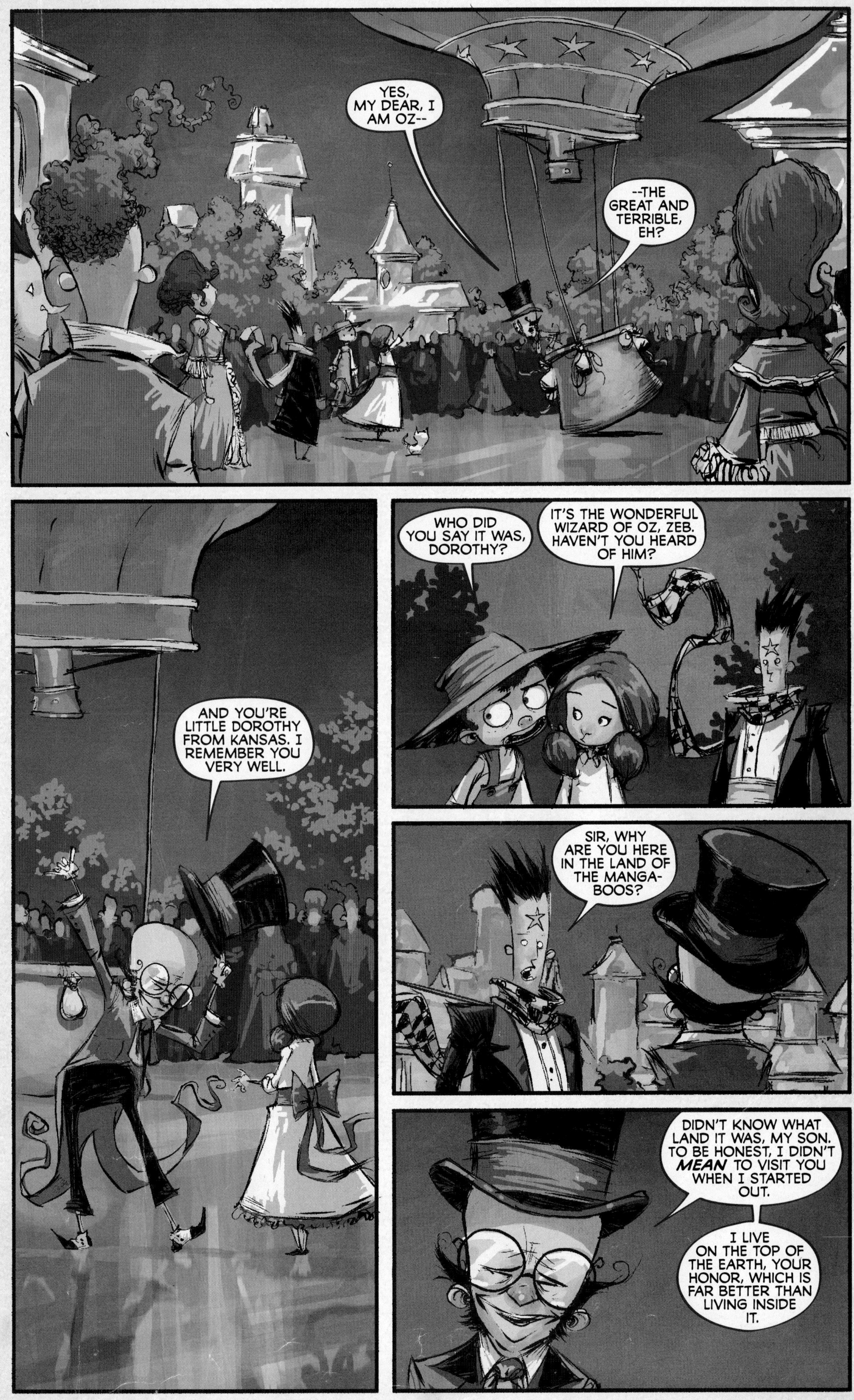
YES, MY DEAR, I AM OZ--
--THE GREAT AND TERRIBLE, EH?
AND YOU'RE LITTLE DOROTHY FROM KANSAS. I REMEMBER YOU VERY WELL.
WHO DID YOU SAY IT WAS, DOROTHY?
IT'S THE WONDERFUL WIZARD OF OZ, ZEB. HAVEN'T YOU HEARD OF HIM?
SIR, WHY ARE YOU HERE IN THE LAND OF THE MANGA-BOOS?
DIDN'T KNOW WHAT LAND IT WAS, MY SON. TO BE HONEST, I DIDN'T MEAN TO VISIT YOU WHEN I STARTED OUT.
I LIVE ON THE TOP OF THE EARTH, YOUR HONOR, WHICH IS FAR BETTER THAN LIVING INSIDE IT.

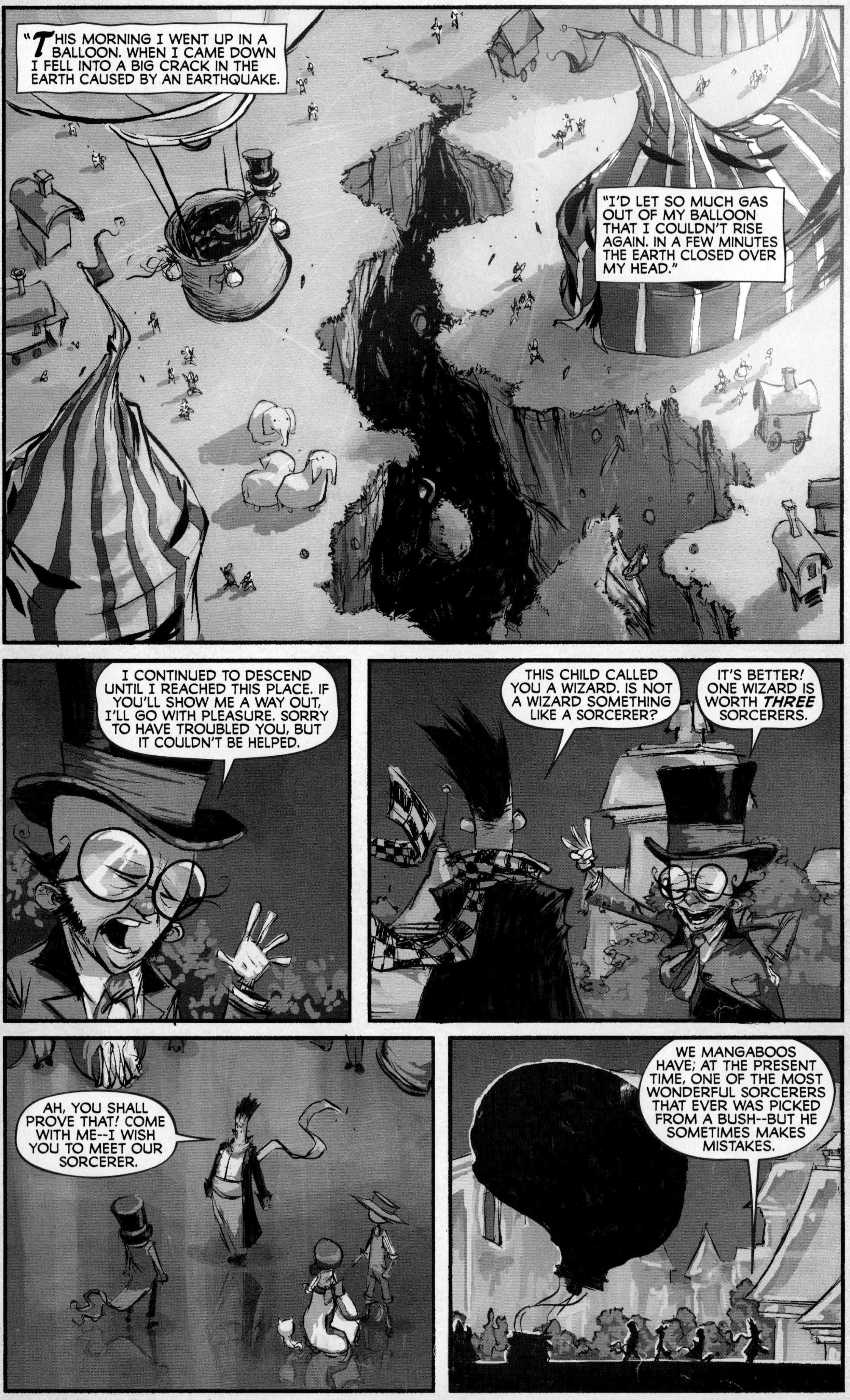
"THIS MORNING I WENT UP IN A BALLOON. WHEN I CAME DOWN I FELL INTO A BIG CRACK IN THE EARTH CAUSED BY AN EARTHQUAKE.
"I'D LET SO MUCH GAS OUT OF MY BALLOON THAT I COULDN'T RISE AGAIN. IN A FEW MINUTES THE EARTH CLOSED OVER MY HEAD."
I CONTINUED TO DESCEND UNTIL I REACHED THIS PLACE. IF YOU'LL SHOW ME A WAY OUT, I'LL GO WITH PLEASURE. SORRY TO HAVE TROUBLED YOU, BUT IT COULDN'T BE HELPED.
THIS CHILD CALLED YOU A WIZARD. IS NOT A WIZARD SOMETHING LIKE A SORCERER?
IT'S BETTER! ONE WIZARD IS WORTH THREE SORCERERS.
AH, YOU SHALL PROVE THAT! COME WITH ME--I WISH YOU TO MEET OUR SORCERER.
WE MANGABOOS HAVE; AT THE PRESENT TIME, ONE OF THE MOST WONDERFUL SORCERERS THAT EVER WAS PICKED FROM A BUSH--BUT HE SOMETIMES MAKES MISTAKES.

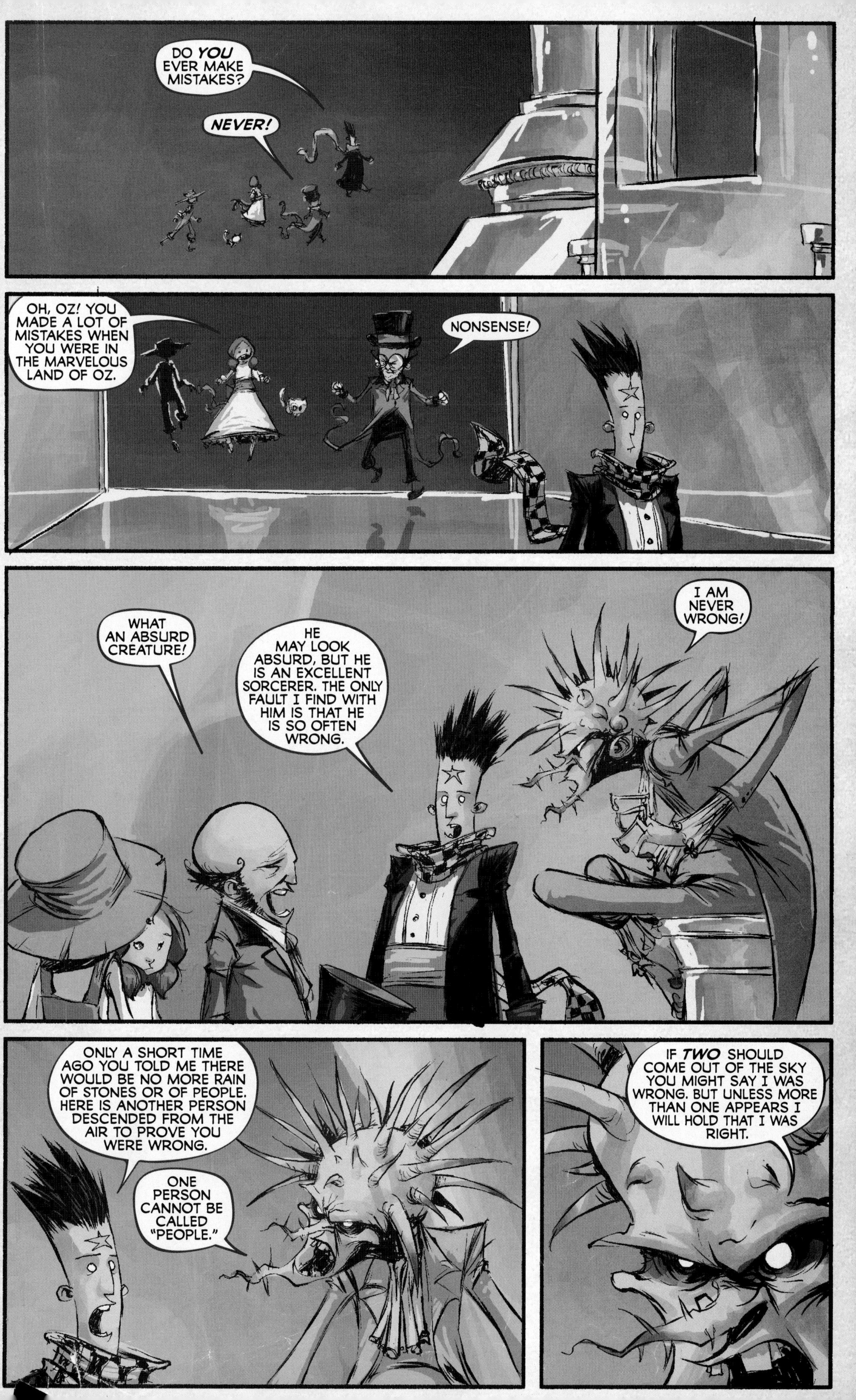
DO YOU EVER MAKE MISTAKES?
NEVER!
OH, OZ! YOU MADE A LOT OF MISTAKES WHEN YOU WERE IN THE MARVELOUS LAND OF OZ.
NONSENSE!
WHAT AN ABSURD CREATURE!
HE MAY LOOK ABSURD, BUT HE IS AN EXCELLENT SORCERER. THE ONLY FAULT I FIND WITH HIM IS THAT HE IS SO OFTEN WRONG.
I AM NEVER WRONG!
ONLY A SHORT TIME AGO YOU TOLD ME THERE WOULD BE NO MORE RAIN OF STONES OR OF PEOPLE. HERE IS ANOTHER PERSON DESCENDED FROM THE AIR TO PROVE YOU WERE WRONG.
ONE PERSON CANNOT BE CALLED "PEOPLE."
IF TWO SHOULD COME OUT OF THE SKY YOU MIGHT SAY I WAS WRONG. BUT UNLESS MORE THAN ONE APPEARS I WILL HOLD THAT I WAS RIGHT.

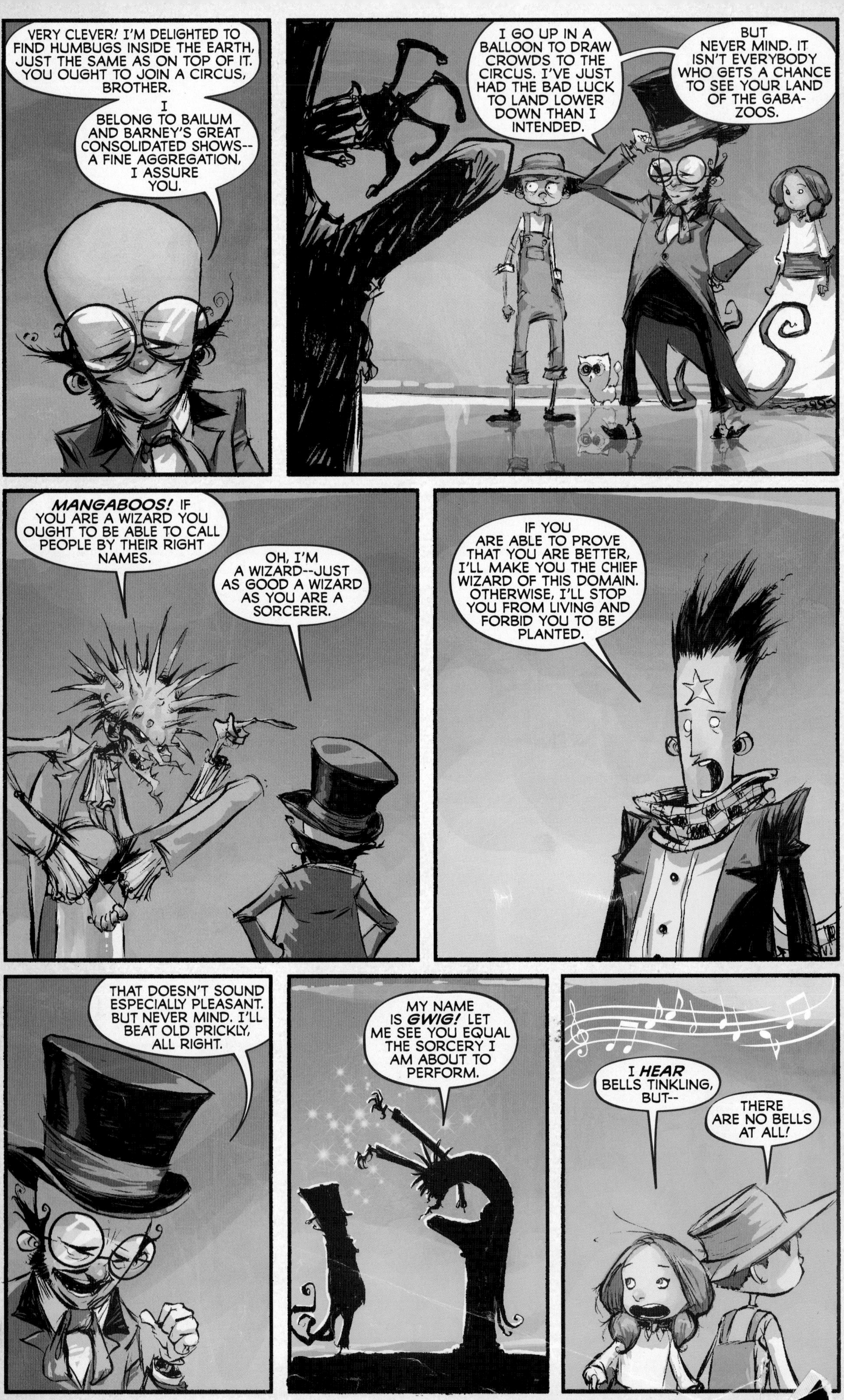
VERY CLEVER! I'M DELIGHTED TO FIND HUMBUGS INSIDE THE EARTH, JUST THE SAME AS ON TOP OF IT. YOU OUGHT TO JOIN A CIRCUS, BROTHER.
I BELONG TO BAILUM AND BARNEY'S GREAT CONSOLIDATED SHOWS-- A FINE AGGREGATION, I ASSURE YOU.
I GO UP IN A BALLOON TO DRAW CROWDS TO THE CIRCUS. I'VE JUST HAD THE BAD LUCK TO LAND LOWER DOWN THAN I INTENDED.
BUT NEVER MIND. IT ISN'T EVERYBODY WHO GETS A CHANCE TO SEE YOUR LAND OF THE GABA-ZOOS.
MANGABOOS! IF YOU ARE A WIZARD YOU OUGHT TO BE ABLE TO CALL PEOPLE BY THEIR RIGHT NAMES.
OH, I'M A WIZARD--JUST AS GOOD A WIZARD AS YOU ARE A SORCERER.
IF YOU ARE ABLE TO PROVE THAT YOU ARE BETTER, I'LL MAKE YOU THE CHIEF WIZARD OF THIS DOMAIN. OTHERWISE, I'LL STOP YOU FROM LIVING AND FORBID YOU TO BE PLANTED.
THAT DOESN'T SOUND ESPECIALLY PLEASANT. BUT NEVER MIND. I'LL BEAT OLD PRICKLY, ALL RIGHT.
MY NAME IS GWIG! LET ME SEE YOU EQUAL THE SORCERY I AM ABOUT TO PERFORM.
I HEAR BELLS TINKLING, BUT--
THERE ARE NO BELLS AT ALL!

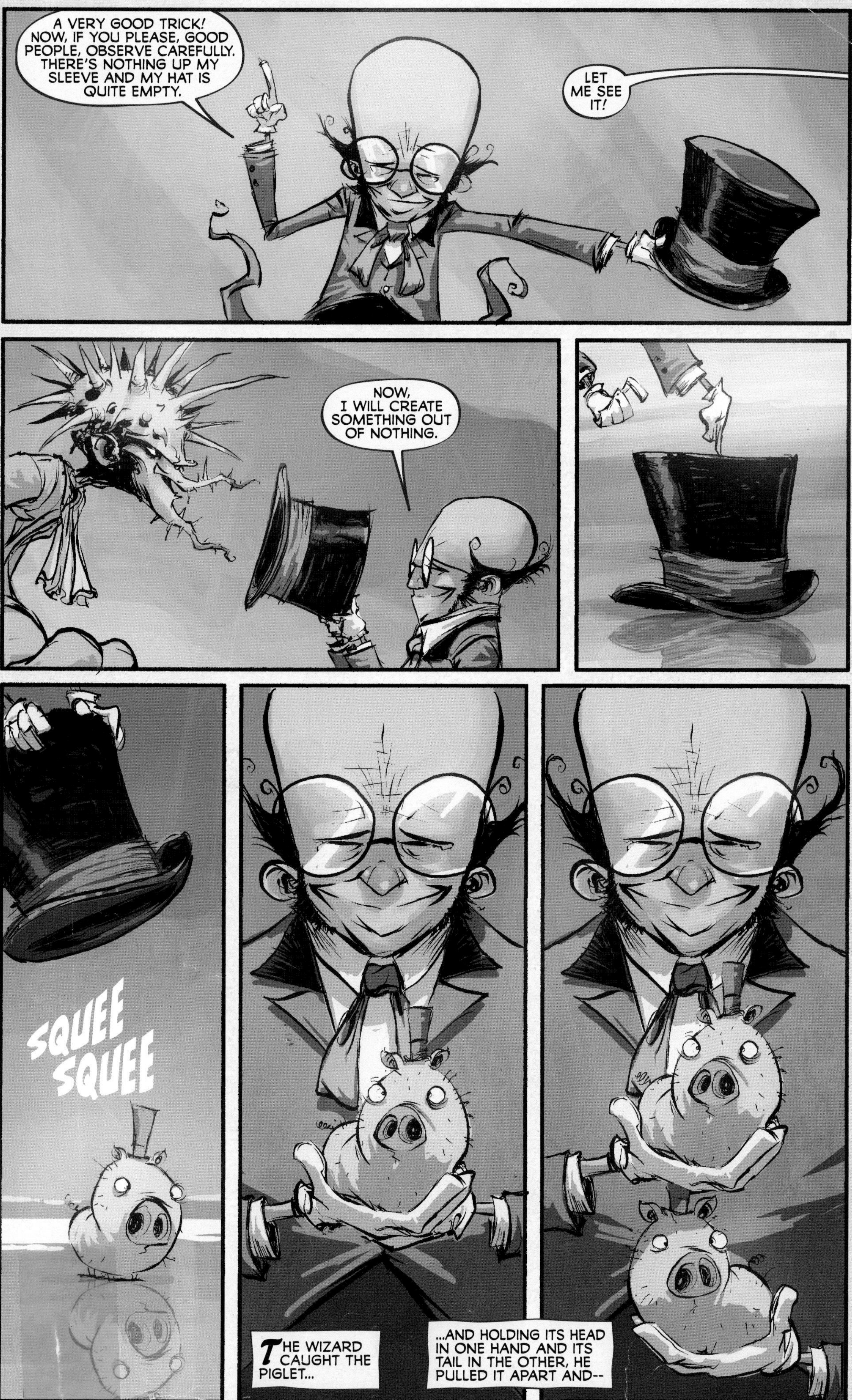
A VERY GOOD TRICK! NOW, IF YOU PLEASE, GOOD PEOPLE, OBSERVE CAREFULLY. THERE'S NOTHING UP MY SLEEVE AND MY HAT IS QUITE EMPTY.
LET ME SEE IT!
NOW, I WILL CREATE SOMETHING OUT OF NOTHING.
SQUEE SQUEE
THE WIZARD CAUGHT THE PIGLET...
...AND HOLDING ITS HEAD IN ONE HAND AND ITS TAIL IN THE OTHER, HE PULLED IT APART AND--

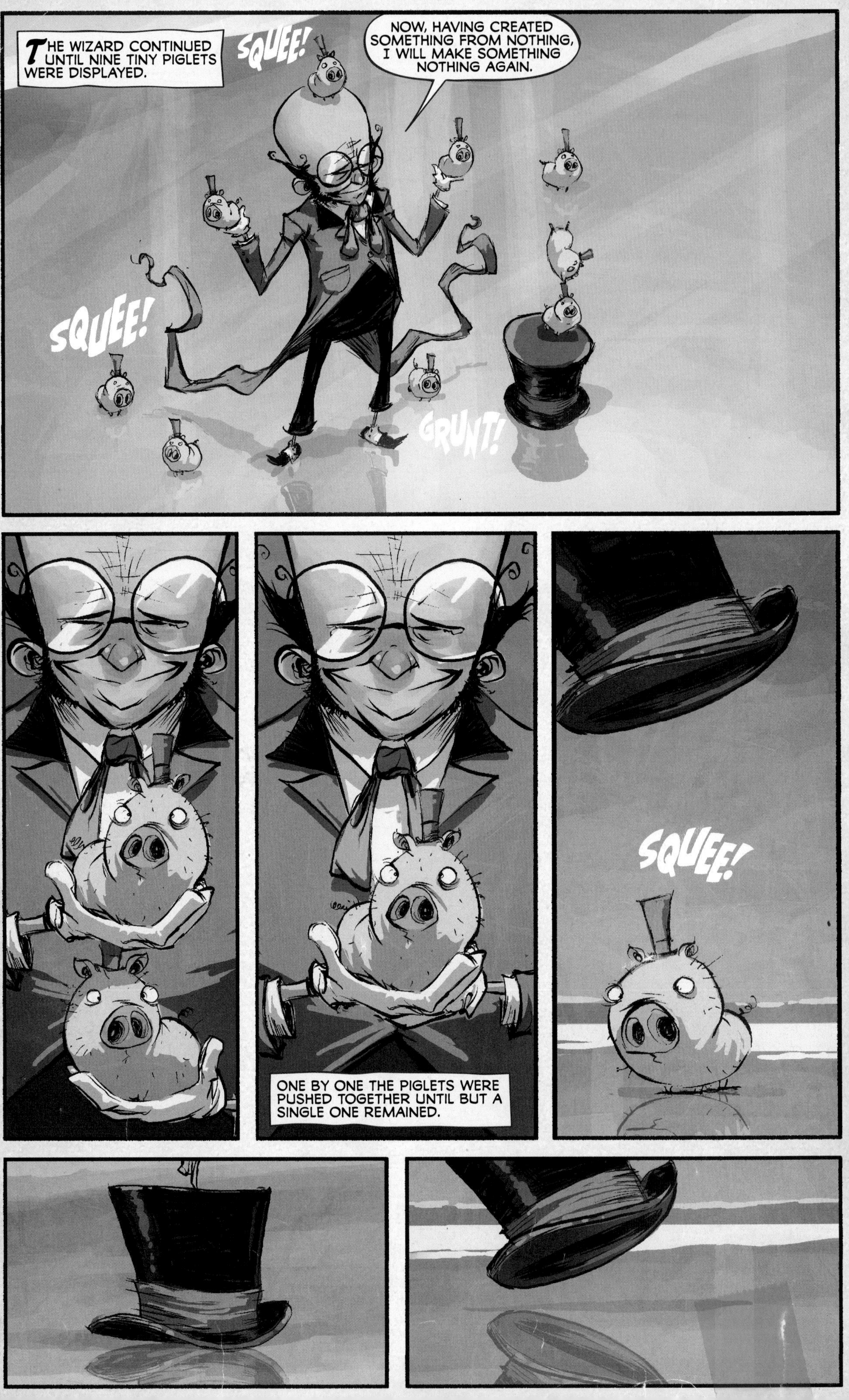
THE WIZARD CONTINUED UNTIL NINE TINY PIGLETS WERE DISPLAYED.
SQUEE!
NOW, HAVING CREATED SOMETHING FROM NOTHING, I WILL MAKE SOMETHING NOTHING AGAIN.
SQUEE!
GRUNT!
ONE BY ONE THE PIGLETS WERE PUSHED TOGETHER UNTIL BUT A SINGLE ONE REMAINED.
SQUEE!

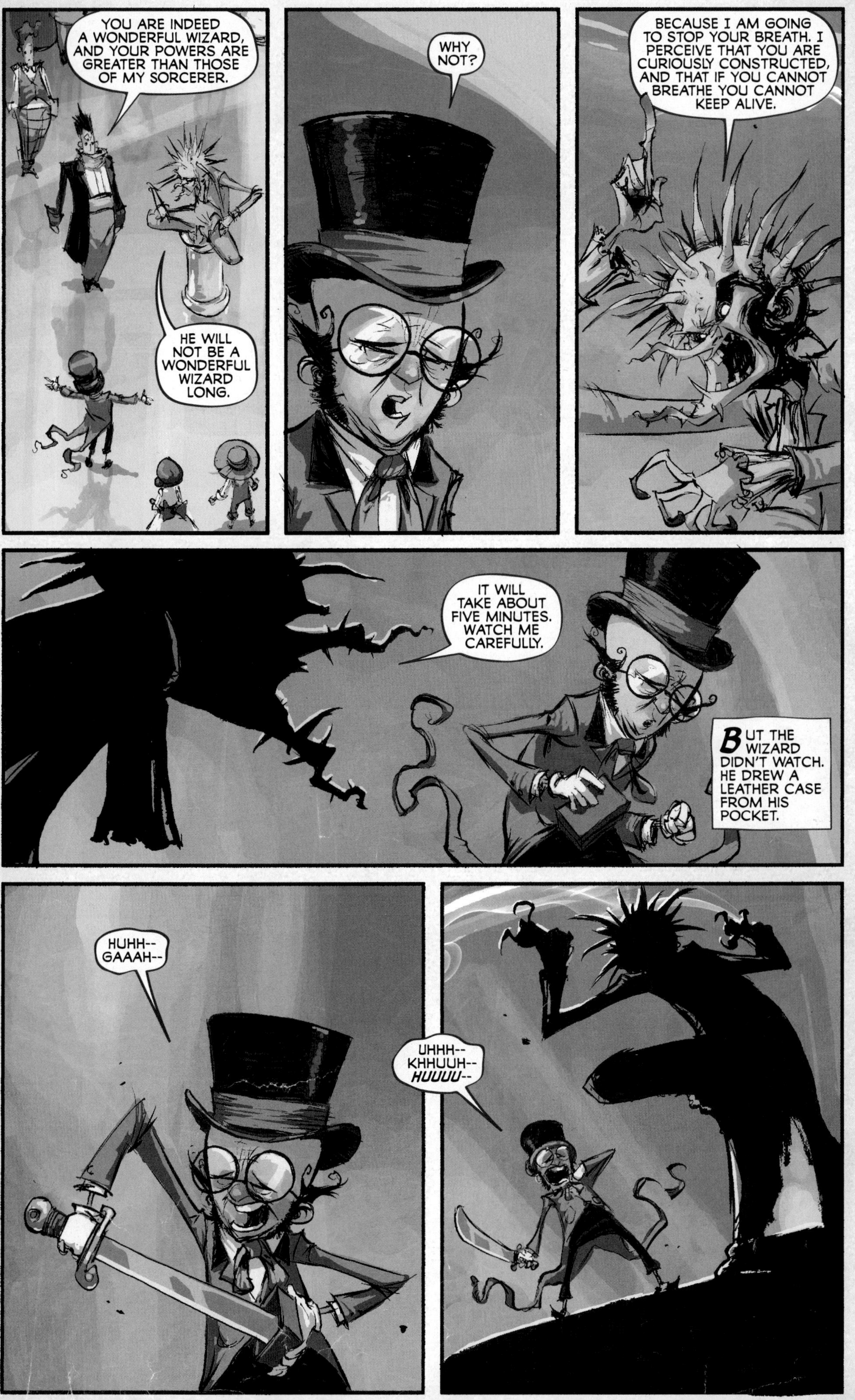
YOU ARE INDEED A WONDERFUL WIZARD, AND YOUR POWERS ARE GREATER THAN THOSE OF MY SORCERER.
HE WILL NOT BE A WONDERFUL WIZARD LONG.
WHY NOT?
BECAUSE I AM GOING TO STOP YOUR BREATH. I PERCEIVE THAT YOU ARE CURIOUSLY CONSTRUCTED, AND THAT IF YOU CANNOT BREATHE YOU CANNOT KEEP ALIVE.
IT WILL TAKE ABOUT FIVE MINUTES. WATCH ME CAREFULLY.
BUT THE WIZARD DIDN'T WATCH. HE DREW A LEATHER CASE FROM HIS POCKET.
HUHH-- GAAAH--
UHHH-- KHHUUH-- *HUUUU*--

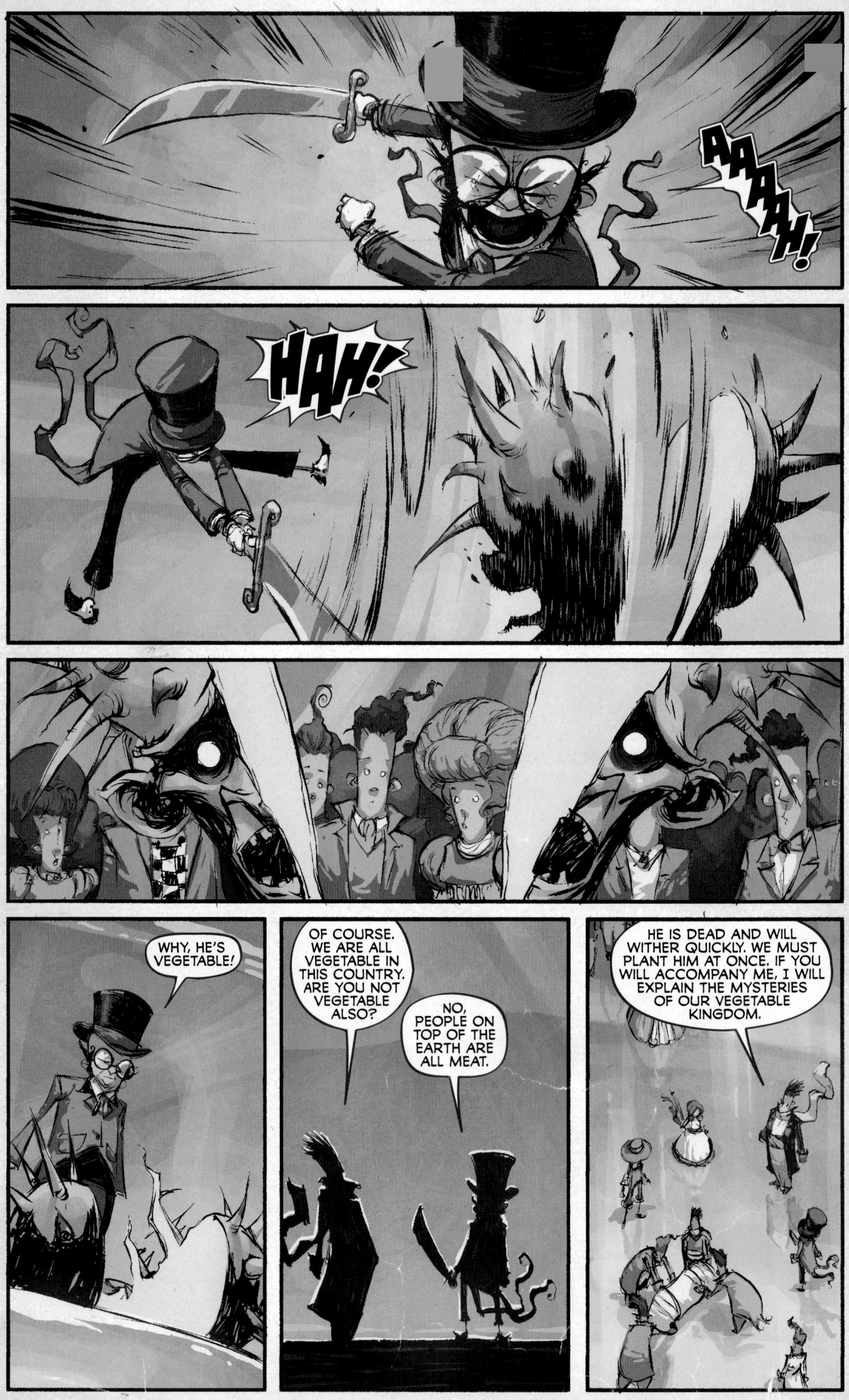
AAAAAH!
HAH!
WHY, HE'S VEGETABLE!
OF COURSE. WE ARE ALL VEGETABLE IN THIS COUNTRY. ARE YOU NOT VEGETABLE ALSO?
NO, PEOPLE ON TOP OF THE EARTH ARE ALL MEAT.
HE IS DEAD AND WILL WITHER QUICKLY. WE MUST PLANT HIM AT ONCE. IF YOU WILL ACCOMPANY ME, I WILL EXPLAIN THE MYSTERIES OF OUR VEGETABLE KINGDOM.

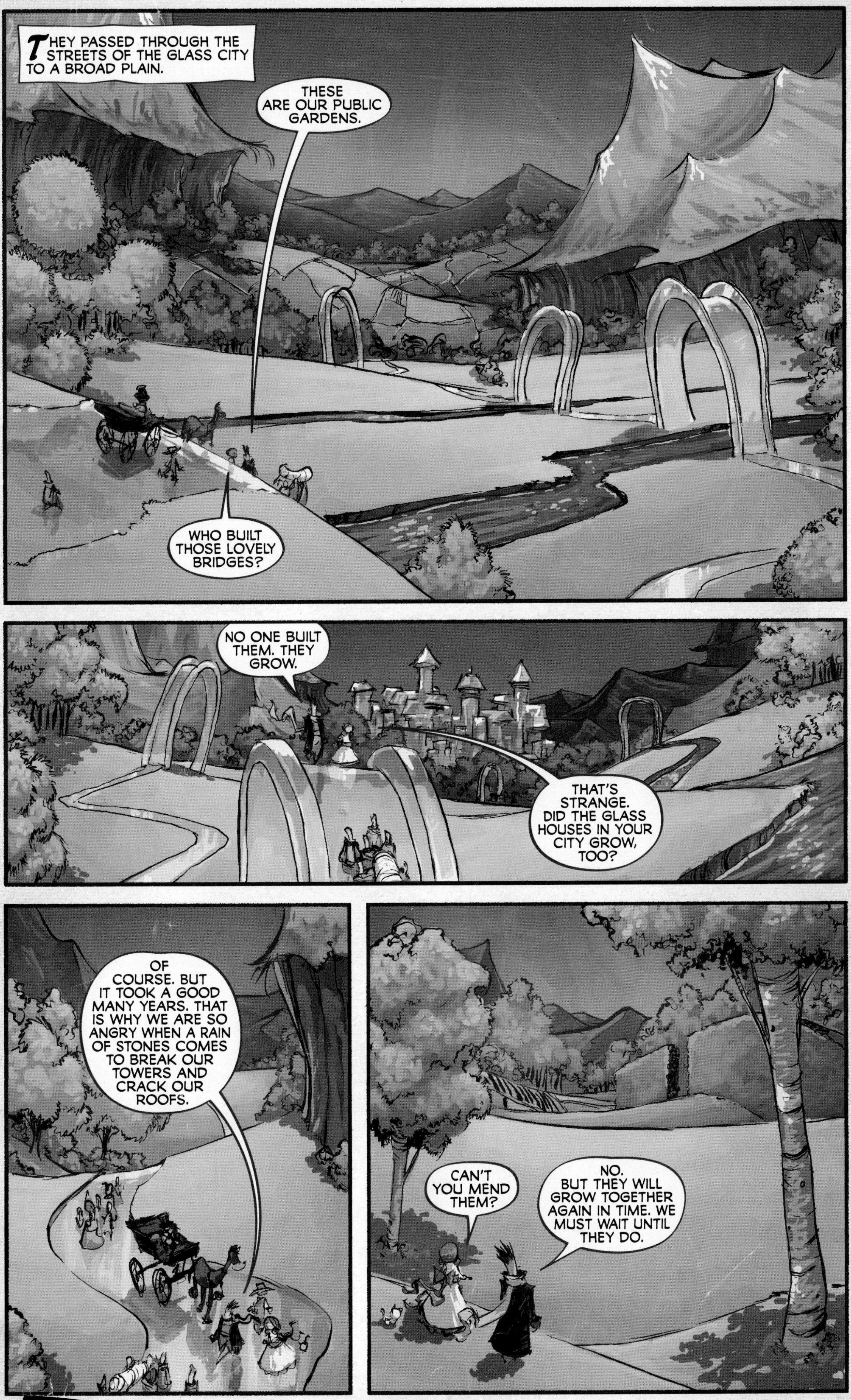
THEY PASSED THROUGH THE STREETS OF THE GLASS CITY TO A BROAD PLAIN.
THESE ARE OUR PUBLIC GARDENS.
WHO BUILT THOSE LOVELY BRIDGES?
NO ONE BUILT THEM. THEY GROW.
THAT'S STRANGE. DID THE GLASS HOUSES IN YOUR CITY GROW, TOO?
OF COURSE. BUT IT TOOK A GOOD MANY YEARS. THAT IS WHY WE ARE SO ANGRY WHEN A RAIN OF STONES COMES TO BREAK OUR TOWERS AND CRACK OUR ROOFS.
CAN'T YOU MEND THEM?
NO. BUT THEY WILL GROW TOGETHER AGAIN IN TIME. WE MUST WAIT UNTIL THEY DO.

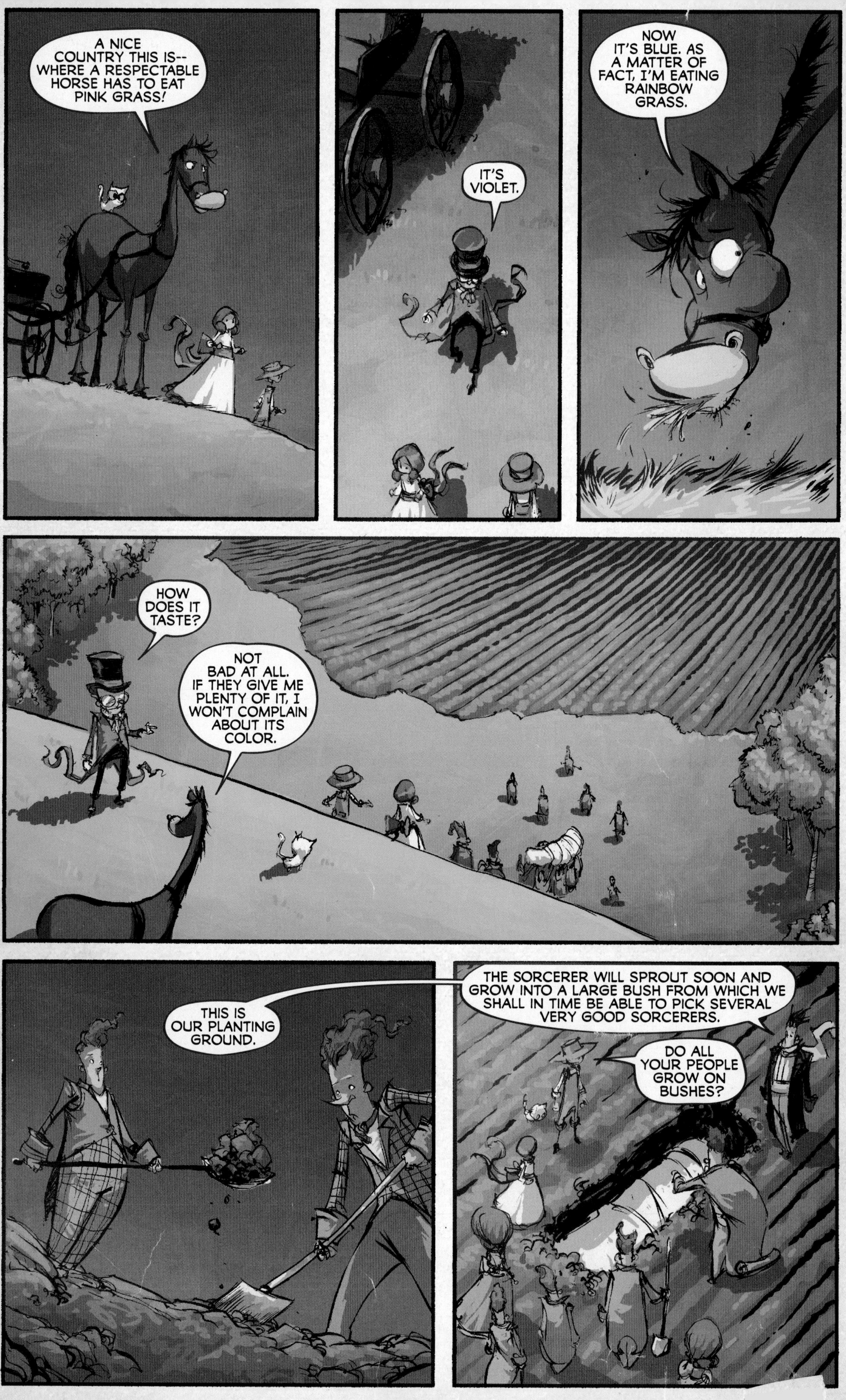
A NICE COUNTRY THIS IS-- WHERE A RESPECTABLE HORSE HAS TO EAT PINK GRASS!
IT'S VIOLET.
NOW IT'S BLUE. AS A MATTER OF FACT, I'M EATING RAINBOW GRASS.
HOW DOES IT TASTE?
NOT BAD AT ALL. IF THEY GIVE ME PLENTY OF IT, I WON'T COMPLAIN ABOUT ITS COLOR.
THIS IS OUR PLANTING GROUND.
THE SORCERER WILL SPROUT SOON AND GROW INTO A LARGE BUSH FROM WHICH WE SHALL IN TIME BE ABLE TO PICK SEVERAL VERY GOOD SORCERERS.
DO ALL YOUR PEOPLE GROW ON BUSHES?

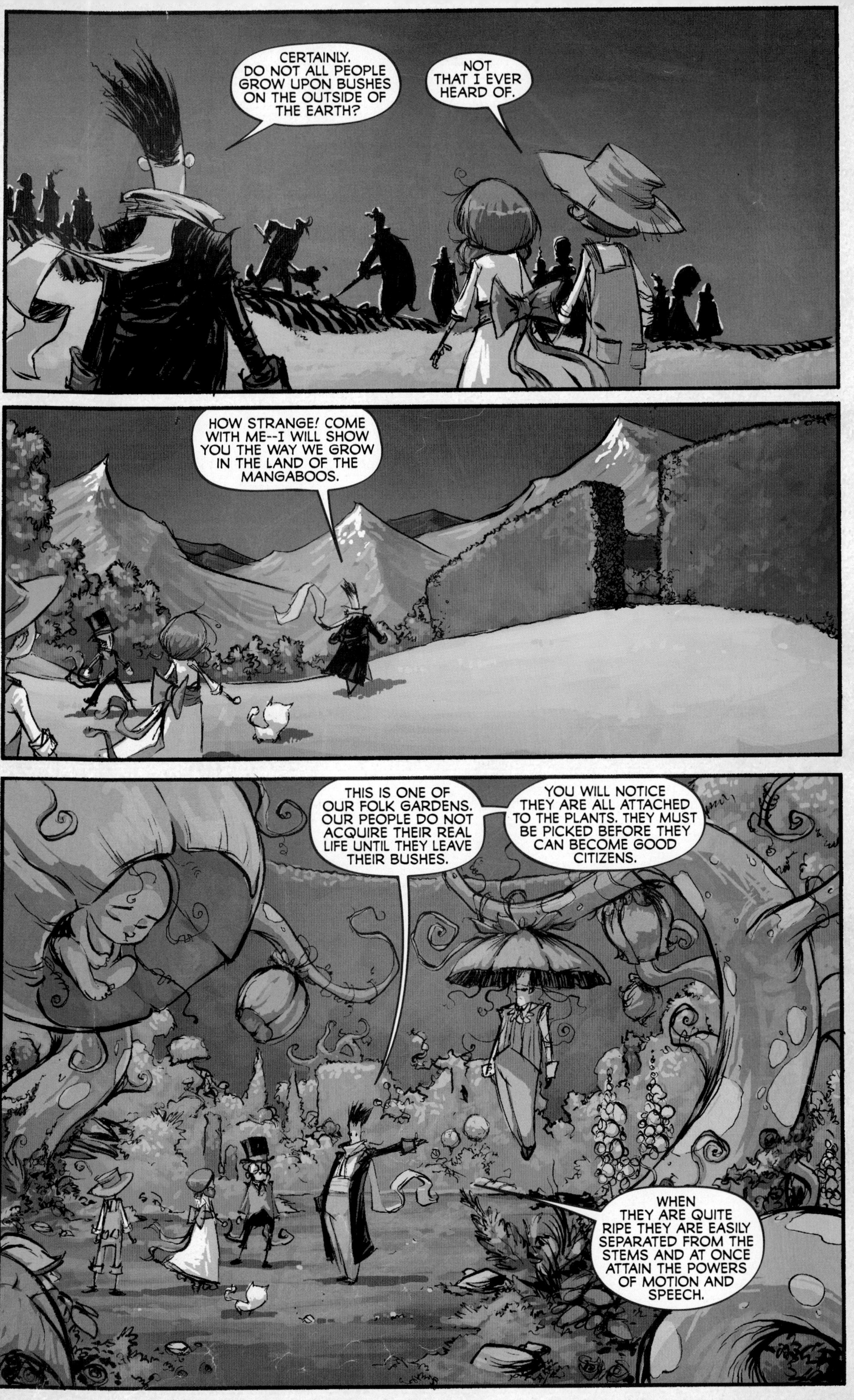
CERTAINLY. DO NOT ALL PEOPLE GROW UPON BUSHES ON THE OUTSIDE OF THE EARTH?
NOT THAT I EVER HEARD OF.
HOW STRANGE! COME WITH ME--I WILL SHOW YOU THE WAY WE GROW IN THE LAND OF THE MANGABOOS.
THIS IS ONE OF OUR FOLK GARDENS. OUR PEOPLE DO NOT ACQUIRE THEIR REAL LIFE UNTIL THEY LEAVE THEIR BUSHES.
YOU WILL NOTICE THEY ARE ALL ATTACHED TO THE PLANTS. THEY MUST BE PICKED BEFORE THEY CAN BECOME GOOD CITIZENS.
WHEN THEY ARE QUITE RIPE THEY ARE EASILY SEPARATED FROM THE STEMS AND AT ONCE ATTAIN THE POWERS OF MOTION AND SPEECH.

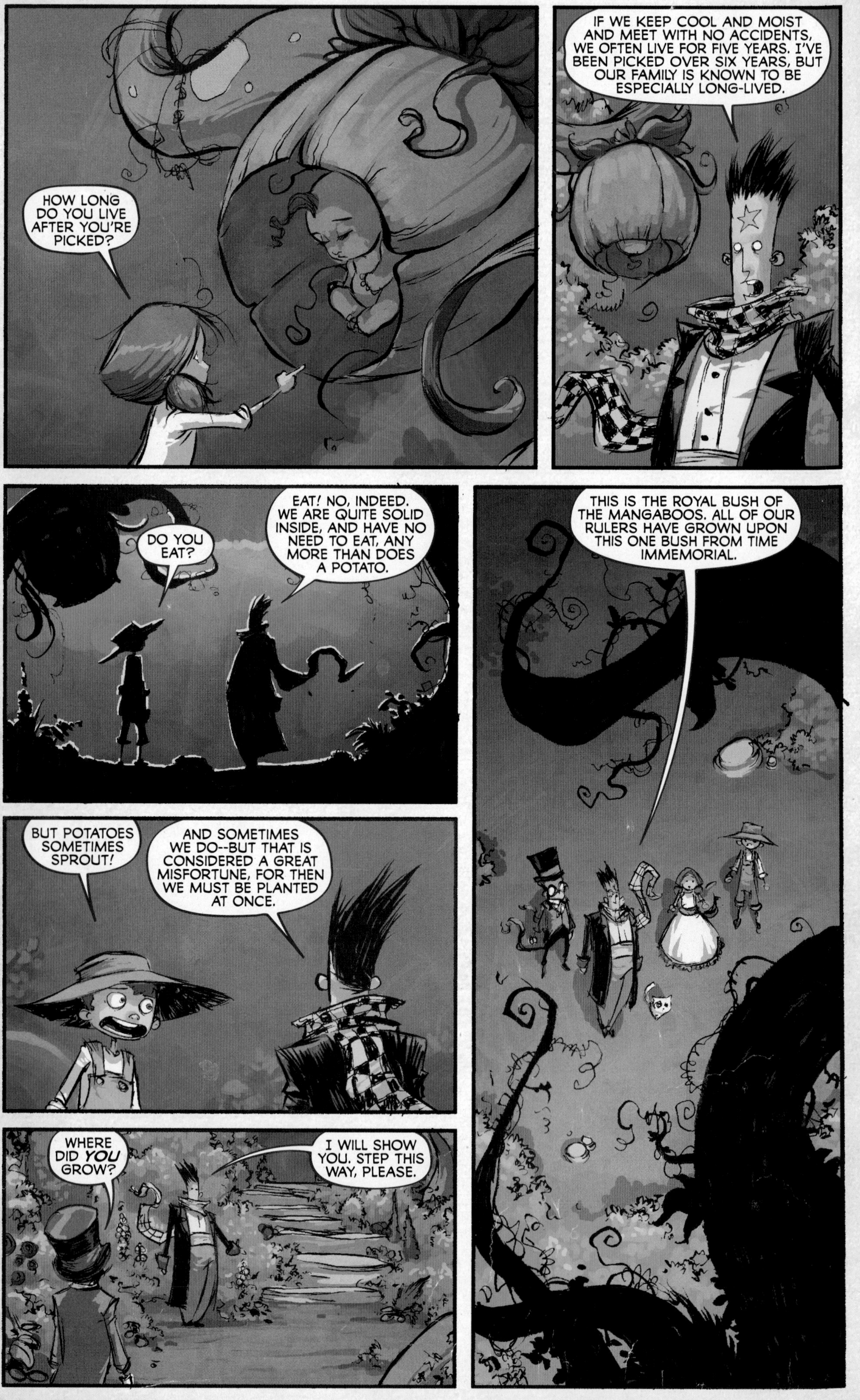
HOW LONG DO YOU LIVE AFTER YOU'RE PICKED?
IF WE KEEP COOL AND MOIST AND MEET WITH NO ACCIDENTS, WE OFTEN LIVE FOR FIVE YEARS. I'VE BEEN PICKED OVER SIX YEARS, BUT OUR FAMILY IS KNOWN TO BE ESPECIALLY LONG-LIVED.
DO YOU EAT?
EAT! NO, INDEED. WE ARE QUITE SOLID INSIDE, AND HAVE NO NEED TO EAT, ANY MORE THAN DOES A POTATO.
BUT POTATOES SOMETIMES SPROUT!
AND SOMETIMES WE DO--BUT THAT IS CONSIDERED A GREAT MISFORTUNE, FOR THEN WE MUST BE PLANTED AT ONCE.
WHERE DID *YOU* GROW?
I WILL SHOW YOU. STEP THIS WAY, PLEASE.
THIS IS THE ROYAL BUSH OF THE MANGABOOS. ALL OF OUR RULERS HAVE GROWN UPON THIS ONE BUSH FROM TIME IMMEMORIAL.

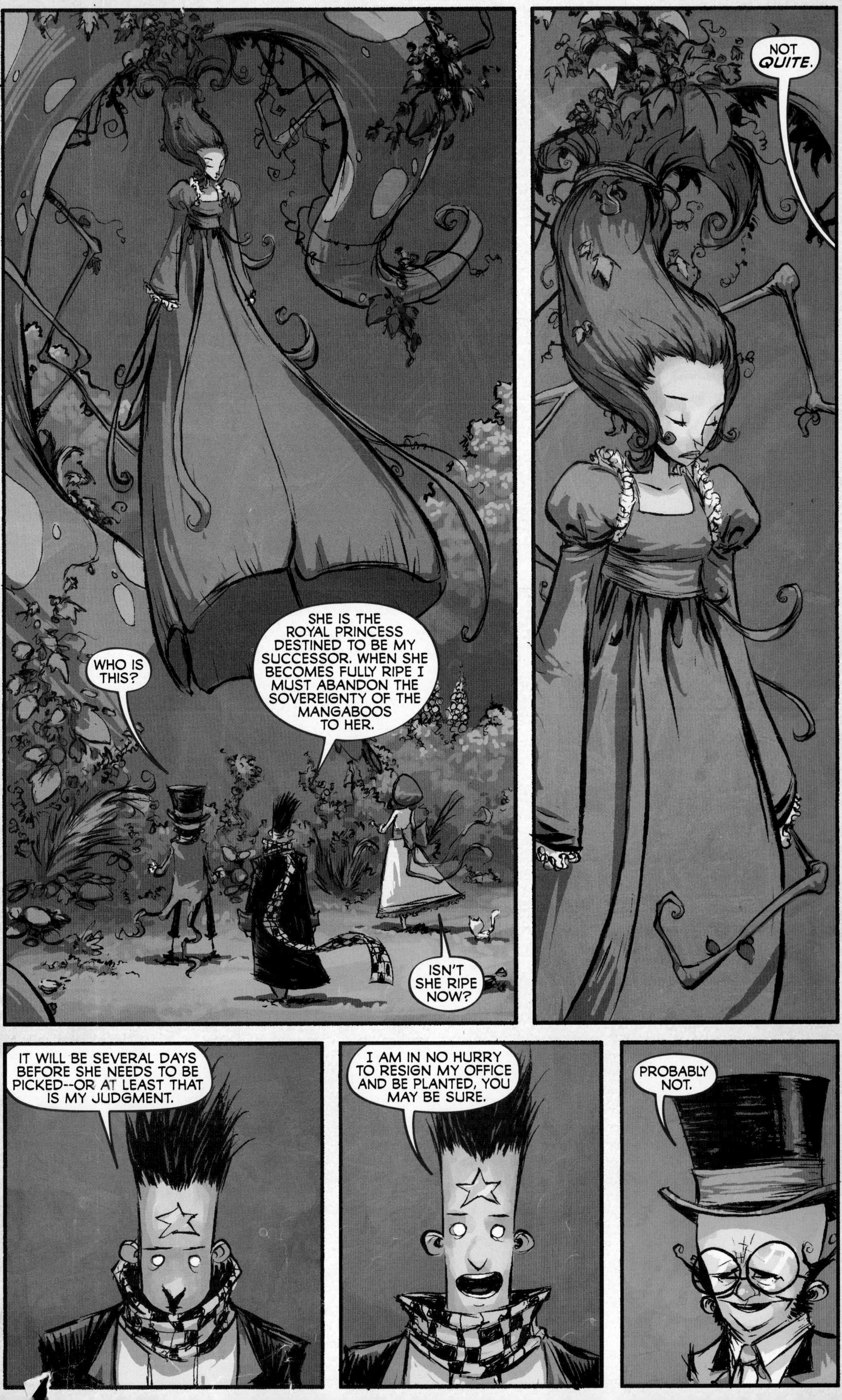
WHO IS THIS?
SHE IS THE ROYAL PRINCESS DESTINED TO BE MY SUCCESSOR. WHEN SHE BECOMES FULLY RIPE I MUST ABANDON THE SOVEREIGNTY OF THE MANGABOOS TO HER.
ISN'T SHE RIPE NOW?
NOT QUITE.
IT WILL BE SEVERAL DAYS BEFORE SHE NEEDS TO BE PICKED--OR AT LEAST THAT IS MY JUDGMENT.
I AM IN NO HURRY TO RESIGN MY OFFICE AND BE PLANTED, YOU MAY BE SURE.
PROBABLY NOT.

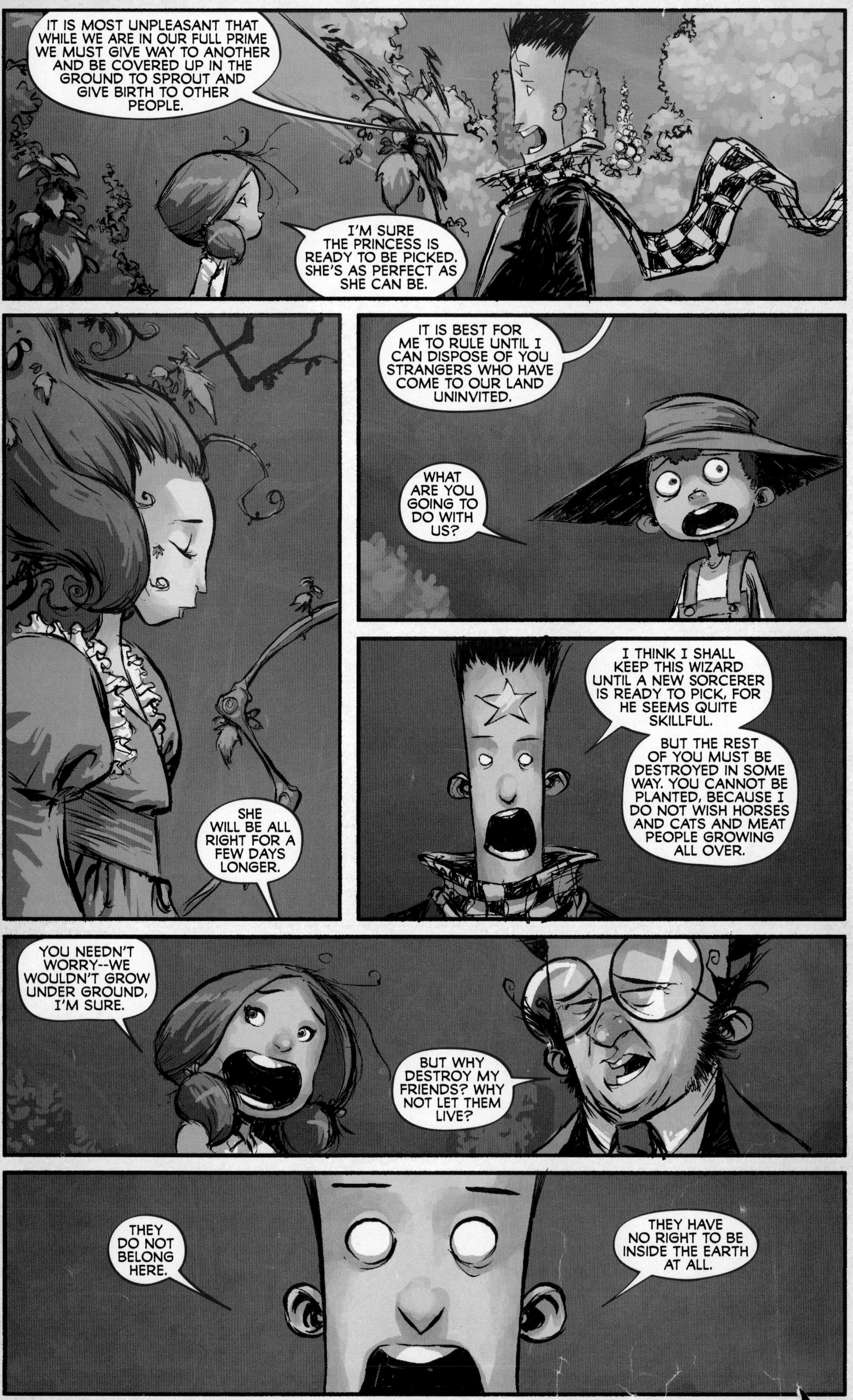
IT IS MOST UNPLEASANT THAT WHILE WE ARE IN OUR FULL PRIME WE MUST GIVE WAY TO ANOTHER AND BE COVERED UP IN THE GROUND TO SPROUT AND GIVE BIRTH TO OTHER PEOPLE.
I'M SURE THE PRINCESS IS READY TO BE PICKED. SHE'S AS PERFECT AS SHE CAN BE.
SHE WILL BE ALL RIGHT FOR A FEW DAYS LONGER.
IT IS BEST FOR ME TO RULE UNTIL I CAN DISPOSE OF YOU STRANGERS WHO HAVE COME TO OUR LAND UNINVITED.
WHAT ARE YOU GOING TO DO WITH US?
I THINK I SHALL KEEP THIS WIZARD UNTIL A NEW SORCERER IS READY TO PICK, FOR HE SEEMS QUITE SKILLFUL.
BUT THE REST OF YOU MUST BE DESTROYED IN SOME WAY. YOU CANNOT BE PLANTED, BECAUSE I DO NOT WISH HORSES AND CATS AND MEAT PEOPLE GROWING ALL OVER.
YOU NEEDN'T WORRY--WE WOULDN'T GROW UNDER GROUND, I'M SURE.
BUT WHY DESTROY MY FRIENDS? WHY NOT LET THEM LIVE?
THEY DO NOT BELONG HERE.
THEY HAVE NO RIGHT TO BE INSIDE THE EARTH AT ALL.

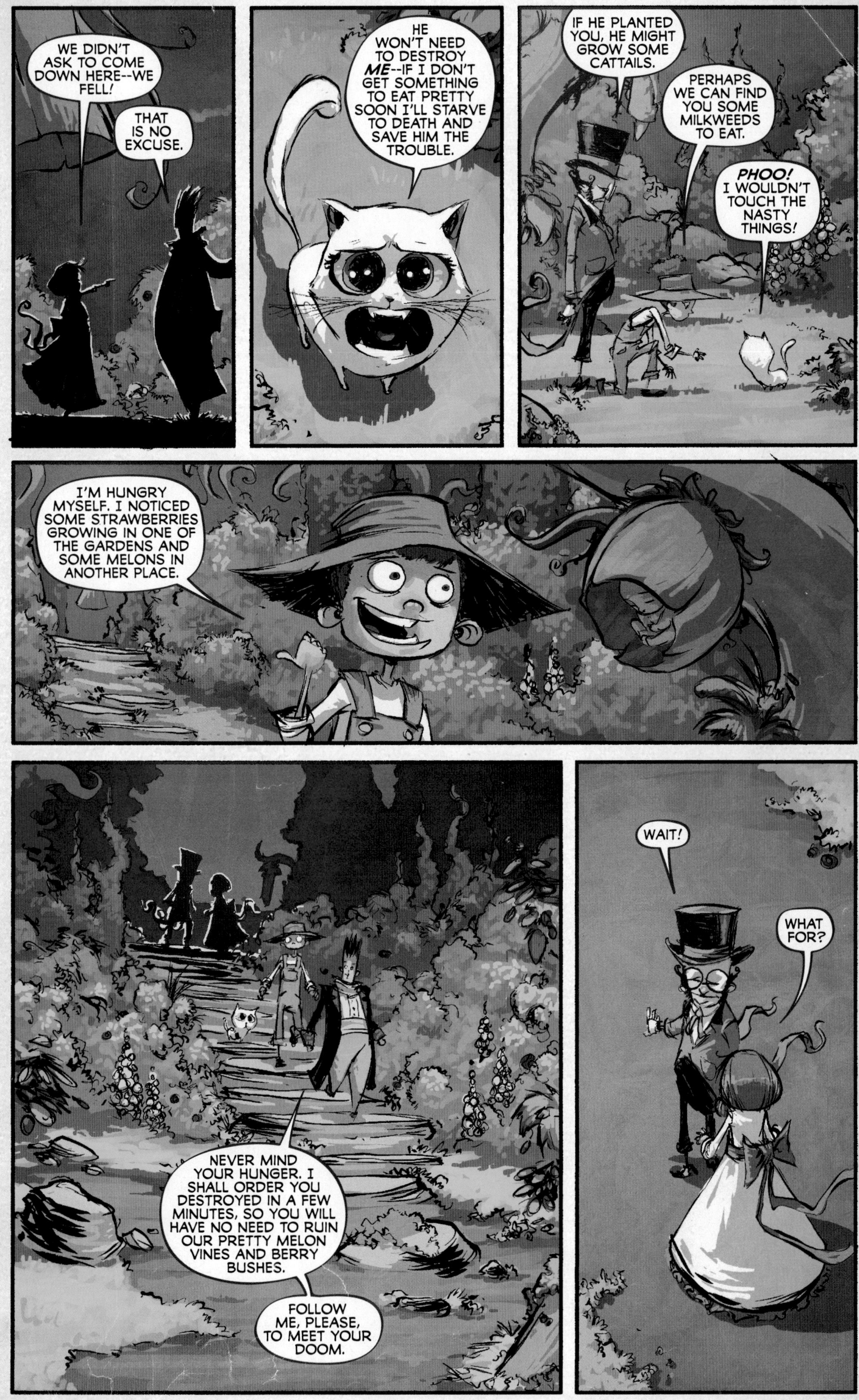
WE DIDN'T ASK TO COME DOWN HERE--WE FELL!
THAT IS NO EXCUSE.
HE WON'T NEED TO DESTROY *ME*--IF I DON'T GET SOMETHING TO EAT PRETTY SOON I'LL STARVE TO DEATH AND SAVE HIM THE TROUBLE.
IF HE PLANTED YOU, HE MIGHT GROW SOME CATTAILS.
PERHAPS WE CAN FIND YOU SOME MILKWEEDS TO EAT.
PHOO! I WOULDN'T TOUCH THE NASTY THINGS!
I'M HUNGRY MYSELF. I NOTICED SOME STRAWBERRIES GROWING IN ONE OF THE GARDENS AND SOME MELONS IN ANOTHER PLACE.
NEVER MIND YOUR HUNGER. I SHALL ORDER YOU DESTROYED IN A FEW MINUTES, SO YOU WILL HAVE NO NEED TO RUIN OUR PRETTY MELON VINES AND BERRY BUSHES.
FOLLOW ME, PLEASE, TO MEET YOUR DOOM.
WAIT!
WHAT FOR?

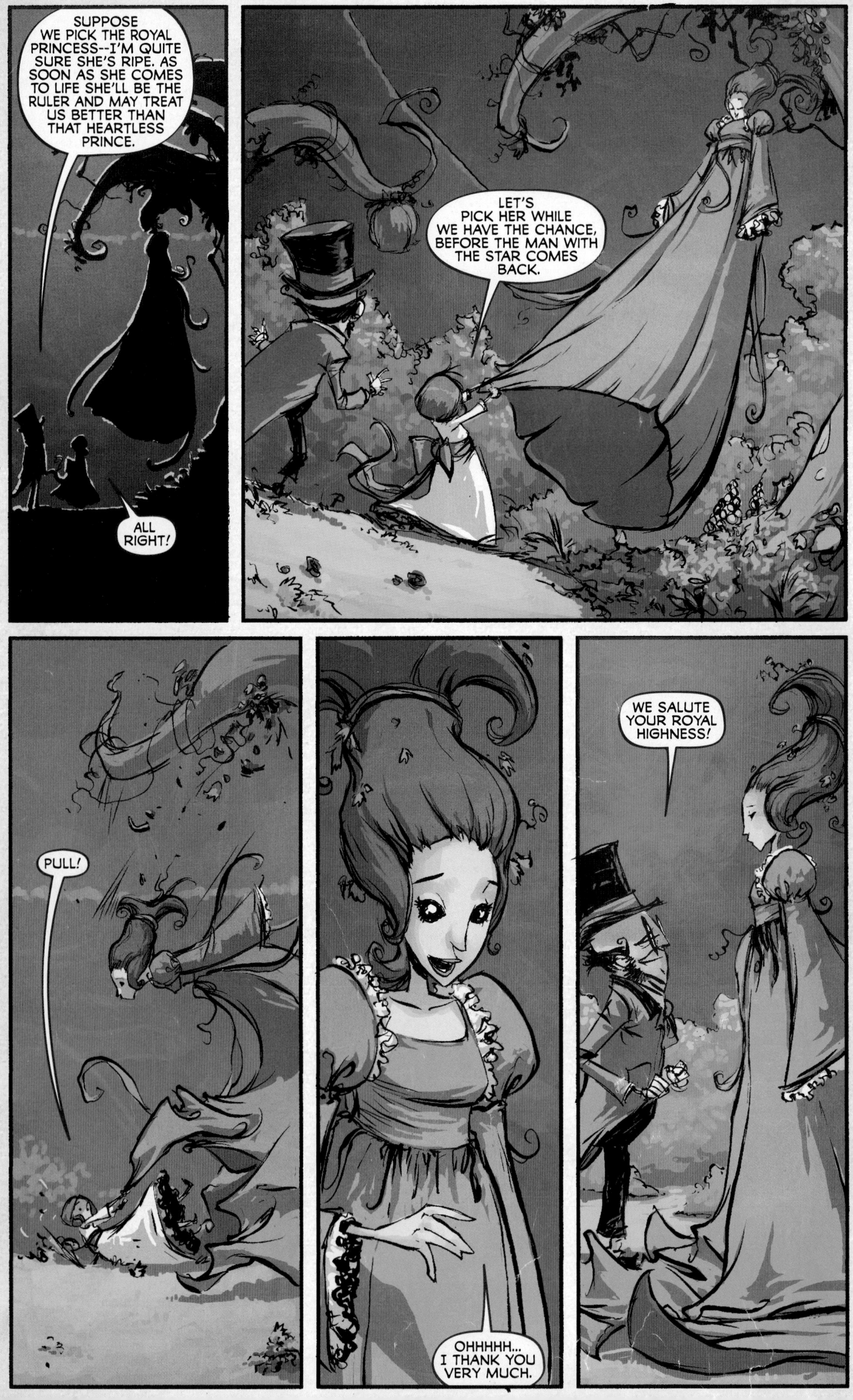
SUPPOSE WE PICK THE ROYAL PRINCESS--I'M QUITE SURE SHE'S RIPE. AS SOON AS SHE COMES TO LIFE SHE'LL BE THE RULER AND MAY TREAT US BETTER THAN THAT HEARTLESS PRINCE.
ALL RIGHT!
LET'S PICK HER WHILE WE HAVE THE CHANCE, BEFORE THE MAN WITH THE STAR COMES BACK.
PULL!
OHHHHH... I THANK YOU VERY MUCH.
WE SALUTE YOUR ROYAL HIGHNESS!

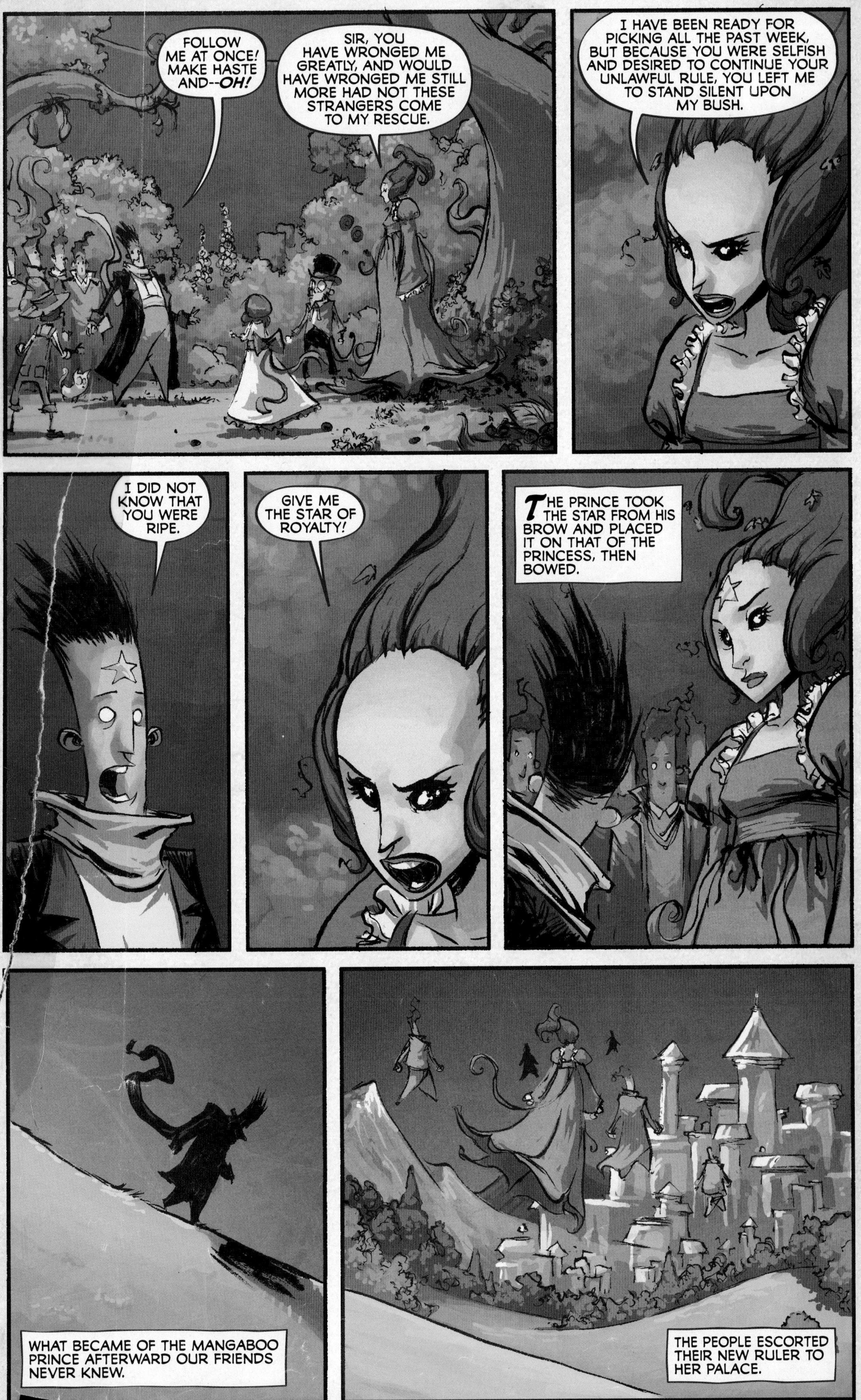
FOLLOW ME AT ONCE! MAKE HASTE AND--OH!
SIR, YOU HAVE WRONGED ME GREATLY, AND WOULD HAVE WRONGED ME STILL MORE HAD NOT THESE STRANGERS COME TO MY RESCUE.
I HAVE BEEN READY FOR PICKING ALL THE PAST WEEK, BUT BECAUSE YOU WERE SELFISH AND DESIRED TO CONTINUE YOUR UNLAWFUL RULE, YOU LEFT ME TO STAND SILENT UPON MY BUSH.
I DID NOT KNOW THAT YOU WERE RIPE.
GIVE ME THE STAR OF ROYALTY!
THE PRINCE TOOK THE STAR FROM HIS BROW AND PLACED IT ON THAT OF THE PRINCESS, THEN BOWED.
WHAT BECAME OF THE MANGABOO PRINCE AFTERWARD OUR FRIENDS NEVER KNEW.
THE PEOPLE ESCORTED THEIR NEW RULER TO HER PALACE.

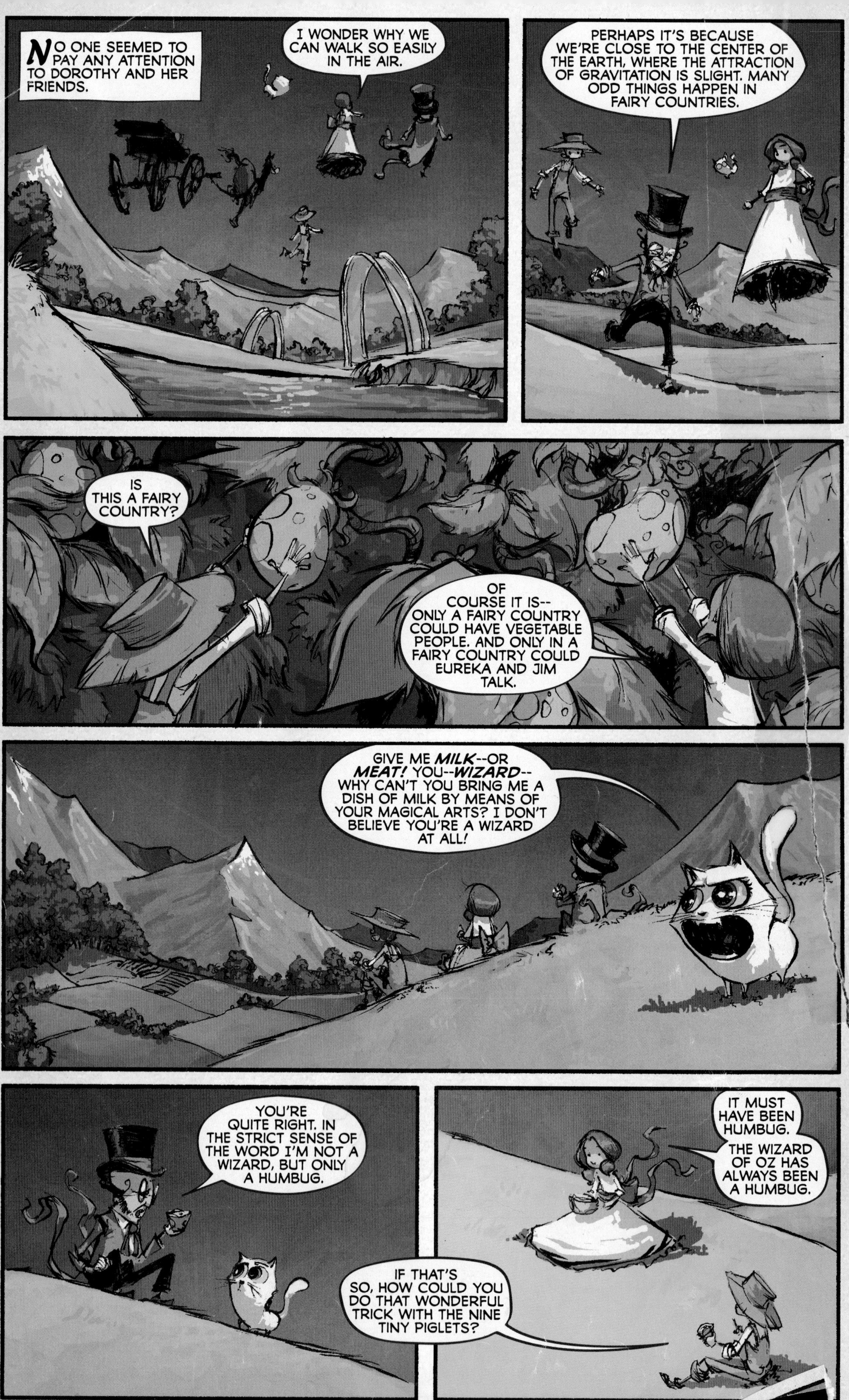
NO ONE SEEMED TO PAY ANY ATTENTION TO DOROTHY AND HER FRIENDS.
I WONDER WHY WE CAN WALK SO EASILY IN THE AIR.
PERHAPS IT'S BECAUSE WE'RE CLOSE TO THE CENTER OF THE EARTH, WHERE THE ATTRACTION OF GRAVITATION IS SLIGHT. MANY ODD THINGS HAPPEN IN FAIRY COUNTRIES.
IS THIS A FAIRY COUNTRY?
OF COURSE IT IS-- ONLY A FAIRY COUNTRY COULD HAVE VEGETABLE PEOPLE. AND ONLY IN A FAIRY COUNTRY COULD EUREKA AND JIM TALK.
GIVE ME **MILK**--OR ***MEAT!*** YOU--***WIZARD***-- WHY CAN'T YOU BRING ME A DISH OF MILK BY MEANS OF YOUR MAGICAL ARTS? I DON'T BELIEVE YOU'RE A WIZARD AT ALL!
YOU'RE QUITE RIGHT. IN THE STRICT SENSE OF THE WORD I'M NOT A WIZARD, BUT ONLY A HUMBUG.
IT MUST HAVE BEEN HUMBUG.
THE WIZARD OF OZ HAS ALWAYS BEEN A HUMBUG.
IF THAT'S SO, HOW COULD YOU DO THAT WONDERFUL TRICK WITH THE NINE TINY PIGLETS?

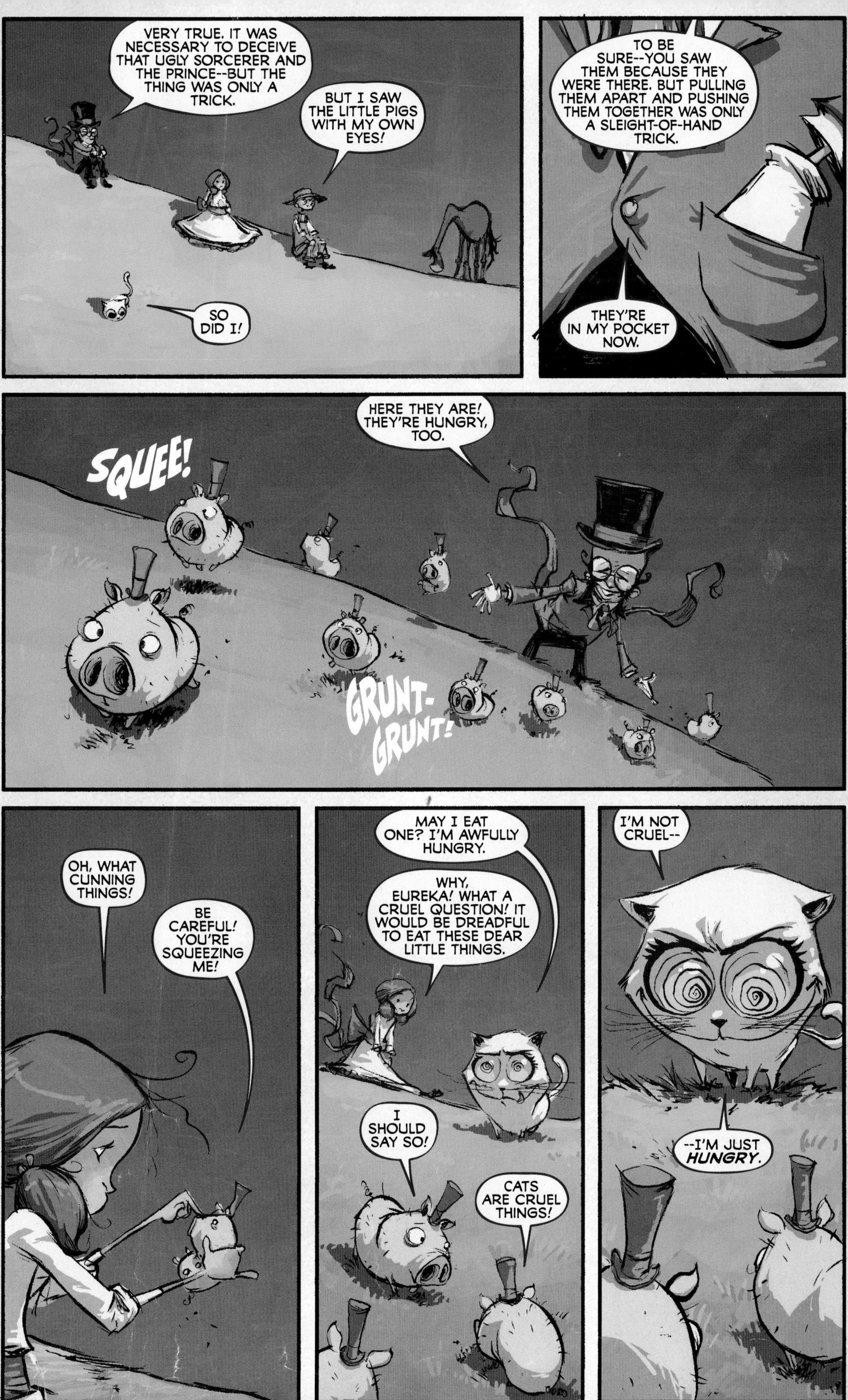

VERY TRUE. IT WAS NECESSARY TO DECEIVE THAT UGLY SORCERER AND THE PRINCE--BUT THE THING WAS ONLY A TRICK.
BUT I SAW THE LITTLE PIGS WITH MY OWN EYES!
SO DID I!
TO BE SURE--YOU SAW THEM BECAUSE THEY WERE THERE. BUT PULLING THEM APART AND PUSHING THEM TOGETHER WAS ONLY A SLEIGHT-OF-HAND TRICK.
THEY'RE IN MY POCKET NOW.
HERE THEY ARE! THEY'RE HUNGRY, TOO.
SQUEE!
GRUNT-GRUNT!
OH, WHAT CUNNING THINGS!
BE CAREFUL! YOU'RE SQUEEZING ME!
MAY I EAT ONE? I'M AWFULLY HUNGRY.
WHY, EUREKA! WHAT A CRUEL QUESTION! IT WOULD BE DREADFUL TO EAT THESE DEAR LITTLE THINGS.
I SHOULD SAY SO!
CATS ARE CRUEL THINGS!
I'M NOT CRUEL--
--I'M JUST HUNGRY.

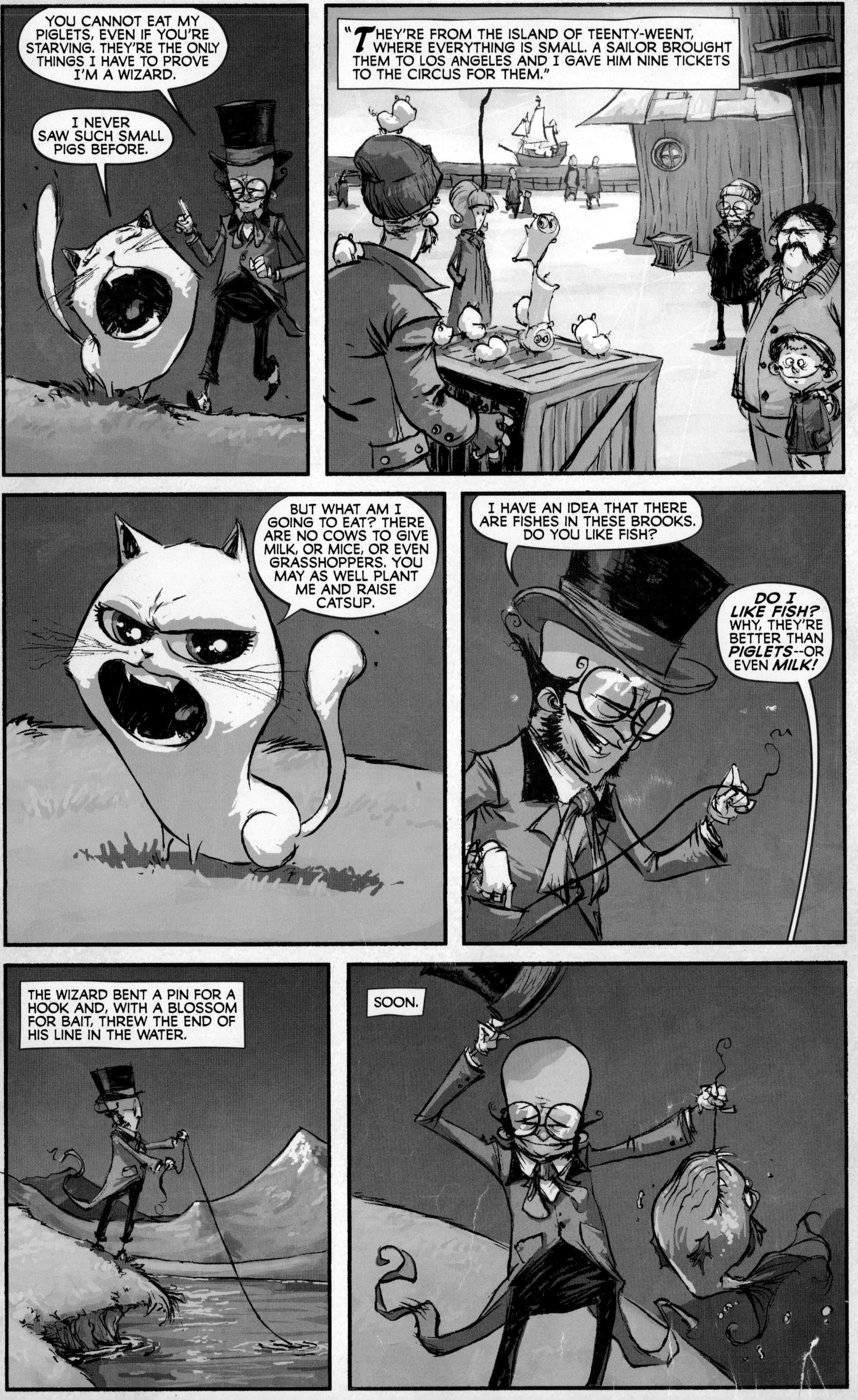
YOU CANNOT EAT MY PIGLETS, EVEN IF YOU'RE STARVING. THEY'RE THE ONLY THINGS I HAVE TO PROVE I'M A WIZARD.
I NEVER SAW SUCH SMALL PIGS BEFORE.
"THEY'RE FROM THE ISLAND OF TEENTY-WEENT, WHERE EVERYTHING IS SMALL. A SAILOR BROUGHT THEM TO LOS ANGELES AND I GAVE HIM NINE TICKETS TO THE CIRCUS FOR THEM."
BUT WHAT AM I GOING TO EAT? THERE ARE NO COWS TO GIVE MILK, OR MICE, OR EVEN GRASSHOPPERS. YOU MAY AS WELL PLANT ME AND RAISE CATSUP.
I HAVE AN IDEA THAT THERE ARE FISHES IN THESE BROOKS. DO YOU LIKE FISH?
DO I LIKE FISH? WHY, THEY'RE BETTER THAN PIGLETS--OR EVEN MILK!
THE WIZARD BENT A PIN FOR A HOOK AND, WITH A BLOSSOM FOR BAIT, THREW THE END OF HIS LINE IN THE WATER.
SOON.

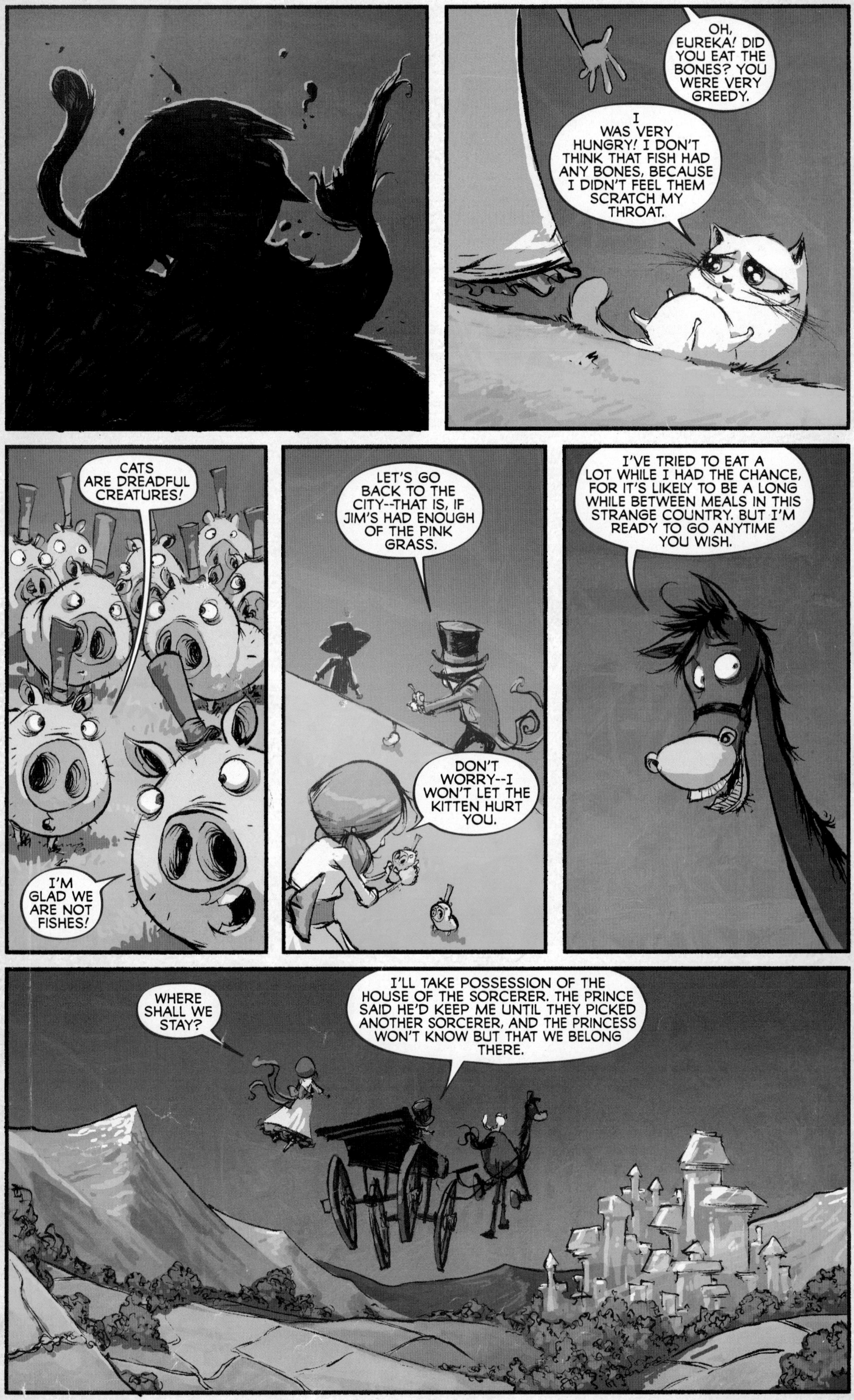
OH, EUREKA! DID YOU EAT THE BONES? YOU WERE VERY GREEDY.
I WAS VERY HUNGRY! I DON'T THINK THAT FISH HAD ANY BONES, BECAUSE I DIDN'T FEEL THEM SCRATCH MY THROAT.
CATS ARE DREADFUL CREATURES!
I'M GLAD WE ARE NOT FISHES!
LET'S GO BACK TO THE CITY--THAT IS, IF JIM'S HAD ENOUGH OF THE PINK GRASS.
DON'T WORRY--I WON'T LET THE KITTEN HURT YOU.
I'VE TRIED TO EAT A LOT WHILE I HAD THE CHANCE, FOR IT'S LIKELY TO BE A LONG WHILE BETWEEN MEALS IN THIS STRANGE COUNTRY. BUT I'M READY TO GO ANYTIME YOU WISH.
WHERE SHALL WE STAY?
I'LL TAKE POSSESSION OF THE HOUSE OF THE SORCERER. THE PRINCE SAID HE'D KEEP ME UNTIL THEY PICKED ANOTHER SORCERER, AND THE PRINCESS WON'T KNOW BUT THAT WE BELONG THERE.

LOOK DOWN!

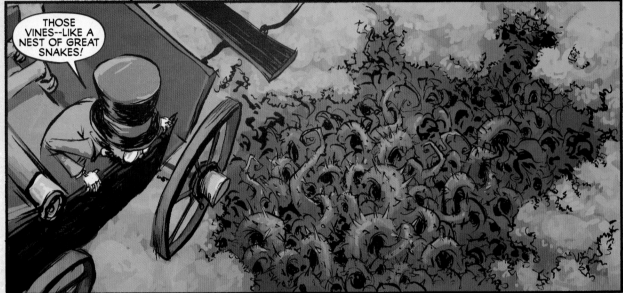

THOSE VINES--LIKE A NEST OF GREAT SNAKES!

THEY'RE ALL TWISTING AND WRITHING!

CRUNCH!

I'M THANKFUL TO HAVE ESCAPED ACCIDENTALLY STROLLING AMONG THEM!

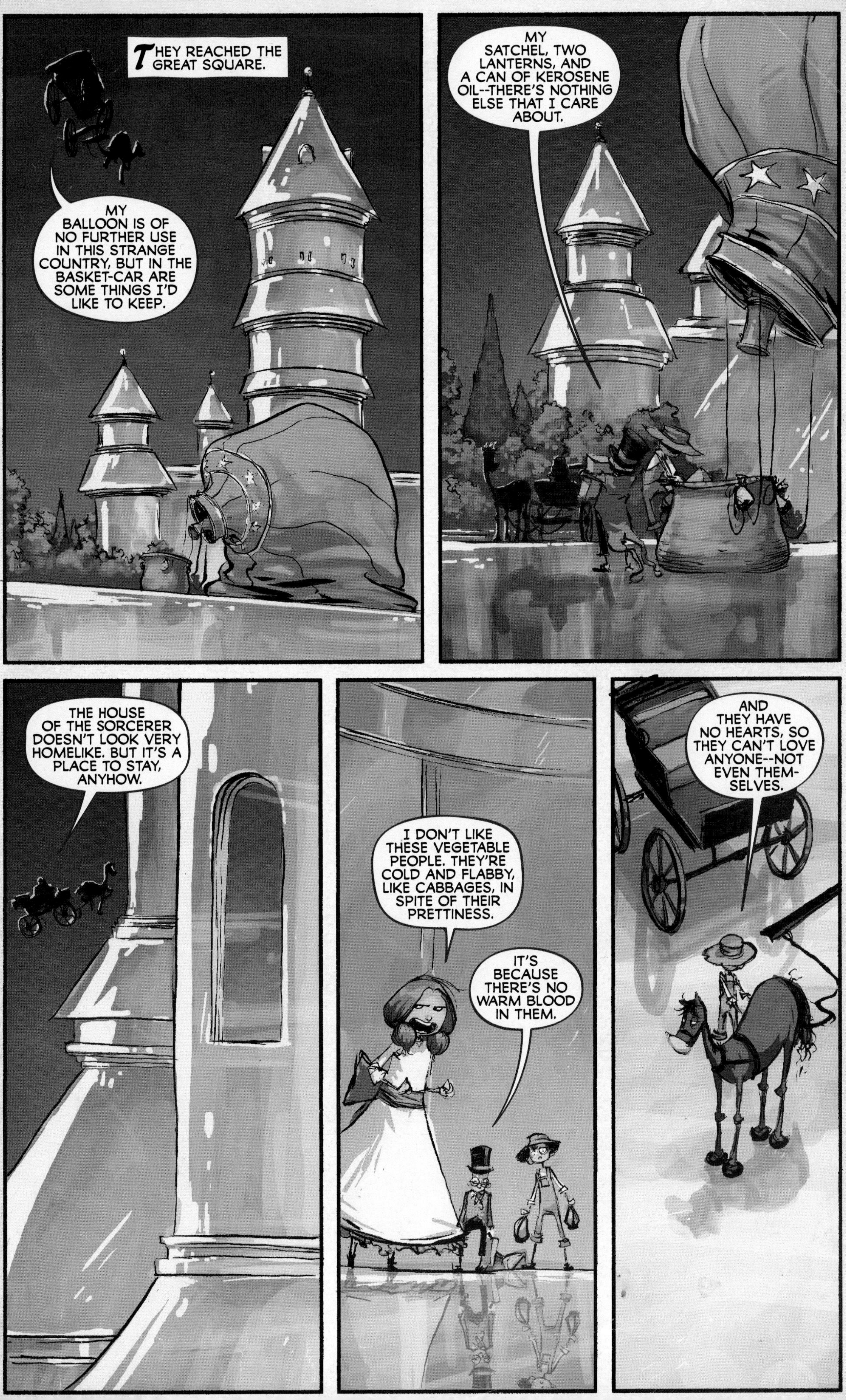
THEY REACHED THE GREAT SQUARE.
MY BALLOON IS OF NO FURTHER USE IN THIS STRANGE COUNTRY, BUT IN THE BASKET-CAR ARE SOME THINGS I'D LIKE TO KEEP.
MY SATCHEL, TWO LANTERNS, AND A CAN OF KEROSENE OIL--THERE'S NOTHING ELSE THAT I CARE ABOUT.
THE HOUSE OF THE SORCERER DOESN'T LOOK VERY HOMELIKE. BUT IT'S A PLACE TO STAY, ANYHOW.
I DON'T LIKE THESE VEGETABLE PEOPLE. THEY'RE COLD AND FLABBY, LIKE CABBAGES, IN SPITE OF THEIR PRETTINESS.
IT'S BECAUSE THERE'S NO WARM BLOOD IN THEM.
AND THEY HAVE NO HEARTS, SO THEY CAN'T LOVE ANYONE--NOT EVEN THEM-SELVES.

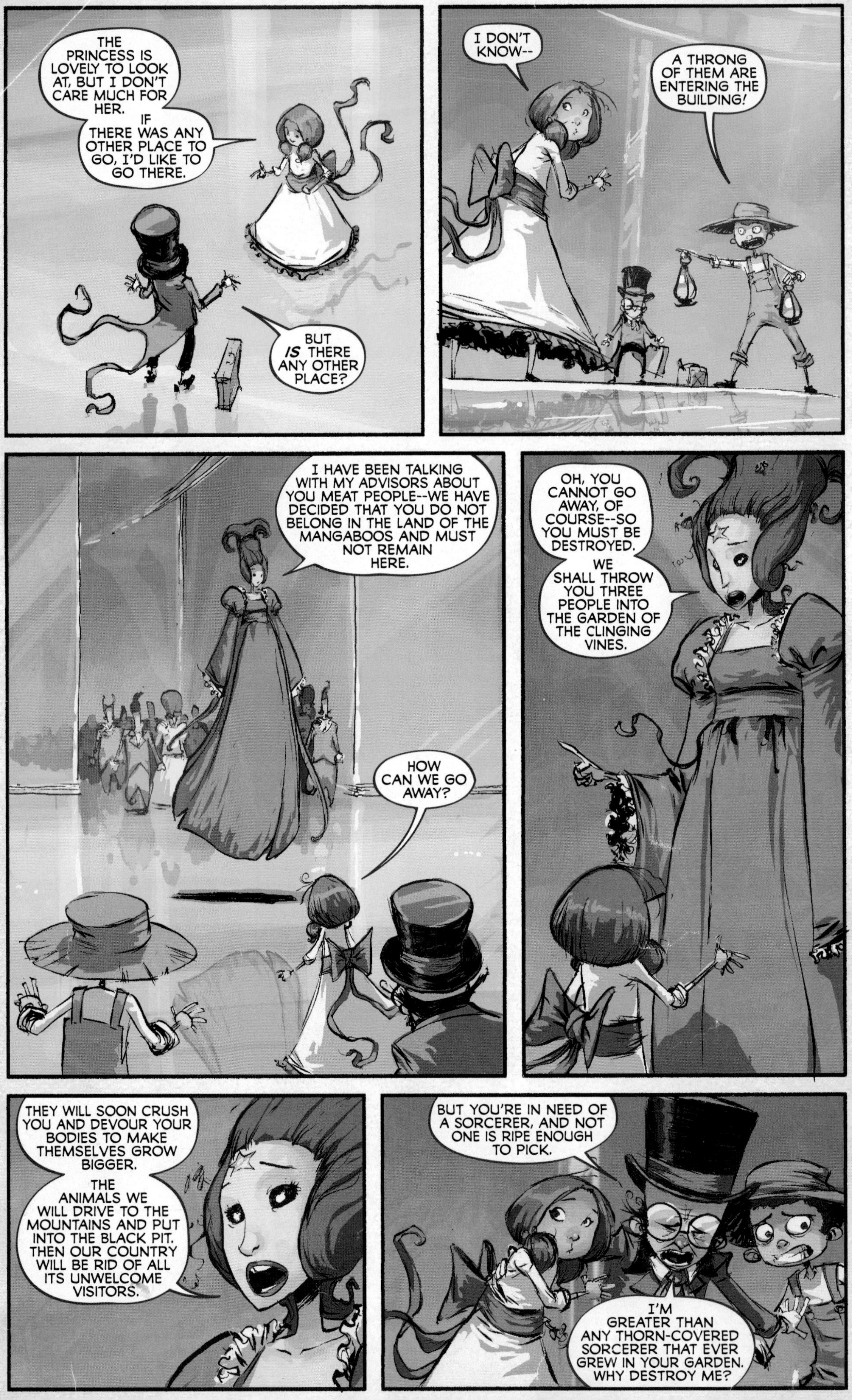
THE PRINCESS IS LOVELY TO LOOK AT, BUT I DON'T CARE MUCH FOR HER.
IF THERE WAS ANY OTHER PLACE TO GO, I'D LIKE TO GO THERE.
BUT *IS* THERE ANY OTHER PLACE?
I DON'T KNOW--
A THRONG OF THEM ARE ENTERING THE BUILDING!
I HAVE BEEN TALKING WITH MY ADVISORS ABOUT YOU MEAT PEOPLE--WE HAVE DECIDED THAT YOU DO NOT BELONG IN THE LAND OF THE MANGABOOS AND MUST NOT REMAIN HERE.
HOW CAN WE GO AWAY?
OH, YOU CANNOT GO AWAY, OF COURSE--SO YOU MUST BE DESTROYED.
WE SHALL THROW YOU THREE PEOPLE INTO THE GARDEN OF THE CLINGING VINES.
THEY WILL SOON CRUSH YOU AND DEVOUR YOUR BODIES TO MAKE THEMSELVES GROW BIGGER.
THE ANIMALS WE WILL DRIVE TO THE MOUNTAINS AND PUT INTO THE BLACK PIT. THEN OUR COUNTRY WILL BE RID OF ALL ITS UNWELCOME VISITORS.
BUT YOU'RE IN NEED OF A SORCERER, AND NOT ONE IS RIPE ENOUGH TO PICK.
I'M GREATER THAN ANY THORN-COVERED SORCERER THAT EVER GREW IN YOUR GARDEN. WHY DESTROY ME?

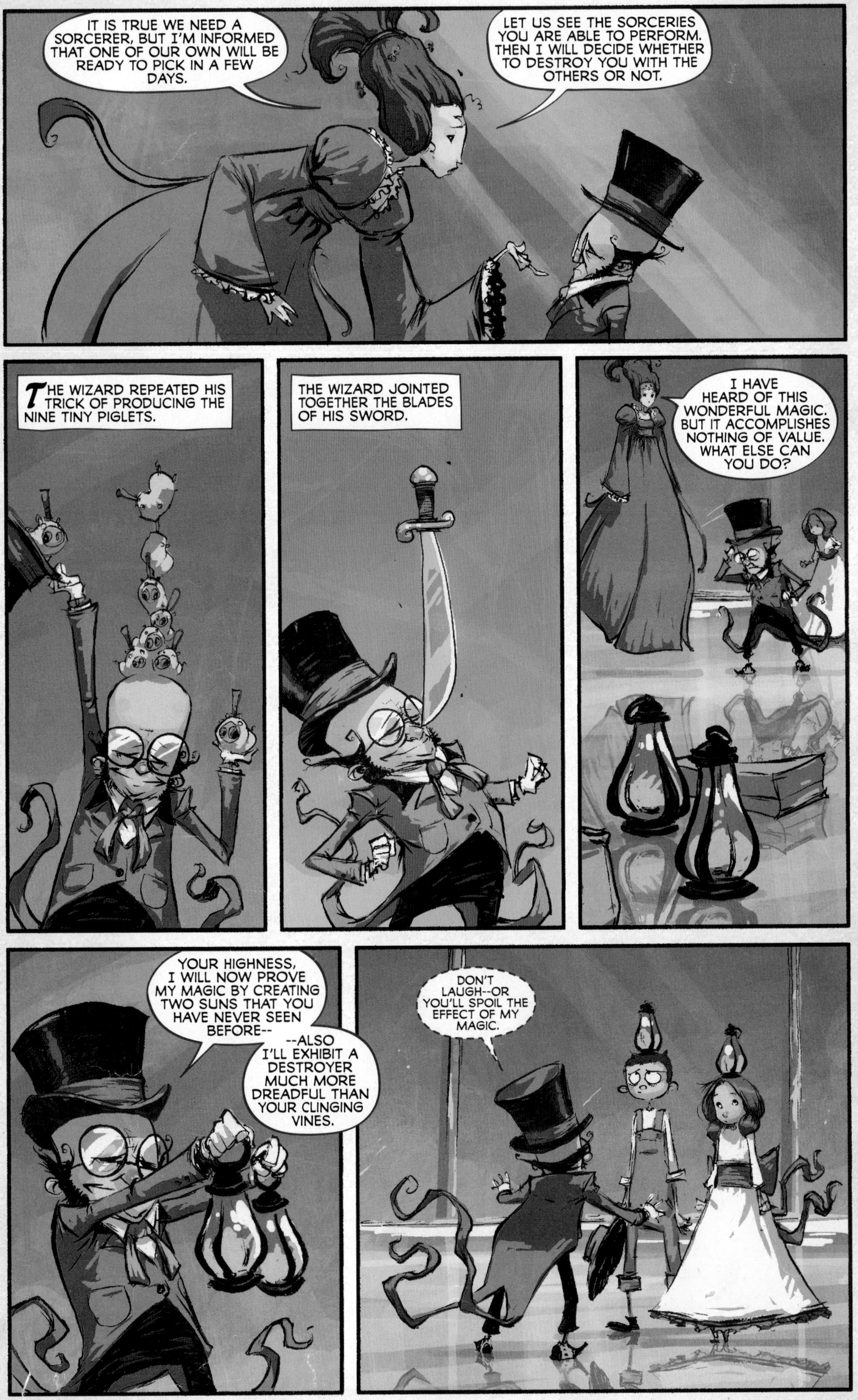
IT IS TRUE WE NEED A SORCERER, BUT I'M INFORMED THAT ONE OF OUR OWN WILL BE READY TO PICK IN A FEW DAYS.
LET US SEE THE SORCERIES YOU ARE ABLE TO PERFORM. THEN I WILL DECIDE WHETHER TO DESTROY YOU WITH THE OTHERS OR NOT.
THE WIZARD REPEATED HIS TRICK OF PRODUCING THE NINE TINY PIGLETS.
THE WIZARD JOINTED TOGETHER THE BLADES OF HIS SWORD.
I HAVE HEARD OF THIS WONDERFUL MAGIC. BUT IT ACCOMPLISHES NOTHING OF VALUE. WHAT ELSE CAN YOU DO?
YOUR HIGHNESS, I WILL NOW PROVE MY MAGIC BY CREATING TWO SUNS THAT YOU HAVE NEVER SEEN BEFORE--
--ALSO I'LL EXHIBIT A DESTROYER MUCH MORE DREADFUL THAN YOUR CLINGING VINES.
DON'T LAUGH--OR YOU'LL SPOIL THE EFFECT OF MY MAGIC.

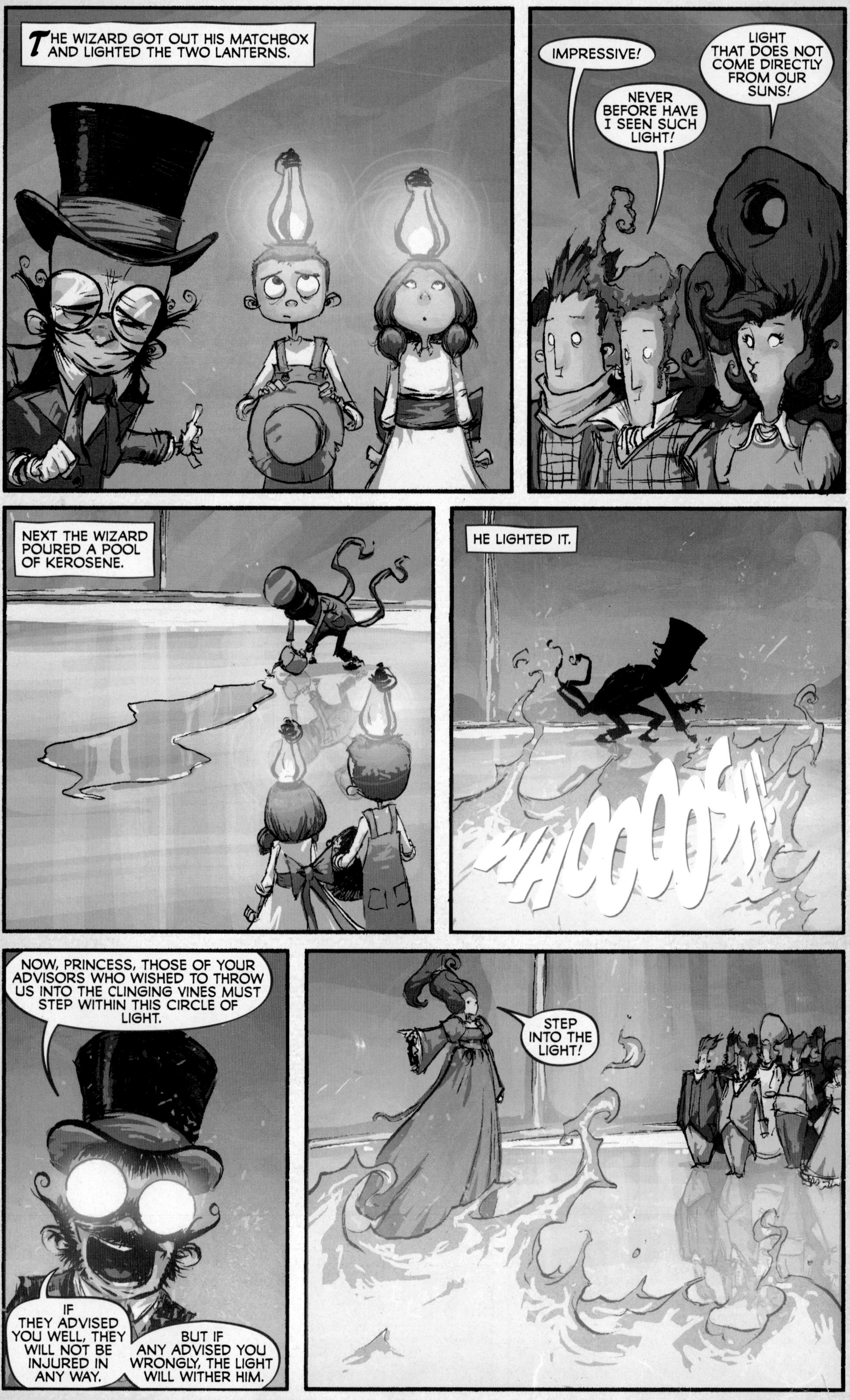
THE WIZARD GOT OUT HIS MATCHBOX AND LIGHTED THE TWO LANTERNS.
IMPRESSIVE!
NEVER BEFORE HAVE I SEEN SUCH LIGHT!
LIGHT THAT DOES NOT COME DIRECTLY FROM OUR SUNS!
NEXT THE WIZARD POURED A POOL OF KEROSENE.
HE LIGHTED IT.
WHOOOOOSH!
NOW, PRINCESS, THOSE OF YOUR ADVISORS WHO WISHED TO THROW US INTO THE CLINGING VINES MUST STEP WITHIN THIS CIRCLE OF LIGHT.
IF THEY ADVISED YOU WELL, THEY WILL NOT BE INJURED IN ANY WAY.
BUT IF ANY ADVISED YOU WRONGLY, THE LIGHT WILL WITHER HIM.
STEP INTO THE LIGHT!

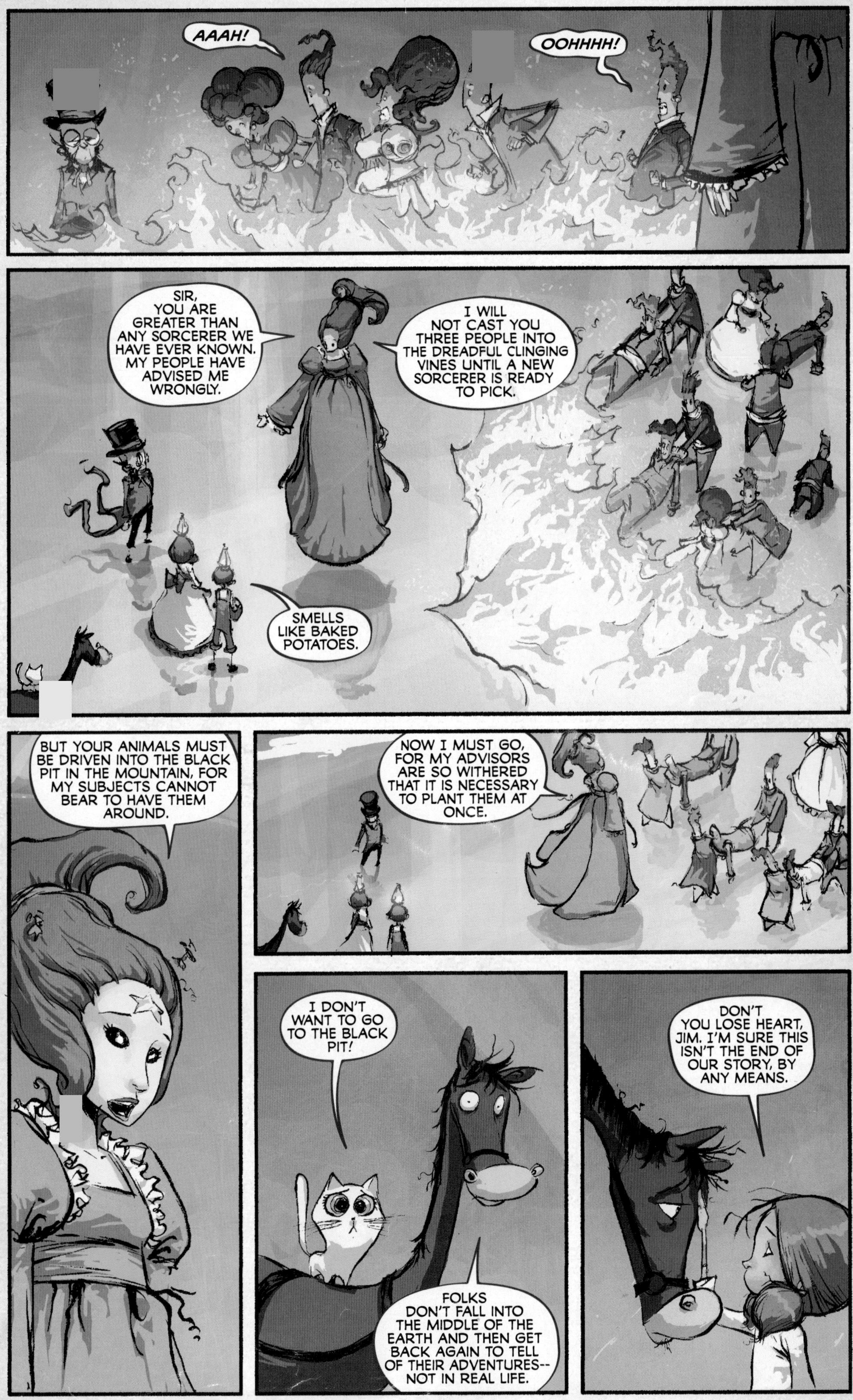
AAAH!
OOHHHH!
SIR, YOU ARE GREATER THAN ANY SORCERER WE HAVE EVER KNOWN. MY PEOPLE HAVE ADVISED ME WRONGLY.
I WILL NOT CAST YOU THREE PEOPLE INTO THE DREADFUL CLINGING VINES UNTIL A NEW SORCERER IS READY TO PICK.
SMELLS LIKE BAKED POTATOES.
BUT YOUR ANIMALS MUST BE DRIVEN INTO THE BLACK PIT IN THE MOUNTAIN, FOR MY SUBJECTS CANNOT BEAR TO HAVE THEM AROUND.
NOW I MUST GO, FOR MY ADVISORS ARE SO WITHERED THAT IT IS NECESSARY TO PLANT THEM AT ONCE.
I DON'T WANT TO GO TO THE BLACK PIT!
FOLKS DON'T FALL INTO THE MIDDLE OF THE EARTH AND THEN GET BACK AGAIN TO TELL OF THEIR ADVENTURES-- NOT IN REAL LIFE.
DON'T YOU LOSE HEART, JIM. I'M SURE THIS ISN'T THE END OF OUR STORY, BY ANY MEANS.

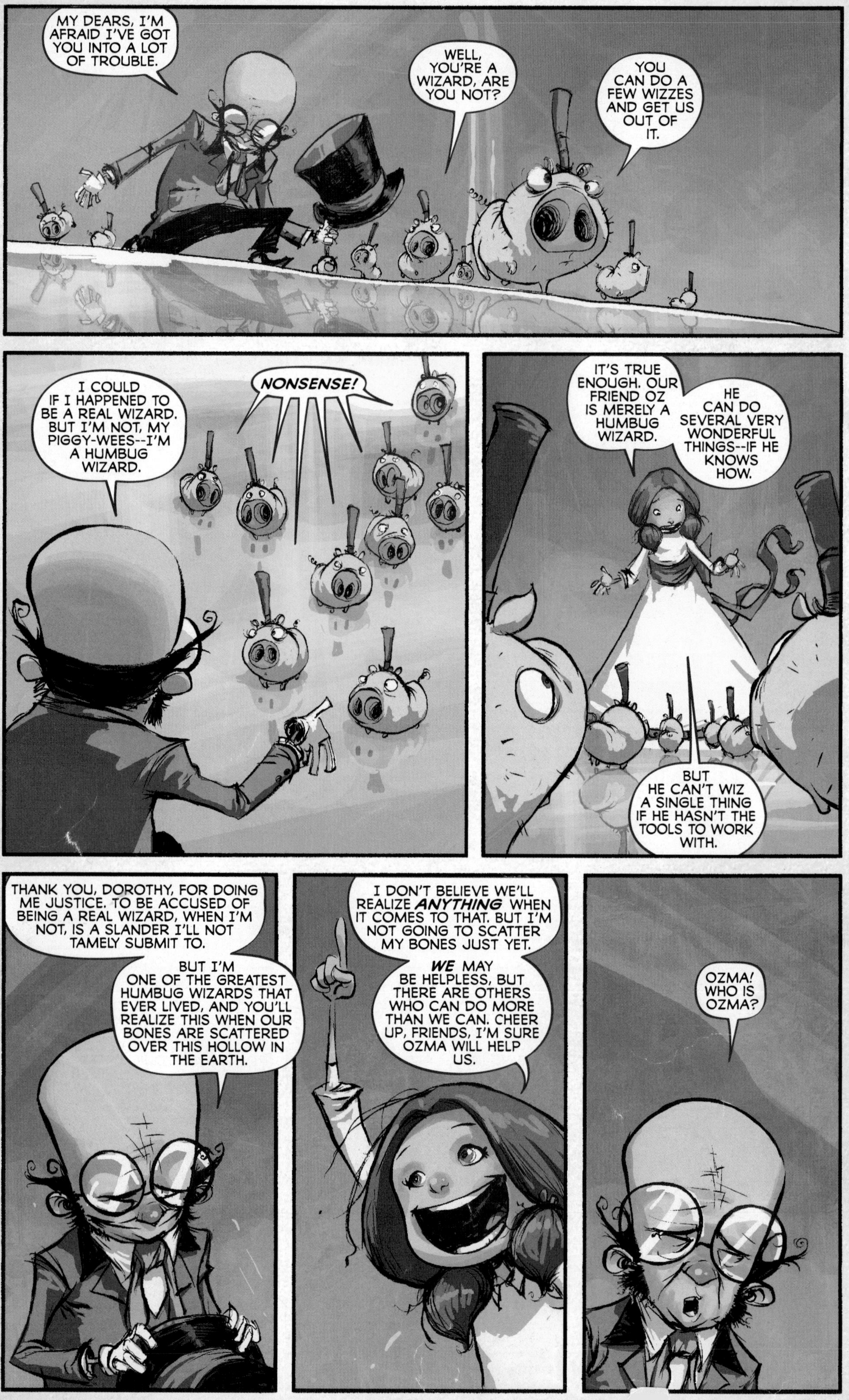
MY DEARS, I'M AFRAID I'VE GOT YOU INTO A LOT OF TROUBLE.
WELL, YOU'RE A WIZARD, ARE YOU NOT?
YOU CAN DO A FEW WIZZES AND GET US OUT OF IT.
I COULD IF I HAPPENED TO BE A REAL WIZARD. BUT I'M NOT, MY PIGGY-WEES--I'M A HUMBUG WIZARD.
NONSENSE!
IT'S TRUE ENOUGH. OUR FRIEND OZ IS MERELY A HUMBUG WIZARD.
HE CAN DO SEVERAL VERY WONDERFUL THINGS--IF HE KNOWS HOW.
BUT HE CAN'T WIZ A SINGLE THING IF HE HASN'T THE TOOLS TO WORK WITH.
THANK YOU, DOROTHY, FOR DOING ME JUSTICE. TO BE ACCUSED OF BEING A REAL WIZARD, WHEN I'M NOT, IS A SLANDER I'LL NOT TAMELY SUBMIT TO.
BUT I'M ONE OF THE GREATEST HUMBUG WIZARDS THAT EVER LIVED, AND YOU'LL REALIZE THIS WHEN OUR BONES ARE SCATTERED OVER THIS HOLLOW IN THE EARTH.
I DON'T BELIEVE WE'LL REALIZE ANYTHING WHEN IT COMES TO THAT. BUT I'M NOT GOING TO SCATTER MY BONES JUST YET.
WE MAY BE HELPLESS, BUT THERE ARE OTHERS WHO CAN DO MORE THAN WE CAN. CHEER UP, FRIENDS, I'M SURE OZMA WILL HELP US.
OZMA! WHO IS OZMA?

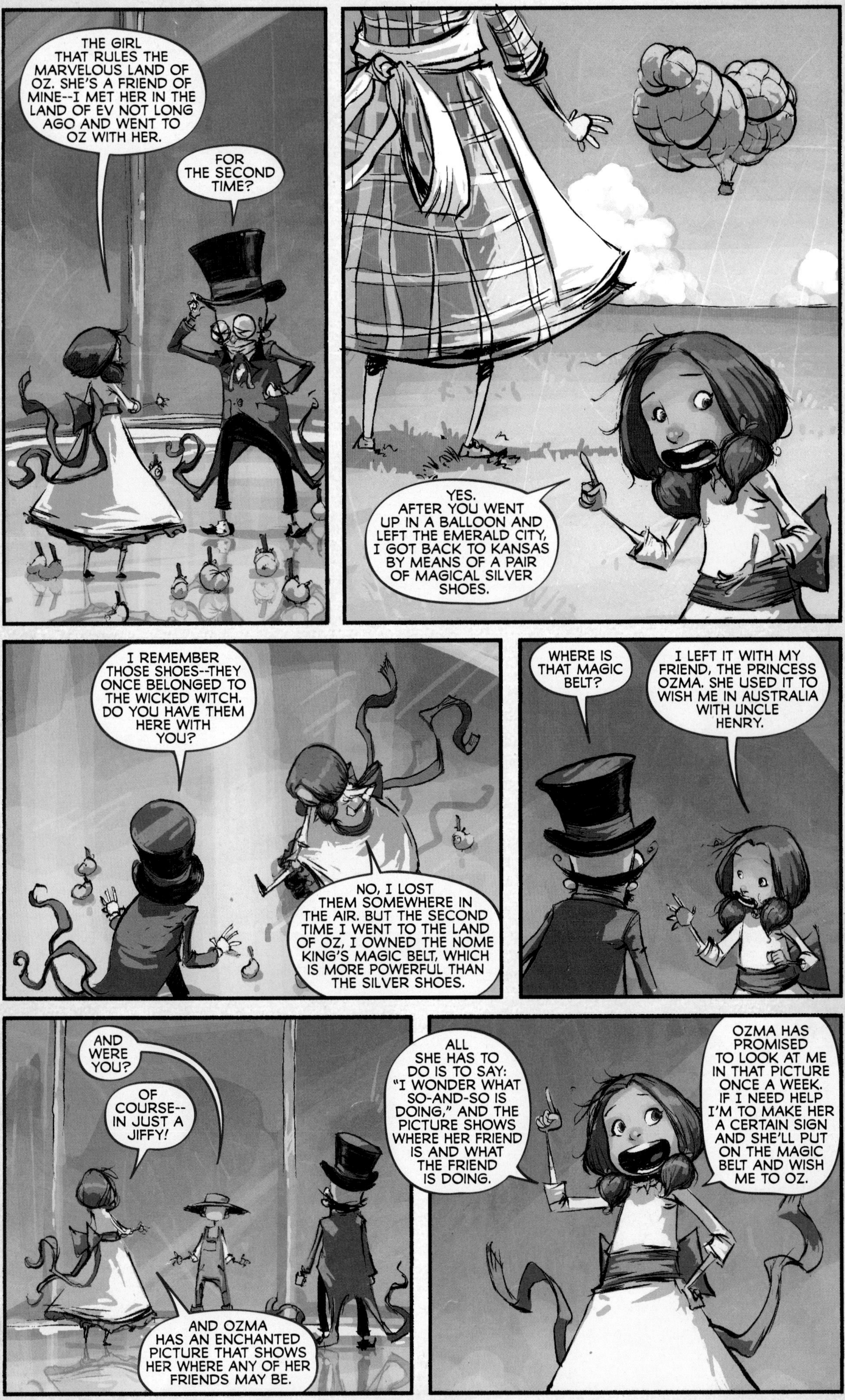
THE GIRL THAT RULES THE MARVELOUS LAND OF OZ. SHE'S A FRIEND OF MINE--I MET HER IN THE LAND OF EV NOT LONG AGO AND WENT TO OZ WITH HER.
FOR THE SECOND TIME?
YES. AFTER YOU WENT UP IN A BALLOON AND LEFT THE EMERALD CITY, I GOT BACK TO KANSAS BY MEANS OF A PAIR OF MAGICAL SILVER SHOES.
I REMEMBER THOSE SHOES--THEY ONCE BELONGED TO THE WICKED WITCH. DO YOU HAVE THEM HERE WITH YOU?
NO, I LOST THEM SOMEWHERE IN THE AIR. BUT THE SECOND TIME I WENT TO THE LAND OF OZ, I OWNED THE NOME KING'S MAGIC BELT, WHICH IS MORE POWERFUL THAN THE SILVER SHOES.
WHERE IS THAT MAGIC BELT?
I LEFT IT WITH MY FRIEND, THE PRINCESS OZMA. SHE USED IT TO WISH ME IN AUSTRALIA WITH UNCLE HENRY.
AND WERE YOU?
OF COURSE-- IN JUST A JIFFY!
AND OZMA HAS AN ENCHANTED PICTURE THAT SHOWS HER WHERE ANY OF HER FRIENDS MAY BE.
ALL SHE HAS TO DO IS TO SAY: "I WONDER WHAT SO-AND-SO IS DOING," AND THE PICTURE SHOWS WHERE HER FRIEND IS AND WHAT THE FRIEND IS DOING.
OZMA HAS PROMISED TO LOOK AT ME IN THAT PICTURE ONCE A WEEK. IF I NEED HELP I'M TO MAKE HER A CERTAIN SIGN AND SHE'LL PUT ON THE MAGIC BELT AND WISH ME TO OZ.

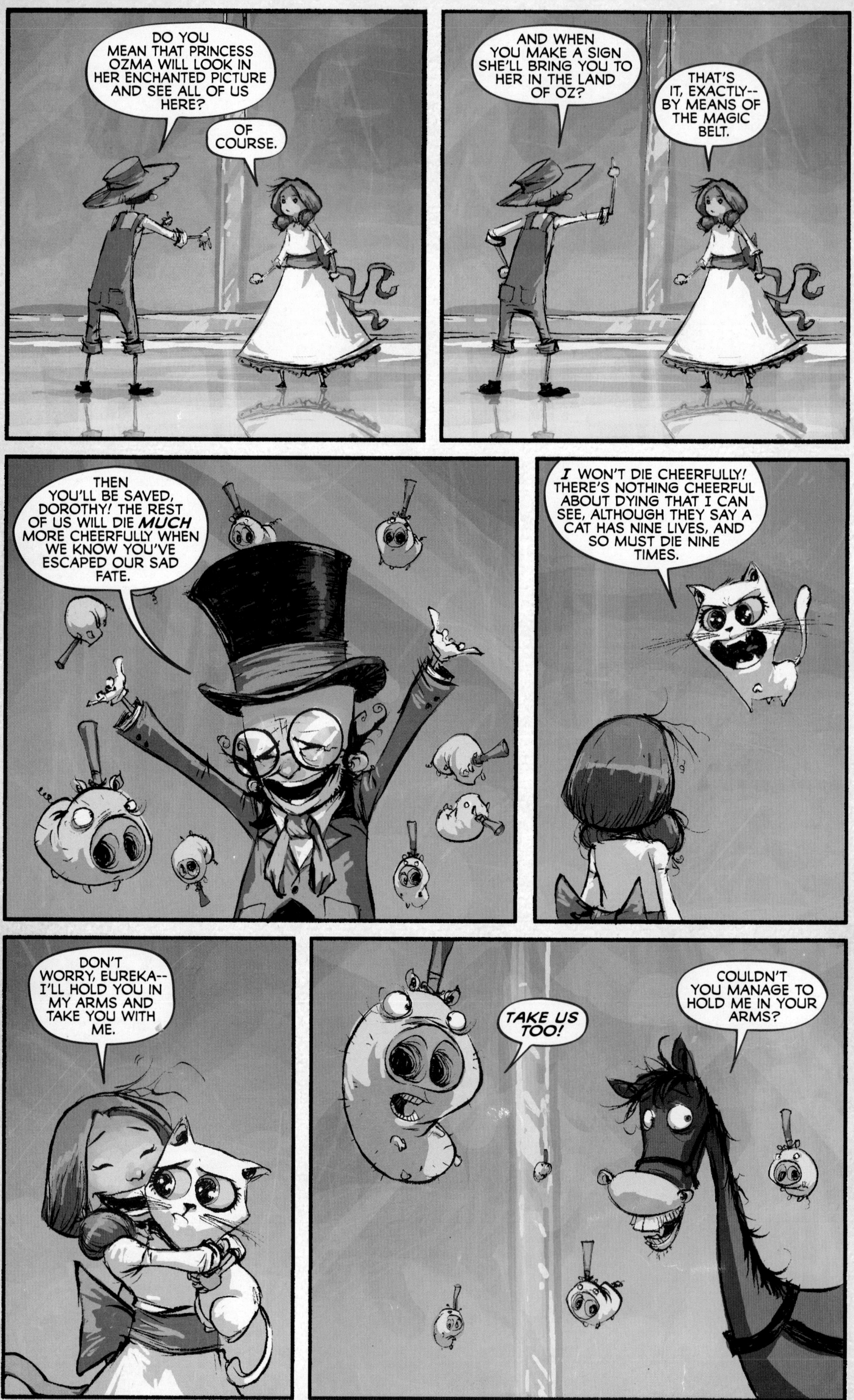
DO YOU MEAN THAT PRINCESS OZMA WILL LOOK IN HER ENCHANTED PICTURE AND SEE ALL OF US HERE?
OF COURSE.
AND WHEN YOU MAKE A SIGN SHE'LL BRING YOU TO HER IN THE LAND OF OZ?
THAT'S IT, EXACTLY-- BY MEANS OF THE MAGIC BELT.
THEN YOU'LL BE SAVED, DOROTHY! THE REST OF US WILL DIE MUCH MORE CHEERFULLY WHEN WE KNOW YOU'VE ESCAPED OUR SAD FATE.
I WON'T DIE CHEERFULLY! THERE'S NOTHING CHEERFUL ABOUT DYING THAT I CAN SEE, ALTHOUGH THEY SAY A CAT HAS NINE LIVES, AND SO MUST DIE NINE TIMES.
DON'T WORRY, EUREKA-- I'LL HOLD YOU IN MY ARMS AND TAKE YOU WITH ME.
TAKE US TOO!
COULDN'T YOU MANAGE TO HOLD ME IN YOUR ARMS?

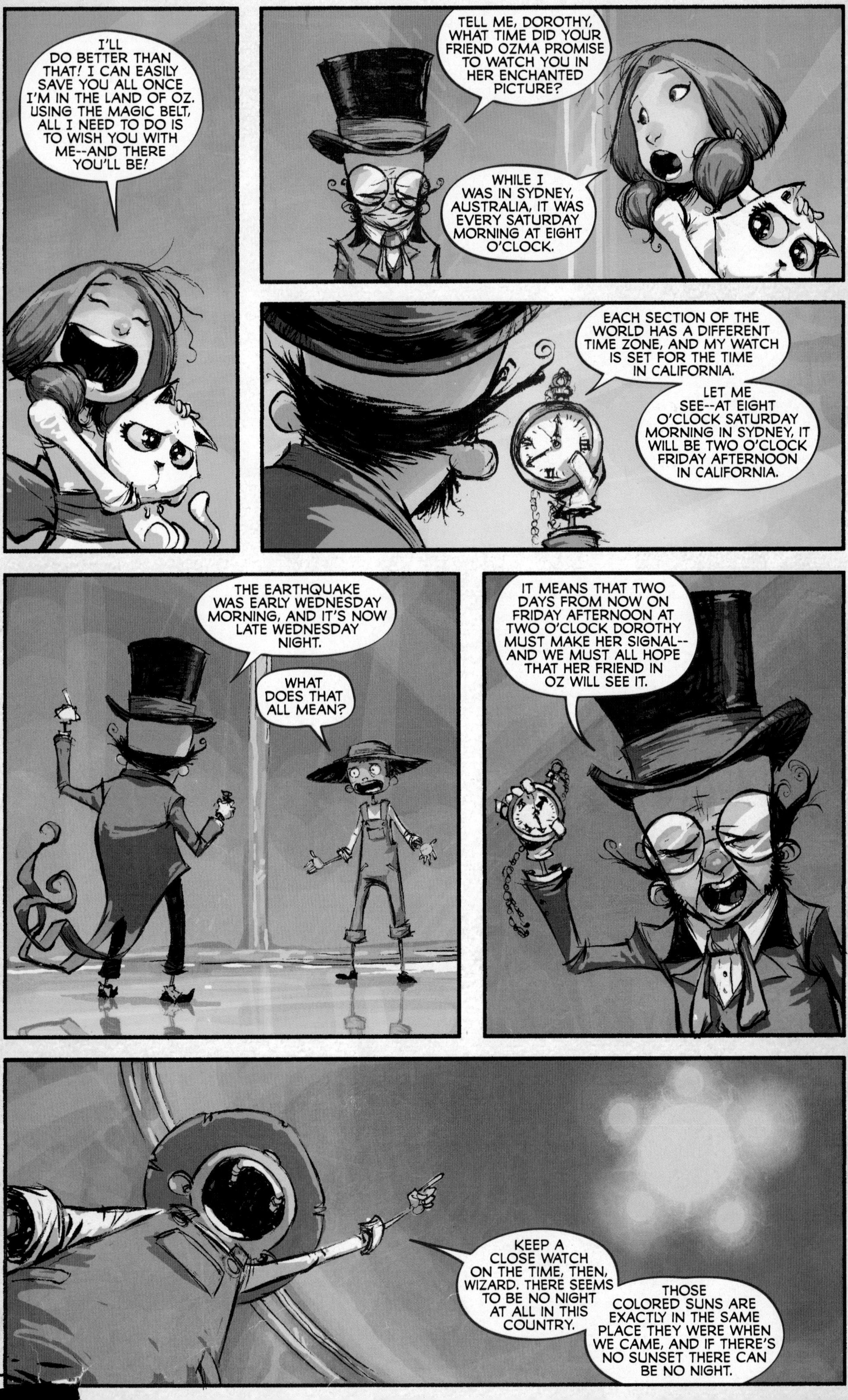
I'LL DO BETTER THAN THAT! I CAN EASILY SAVE YOU ALL ONCE I'M IN THE LAND OF OZ. USING THE MAGIC BELT, ALL I NEED TO DO IS TO WISH YOU WITH ME--AND THERE YOU'LL BE!
TELL ME, DOROTHY, WHAT TIME DID YOUR FRIEND OZMA PROMISE TO WATCH YOU IN HER ENCHANTED PICTURE?
WHILE I WAS IN SYDNEY, AUSTRALIA, IT WAS EVERY SATURDAY MORNING AT EIGHT O'CLOCK.
EACH SECTION OF THE WORLD HAS A DIFFERENT TIME ZONE, AND MY WATCH IS SET FOR THE TIME IN CALIFORNIA.
LET ME SEE--AT EIGHT O'CLOCK SATURDAY MORNING IN SYDNEY, IT WILL BE TWO O'CLOCK FRIDAY AFTERNOON IN CALIFORNIA.
THE EARTHQUAKE WAS EARLY WEDNESDAY MORNING, AND IT'S NOW LATE WEDNESDAY NIGHT.
WHAT DOES THAT ALL MEAN?
IT MEANS THAT TWO DAYS FROM NOW ON FRIDAY AFTERNOON AT TWO O'CLOCK DOROTHY MUST MAKE HER SIGNAL--AND WE MUST ALL HOPE THAT HER FRIEND IN OZ WILL SEE IT.
KEEP A CLOSE WATCH ON THE TIME, THEN, WIZARD. THERE SEEMS TO BE NO NIGHT AT ALL IN THIS COUNTRY.
THOSE COLORED SUNS ARE EXACTLY IN THE SAME PLACE THEY WERE WHEN WE CAME, AND IF THERE'S NO SUNSET THERE CAN BE NO NIGHT.

VERY TRUE. IT'S A LONG TIME SINCE I'VE HAD ANY SLEEP. I WONDER WHERE WE CAN FIND SOME BEDS.

WHAT ARE THOSE HOLES UP THERE? THEY LOOK LIKE DOORWAYS, ONLY THERE ARE NO STAIRS TO GET TO THEM.

YOU FORGET THAT STAIRS ARE UNNECESSARY. LET'S WALK UP AND SEE WHERE THE DOORS LEAD TO.

THIS DOORWAY LEADS INTO A HALL.

THERE ARE MANY ROOMS--BUT NO BEDS.

I WONDER IF THESE PEOPLE NEVER SLEEP.

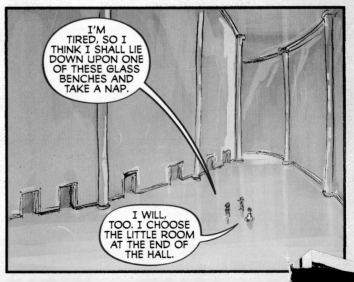

I'M TIRED, SO I THINK I SHALL LIE DOWN UPON ONE OF THESE GLASS BENCHES AND TAKE A NAP.

I WILL, TOO. I CHOOSE THE LITTLE ROOM AT THE END OF THE HALL.

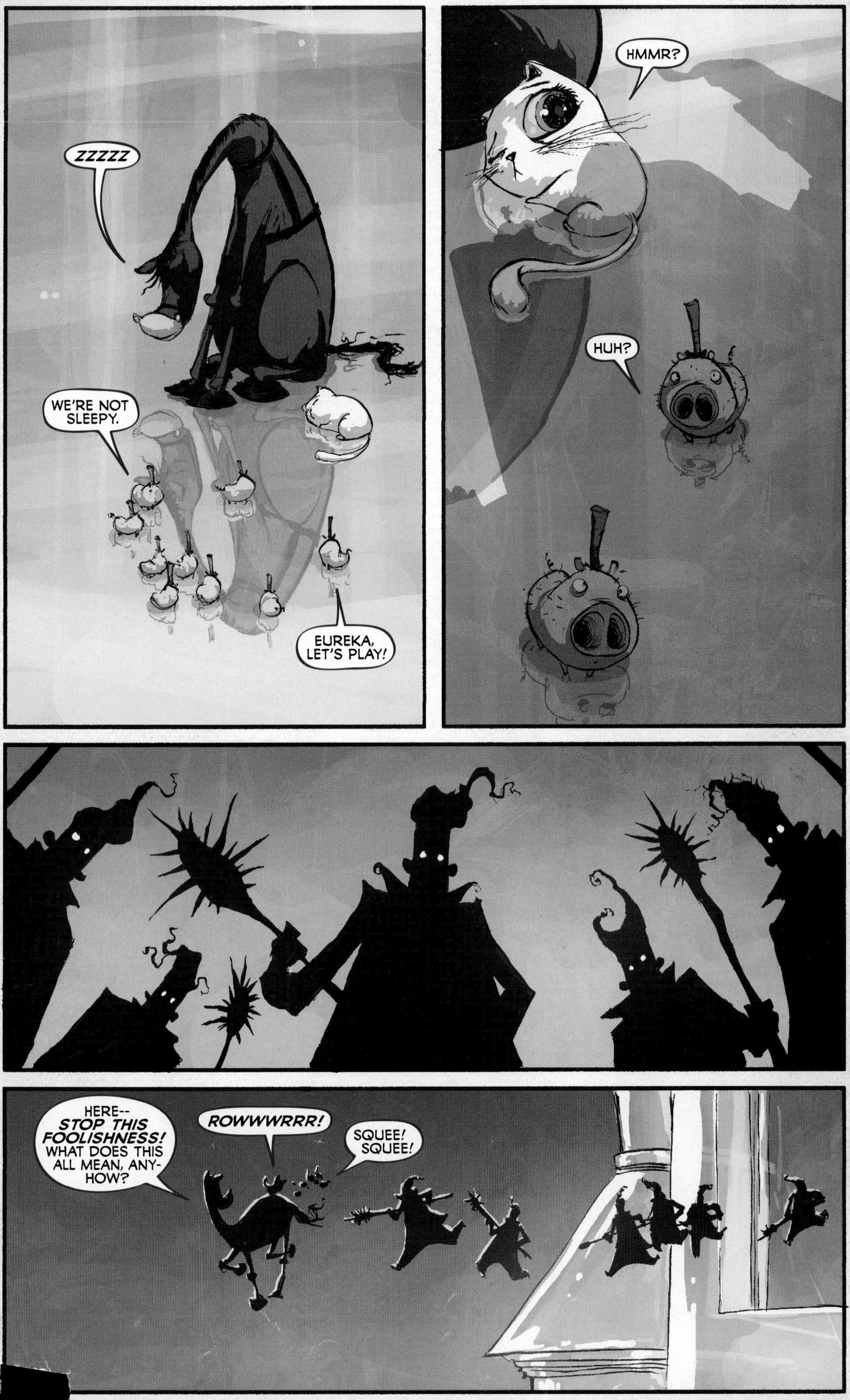
ZZZZZ
WE'RE NOT SLEEPY.
EUREKA, LET'S PLAY!
HMMR?
HUH?
HERE-- **STOP THIS FOOLISHNESS!** WHAT DOES THIS ALL MEAN, ANY-HOW?
ROWWWRRR!
SQUEE! SQUEE!

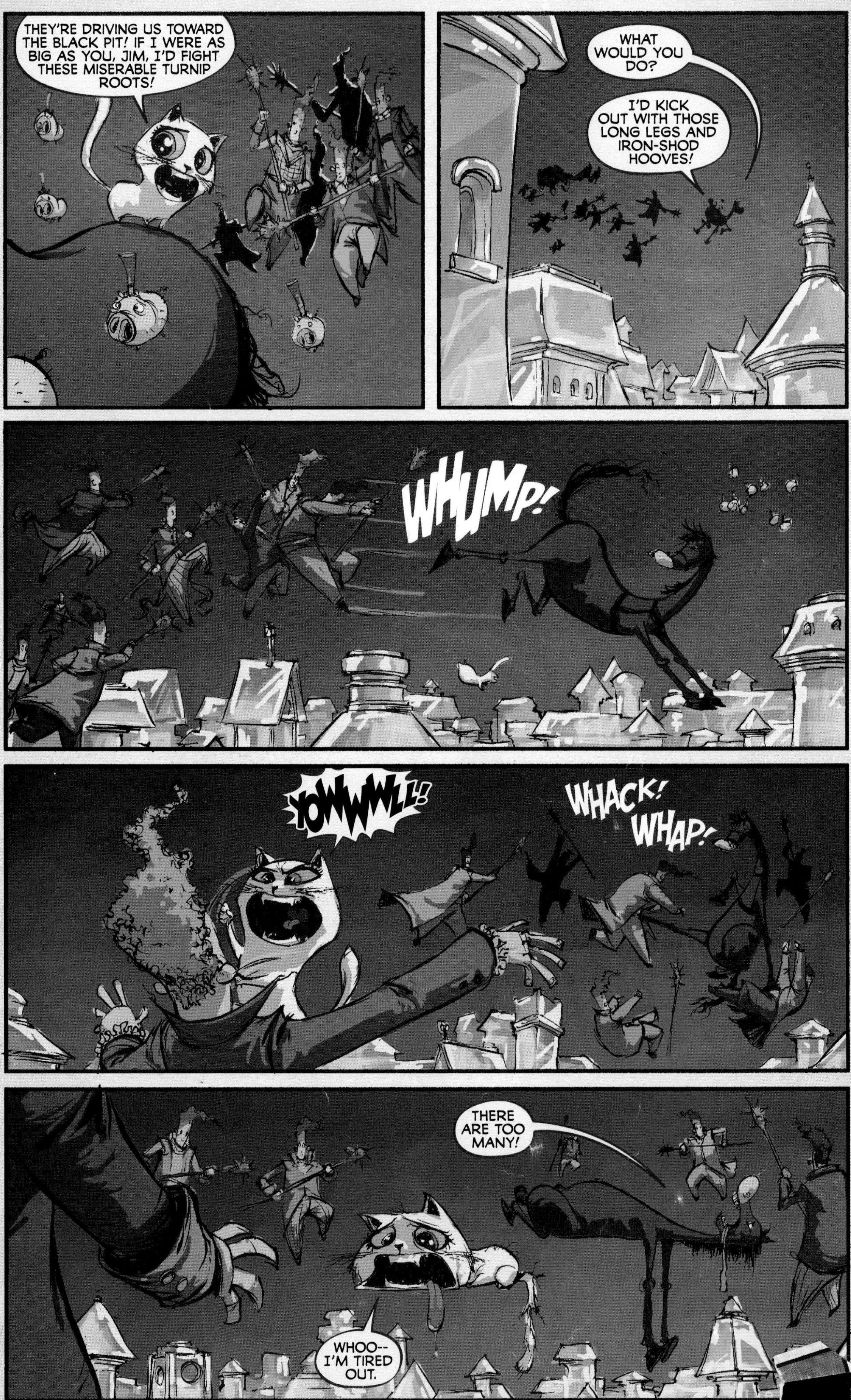
THEY'RE DRIVING US TOWARD THE BLACK PIT! IF I WERE AS BIG AS YOU, JIM, I'D FIGHT THESE MISERABLE TURNIP ROOTS!
WHAT WOULD YOU DO?
I'D KICK OUT WITH THOSE LONG LEGS AND IRON-SHOD HOOVES!
WHUMP!
YOWWWLL!
WHACK!
WHAP!
THERE ARE TOO MANY!
WHOO-- I'M TIRED OUT.

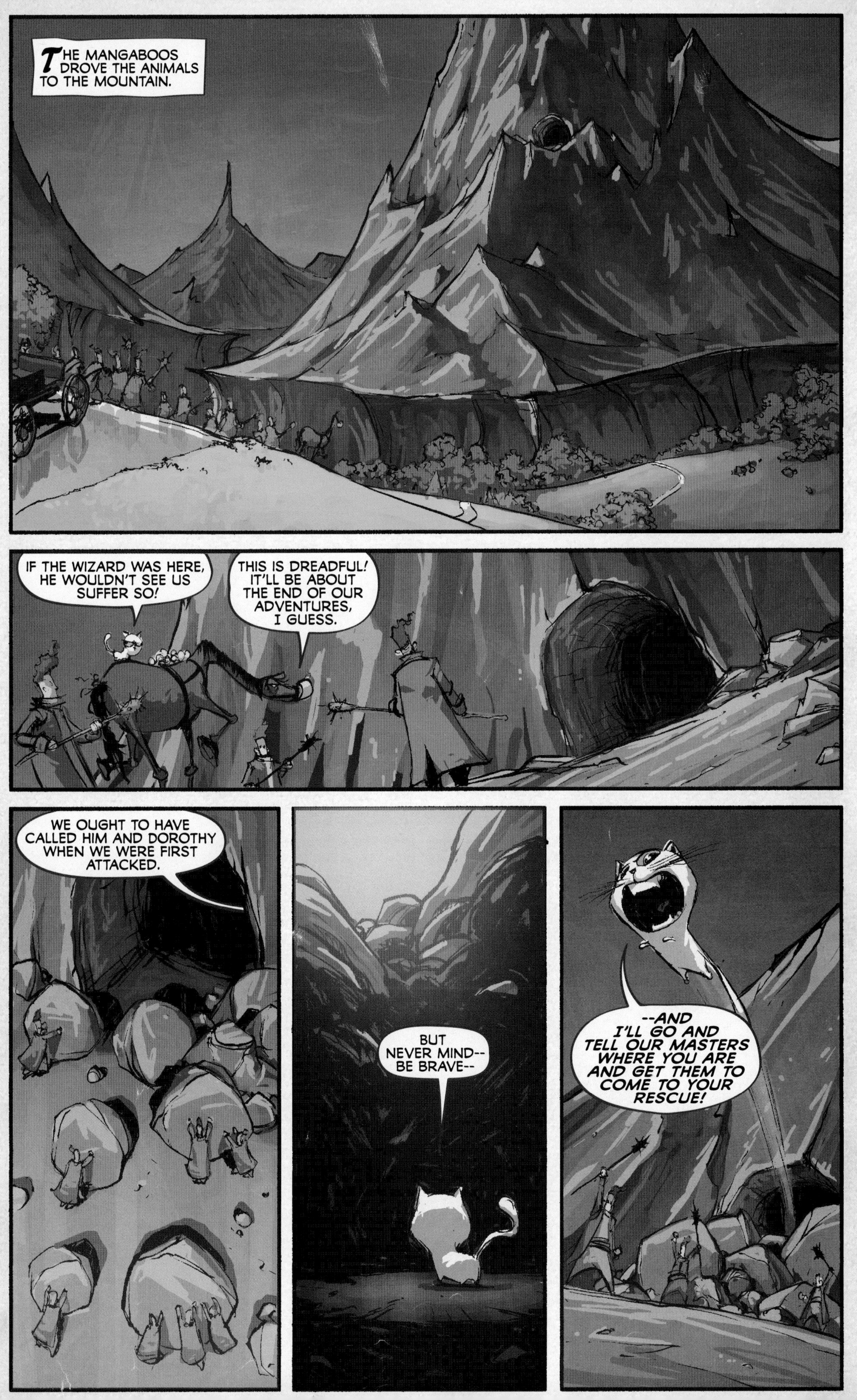
THE MANGABOOS DROVE THE ANIMALS TO THE MOUNTAIN.
IF THE WIZARD WAS HERE, HE WOULDN'T SEE US SUFFER SO!
THIS IS DREADFUL! IT'LL BE ABOUT THE END OF OUR ADVENTURES, I GUESS.
WE OUGHT TO HAVE CALLED HIM AND DOROTHY WHEN WE WERE FIRST ATTACKED.
BUT NEVER MIND-- BE BRAVE--
--AND I'LL GO AND TELL OUR MASTERS WHERE YOU ARE AND GET THEM TO COME TO YOUR RESCUE!

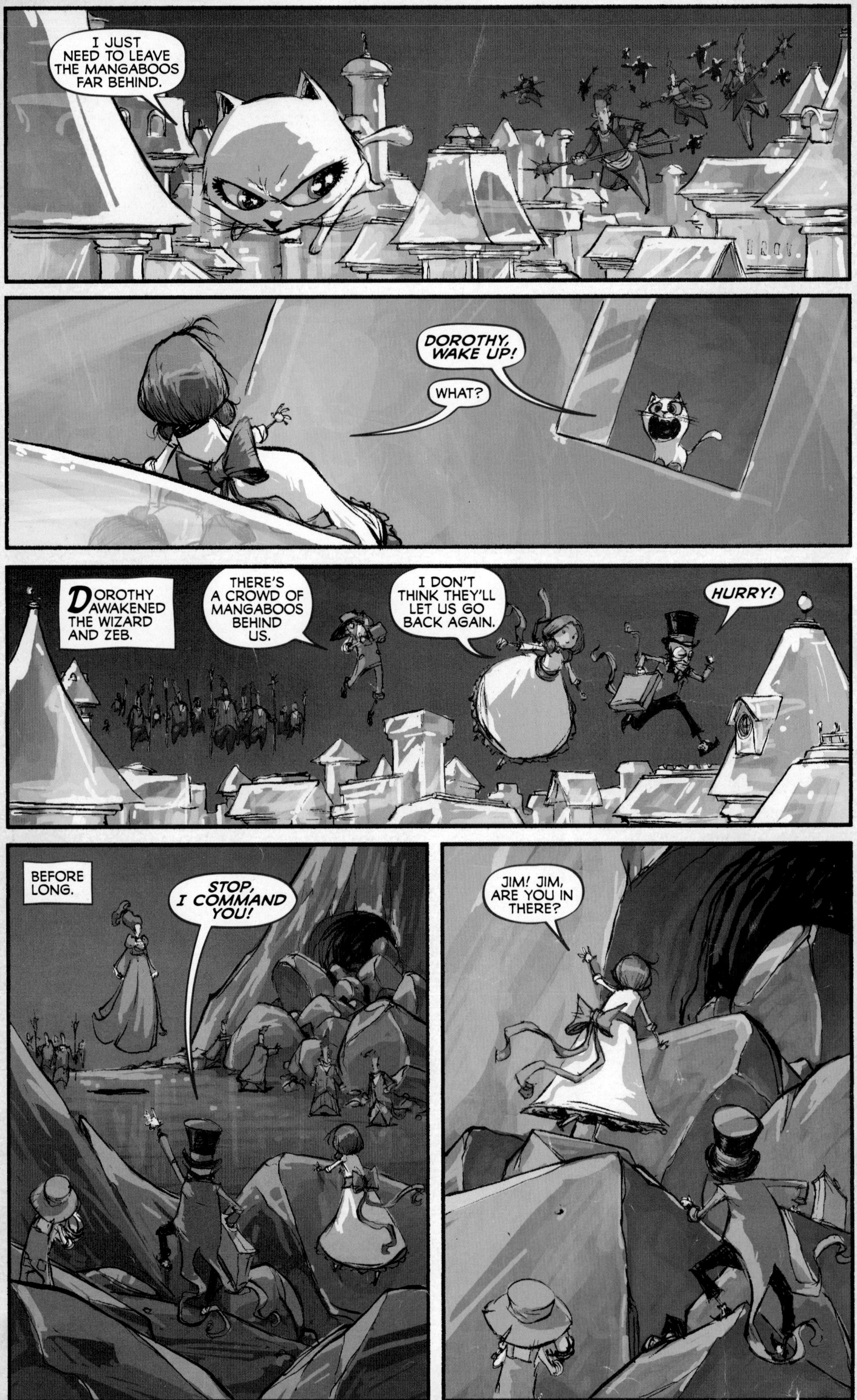
I JUST NEED TO LEAVE THE MANGABOOS FAR BEHIND.
DOROTHY, WAKE UP!
WHAT?
DOROTHY AWAKENED THE WIZARD AND ZEB.
THERE'S A CROWD OF MANGABOOS BEHIND US.
I DON'T THINK THEY'LL LET US GO BACK AGAIN.
HURRY!
BEFORE LONG.
STOP, I COMMAND YOU!
JIM! JIM, ARE YOU IN THERE?

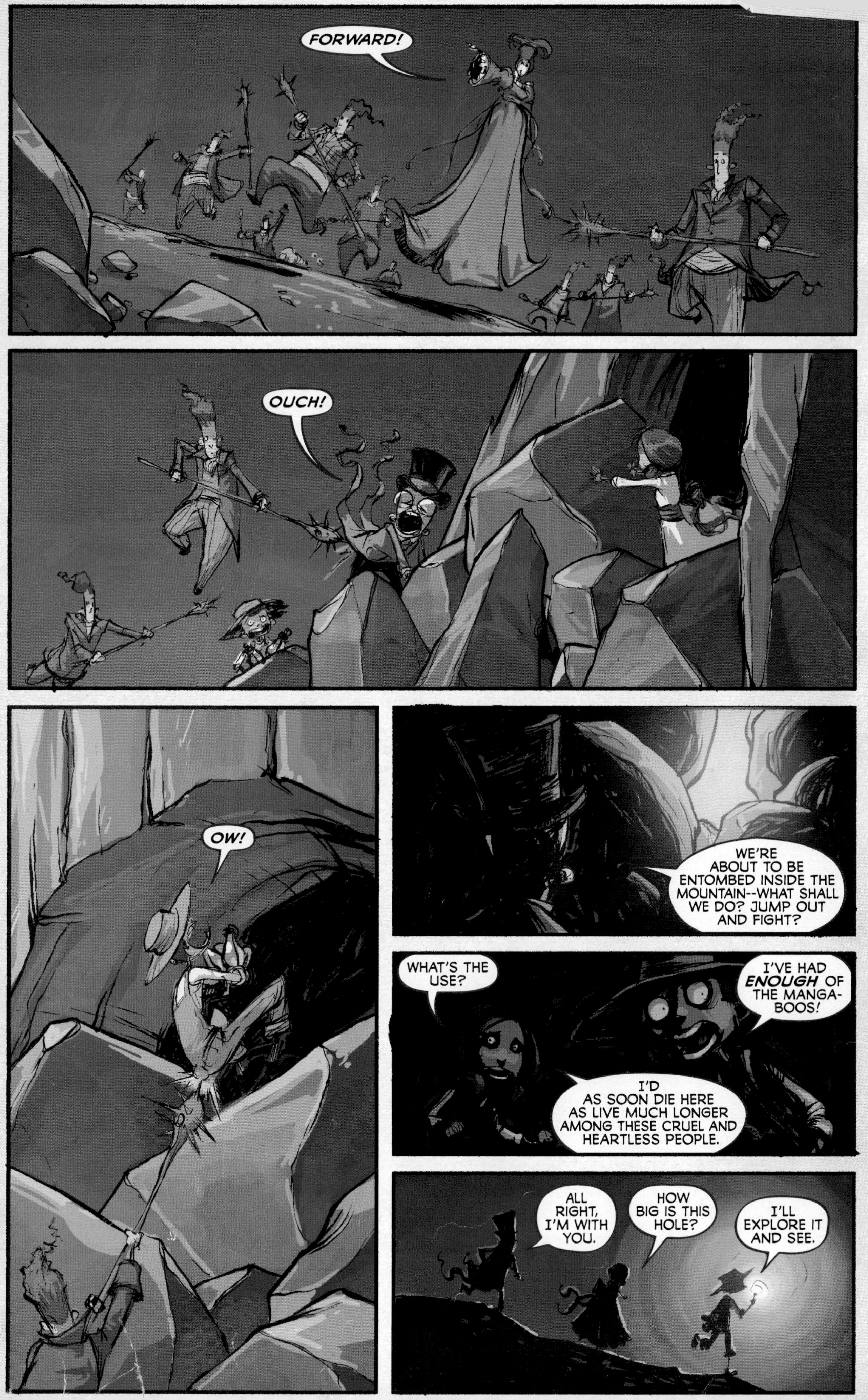
FORWARD!
OUCH!
OW!
WE'RE ABOUT TO BE ENTOMBED INSIDE THE MOUNTAIN--WHAT SHALL WE DO? JUMP OUT AND FIGHT?
WHAT'S THE USE?
I'VE HAD ENOUGH OF THE MANGA-BOOS!
I'D AS SOON DIE HERE AS LIVE MUCH LONGER AMONG THESE CRUEL AND HEARTLESS PEOPLE.
ALL RIGHT, I'M WITH YOU.
HOW BIG IS THIS HOLE?
I'LL EXPLORE IT AND SEE.

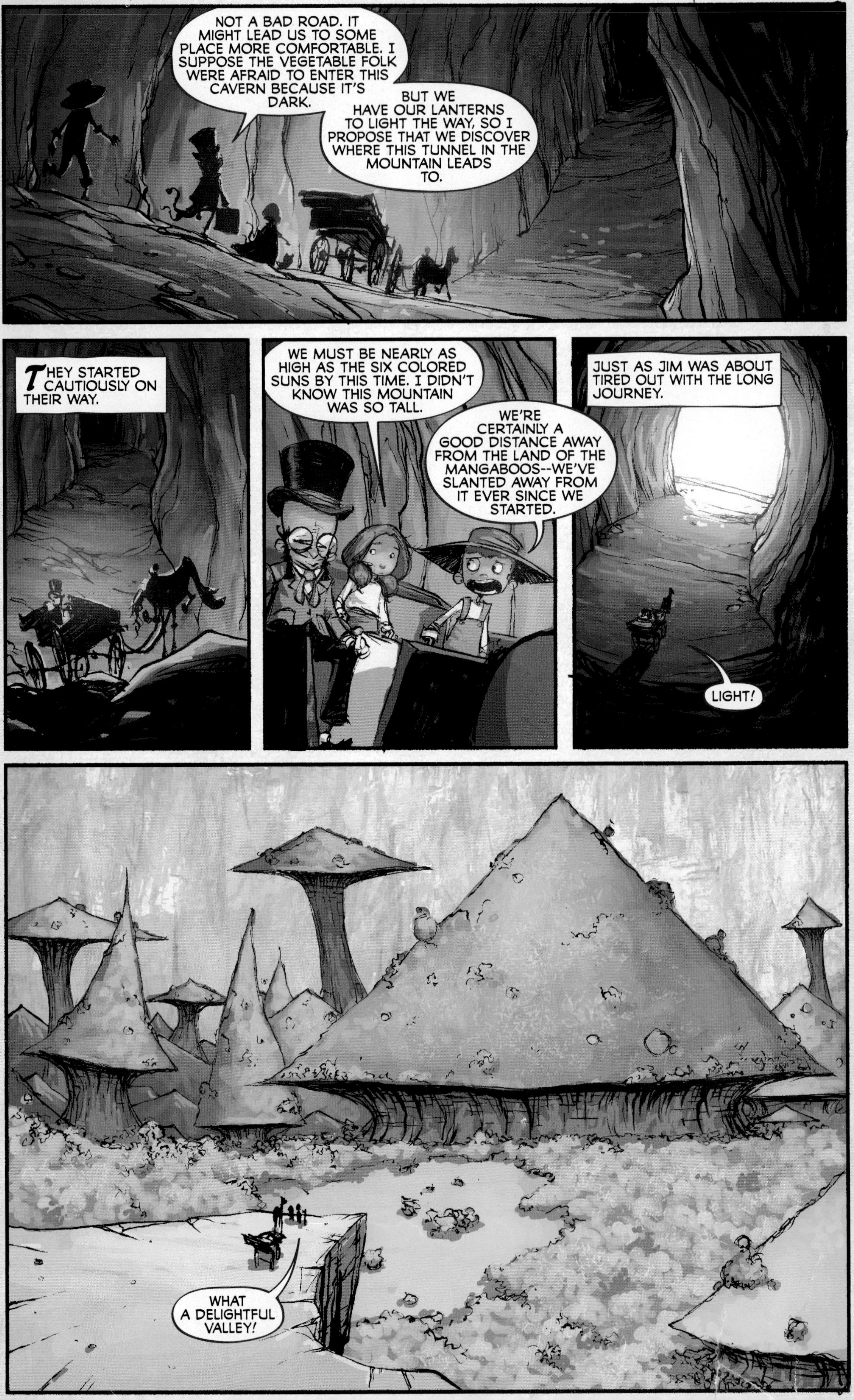
NOT A BAD ROAD. IT MIGHT LEAD US TO SOME PLACE MORE COMFORTABLE. I SUPPOSE THE VEGETABLE FOLK WERE AFRAID TO ENTER THIS CAVERN BECAUSE IT'S DARK.
BUT WE HAVE OUR LANTERNS TO LIGHT THE WAY, SO I PROPOSE THAT WE DISCOVER WHERE THIS TUNNEL IN THE MOUNTAIN LEADS TO.
THEY STARTED CAUTIOUSLY ON THEIR WAY.
WE MUST BE NEARLY AS HIGH AS THE SIX COLORED SUNS BY THIS TIME. I DIDN'T KNOW THIS MOUNTAIN WAS SO TALL.
WE'RE CERTAINLY A GOOD DISTANCE AWAY FROM THE LAND OF THE MANGABOOS--WE'VE SLANTED AWAY FROM IT EVER SINCE WE STARTED.
JUST AS JIM WAS ABOUT TIRED OUT WITH THE LONG JOURNEY.
LIGHT!
WHAT A DELIGHTFUL VALLEY!

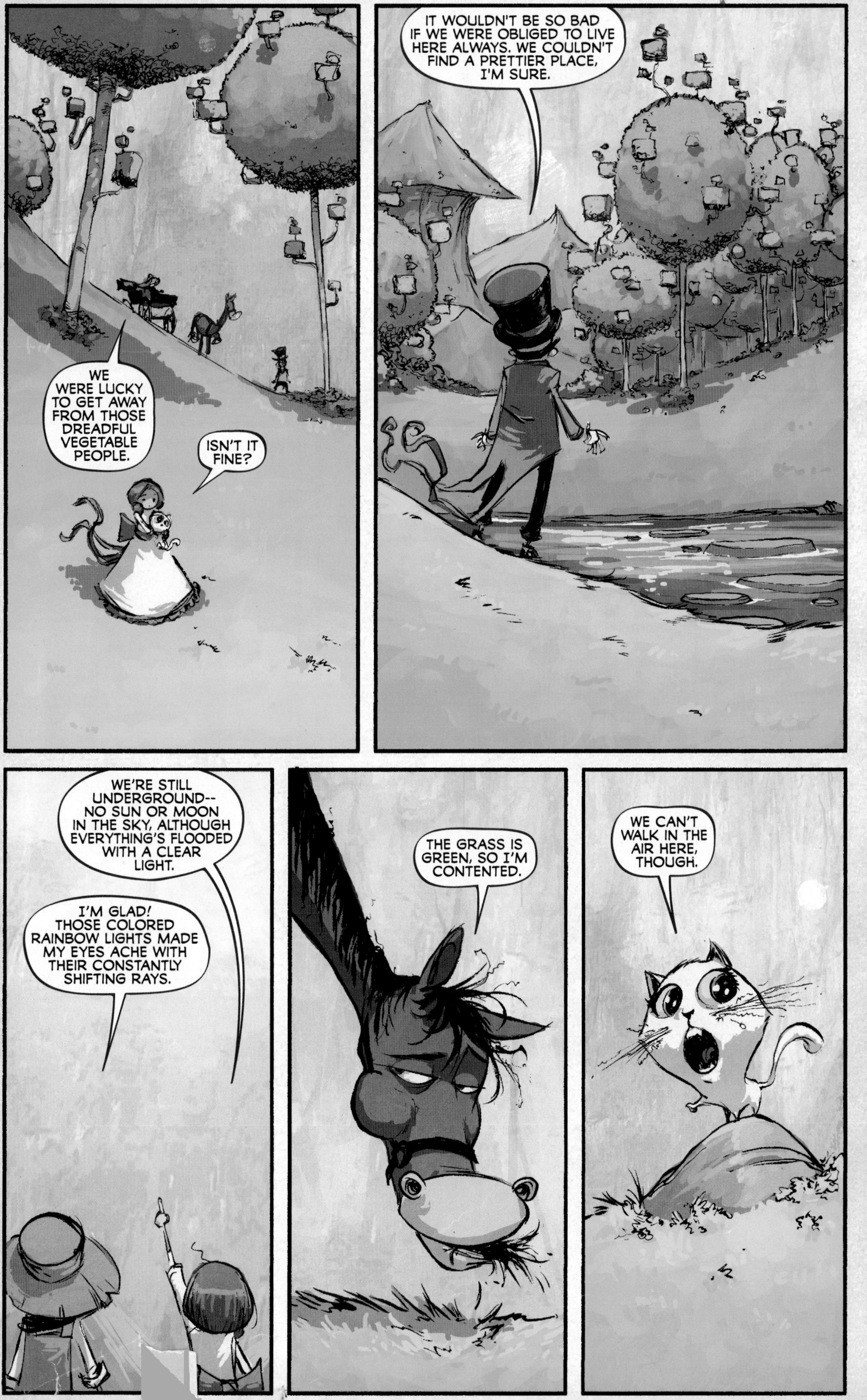
WE WERE LUCKY TO GET AWAY FROM THOSE DREADFUL VEGETABLE PEOPLE.
ISN'T IT FINE?
IT WOULDN'T BE SO BAD IF WE WERE OBLIGED TO LIVE HERE ALWAYS. WE COULDN'T FIND A PRETTIER PLACE, I'M SURE.
WE'RE STILL UNDERGROUND-- NO SUN OR MOON IN THE SKY, ALTHOUGH EVERYTHING'S FLOODED WITH A CLEAR LIGHT.
I'M GLAD! THOSE COLORED RAINBOW LIGHTS MADE MY EYES ACHE WITH THEIR CONSTANTLY SHIFTING RAYS.
THE GRASS IS GREEN, SO I'M CONTENTED.
WE CAN'T WALK IN THE AIR HERE, THOUGH.

WE MUST BE NEARER THE SURFACE OF THE EARTH. EVERYTHING IS MORE HOMELIKE AND NATURAL.

BUT WHERE ARE THE PEOPLE?

CHIRP CHIRP CHIIIRR-UPP

I HEAR A BIRD--BUT I DON'T SEE IT.

I CAN'T FIND BIRDS ANYWHERE.

BUT I SMELL SOMETHING DELICIOUS!

THAT STRANGE FRUIT--

WHAT IS IT, DO YOU S'POSE?

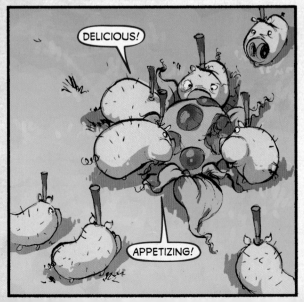

DELICIOUS!

APPETIZING!

IT'S GOOD, ANYWAY, OR THOSE LITTLE RASCALS WOULDN'T GOBBLE IT UP SO GREEDILY.

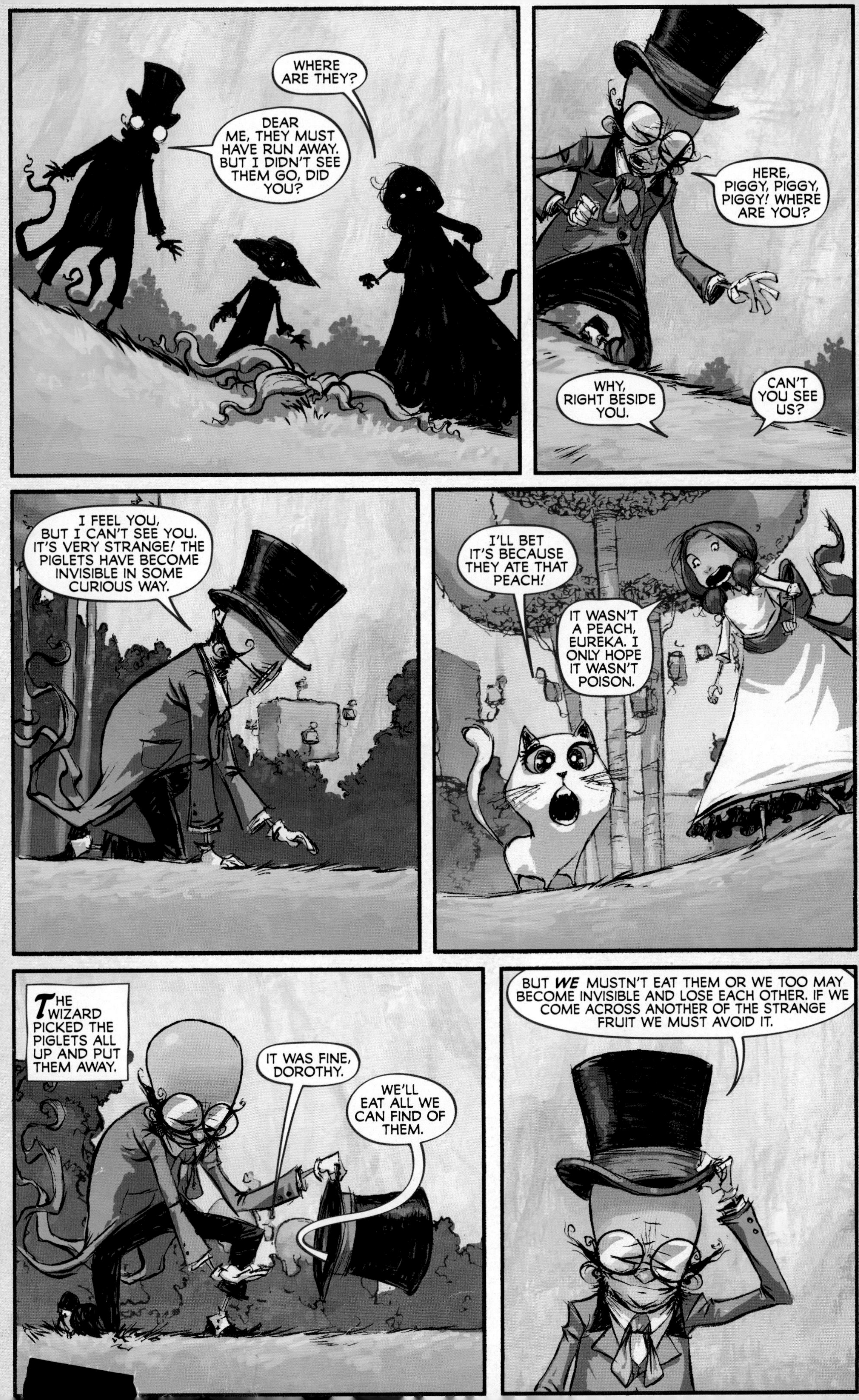
WHERE ARE THEY?
DEAR ME, THEY MUST HAVE RUN AWAY. BUT I DIDN'T SEE THEM GO, DID YOU?
HERE, PIGGY, PIGGY, PIGGY! WHERE ARE YOU?
WHY, RIGHT BESIDE YOU.
CAN'T YOU SEE US?
I FEEL YOU, BUT I CAN'T SEE YOU. IT'S VERY STRANGE! THE PIGLETS HAVE BECOME INVISIBLE IN SOME CURIOUS WAY.
I'LL BET IT'S BECAUSE THEY ATE THAT PEACH!
IT WASN'T A PEACH, EUREKA. I ONLY HOPE IT WASN'T POISON.
THE WIZARD PICKED THE PIGLETS ALL UP AND PUT THEM AWAY.
IT WAS FINE, DOROTHY.
WE'LL EAT ALL WE CAN FIND OF THEM.
BUT WE MUSTN'T EAT THEM OR WE TOO MAY BECOME INVISIBLE AND LOSE EACH OTHER. IF WE COME ACROSS ANOTHER OF THE STRANGE FRUIT WE MUST AVOID IT.

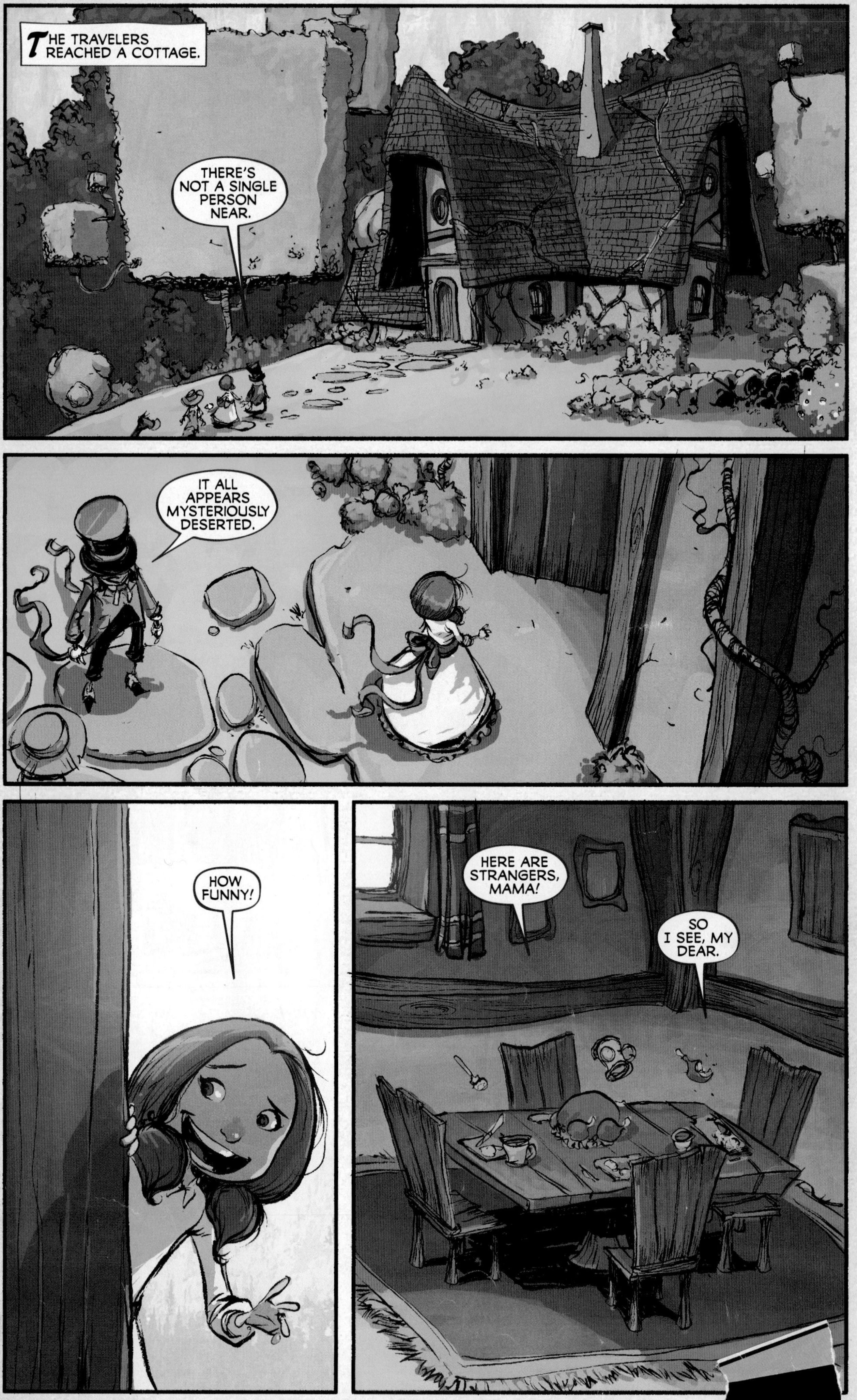
THE TRAVELERS REACHED A COTTAGE.
THERE'S NOT A SINGLE PERSON NEAR.
IT ALL APPEARS MYSTERIOUSLY DESERTED.
HOW FUNNY!
HERE ARE STRANGERS, MAMA!
SO I SEE, MY DEAR.

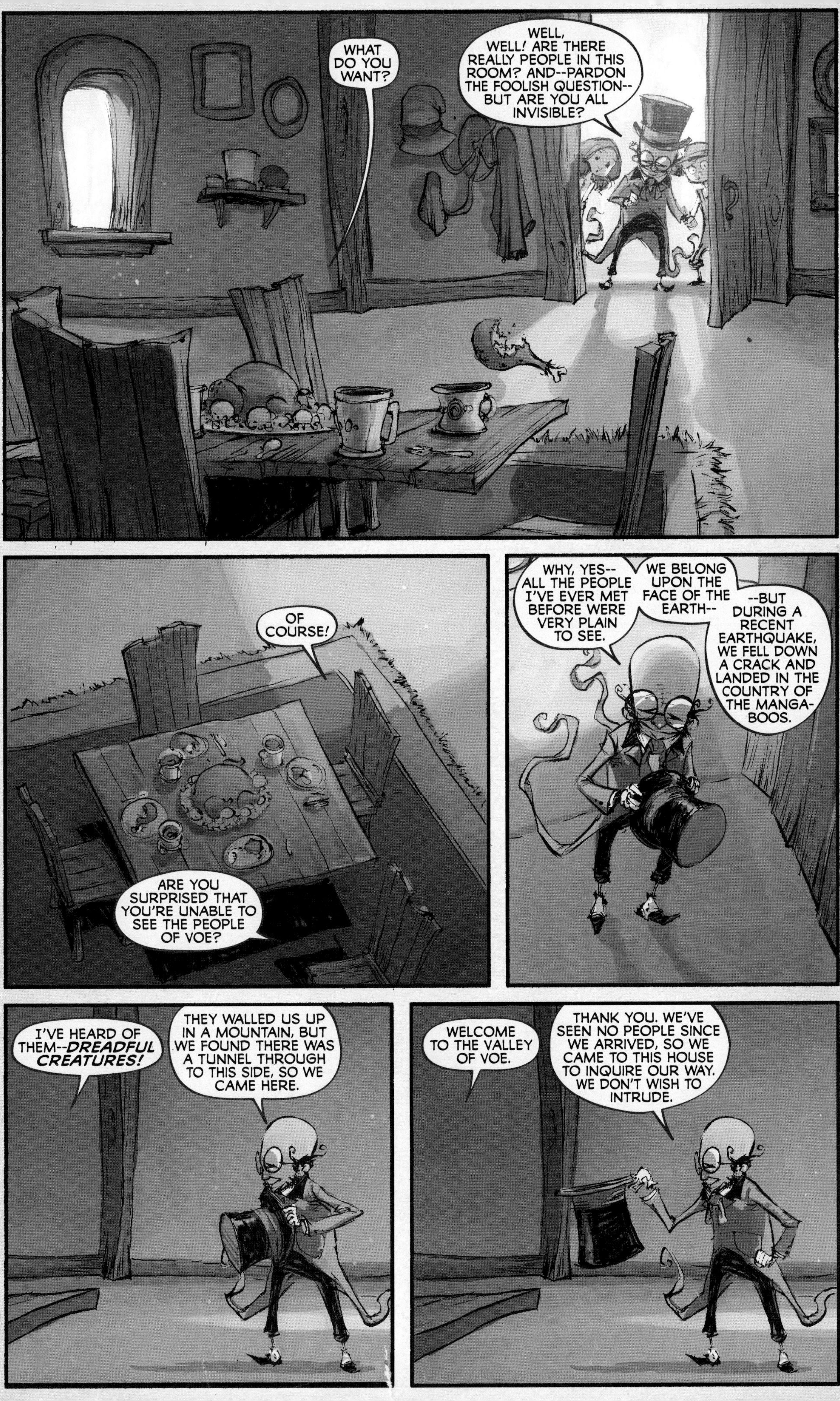

WHAT DO YOU WANT?
WELL, WELL! ARE THERE REALLY PEOPLE IN THIS ROOM? AND--PARDON THE FOOLISH QUESTION--BUT ARE YOU ALL INVISIBLE?
OF COURSE!
ARE YOU SURPRISED THAT YOU'RE UNABLE TO SEE THE PEOPLE OF VOE?
WHY, YES--ALL THE PEOPLE I'VE EVER MET BEFORE WERE VERY PLAIN TO SEE.
WE BELONG UPON THE FACE OF THE EARTH--
--BUT DURING A RECENT EARTHQUAKE, WE FELL DOWN A CRACK AND LANDED IN THE COUNTRY OF THE MANGA-BOOS.
I'VE HEARD OF THEM--*DREADFUL CREATURES!*
THEY WALLED US UP IN A MOUNTAIN, BUT WE FOUND THERE WAS A TUNNEL THROUGH TO THIS SIDE, SO WE CAME HERE.
WELCOME TO THE VALLEY OF VOE.
THANK YOU. WE'VE SEEN NO PEOPLE SINCE WE ARRIVED, SO WE CAME TO THIS HOUSE TO INQUIRE OUR WAY. WE DON'T WISH TO INTRUDE.

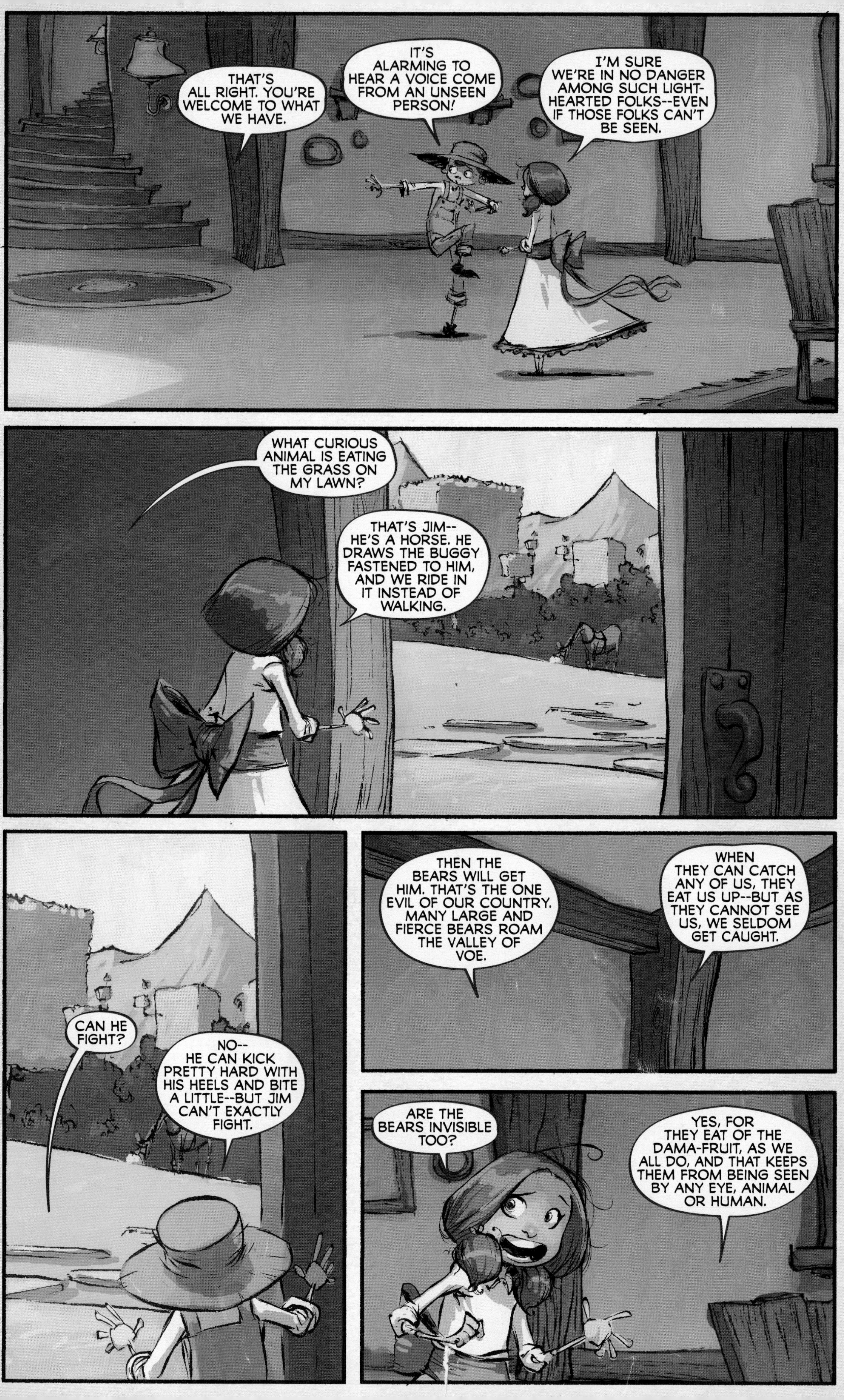
THAT'S ALL RIGHT. YOU'RE WELCOME TO WHAT WE HAVE.
IT'S ALARMING TO HEAR A VOICE COME FROM AN UNSEEN PERSON!
I'M SURE WE'RE IN NO DANGER AMONG SUCH LIGHT-HEARTED FOLKS--EVEN IF THOSE FOLKS CAN'T BE SEEN.
WHAT CURIOUS ANIMAL IS EATING THE GRASS ON MY LAWN?
THAT'S JIM--HE'S A HORSE. HE DRAWS THE BUGGY FASTENED TO HIM, AND WE RIDE IN IT INSTEAD OF WALKING.
CAN HE FIGHT?
NO--HE CAN KICK PRETTY HARD WITH HIS HEELS AND BITE A LITTLE--BUT JIM CAN'T EXACTLY FIGHT.
THEN THE BEARS WILL GET HIM. THAT'S THE ONE EVIL OF OUR COUNTRY. MANY LARGE AND FIERCE BEARS ROAM THE VALLEY OF VOE.
WHEN THEY CAN CATCH ANY OF US, THEY EAT US UP--BUT AS THEY CANNOT SEE US, WE SELDOM GET CAUGHT.
ARE THE BEARS INVISIBLE TOO?
YES, FOR THEY EAT OF THE DAMA-FRUIT, AS WE ALL DO, AND THAT KEEPS THEM FROM BEING SEEN BY ANY EYE, ANIMAL OR HUMAN.

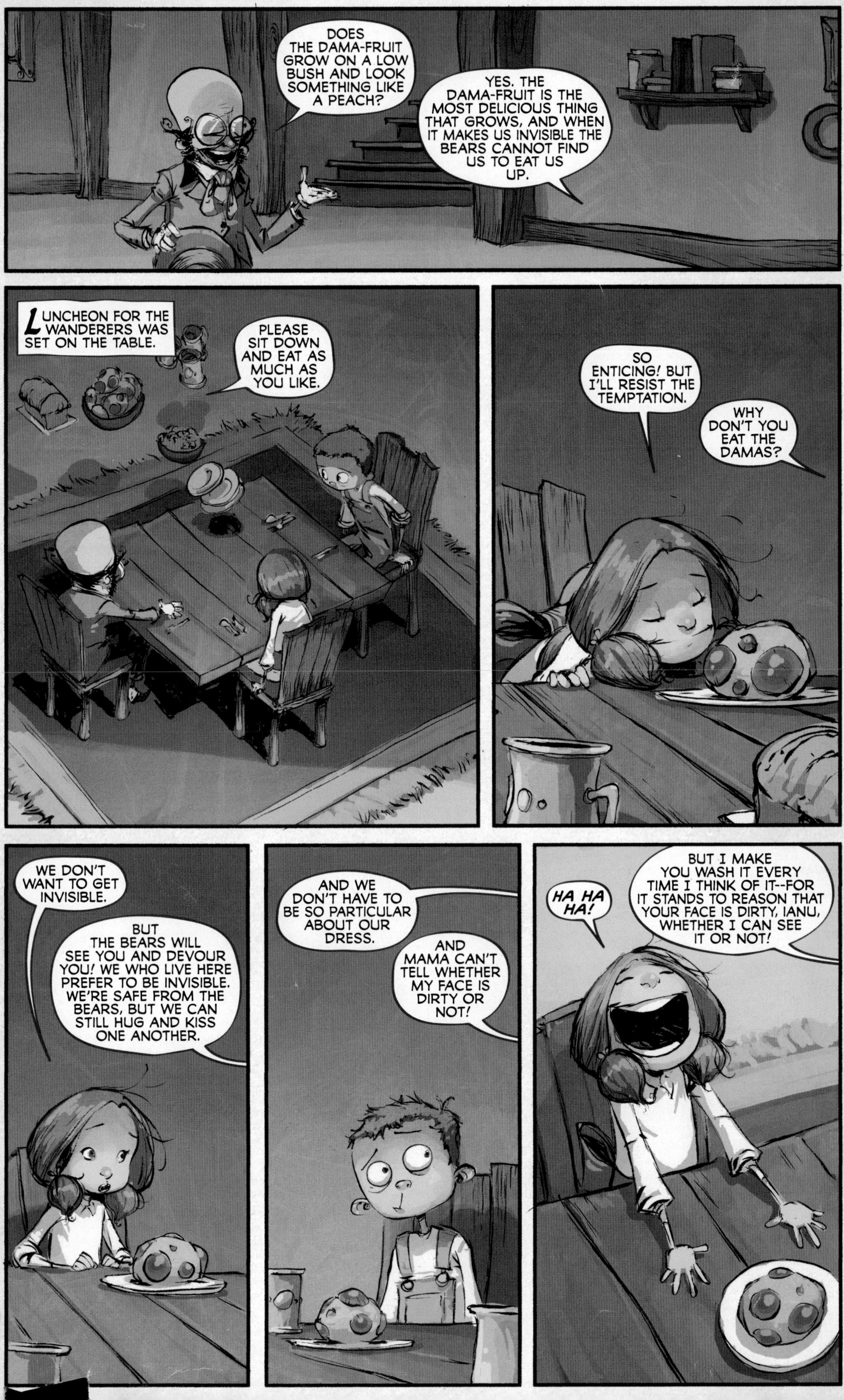
DOES THE DAMA-FRUIT GROW ON A LOW BUSH AND LOOK SOMETHING LIKE A PEACH?
YES. THE DAMA-FRUIT IS THE MOST DELICIOUS THING THAT GROWS, AND WHEN IT MAKES US INVISIBLE THE BEARS CANNOT FIND US TO EAT US UP.
LUNCHEON FOR THE WANDERERS WAS SET ON THE TABLE.
PLEASE SIT DOWN AND EAT AS MUCH AS YOU LIKE.
SO ENTICING! BUT I'LL RESIST THE TEMPTATION.
WHY DON'T YOU EAT THE DAMAS?
WE DON'T WANT TO GET INVISIBLE.
BUT THE BEARS WILL SEE YOU AND DEVOUR YOU! WE WHO LIVE HERE PREFER TO BE INVISIBLE. WE'RE SAFE FROM THE BEARS, BUT WE CAN STILL HUG AND KISS ONE ANOTHER.
AND WE DON'T HAVE TO BE SO PARTICULAR ABOUT OUR DRESS.
AND MAMA CAN'T TELL WHETHER MY FACE IS DIRTY OR NOT!
HA HA HA!
BUT I MAKE YOU WASH IT EVERY TIME I THINK OF IT--FOR IT STANDS TO REASON THAT YOUR FACE IS DIRTY, IANU, WHETHER I CAN SEE IT OR NOT!

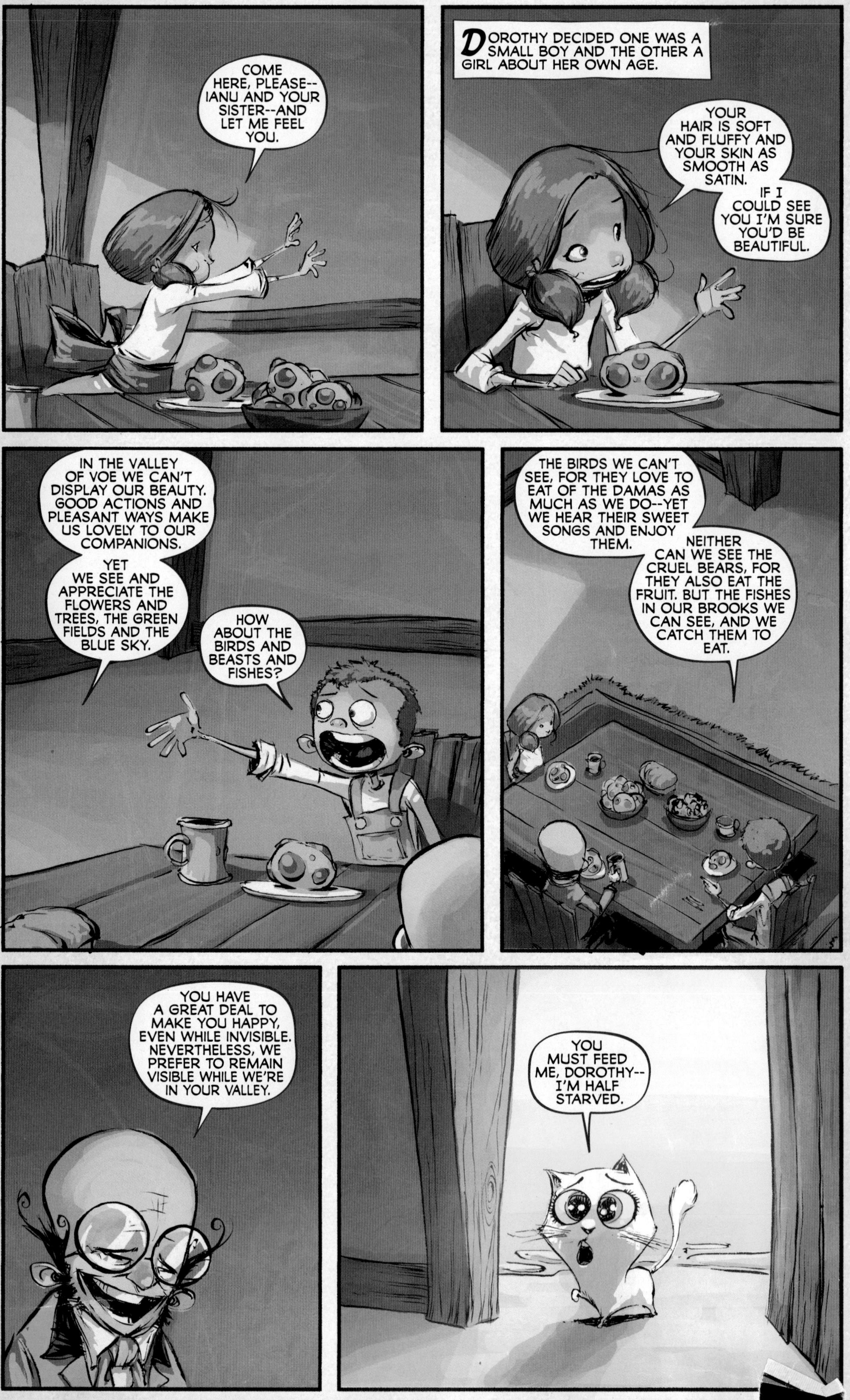
COME HERE, PLEASE--IANU AND YOUR SISTER--AND LET ME FEEL YOU.
DOROTHY DECIDED ONE WAS A SMALL BOY AND THE OTHER A GIRL ABOUT HER OWN AGE.
YOUR HAIR IS SOFT AND FLUFFY AND YOUR SKIN AS SMOOTH AS SATIN.
IF I COULD SEE YOU I'M SURE YOU'D BE BEAUTIFUL.
IN THE VALLEY OF VOE WE CAN'T DISPLAY OUR BEAUTY. GOOD ACTIONS AND PLEASANT WAYS MAKE US LOVELY TO OUR COMPANIONS.
YET WE SEE AND APPRECIATE THE FLOWERS AND TREES, THE GREEN FIELDS AND THE BLUE SKY.
HOW ABOUT THE BIRDS AND BEASTS AND FISHES?
THE BIRDS WE CAN'T SEE, FOR THEY LOVE TO EAT OF THE DAMAS AS MUCH AS WE DO--YET WE HEAR THEIR SWEET SONGS AND ENJOY THEM.
NEITHER CAN WE SEE THE CRUEL BEARS, FOR THEY ALSO EAT THE FRUIT. BUT THE FISHES IN OUR BROOKS WE CAN SEE, AND WE CATCH THEM TO EAT.
YOU HAVE A GREAT DEAL TO MAKE YOU HAPPY, EVEN WHILE INVISIBLE. NEVERTHELESS, WE PREFER TO REMAIN VISIBLE WHILE WE'RE IN YOUR VALLEY.
YOU MUST FEED ME, DOROTHY--I'M HALF STARVED.

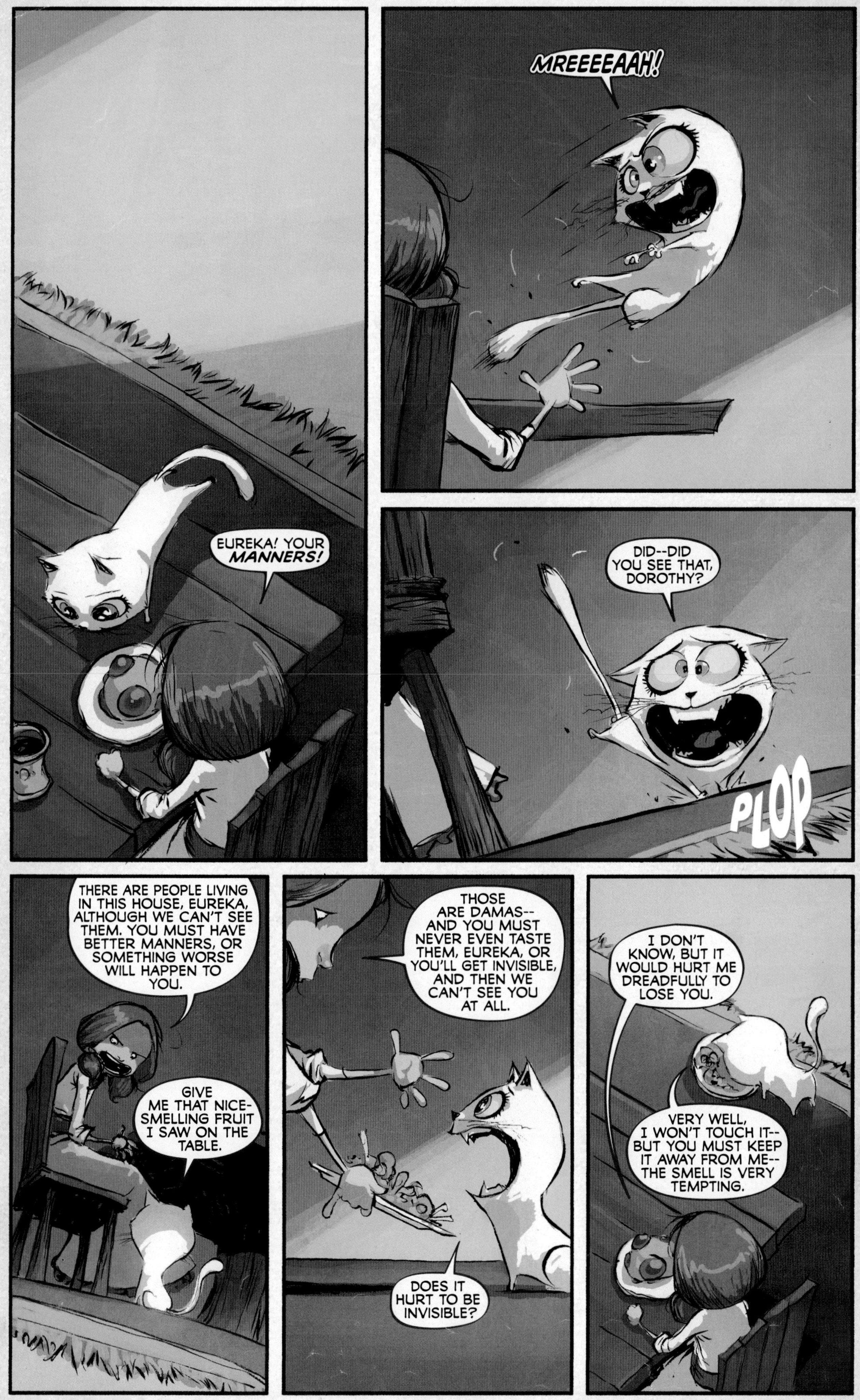

EUREKA! YOUR MANNERS!
MREEEEAAH!
DID--DID YOU SEE THAT, DOROTHY?
PLOP
THERE ARE PEOPLE LIVING IN THIS HOUSE, EUREKA, ALTHOUGH WE CAN'T SEE THEM. YOU MUST HAVE BETTER MANNERS, OR SOMETHING WORSE WILL HAPPEN TO YOU.
GIVE ME THAT NICE-SMELLING FRUIT I SAW ON THE TABLE.
THOSE ARE DAMAS--AND YOU MUST NEVER EVEN TASTE THEM, EUREKA, OR YOU'LL GET INVISIBLE, AND THEN WE CAN'T SEE YOU AT ALL.
DOES IT HURT TO BE INVISIBLE?
I DON'T KNOW, BUT IT WOULD HURT ME DREADFULLY TO LOSE YOU.
VERY WELL, I WON'T TOUCH IT--BUT YOU MUST KEEP IT AWAY FROM ME--THE SMELL IS VERY TEMPTING.

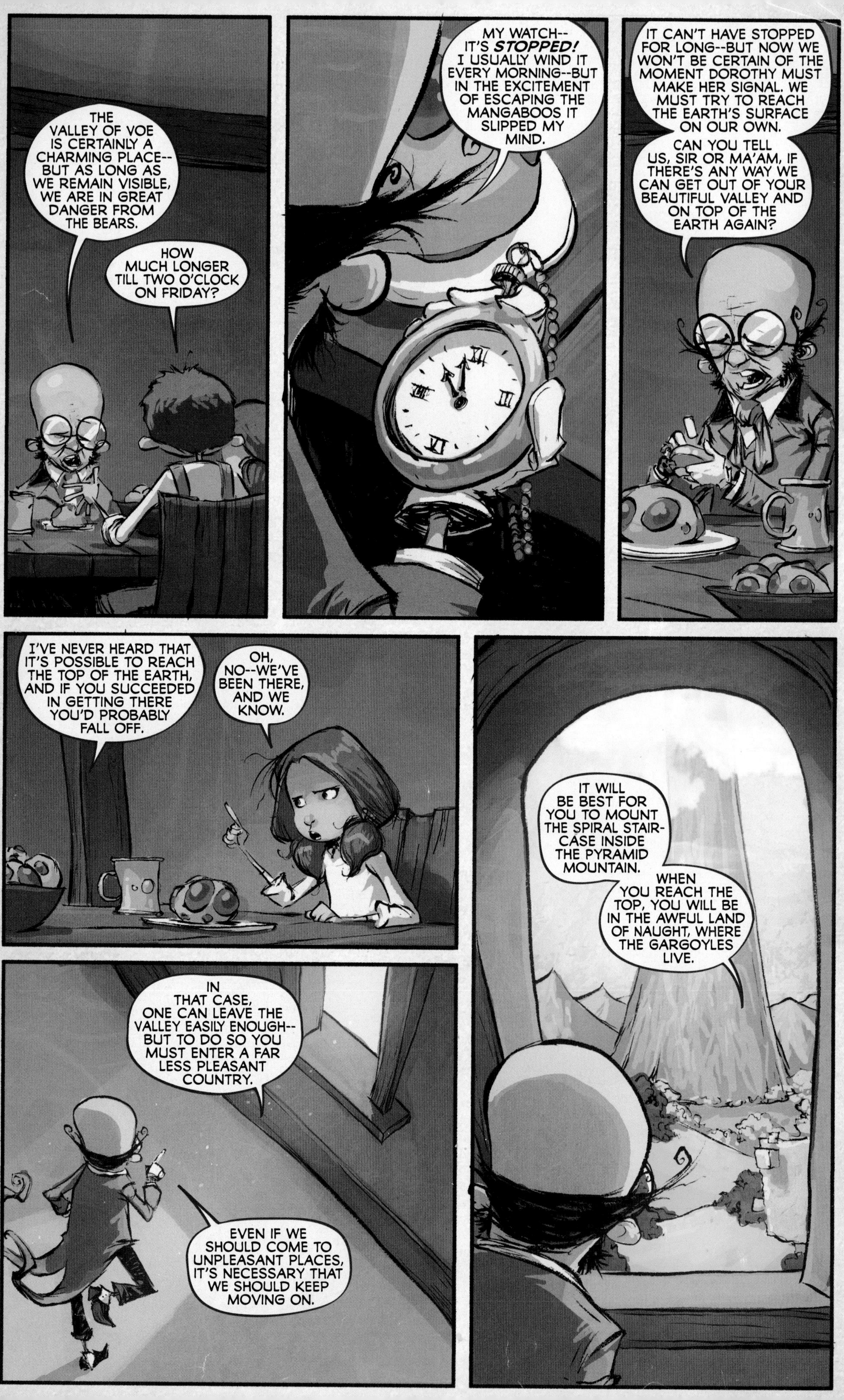
THE VALLEY OF VOE IS CERTAINLY A CHARMING PLACE--BUT AS LONG AS WE REMAIN VISIBLE, WE ARE IN GREAT DANGER FROM THE BEARS.
HOW MUCH LONGER TILL TWO O'CLOCK ON FRIDAY?
MY WATCH--IT'S STOPPED! I USUALLY WIND IT EVERY MORNING--BUT IN THE EXCITEMENT OF ESCAPING THE MANGABOOS IT SLIPPED MY MIND.
IT CAN'T HAVE STOPPED FOR LONG--BUT NOW WE WON'T BE CERTAIN OF THE MOMENT DOROTHY MUST MAKE HER SIGNAL. WE MUST TRY TO REACH THE EARTH'S SURFACE ON OUR OWN.
CAN YOU TELL US, SIR OR MA'AM, IF THERE'S ANY WAY WE CAN GET OUT OF YOUR BEAUTIFUL VALLEY AND ON TOP OF THE EARTH AGAIN?
I'VE NEVER HEARD THAT IT'S POSSIBLE TO REACH THE TOP OF THE EARTH, AND IF YOU SUCCEEDED IN GETTING THERE YOU'D PROBABLY FALL OFF.
OH, NO--WE'VE BEEN THERE, AND WE KNOW.
IN THAT CASE, ONE CAN LEAVE THE VALLEY EASILY ENOUGH--BUT TO DO SO YOU MUST ENTER A FAR LESS PLEASANT COUNTRY.
EVEN IF WE SHOULD COME TO UNPLEASANT PLACES, IT'S NECESSARY THAT WE SHOULD KEEP MOVING ON.
IT WILL BE BEST FOR YOU TO MOUNT THE SPIRAL STAIR-CASE INSIDE THE PYRAMID MOUNTAIN.
WHEN YOU REACH THE TOP, YOU WILL BE IN THE AWFUL LAND OF NAUGHT, WHERE THE GARGOYLES LIVE.

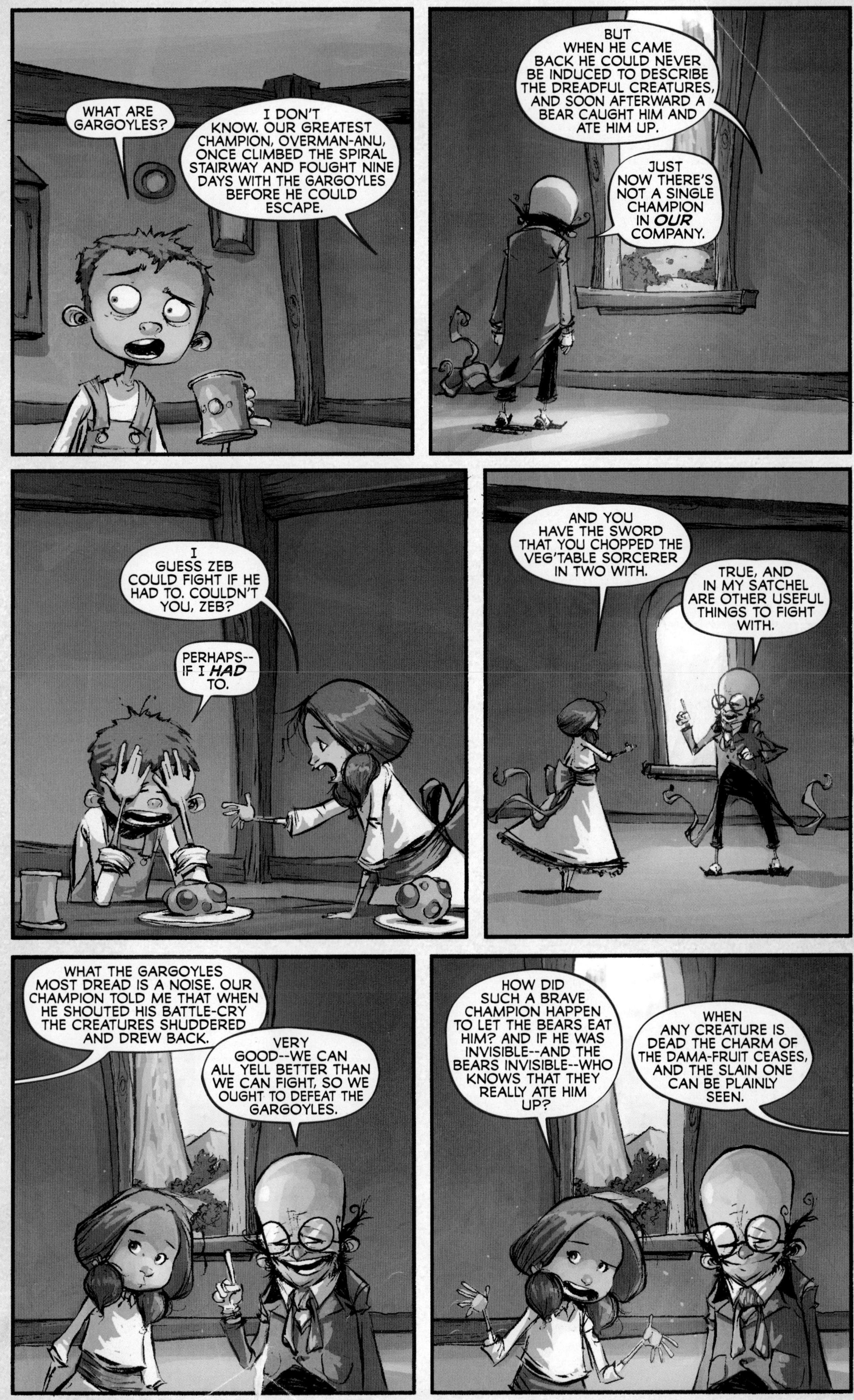
WHAT ARE GARGOYLES?
I DON'T KNOW. OUR GREATEST CHAMPION, OVERMAN-ANU, ONCE CLIMBED THE SPIRAL STAIRWAY AND FOUGHT NINE DAYS WITH THE GARGOYLES BEFORE HE COULD ESCAPE.
BUT WHEN HE CAME BACK HE COULD NEVER BE INDUCED TO DESCRIBE THE DREADFUL CREATURES, AND SOON AFTERWARD A BEAR CAUGHT HIM AND ATE HIM UP.
JUST NOW THERE'S NOT A SINGLE CHAMPION IN OUR COMPANY.
I GUESS ZEB COULD FIGHT IF HE HAD TO. COULDN'T YOU, ZEB?
PERHAPS-- IF I HAD TO.
AND YOU HAVE THE SWORD THAT YOU CHOPPED THE VEG'TABLE SORCERER IN TWO WITH.
TRUE, AND IN MY SATCHEL ARE OTHER USEFUL THINGS TO FIGHT WITH.
WHAT THE GARGOYLES MOST DREAD IS A NOISE. OUR CHAMPION TOLD ME THAT WHEN HE SHOUTED HIS BATTLE-CRY THE CREATURES SHUDDERED AND DREW BACK.
VERY GOOD--WE CAN ALL YELL BETTER THAN WE CAN FIGHT, SO WE OUGHT TO DEFEAT THE GARGOYLES.
HOW DID SUCH A BRAVE CHAMPION HAPPEN TO LET THE BEARS EAT HIM? AND IF HE WAS INVISIBLE--AND THE BEARS INVISIBLE--WHO KNOWS THAT THEY REALLY ATE HIM UP?
WHEN ANY CREATURE IS DEAD THE CHARM OF THE DAMA-FRUIT CEASES, AND THE SLAIN ONE CAN BE PLAINLY SEEN.

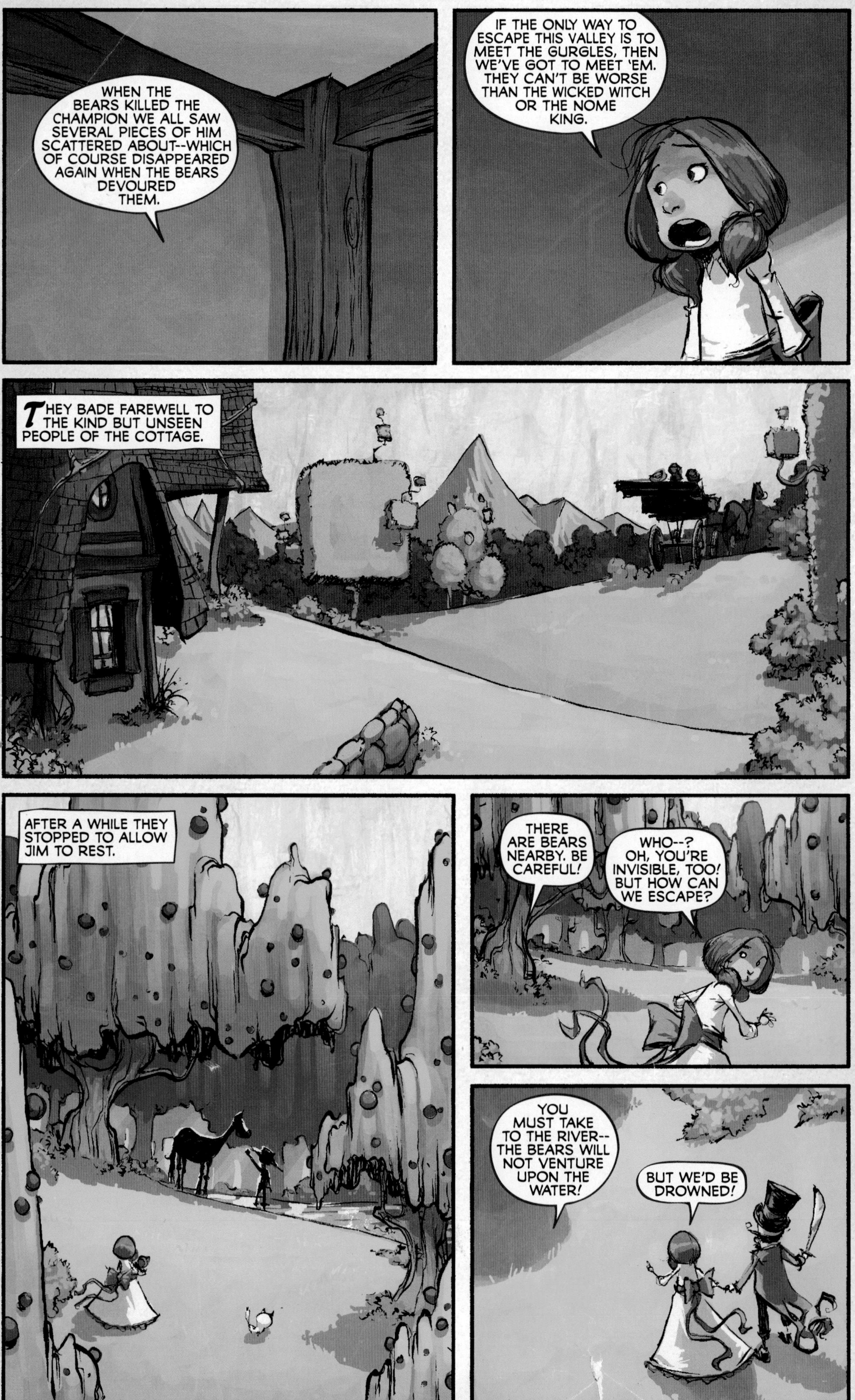
WHEN THE BEARS KILLED THE CHAMPION WE ALL SAW SEVERAL PIECES OF HIM SCATTERED ABOUT--WHICH OF COURSE DISAPPEARED AGAIN WHEN THE BEARS DEVOURED THEM.
IF THE ONLY WAY TO ESCAPE THIS VALLEY IS TO MEET THE GURGLES, THEN WE'VE GOT TO MEET 'EM. THEY CAN'T BE WORSE THAN THE WICKED WITCH OR THE NOME KING.
THEY BADE FAREWELL TO THE KIND BUT UNSEEN PEOPLE OF THE COTTAGE.
AFTER A WHILE THEY STOPPED TO ALLOW JIM TO REST.
THERE ARE BEARS NEARBY. BE CAREFUL!
WHO--? OH, YOU'RE INVISIBLE, TOO! BUT HOW CAN WE ESCAPE?
YOU MUST TAKE TO THE RIVER-- THE BEARS WILL NOT VENTURE UPON THE WATER!
BUT WE'D BE DROWNED!

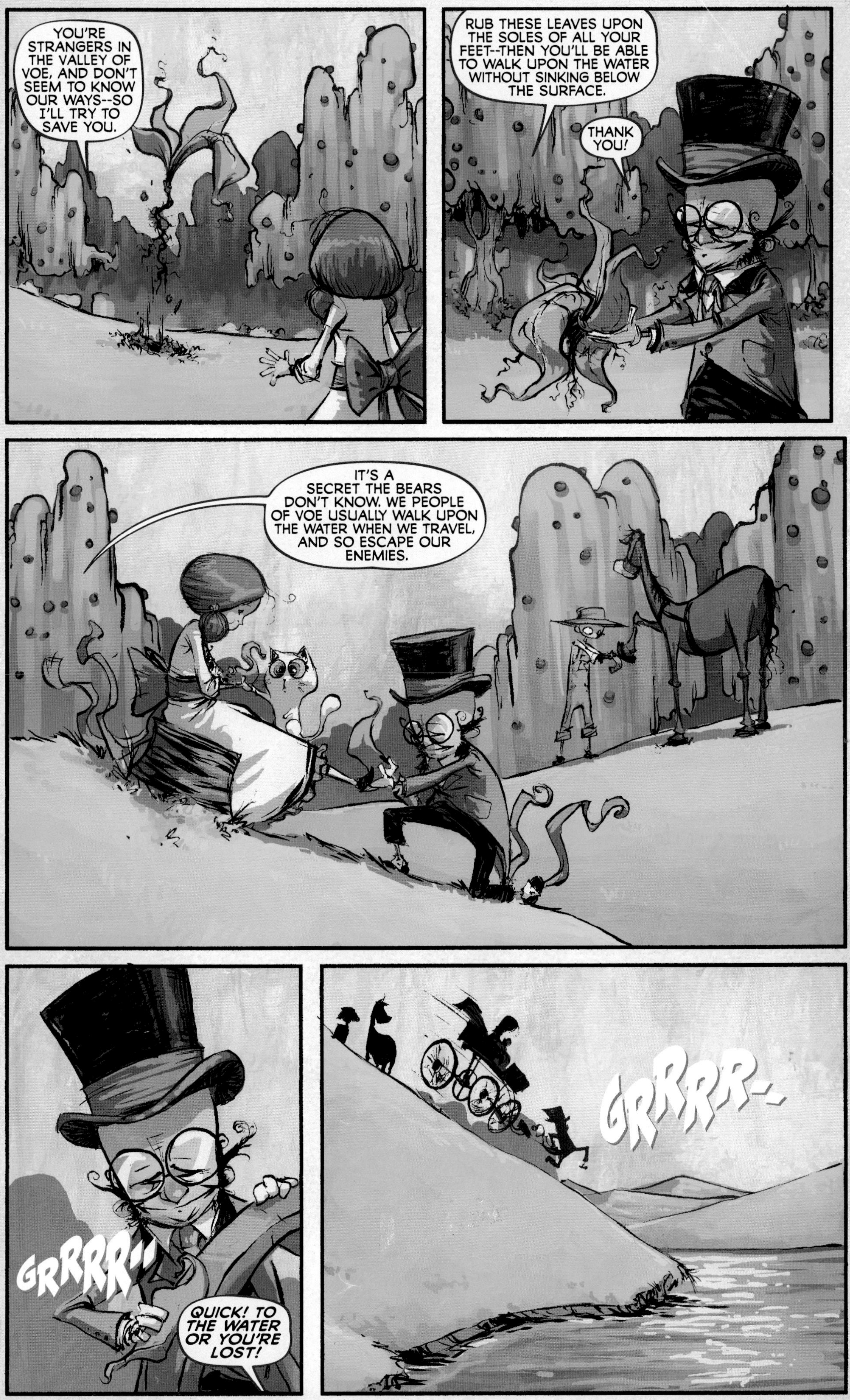
YOU'RE STRANGERS IN THE VALLEY OF VOE, AND DON'T SEEM TO KNOW OUR WAYS--SO I'LL TRY TO SAVE YOU.
RUB THESE LEAVES UPON THE SOLES OF ALL YOUR FEET--THEN YOU'LL BE ABLE TO WALK UPON THE WATER WITHOUT SINKING BELOW THE SURFACE.
THANK YOU!
IT'S A SECRET THE BEARS DON'T KNOW. WE PEOPLE OF VOE USUALLY WALK UPON THE WATER WHEN WE TRAVEL, AND SO ESCAPE OUR ENEMIES.
GRRRR--
QUICK! TO THE WATER OR YOU'RE LOST!
GRRRR--

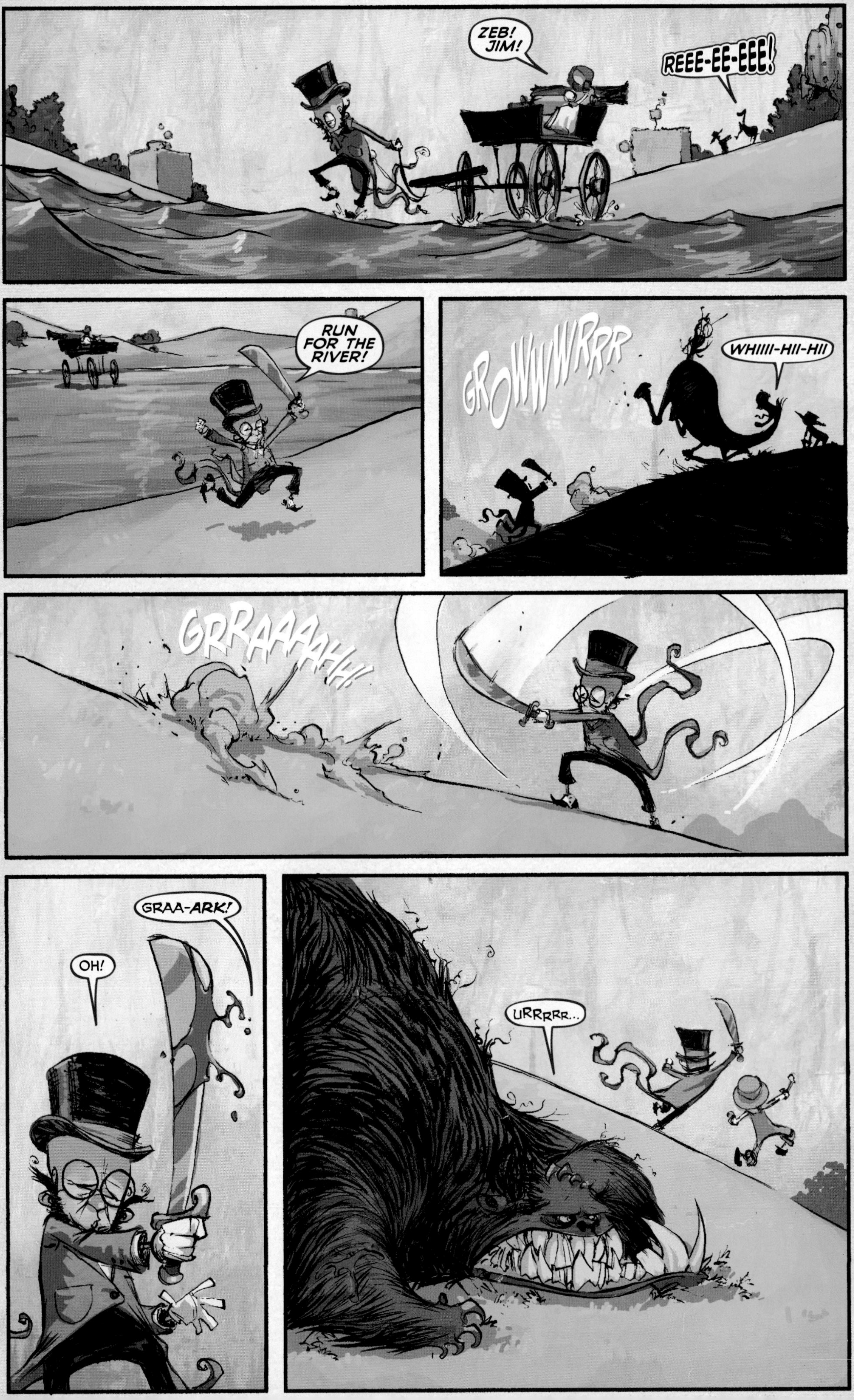
ZEB! JIM!
REEE-EE-EEE!
RUN FOR THE RIVER!
GROWWWRRR
WHIIII-HII-HII
GRRAAAAAHH!
GRAA-ARK!
OH!
URRRRR...

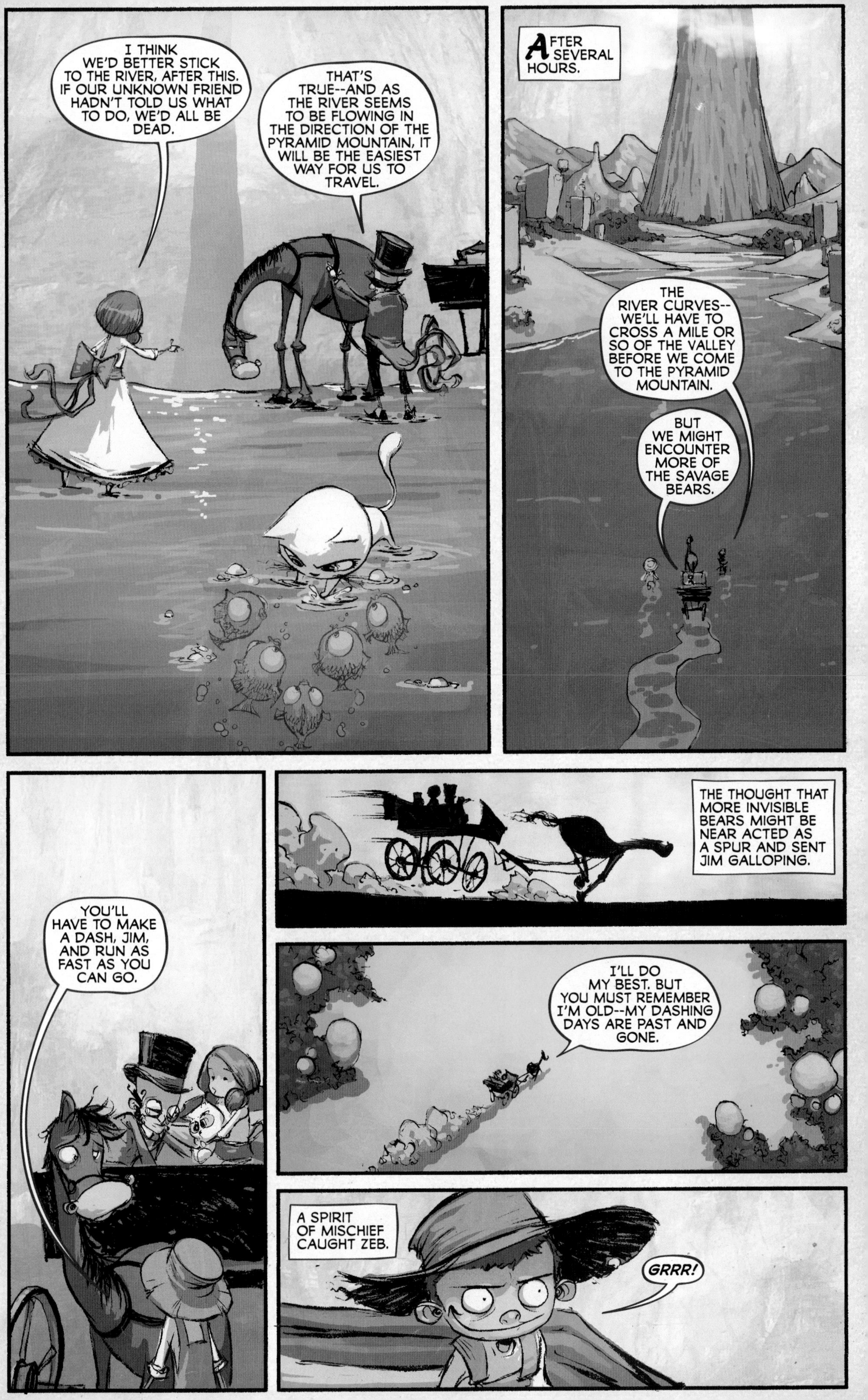

I THINK WE'D BETTER STICK TO THE RIVER, AFTER THIS. IF OUR UNKNOWN FRIEND HADN'T TOLD US WHAT TO DO, WE'D ALL BE DEAD.
THAT'S TRUE--AND AS THE RIVER SEEMS TO BE FLOWING IN THE DIRECTION OF THE PYRAMID MOUNTAIN, IT WILL BE THE EASIEST WAY FOR US TO TRAVEL.
AFTER SEVERAL HOURS.
THE RIVER CURVES--WE'LL HAVE TO CROSS A MILE OR SO OF THE VALLEY BEFORE WE COME TO THE PYRAMID MOUNTAIN.
BUT WE MIGHT ENCOUNTER MORE OF THE SAVAGE BEARS.
YOU'LL HAVE TO MAKE A DASH, JIM, AND RUN AS FAST AS YOU CAN GO.
THE THOUGHT THAT MORE INVISIBLE BEARS MIGHT BE NEAR ACTED AS A SPUR AND SENT JIM GALLOPING.
I'LL DO MY BEST. BUT YOU MUST REMEMBER I'M OLD--MY DASHING DAYS ARE PAST AND GONE.
A SPIRIT OF MISCHIEF CAUGHT ZEB.
GRRR!

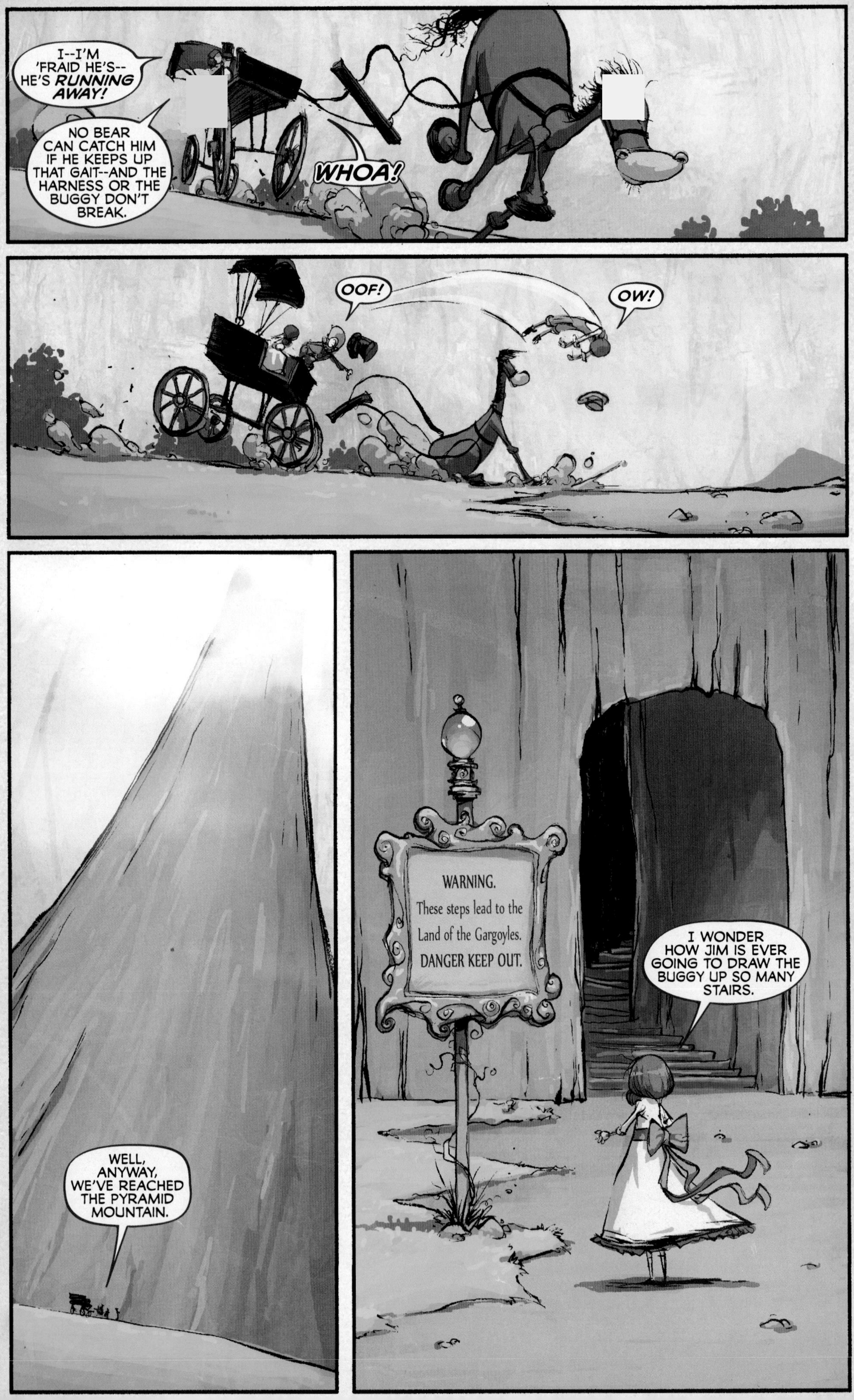
I--I'M 'FRAID HE'S-- HE'S *RUNNING AWAY!*
NO BEAR CAN CATCH HIM IF HE KEEPS UP THAT GAIT--AND THE HARNESS OR THE BUGGY DON'T BREAK.
WHOA!
OOF!
OW!
WELL, ANYWAY, WE'VE REACHED THE PYRAMID MOUNTAIN.
WARNING.
These steps lead to the Land of the Gargoyles.
DANGER KEEP OUT.
I WONDER HOW JIM IS EVER GOING TO DRAW THE BUGGY UP SO MANY STAIRS.

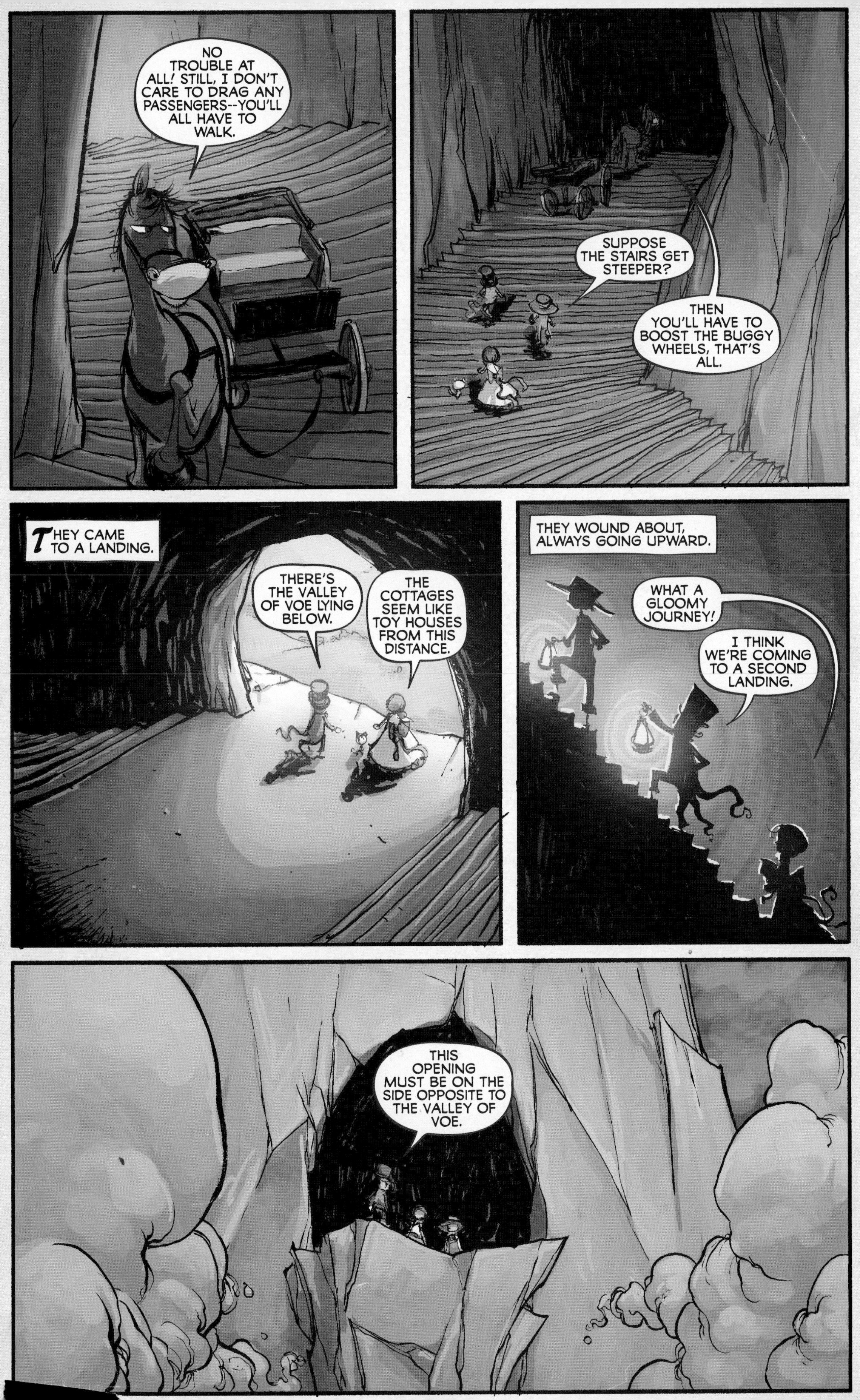
NO TROUBLE AT ALL! STILL, I DON'T CARE TO DRAG ANY PASSENGERS--YOU'LL ALL HAVE TO WALK.
SUPPOSE THE STAIRS GET STEEPER?
THEN YOU'LL HAVE TO BOOST THE BUGGY WHEELS, THAT'S ALL.
THEY CAME TO A LANDING.
THERE'S THE VALLEY OF VOE LYING BELOW.
THE COTTAGES SEEM LIKE TOY HOUSES FROM THIS DISTANCE.
THEY WOUND ABOUT, ALWAYS GOING UPWARD.
WHAT A GLOOMY JOURNEY!
I THINK WE'RE COMING TO A SECOND LANDING.
THIS OPENING MUST BE ON THE SIDE OPPOSITE TO THE VALLEY OF VOE.

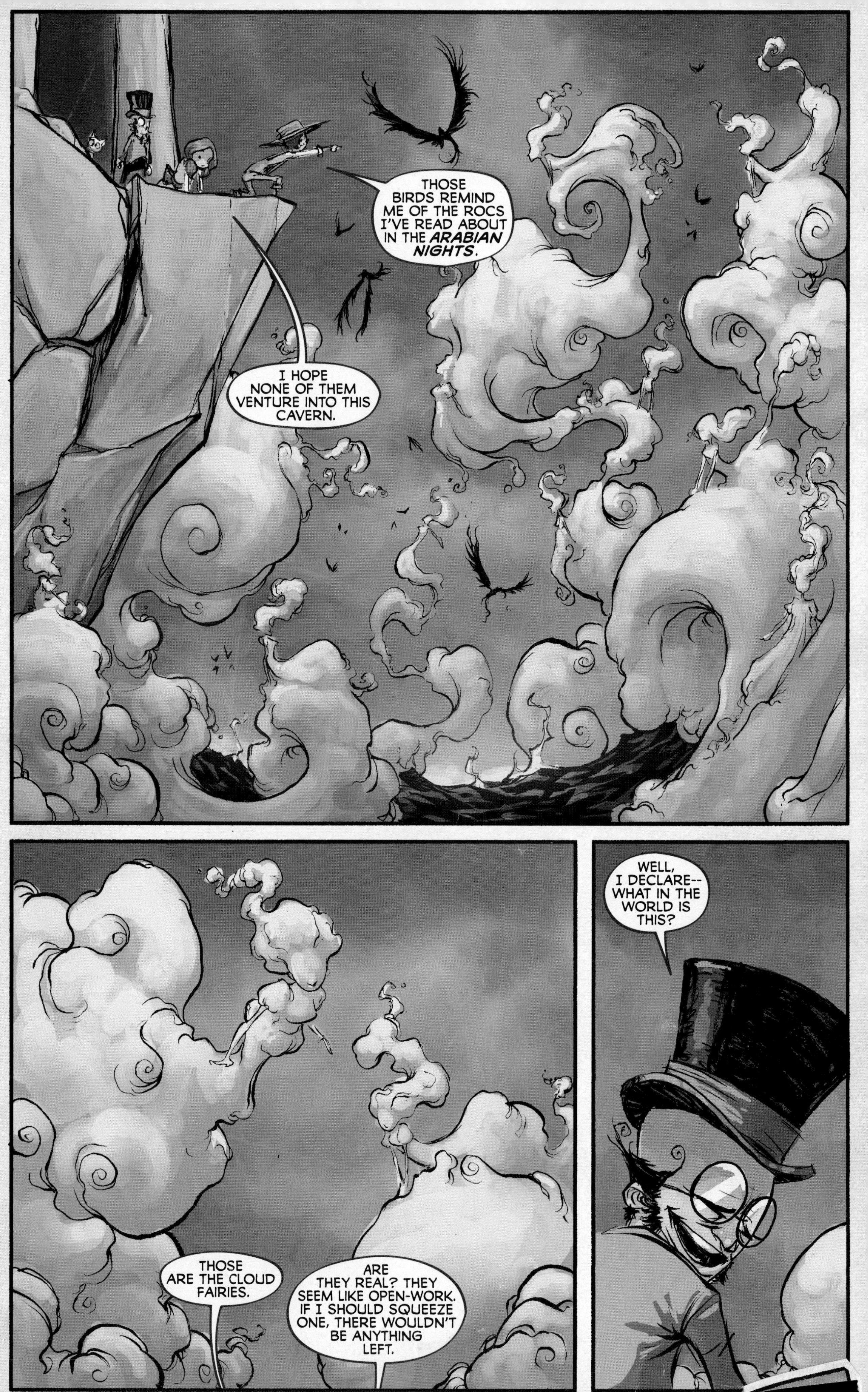
THOSE BIRDS REMIND ME OF THE ROCS I'VE READ ABOUT IN THE *ARABIAN NIGHTS*.
I HOPE NONE OF THEM VENTURE INTO THIS CAVERN.
WELL, I DECLARE-- WHAT IN THE WORLD IS THIS?
THOSE ARE THE CLOUD FAIRIES.
ARE THEY REAL? THEY SEEM LIKE OPEN-WORK. IF I SHOULD SQUEEZE ONE, THERE WOULDN'T BE ANYTHING LEFT.

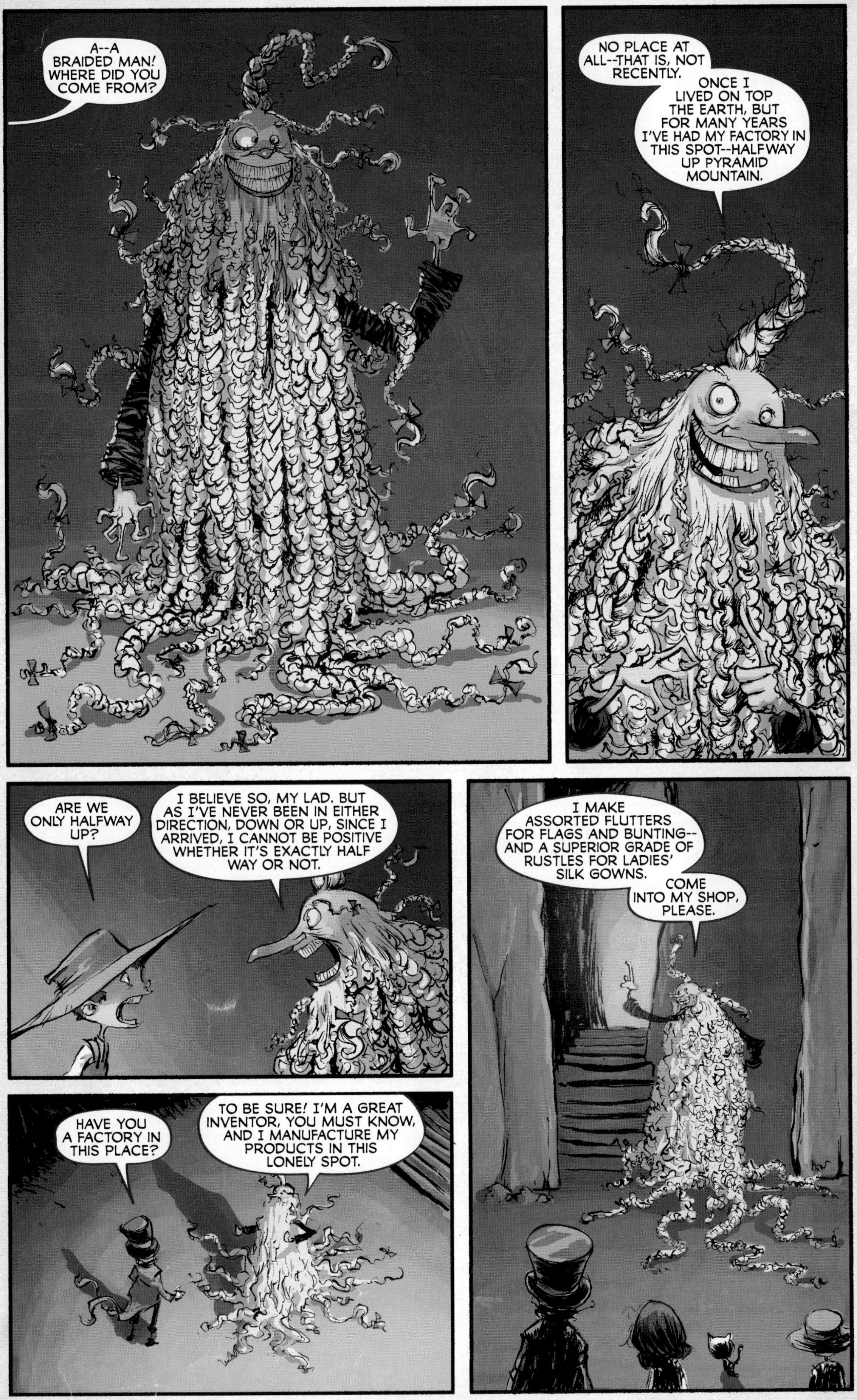
A--A BRAIDED MAN! WHERE DID YOU COME FROM?
NO PLACE AT ALL--THAT IS, NOT RECENTLY.
ONCE I LIVED ON TOP THE EARTH, BUT FOR MANY YEARS I'VE HAD MY FACTORY IN THIS SPOT--HALFWAY UP PYRAMID MOUNTAIN.
ARE WE ONLY HALFWAY UP?
I BELIEVE SO, MY LAD. BUT AS I'VE NEVER BEEN IN EITHER DIRECTION, DOWN OR UP, SINCE I ARRIVED, I CANNOT BE POSITIVE WHETHER IT'S EXACTLY HALF WAY OR NOT.
HAVE YOU A FACTORY IN THIS PLACE?
TO BE SURE! I'M A GREAT INVENTOR, YOU MUST KNOW, AND I MANUFACTURE MY PRODUCTS IN THIS LONELY SPOT.
I MAKE ASSORTED FLUTTERS FOR FLAGS AND BUNTING--AND A SUPERIOR GRADE OF RUSTLES FOR LADIES' SILK GOWNS.
COME INTO MY SHOP, PLEASE.

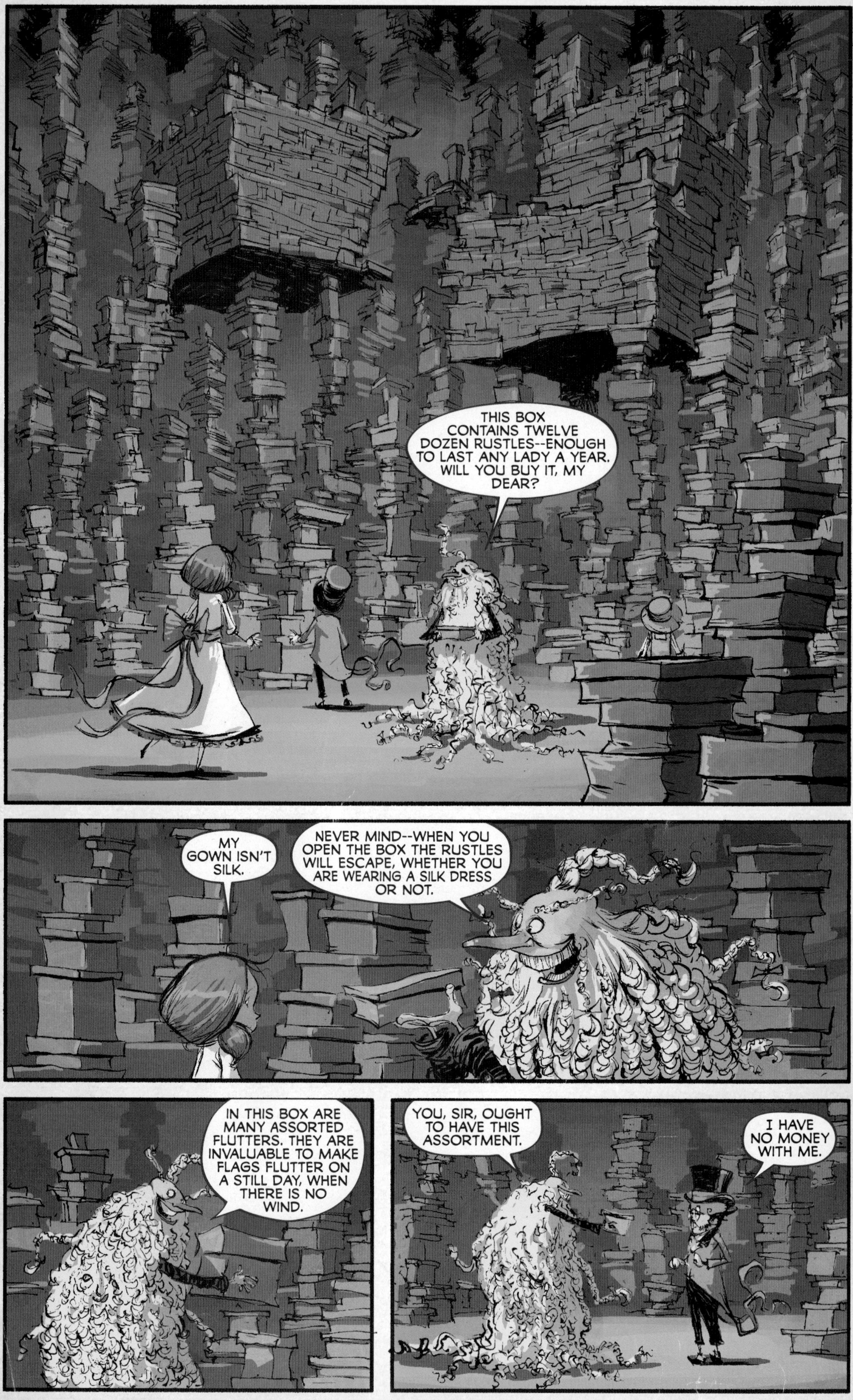
THIS BOX CONTAINS TWELVE DOZEN RUSTLES--ENOUGH TO LAST ANY LADY A YEAR. WILL YOU BUY IT, MY DEAR?
MY GOWN ISN'T SILK.
NEVER MIND--WHEN YOU OPEN THE BOX THE RUSTLES WILL ESCAPE, WHETHER YOU ARE WEARING A SILK DRESS OR NOT.
IN THIS BOX ARE MANY ASSORTED FLUTTERS. THEY ARE INVALUABLE TO MAKE FLAGS FLUTTER ON A STILL DAY, WHEN THERE IS NO WIND.
YOU, SIR, OUGHT TO HAVE THIS ASSORTMENT.
I HAVE NO MONEY WITH ME.

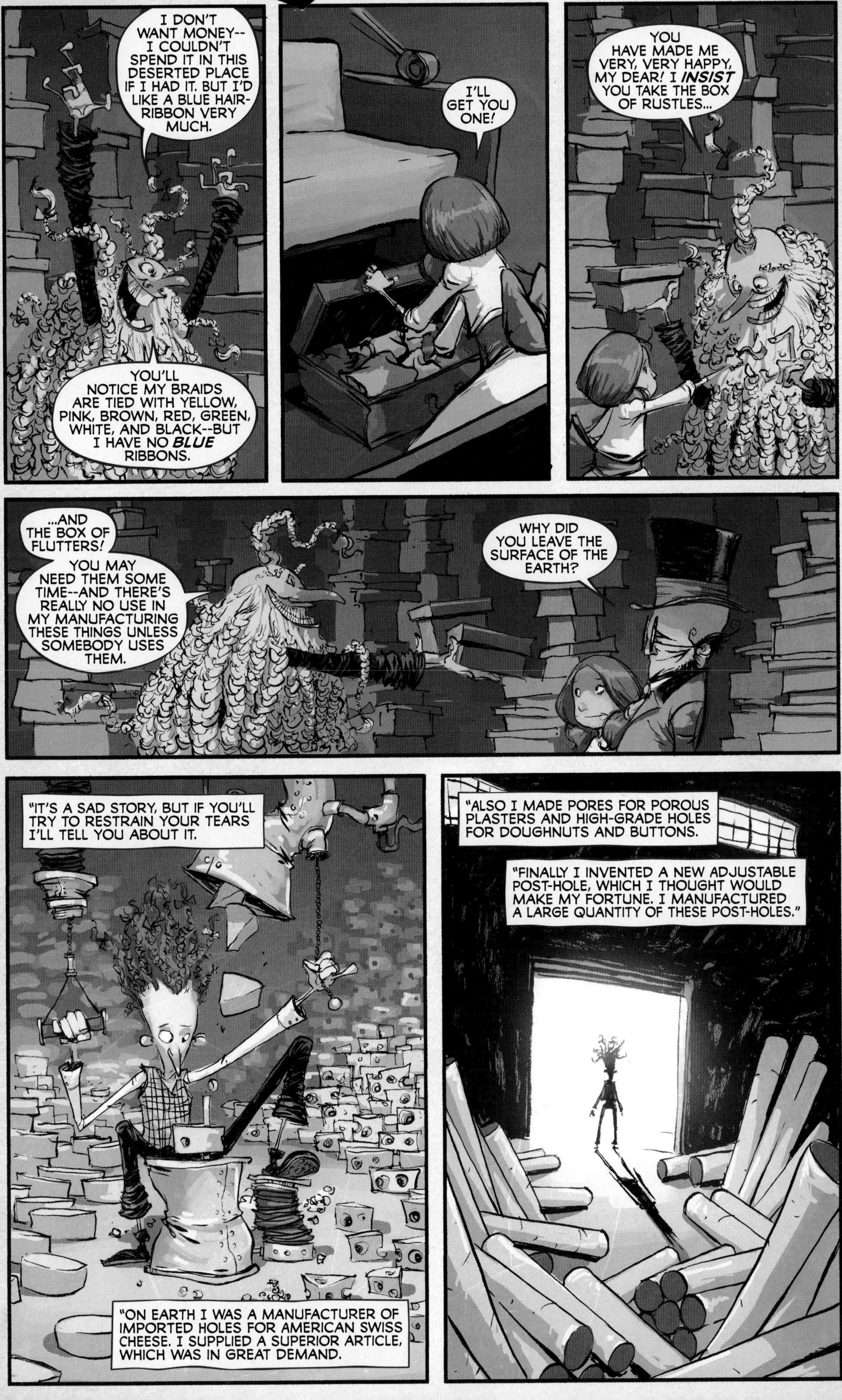
I DON'T WANT MONEY--I COULDN'T SPEND IT IN THIS DESERTED PLACE IF I HAD IT. BUT I'D LIKE A BLUE HAIR-RIBBON VERY MUCH.
YOU'LL NOTICE MY BRAIDS ARE TIED WITH YELLOW, PINK, BROWN, RED, GREEN, WHITE, AND BLACK--BUT I HAVE NO *BLUE* RIBBONS.
I'LL GET YOU ONE!
YOU HAVE MADE ME VERY, VERY HAPPY, MY DEAR! I *INSIST* YOU TAKE THE BOX OF RUSTLES...
...AND THE BOX OF FLUTTERS!
YOU MAY NEED THEM SOME TIME--AND THERE'S REALLY NO USE IN MY MANUFACTURING THESE THINGS UNLESS SOMEBODY USES THEM.
WHY DID YOU LEAVE THE SURFACE OF THE EARTH?
"IT'S A SAD STORY, BUT IF YOU'LL TRY TO RESTRAIN YOUR TEARS I'LL TELL YOU ABOUT IT.
"ON EARTH I WAS A MANUFACTURER OF IMPORTED HOLES FOR AMERICAN SWISS CHEESE. I SUPPLIED A SUPERIOR ARTICLE, WHICH WAS IN GREAT DEMAND.
"ALSO I MADE PORES FOR POROUS PLASTERS AND HIGH-GRADE HOLES FOR DOUGHNUTS AND BUTTONS.
"FINALLY I INVENTED A NEW ADJUSTABLE POST-HOLE, WHICH I THOUGHT WOULD MAKE MY FORTUNE. I MANUFACTURED A LARGE QUANTITY OF THESE POST-HOLES."

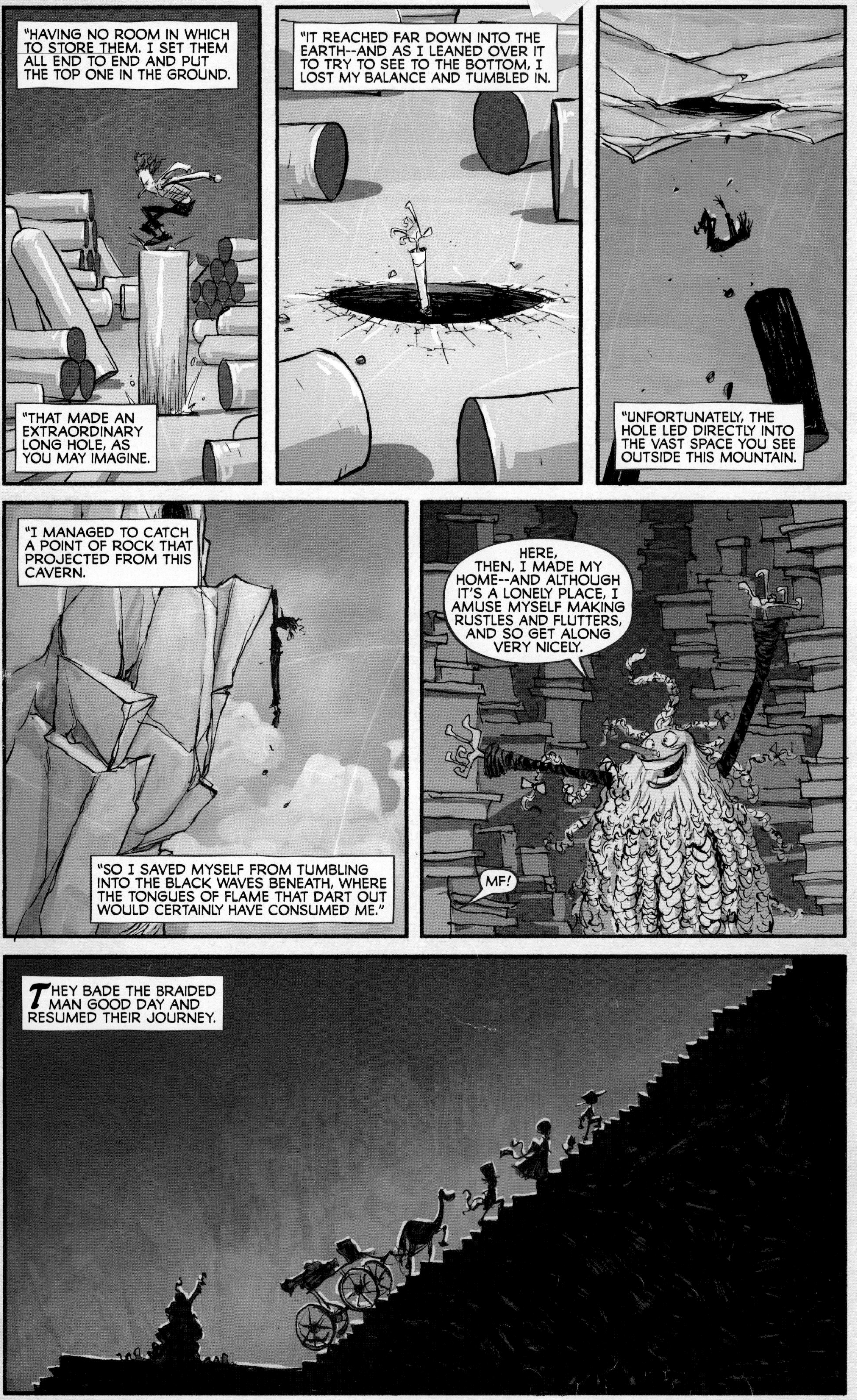
"HAVING NO ROOM IN WHICH TO STORE THEM. I SET THEM ALL END TO END AND PUT THE TOP ONE IN THE GROUND.
"THAT MADE AN EXTRAORDINARY LONG HOLE, AS YOU MAY IMAGINE.
"IT REACHED FAR DOWN INTO THE EARTH--AND AS I LEANED OVER IT TO TRY TO SEE TO THE BOTTOM, I LOST MY BALANCE AND TUMBLED IN.
"UNFORTUNATELY, THE HOLE LED DIRECTLY INTO THE VAST SPACE YOU SEE OUTSIDE THIS MOUNTAIN.
"I MANAGED TO CATCH A POINT OF ROCK THAT PROJECTED FROM THIS CAVERN.
"SO I SAVED MYSELF FROM TUMBLING INTO THE BLACK WAVES BENEATH, WHERE THE TONGUES OF FLAME THAT DART OUT WOULD CERTAINLY HAVE CONSUMED ME."
HERE, THEN, I MADE MY HOME--AND ALTHOUGH IT'S A LONELY PLACE, I AMUSE MYSELF MAKING RUSTLES AND FLUTTERS, AND SO GET ALONG VERY NICELY.
MF!
THEY BADE THE BRAIDED MAN GOOD DAY AND RESUMED THEIR JOURNEY.

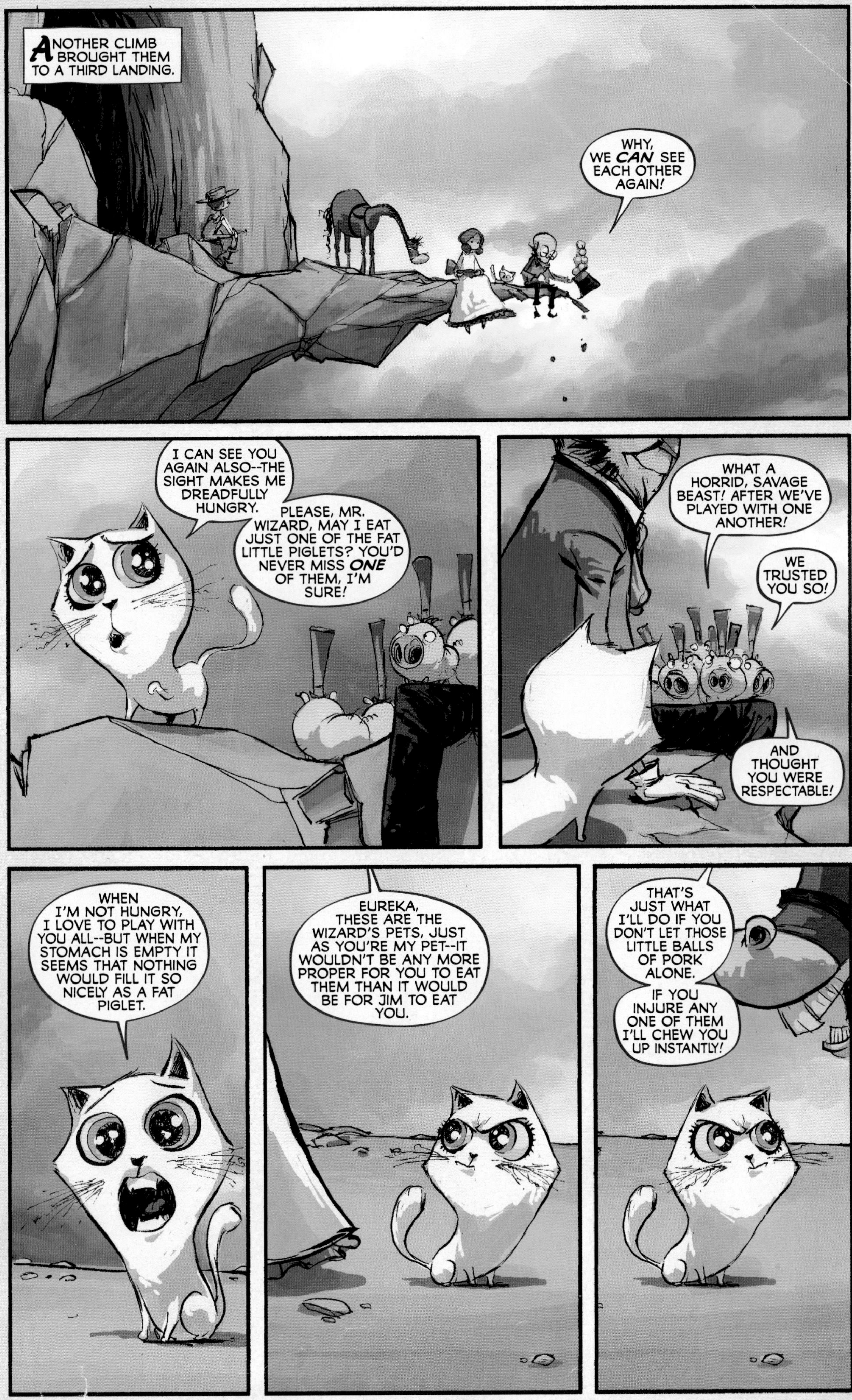
ANOTHER CLIMB BROUGHT THEM TO A THIRD LANDING.
WHY, WE CAN SEE EACH OTHER AGAIN!
I CAN SEE YOU AGAIN ALSO--THE SIGHT MAKES ME DREADFULLY HUNGRY.
PLEASE, MR. WIZARD, MAY I EAT JUST ONE OF THE FAT LITTLE PIGLETS? YOU'D NEVER MISS ONE OF THEM, I'M SURE!
WHAT A HORRID, SAVAGE BEAST! AFTER WE'VE PLAYED WITH ONE ANOTHER!
WE TRUSTED YOU SO!
AND THOUGHT YOU WERE RESPECTABLE!
WHEN I'M NOT HUNGRY, I LOVE TO PLAY WITH YOU ALL--BUT WHEN MY STOMACH IS EMPTY IT SEEMS THAT NOTHING WOULD FILL IT SO NICELY AS A FAT PIGLET.
EUREKA, THESE ARE THE WIZARD'S PETS, JUST AS YOU'RE MY PET--IT WOULDN'T BE ANY MORE PROPER FOR YOU TO EAT THEM THAN IT WOULD BE FOR JIM TO EAT YOU.
THAT'S JUST WHAT I'LL DO IF YOU DON'T LET THOSE LITTLE BALLS OF PORK ALONE.
IF YOU INJURE ANY ONE OF THEM I'LL CHEW YOU UP INSTANTLY!

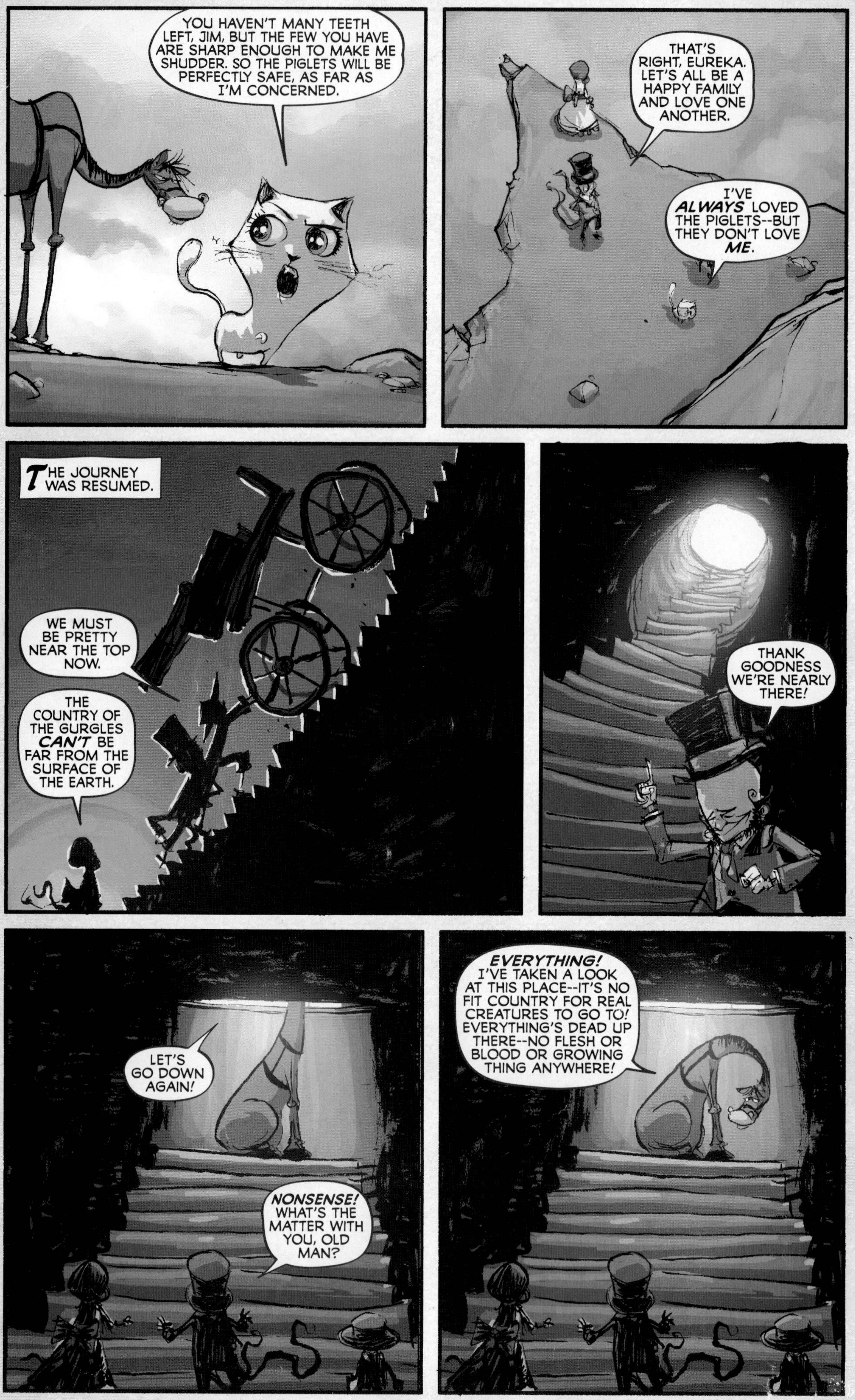
YOU HAVEN'T MANY TEETH LEFT, JIM, BUT THE FEW YOU HAVE ARE SHARP ENOUGH TO MAKE ME SHUDDER. SO THE PIGLETS WILL BE PERFECTLY SAFE, AS FAR AS I'M CONCERNED.
THAT'S RIGHT, EUREKA. LET'S ALL BE A HAPPY FAMILY AND LOVE ONE ANOTHER.
I'VE ALWAYS LOVED THE PIGLETS--BUT THEY DON'T LOVE ME.
THE JOURNEY WAS RESUMED.
WE MUST BE PRETTY NEAR THE TOP NOW.
THE COUNTRY OF THE GURGLES CAN'T BE FAR FROM THE SURFACE OF THE EARTH.
THANK GOODNESS WE'RE NEARLY THERE!
LET'S GO DOWN AGAIN!
NONSENSE! WHAT'S THE MATTER WITH YOU, OLD MAN?
EVERYTHING! I'VE TAKEN A LOOK AT THIS PLACE--IT'S NO FIT COUNTRY FOR REAL CREATURES TO GO TO! EVERYTHING'S DEAD UP THERE--NO FLESH OR BLOOD OR GROWING THING ANYWHERE!

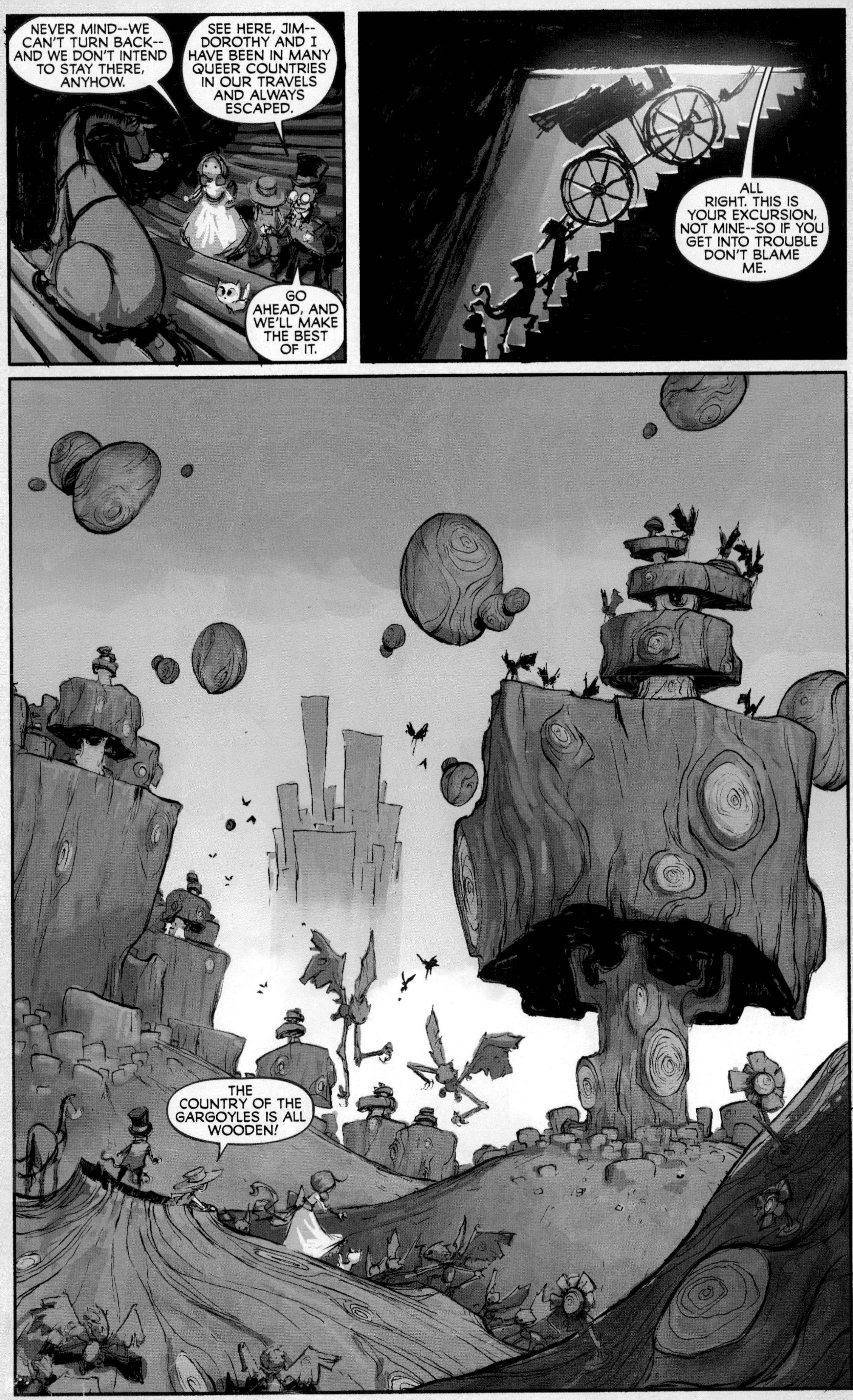
NEVER MIND--WE CAN'T TURN BACK--AND WE DON'T INTEND TO STAY THERE, ANYHOW.
SEE HERE, JIM--DOROTHY AND I HAVE BEEN IN MANY QUEER COUNTRIES IN OUR TRAVELS AND ALWAYS ESCAPED.
GO AHEAD, AND WE'LL MAKE THE BEST OF IT.
ALL RIGHT. THIS IS YOUR EXCURSION, NOT MINE--SO IF YOU GET INTO TROUBLE DON'T BLAME ME.
THE COUNTRY OF THE GARGOYLES IS ALL WOODEN!

THE MOST PECULIAR THING ABOUT THESE GURGLES IS THEY MAKE NO SOUNDS AT ALL.

THERE'S GOING TO BE TROUBLE, I'M SURE. UNHITCH ME, ZEB, SO I CAN FIGHT.

JIM'S RIGHT. MY SWORD ISN'T STOUT ENOUGH TO CUT UP THOSE WOODEN BODIES-- SO I'LL HAVE TO GET OUT MY REVOLVERS.

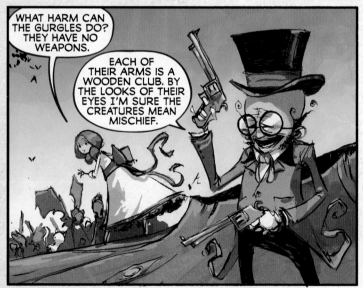

WHAT HARM CAN THE GURGLES DO? THEY HAVE NO WEAPONS.

EACH OF THEIR ARMS IS A WOODEN CLUB. BY THE LOOKS OF THEIR EYES I'M SURE THE CREATURES MEAN MISCHIEF.

EVEN THESE REVOLVERS CAN MERELY SUCCEED IN DAMAGING A FEW OF THEIR WOODEN BODIES. AFTER THAT WE'LL BE AT THEIR MERCY.

BUT WHY FIGHT AT ALL, IN THAT CASE?

SO I MAY DIE WITH A CLEAR CONSCIENCE. IT'S EVERY MAN'S DUTY TO DO THE BEST HE KNOWS HOW-- AND I'M GOING TO DO IT.

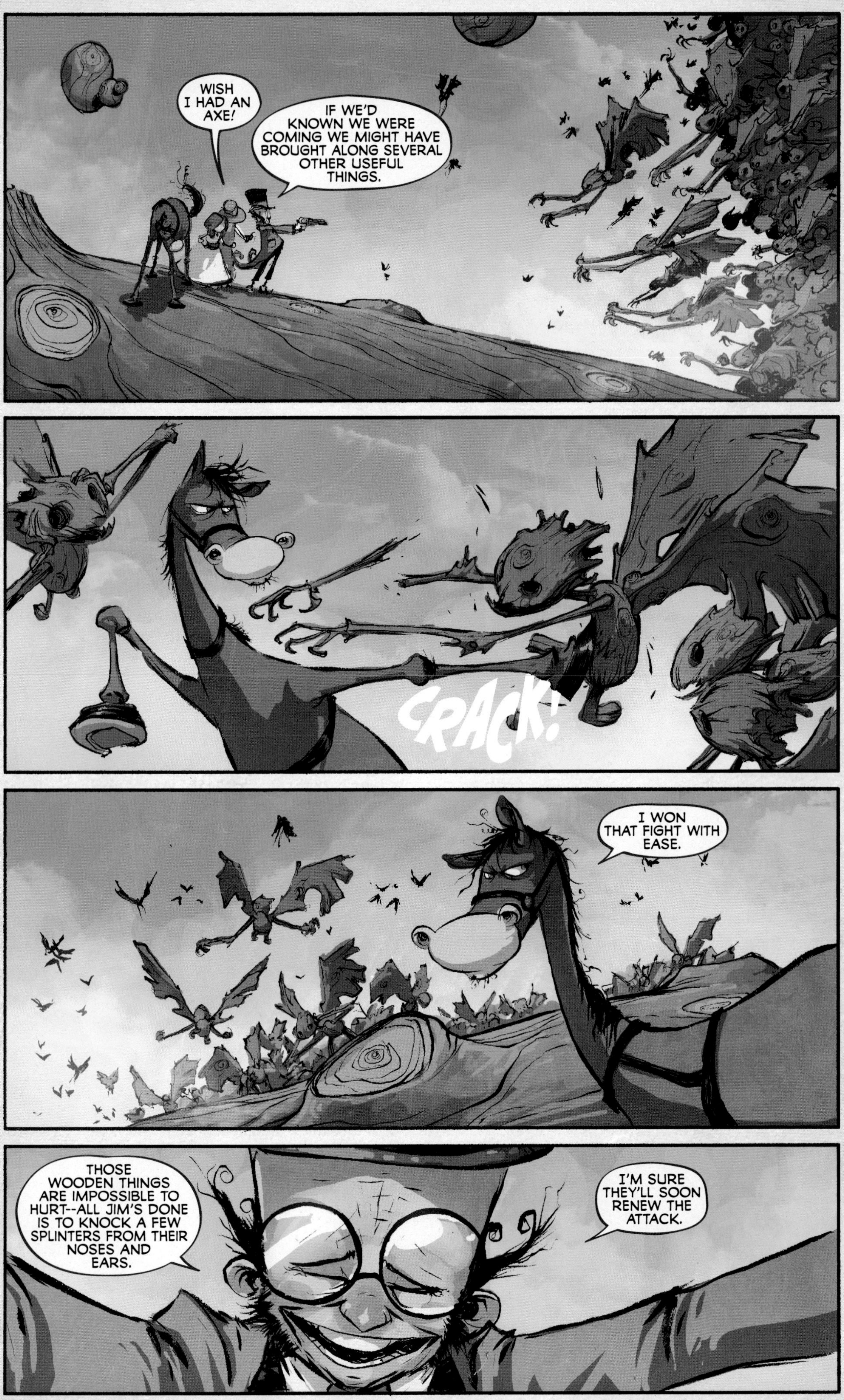
WISH I HAD AN AXE!
IF WE'D KNOWN WE WERE COMING WE MIGHT HAVE BROUGHT ALONG SEVERAL OTHER USEFUL THINGS.
CRACK!
I WON THAT FIGHT WITH EASE.
THOSE WOODEN THINGS ARE IMPOSSIBLE TO HURT--ALL JIM'S DONE IS TO KNOCK A FEW SPLINTERS FROM THEIR NOSES AND EARS.
I'M SURE THEY'LL SOON RENEW THE ATTACK.

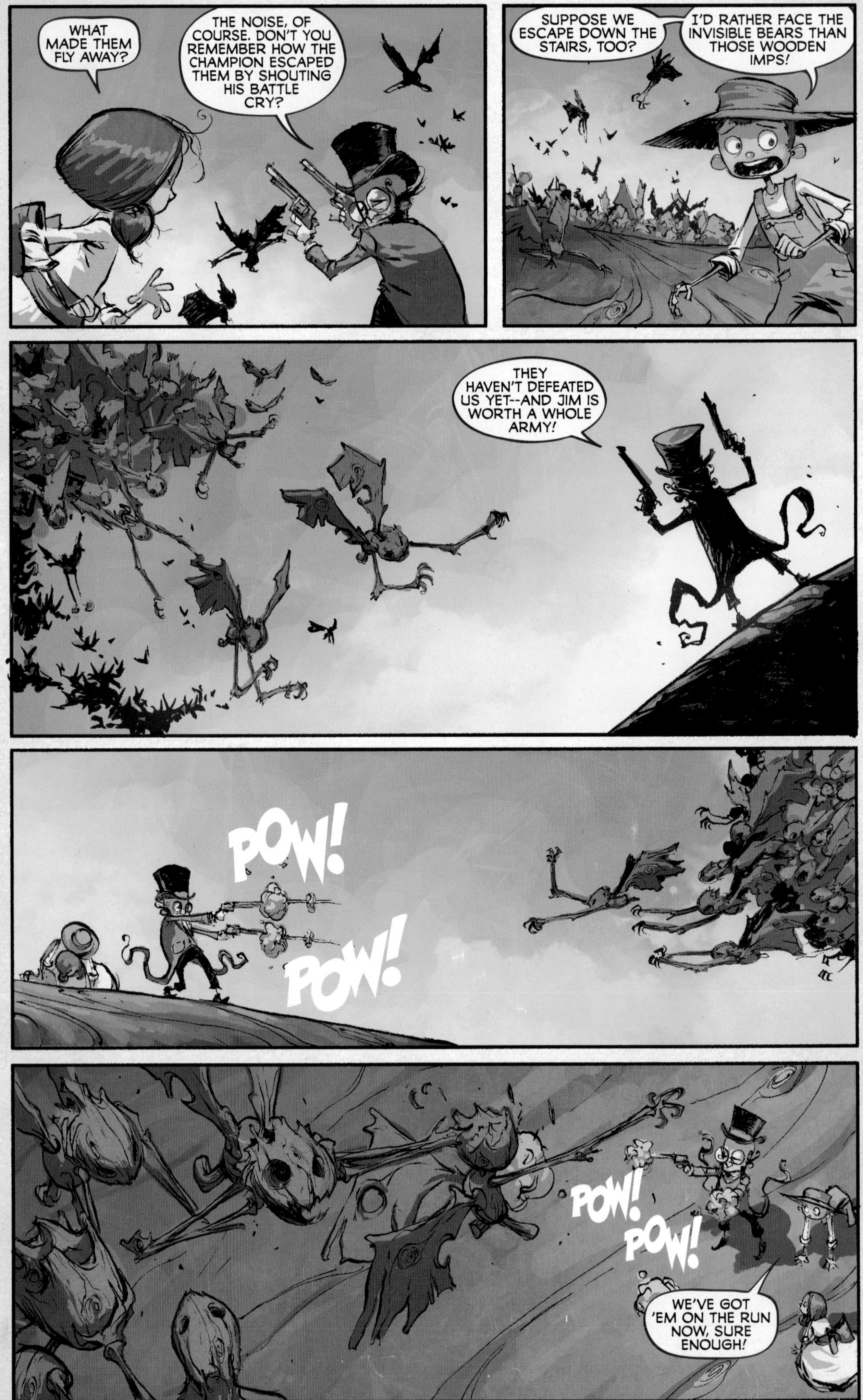
WHAT MADE THEM FLY AWAY?
THE NOISE, OF COURSE. DON'T YOU REMEMBER HOW THE CHAMPION ESCAPED THEM BY SHOUTING HIS BATTLE CRY?
SUPPOSE WE ESCAPE DOWN THE STAIRS, TOO?
I'D RATHER FACE THE INVISIBLE BEARS THAN THOSE WOODEN IMPS!
THEY HAVEN'T DEFEATED US YET--AND JIM IS WORTH A WHOLE ARMY!
POW!
POW!
POW!
POW!
WE'VE GOT 'EM ON THE RUN NOW, SURE ENOUGH!

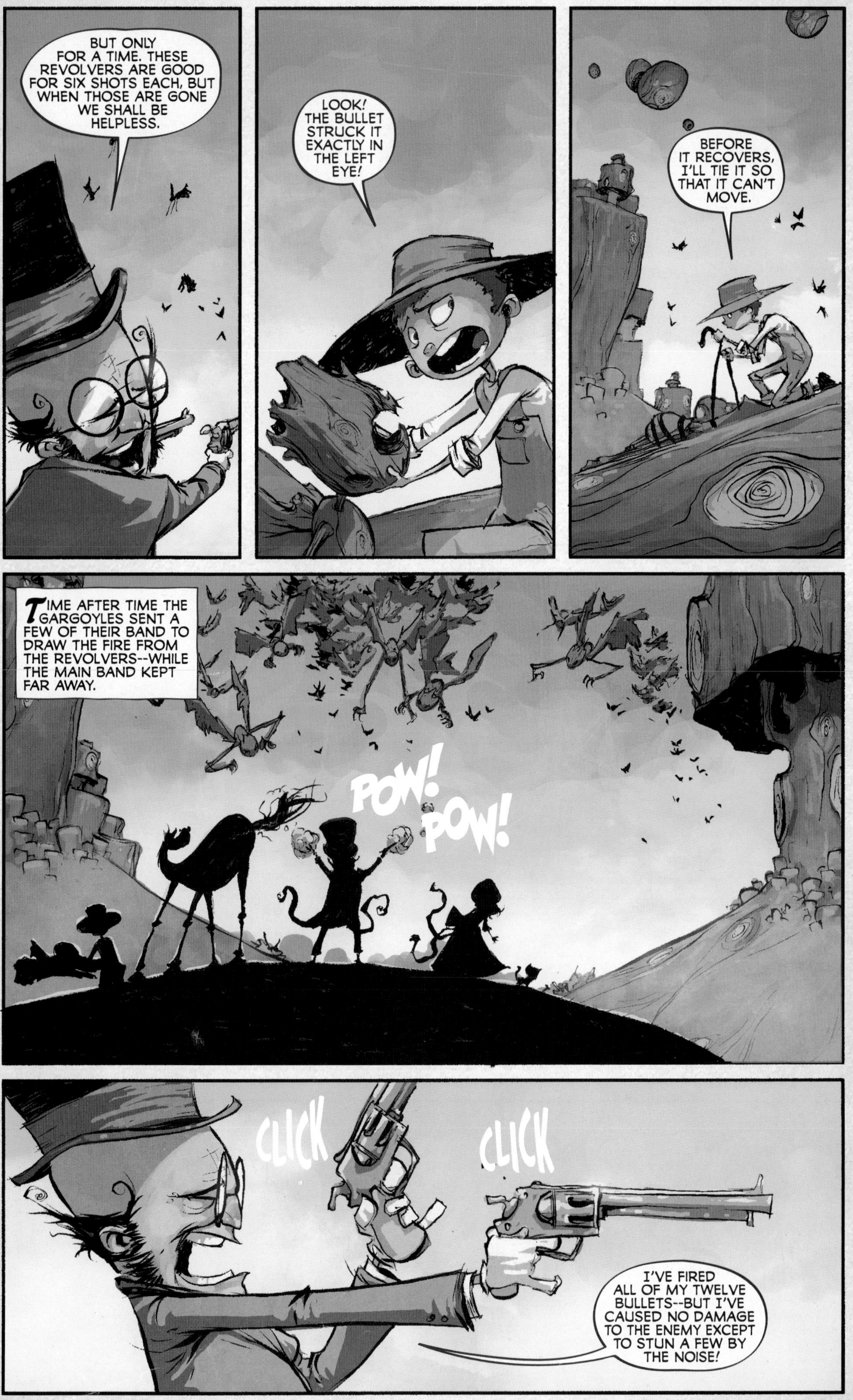

BUT ONLY FOR A TIME. THESE REVOLVERS ARE GOOD FOR SIX SHOTS EACH, BUT WHEN THOSE ARE GONE WE SHALL BE HELPLESS.
LOOK! THE BULLET STRUCK IT EXACTLY IN THE LEFT EYE!
BEFORE IT RECOVERS, I'LL TIE IT SO THAT IT CAN'T MOVE.
TIME AFTER TIME THE GARGOYLES SENT A FEW OF THEIR BAND TO DRAW THE FIRE FROM THE REVOLVERS--WHILE THE MAIN BAND KEPT FAR AWAY.
POW!
POW!
CLICK
CLICK
I'VE FIRED ALL OF MY TWELVE BULLETS--BUT I'VE CAUSED NO DAMAGE TO THE ENEMY EXCEPT TO STUN A FEW BY THE NOISE!

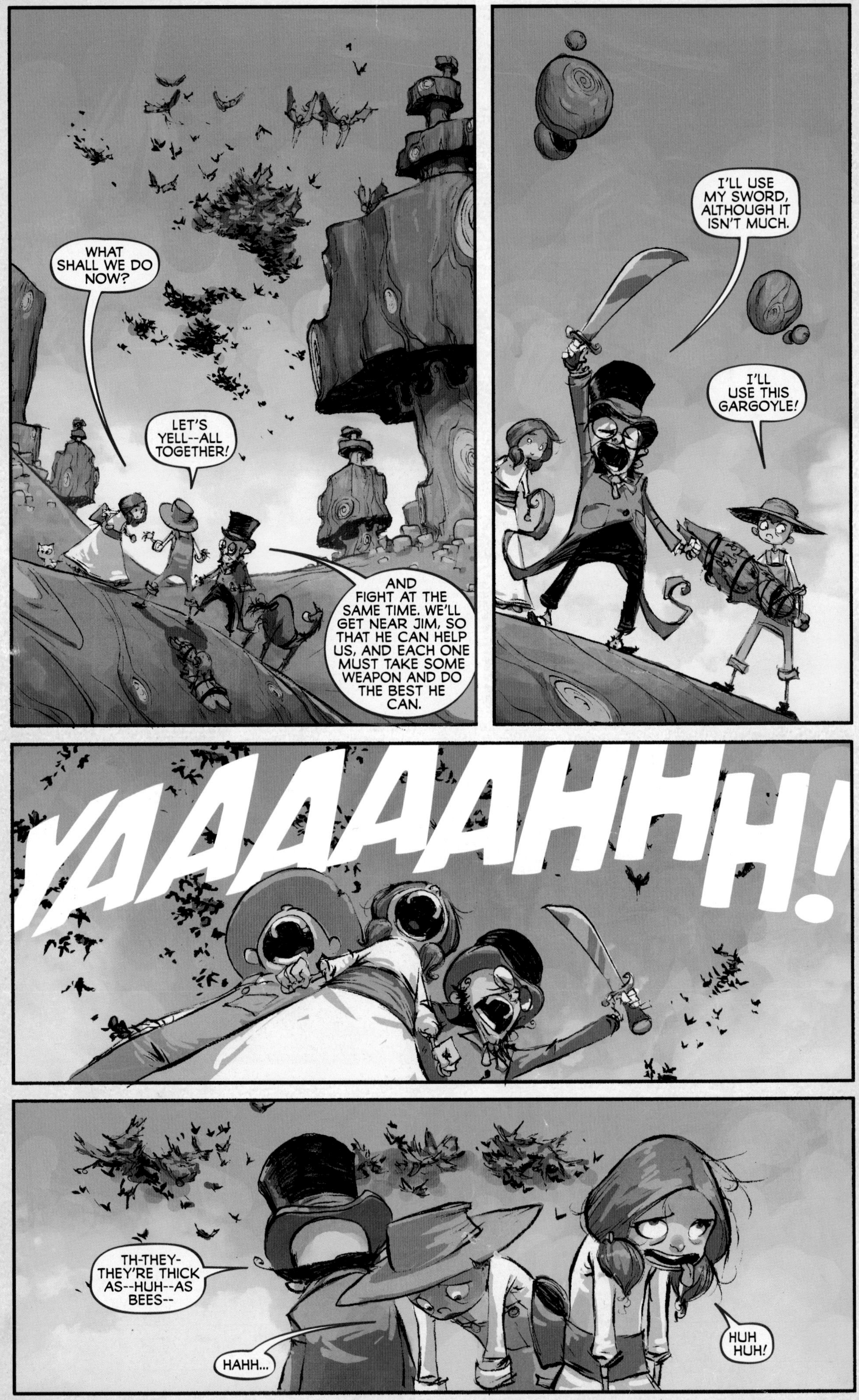
WHAT SHALL WE DO NOW?
LET'S YELL--ALL TOGETHER!
AND FIGHT AT THE SAME TIME. WE'LL GET NEAR JIM, SO THAT HE CAN HELP US, AND EACH ONE MUST TAKE SOME WEAPON AND DO THE BEST HE CAN.
I'LL USE MY SWORD, ALTHOUGH IT ISN'T MUCH.
I'LL USE THIS GARGOYLE!
YAAAAAHHH!
TH-THEY-THEY'RE THICK AS--HUH--AS BEES--
HAHH...
HUH HUH!

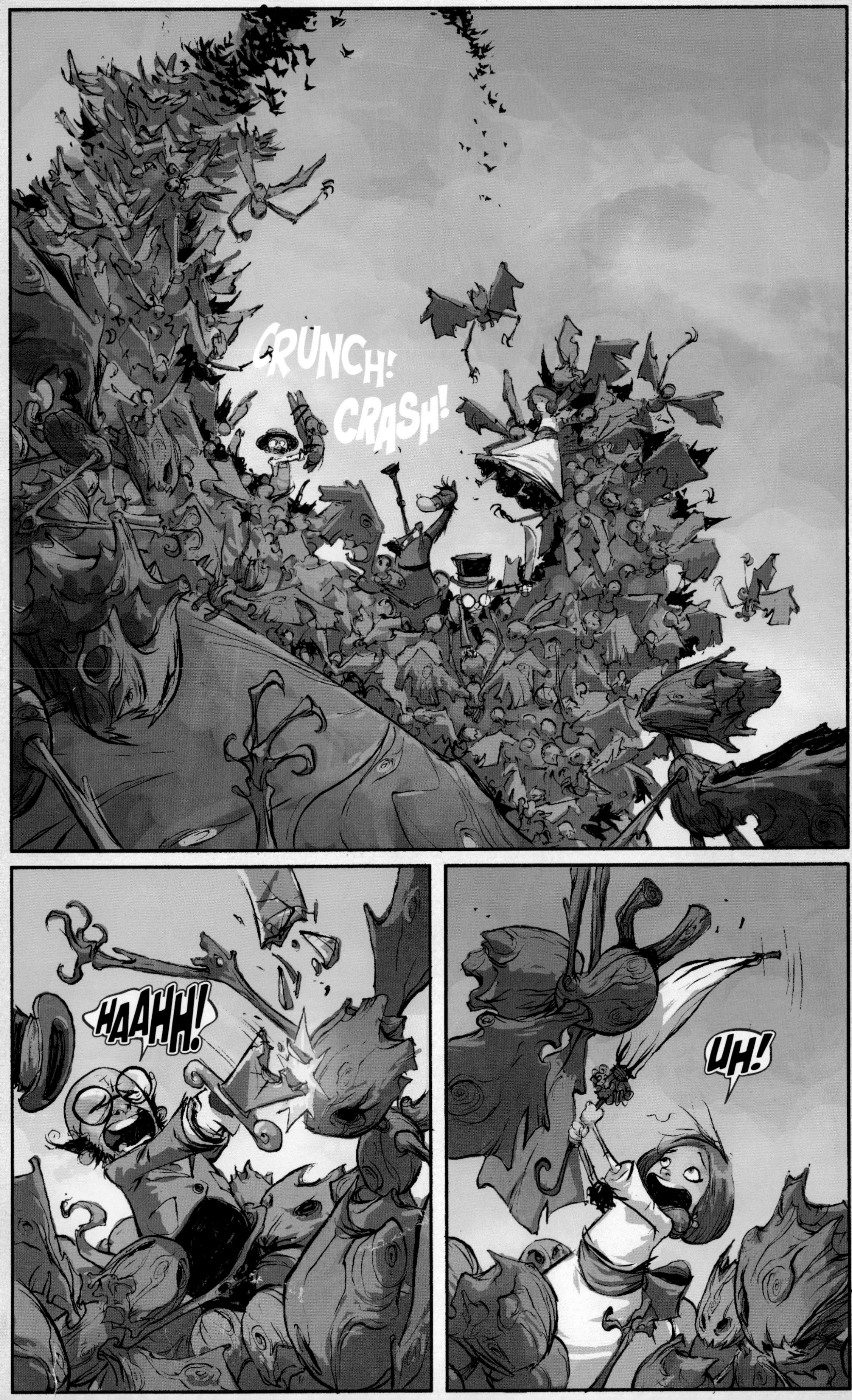
CRUNCH!
CRASH!
HAAHH!
UH!

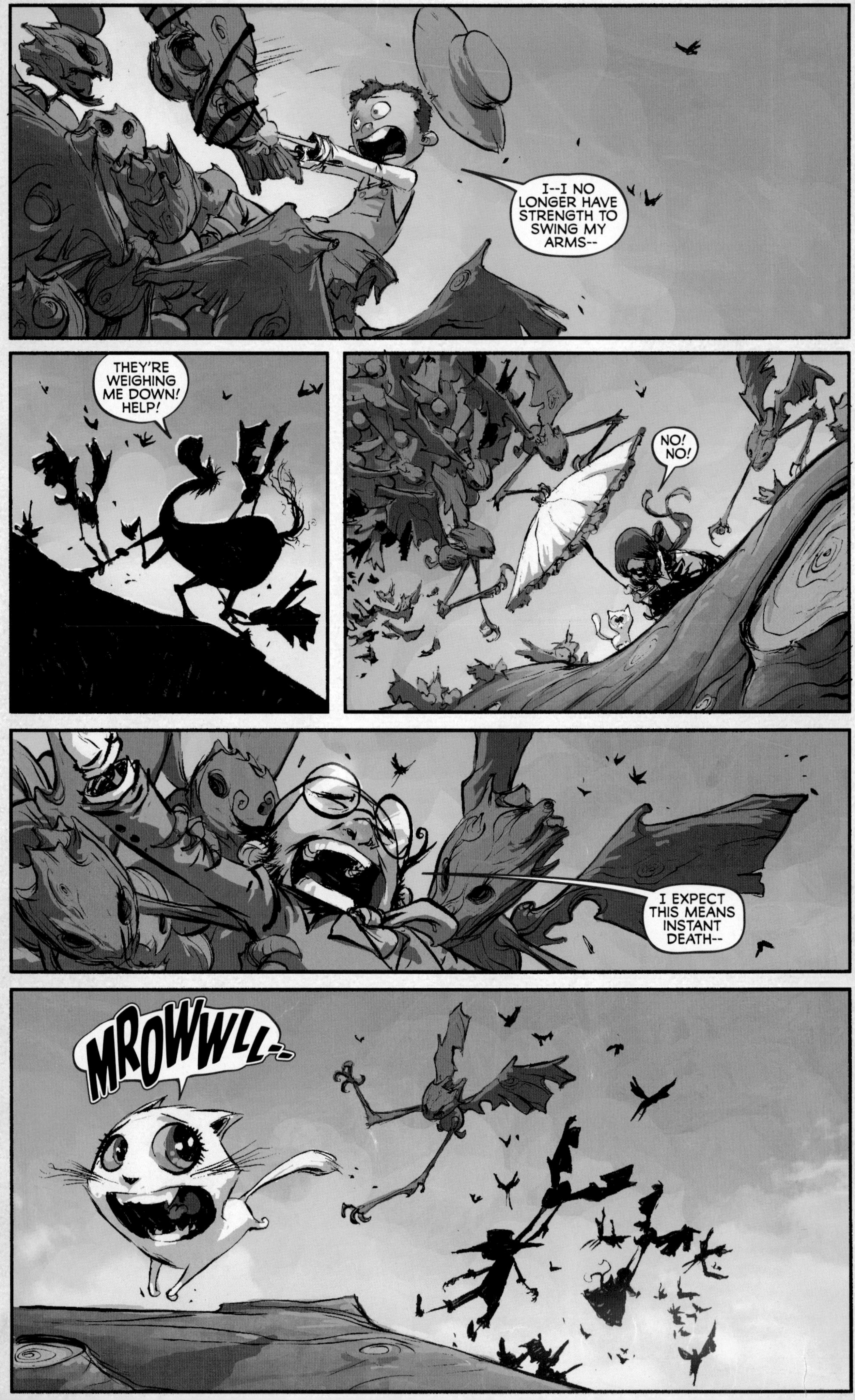
I--I NO LONGER HAVE STRENGTH TO SWING MY ARMS--
THEY'RE WEIGHING ME DOWN! HELP!
NO! NO!
I EXPECT THIS MEANS INSTANT DEATH--
MROWWLL--

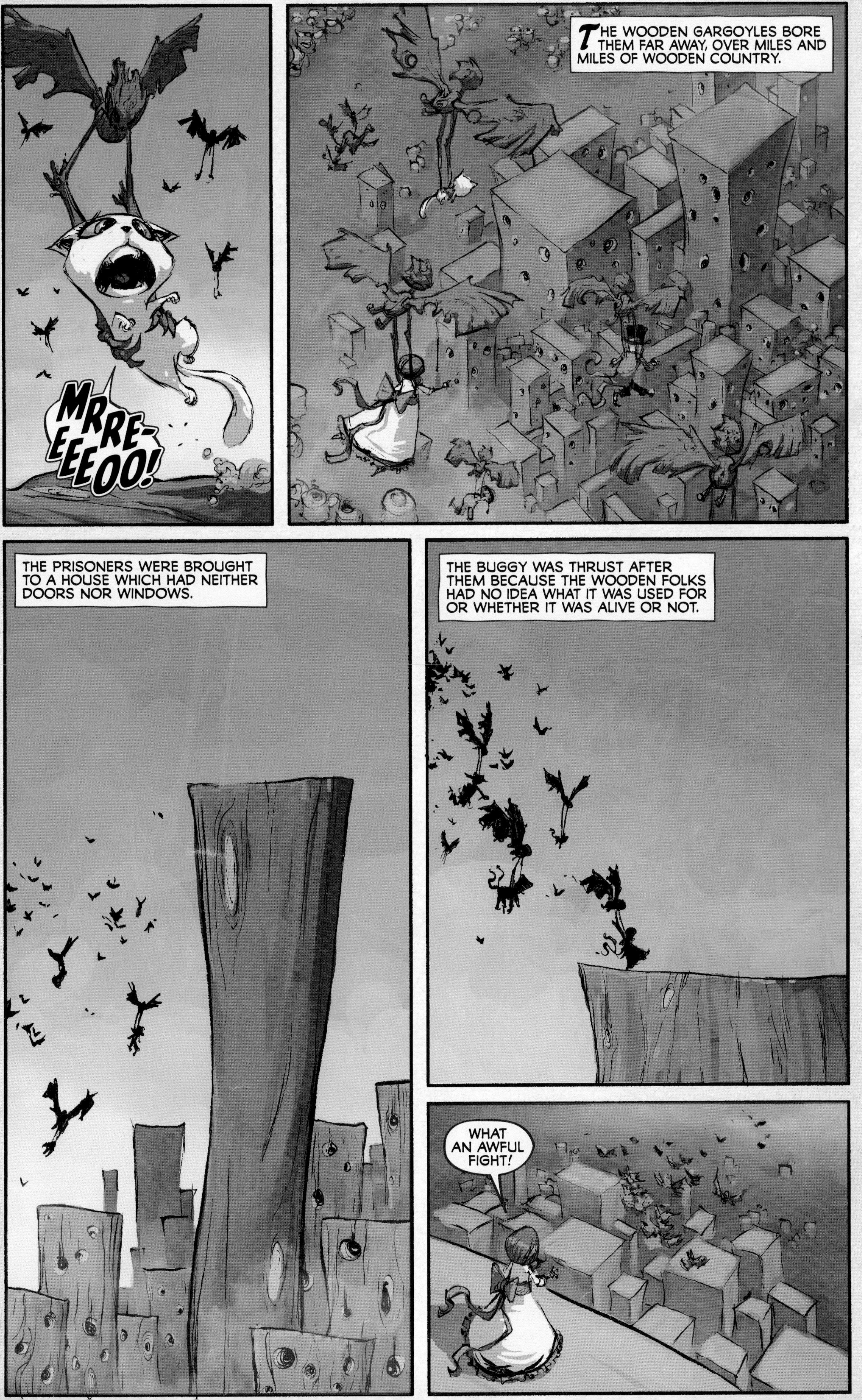
MRRE-EEEOO!
THE WOODEN GARGOYLES BORE THEM FAR AWAY, OVER MILES AND MILES OF WOODEN COUNTRY.
THE PRISONERS WERE BROUGHT TO A HOUSE WHICH HAD NEITHER DOORS NOR WINDOWS.
THE BUGGY WAS THRUST AFTER THEM BECAUSE THE WOODEN FOLKS HAD NO IDEA WHAT IT WAS USED FOR OR WHETHER IT WAS ALIVE OR NOT.
WHAT AN AWFUL FIGHT!

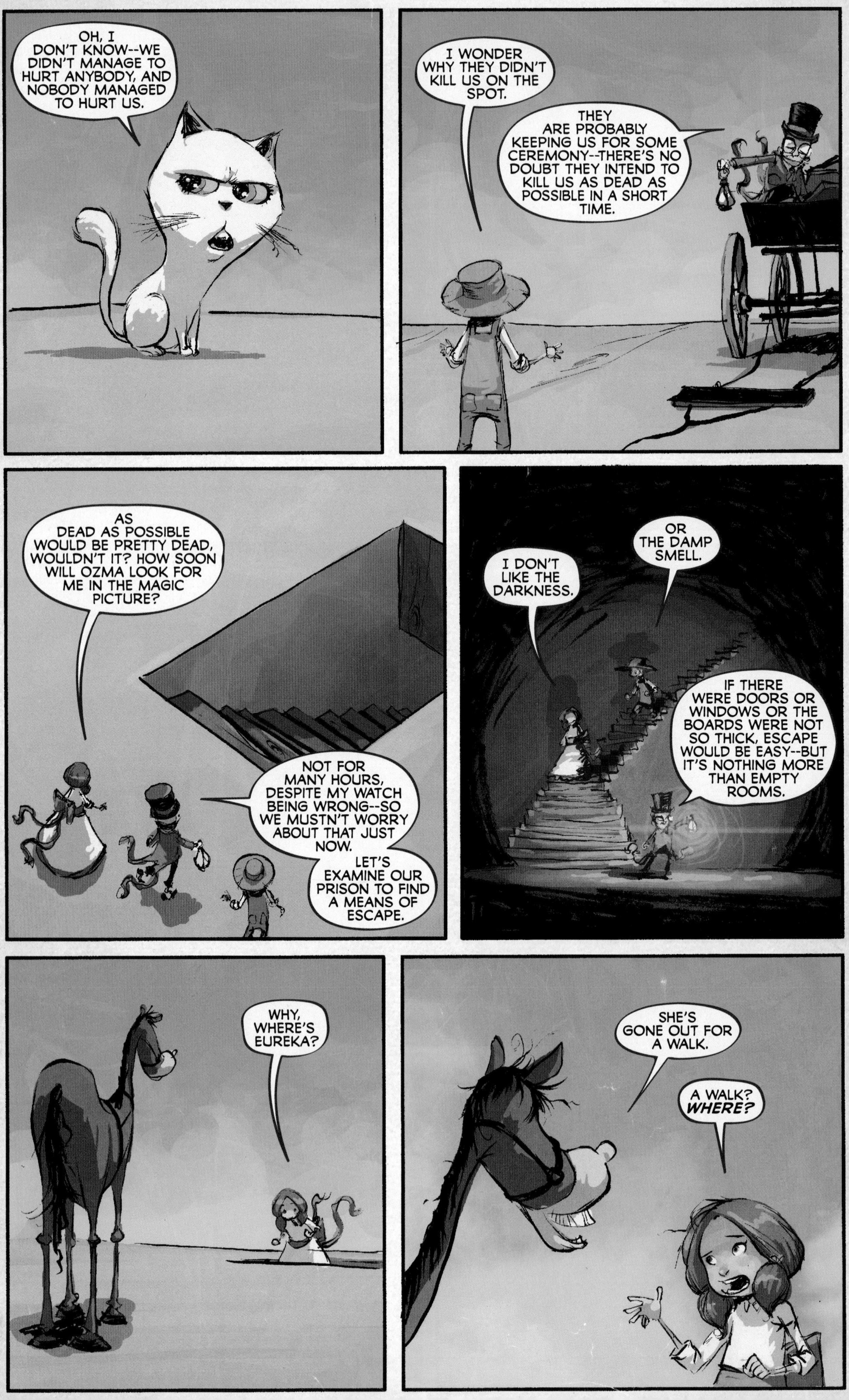
OH, I DON'T KNOW--WE DIDN'T MANAGE TO HURT ANYBODY, AND NOBODY MANAGED TO HURT US.
I WONDER WHY THEY DIDN'T KILL US ON THE SPOT.
THEY ARE PROBABLY KEEPING US FOR SOME CEREMONY--THERE'S NO DOUBT THEY INTEND TO KILL US AS DEAD AS POSSIBLE IN A SHORT TIME.
AS DEAD AS POSSIBLE WOULD BE PRETTY DEAD, WOULDN'T IT? HOW SOON WILL OZMA LOOK FOR ME IN THE MAGIC PICTURE?
NOT FOR MANY HOURS, DESPITE MY WATCH BEING WRONG--SO WE MUSTN'T WORRY ABOUT THAT JUST NOW.
LET'S EXAMINE OUR PRISON TO FIND A MEANS OF ESCAPE.
I DON'T LIKE THE DARKNESS.
OR THE DAMP SMELL.
IF THERE WERE DOORS OR WINDOWS OR THE BOARDS WERE NOT SO THICK, ESCAPE WOULD BE EASY--BUT IT'S NOTHING MORE THAN EMPTY ROOMS.
WHY, WHERE'S EUREKA?
SHE'S GONE OUT FOR A WALK.
A WALK? *WHERE?*

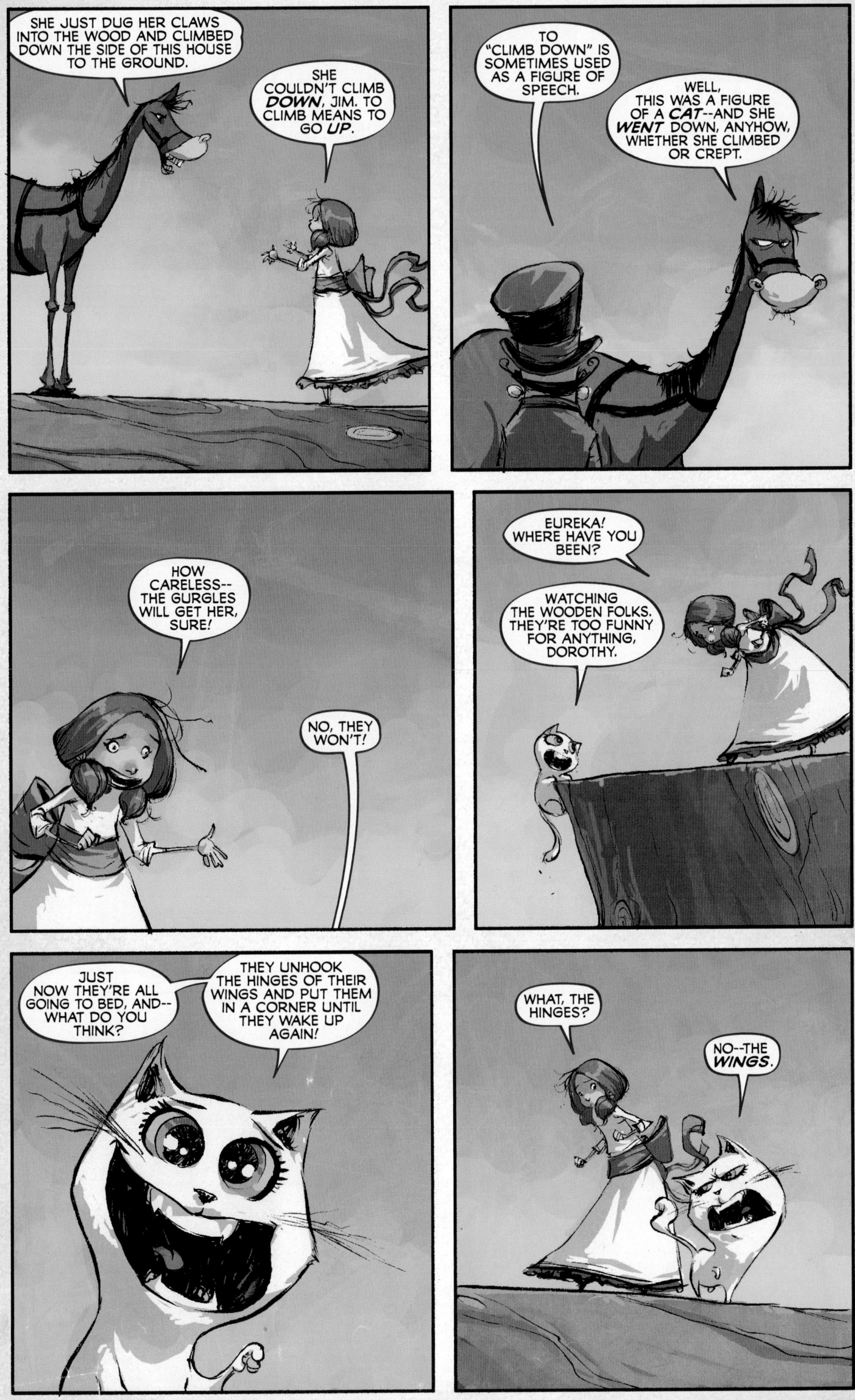
SHE JUST DUG HER CLAWS INTO THE WOOD AND CLIMBED DOWN THE SIDE OF THIS HOUSE TO THE GROUND.
SHE COULDN'T CLIMB *DOWN*, JIM. TO CLIMB MEANS TO GO *UP*.
TO "CLIMB DOWN" IS SOMETIMES USED AS A FIGURE OF SPEECH.
WELL, THIS WAS A FIGURE OF A *CAT*--AND SHE *WENT* DOWN, ANYHOW, WHETHER SHE CLIMBED OR CREPT.
HOW CARELESS-- THE GURGLES WILL GET HER, SURE!
NO, THEY WON'T!
EUREKA! WHERE HAVE YOU BEEN?
WATCHING THE WOODEN FOLKS. THEY'RE TOO FUNNY FOR ANYTHING, DOROTHY.
JUST NOW THEY'RE ALL GOING TO BED, AND-- WHAT DO YOU THINK?
THEY UNHOOK THE HINGES OF THEIR WINGS AND PUT THEM IN A CORNER UNTIL THEY WAKE UP AGAIN!
WHAT, THE HINGES?
NO--THE *WINGS*.

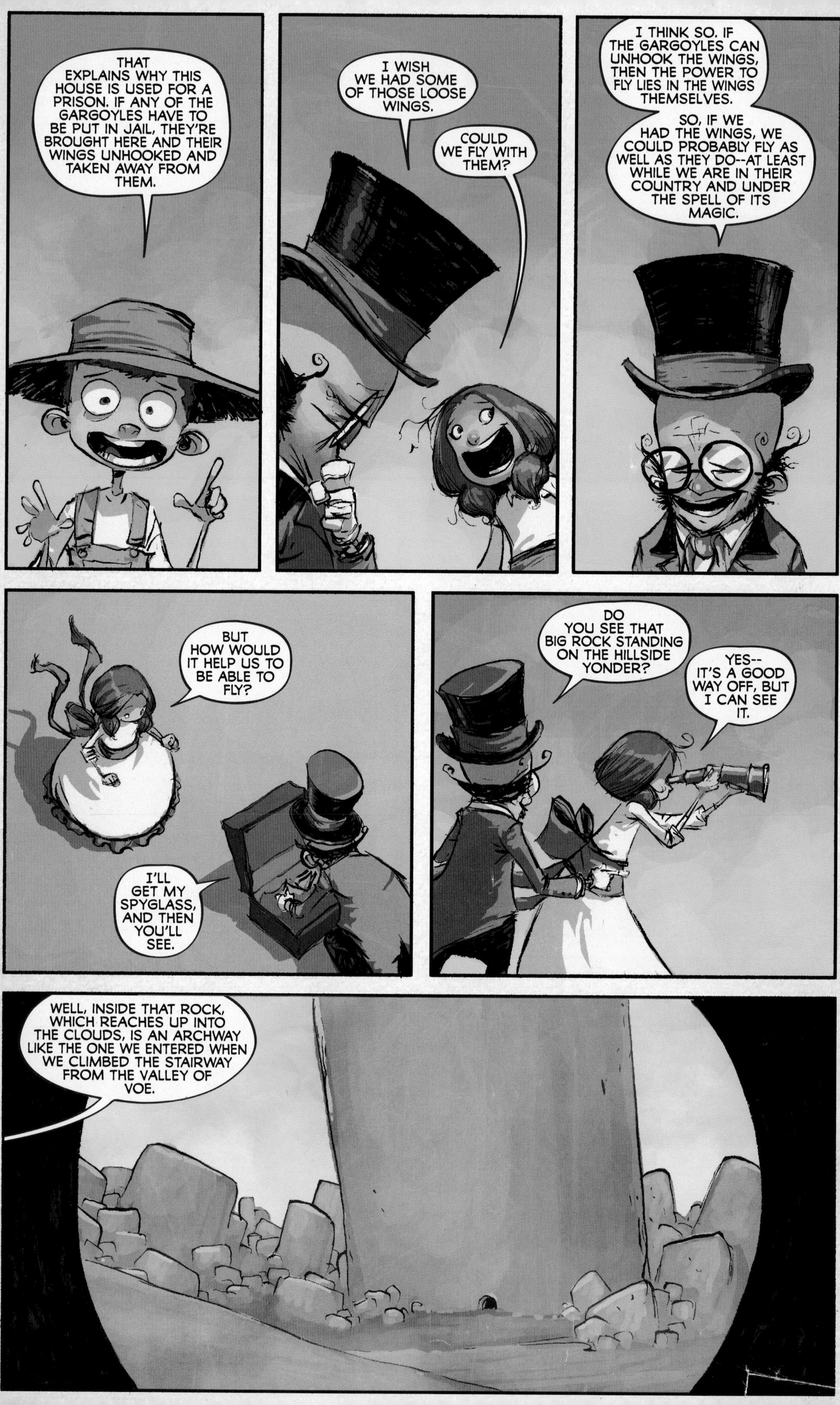
THAT EXPLAINS WHY THIS HOUSE IS USED FOR A PRISON. IF ANY OF THE GARGOYLES HAVE TO BE PUT IN JAIL, THEY'RE BROUGHT HERE AND THEIR WINGS UNHOOKED AND TAKEN AWAY FROM THEM.
I WISH WE HAD SOME OF THOSE LOOSE WINGS.
COULD WE FLY WITH THEM?
I THINK SO. IF THE GARGOYLES CAN UNHOOK THE WINGS, THEN THE POWER TO FLY LIES IN THE WINGS THEMSELVES.
SO, IF WE HAD THE WINGS, WE COULD PROBABLY FLY AS WELL AS THEY DO--AT LEAST WHILE WE ARE IN THEIR COUNTRY AND UNDER THE SPELL OF ITS MAGIC.
BUT HOW WOULD IT HELP US TO BE ABLE TO FLY?
I'LL GET MY SPYGLASS, AND THEN YOU'LL SEE.
DO YOU SEE THAT BIG ROCK STANDING ON THE HILLSIDE YONDER?
YES-- IT'S A GOOD WAY OFF, BUT I CAN SEE IT.
WELL, INSIDE THAT ROCK, WHICH REACHES UP INTO THE CLOUDS, IS AN ARCHWAY LIKE THE ONE WE ENTERED WHEN WE CLIMBED THE STAIRWAY FROM THE VALLEY OF VOE.

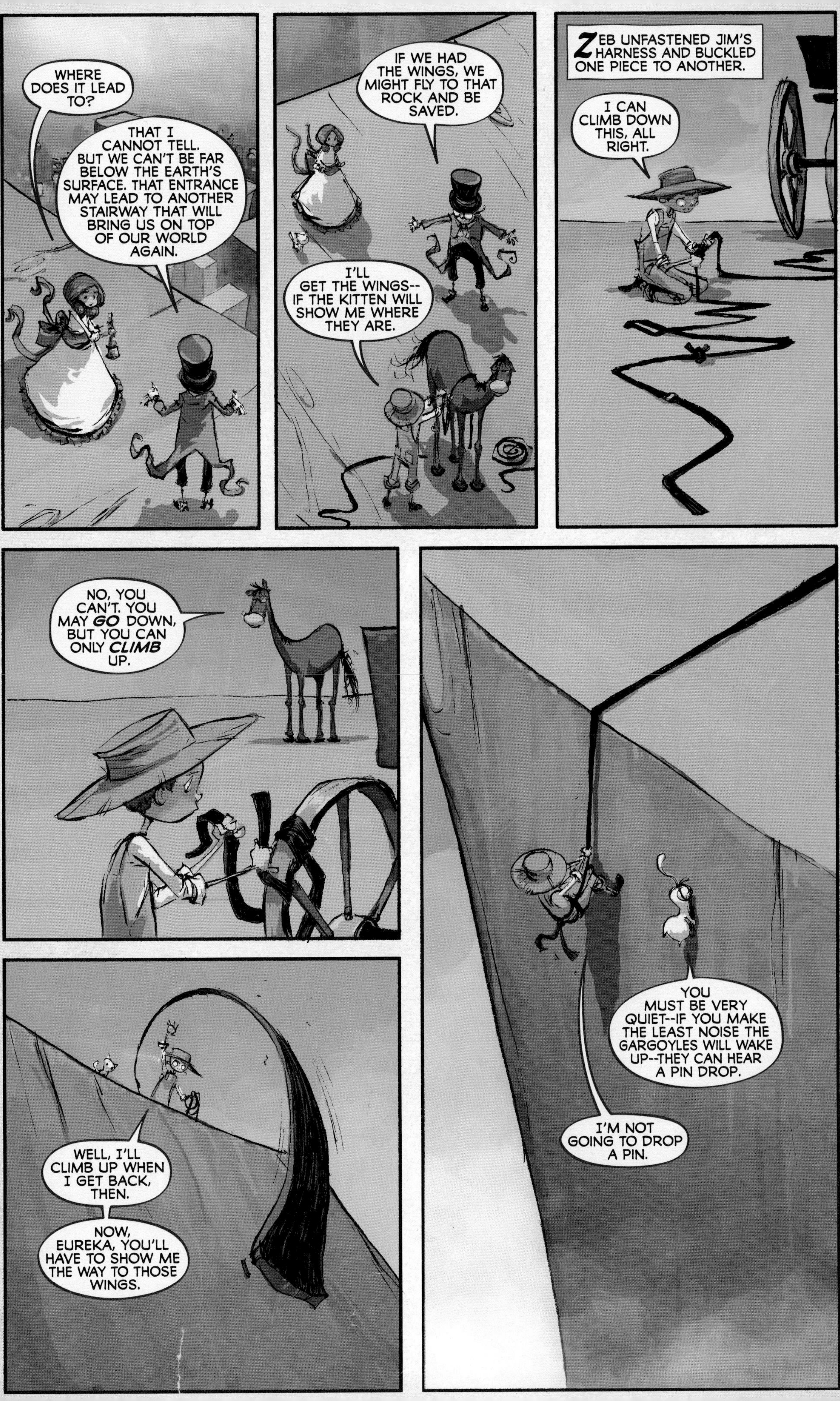
WHERE DOES IT LEAD TO?
THAT I CANNOT TELL. BUT WE CAN'T BE FAR BELOW THE EARTH'S SURFACE. THAT ENTRANCE MAY LEAD TO ANOTHER STAIRWAY THAT WILL BRING US ON TOP OF OUR WORLD AGAIN.
IF WE HAD THE WINGS, WE MIGHT FLY TO THAT ROCK AND BE SAVED.
I'LL GET THE WINGS--IF THE KITTEN WILL SHOW ME WHERE THEY ARE.
ZEB UNFASTENED JIM'S HARNESS AND BUCKLED ONE PIECE TO ANOTHER.
I CAN CLIMB DOWN THIS, ALL RIGHT.
NO, YOU CAN'T. YOU MAY *GO* DOWN, BUT YOU CAN ONLY *CLIMB* UP.
WELL, I'LL CLIMB UP WHEN I GET BACK, THEN.
NOW, EUREKA, YOU'LL HAVE TO SHOW ME THE WAY TO THOSE WINGS.
YOU MUST BE VERY QUIET--IF YOU MAKE THE LEAST NOISE THE GARGOYLES WILL WAKE UP--THEY CAN HEAR A PIN DROP.
I'M NOT GOING TO DROP A PIN.

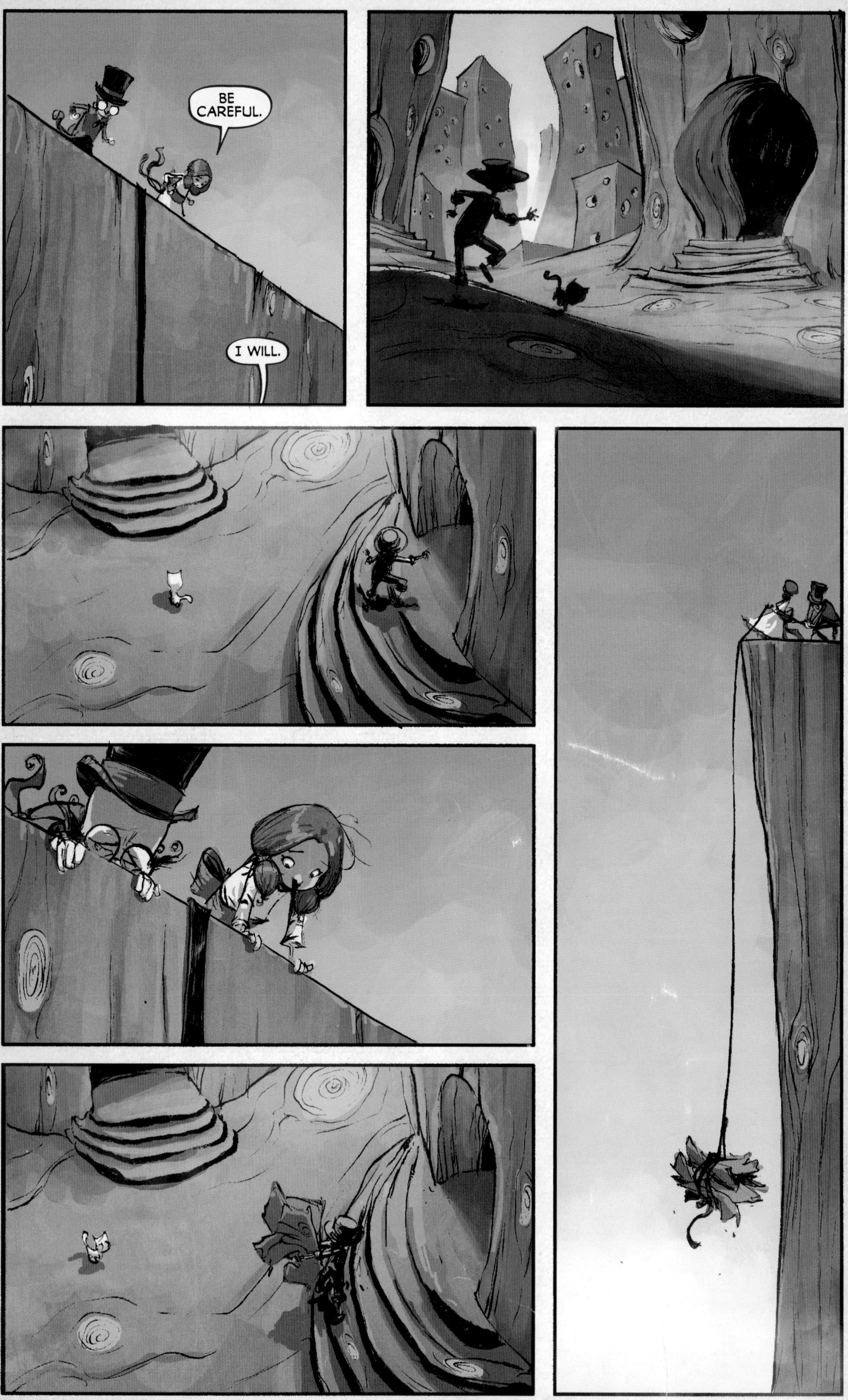
BE CAREFUL.
I WILL.

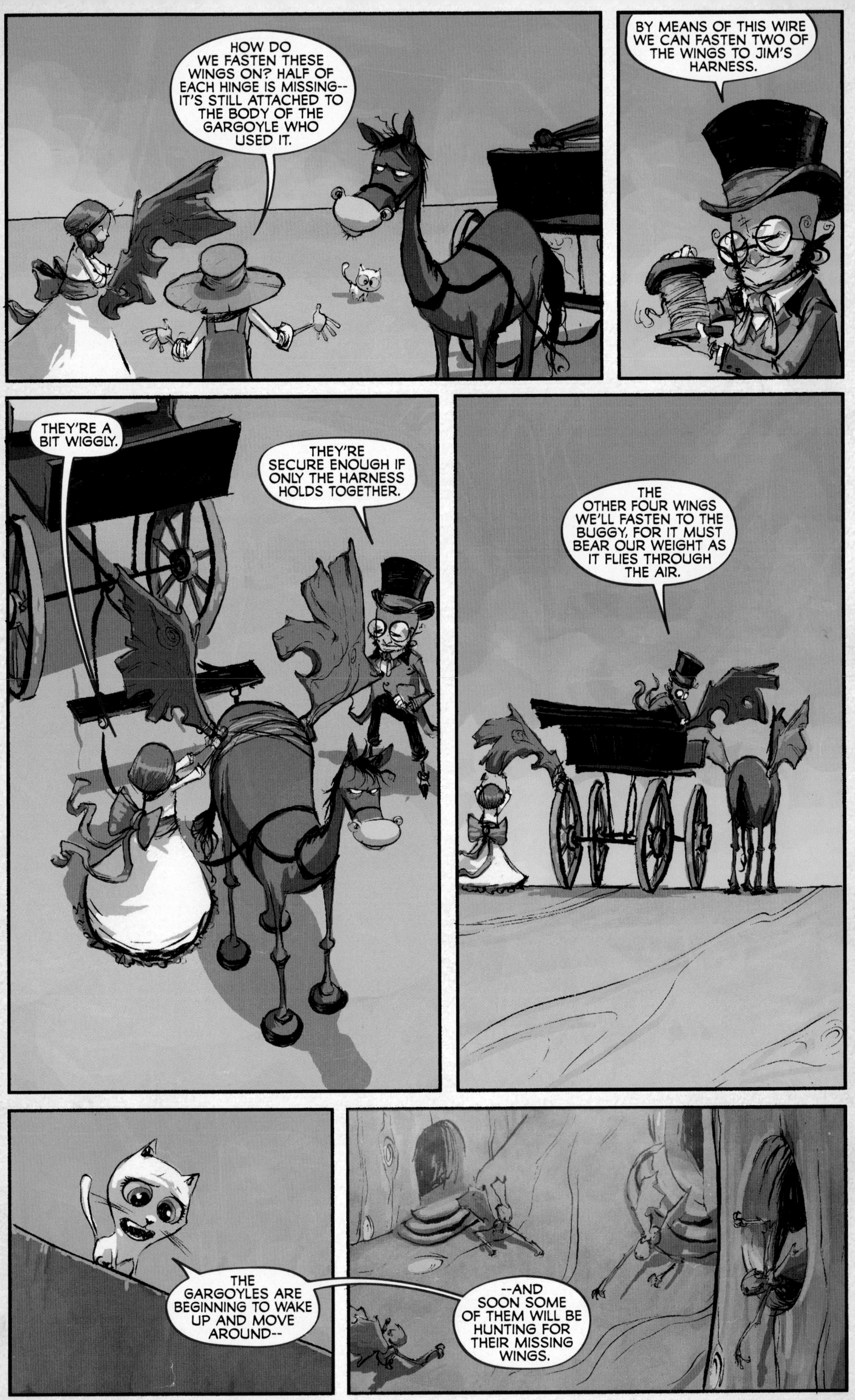
HOW DO WE FASTEN THESE WINGS ON? HALF OF EACH HINGE IS MISSING-- IT'S STILL ATTACHED TO THE BODY OF THE GARGOYLE WHO USED IT.
BY MEANS OF THIS WIRE WE CAN FASTEN TWO OF THE WINGS TO JIM'S HARNESS.
THEY'RE A BIT WIGGLY.
THEY'RE SECURE ENOUGH IF ONLY THE HARNESS HOLDS TOGETHER.
THE OTHER FOUR WINGS WE'LL FASTEN TO THE BUGGY, FOR IT MUST BEAR OUR WEIGHT AS IT FLIES THROUGH THE AIR.
THE GARGOYLES ARE BEGINNING TO WAKE UP AND MOVE AROUND--
--AND SOON SOME OF THEM WILL BE HUNTING FOR THEIR MISSING WINGS.

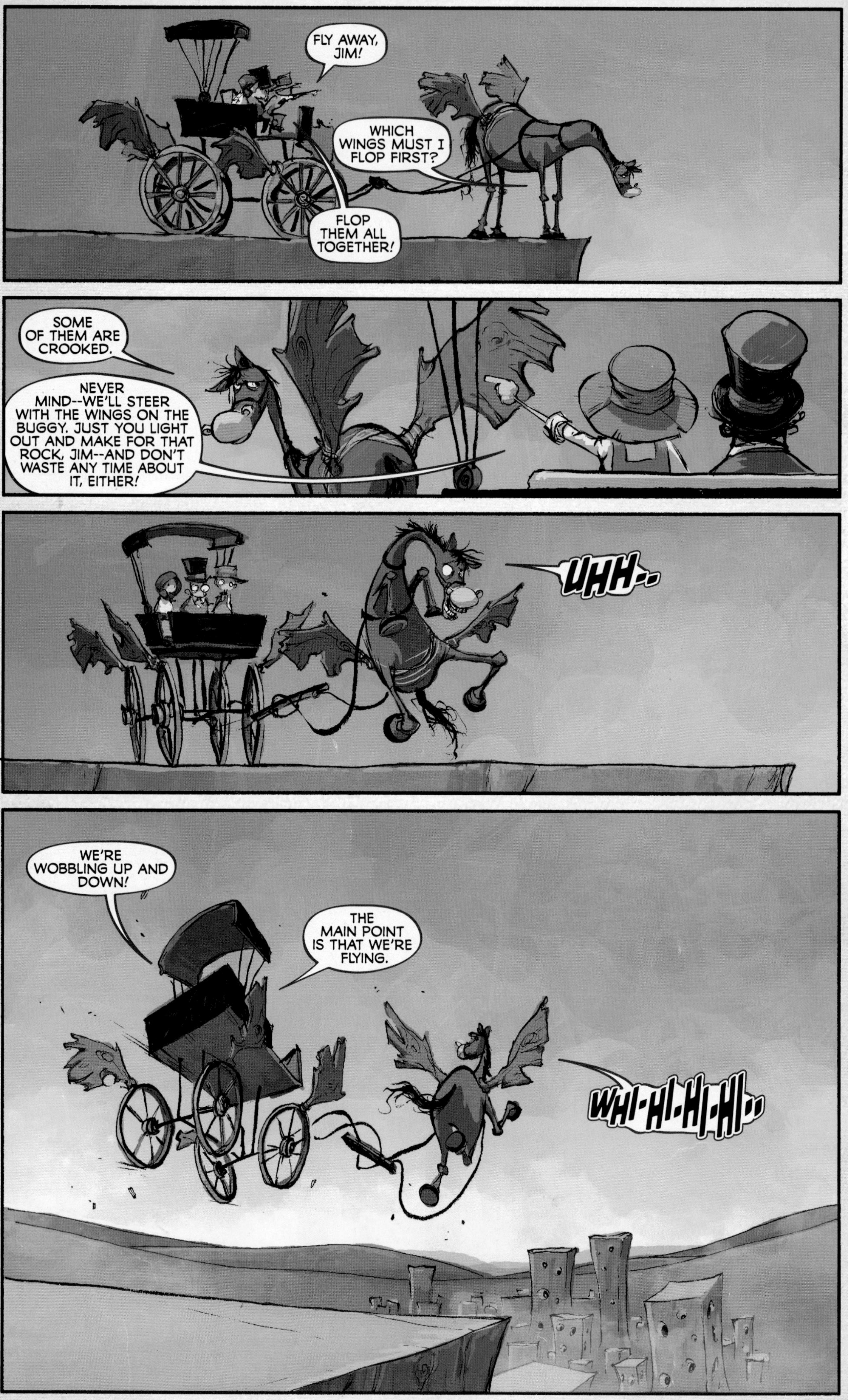
FLY AWAY, JIM!
WHICH WINGS MUST I FLOP FIRST?
FLOP THEM ALL TOGETHER!
SOME OF THEM ARE CROOKED.
NEVER MIND--WE'LL STEER WITH THE WINGS ON THE BUGGY. JUST YOU LIGHT OUT AND MAKE FOR THAT ROCK, JIM--AND DON'T WASTE ANY TIME ABOUT IT, EITHER!
UHH--
WE'RE WOBBLING UP AND DOWN!
THE MAIN POINT IS THAT WE'RE FLYING.
WHI-HI-HI-HI--

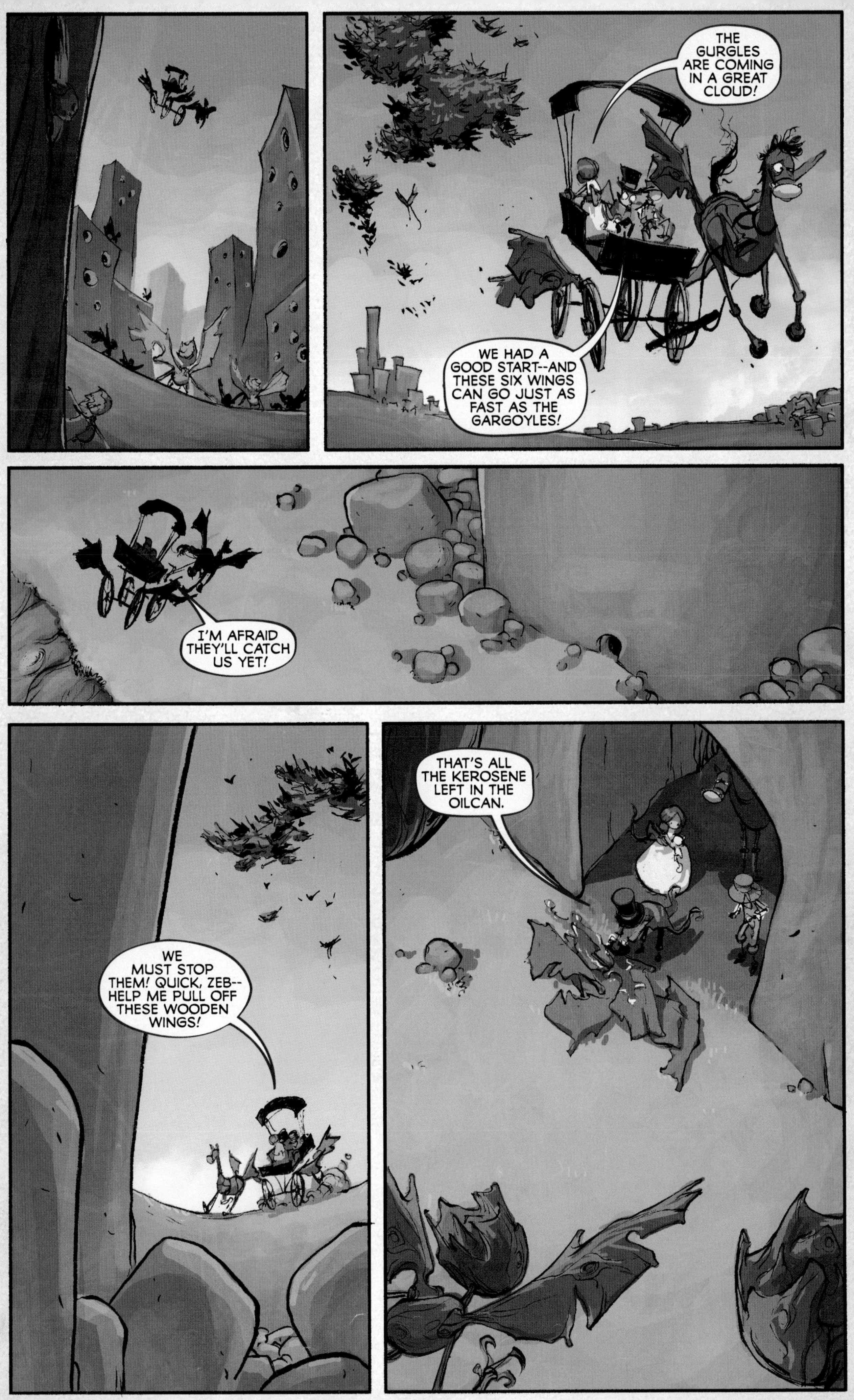
THE GURGLES ARE COMING IN A GREAT CLOUD!
WE HAD A GOOD START--AND THESE SIX WINGS CAN GO JUST AS FAST AS THE GARGOYLES!
I'M AFRAID THEY'LL CATCH US YET!
WE MUST STOP THEM! QUICK, ZEB--HELP ME PULL OFF THESE WOODEN WINGS!
THAT'S ALL THE KEROSENE LEFT IN THE OILCAN.

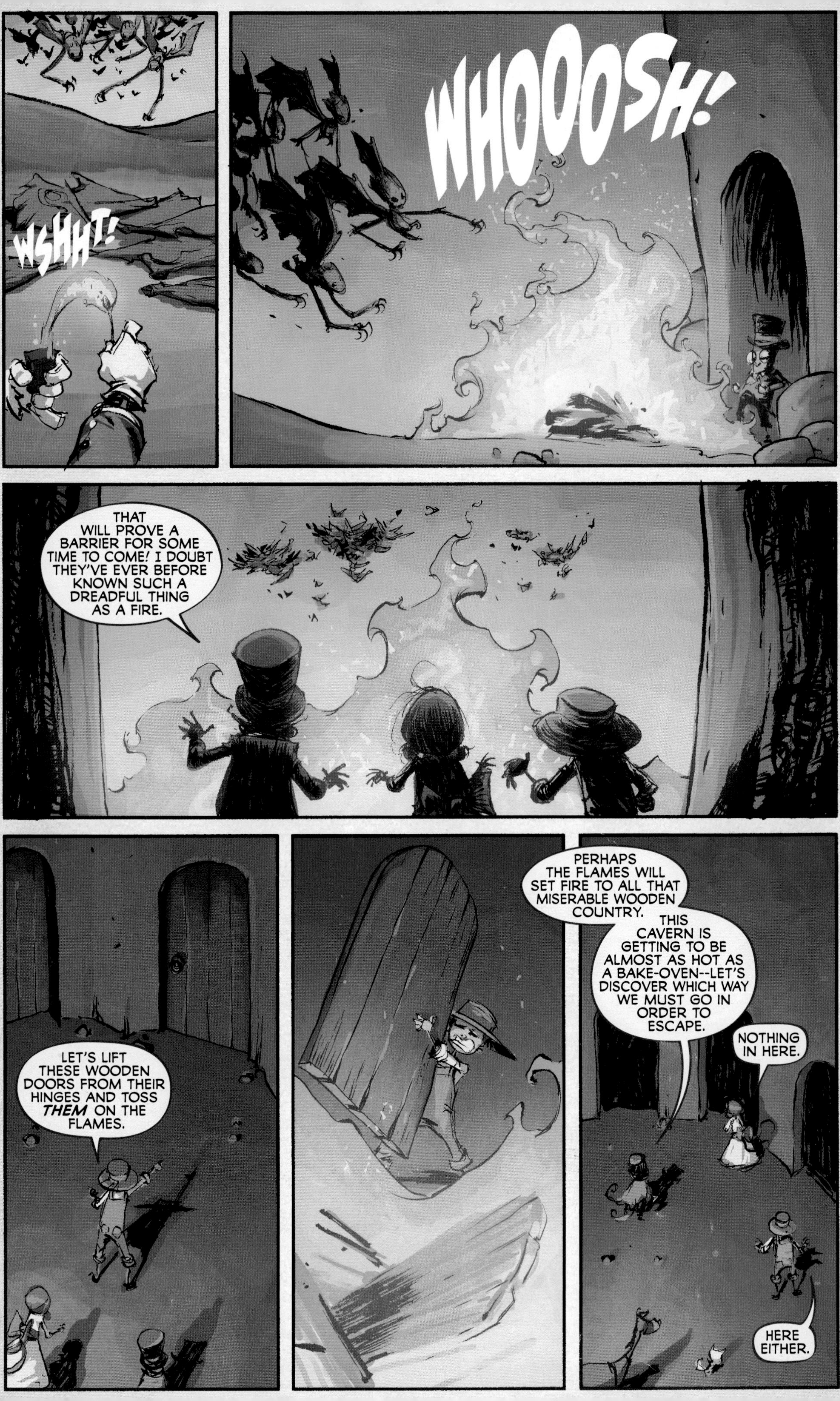
WSHHT!
WHOOOSH!
THAT WILL PROVE A BARRIER FOR SOME TIME TO COME! I DOUBT THEY'VE EVER BEFORE KNOWN SUCH A DREADFUL THING AS A FIRE.
LET'S LIFT THESE WOODEN DOORS FROM THEIR HINGES AND TOSS *THEM* ON THE FLAMES.
PERHAPS THE FLAMES WILL SET FIRE TO ALL THAT MISERABLE WOODEN COUNTRY.
THIS CAVERN IS GETTING TO BE ALMOST AS HOT AS A BAKE-OVEN--LET'S DISCOVER WHICH WAY WE MUST GO IN ORDER TO ESCAPE.
NOTHING IN HERE.
HERE EITHER.

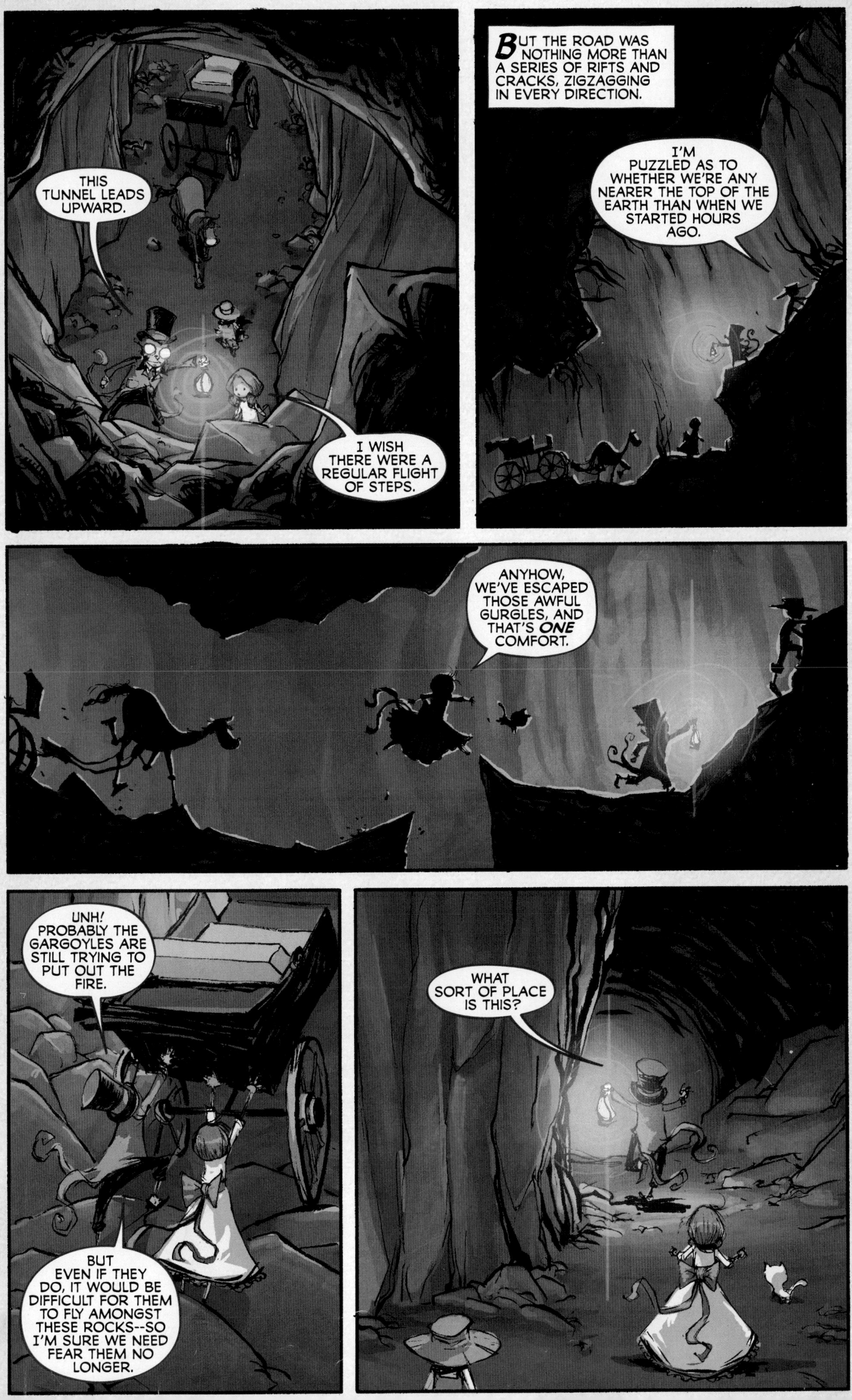
THIS TUNNEL LEADS UPWARD.
I WISH THERE WERE A REGULAR FLIGHT OF STEPS.
BUT THE ROAD WAS NOTHING MORE THAN A SERIES OF RIFTS AND CRACKS, ZIGZAGGING IN EVERY DIRECTION.
I'M PUZZLED AS TO WHETHER WE'RE ANY NEARER THE TOP OF THE EARTH THAN WHEN WE STARTED HOURS AGO.
ANYHOW, WE'VE ESCAPED THOSE AWFUL GURGLES, AND THAT'S ONE COMFORT.
UNH! PROBABLY THE GARGOYLES ARE STILL TRYING TO PUT OUT THE FIRE.
BUT EVEN IF THEY DO, IT WOULD BE DIFFICULT FOR THEM TO FLY AMONGST THESE ROCKS--SO I'M SURE WE NEED FEAR THEM NO LONGER.
WHAT SORT OF PLACE IS THIS?

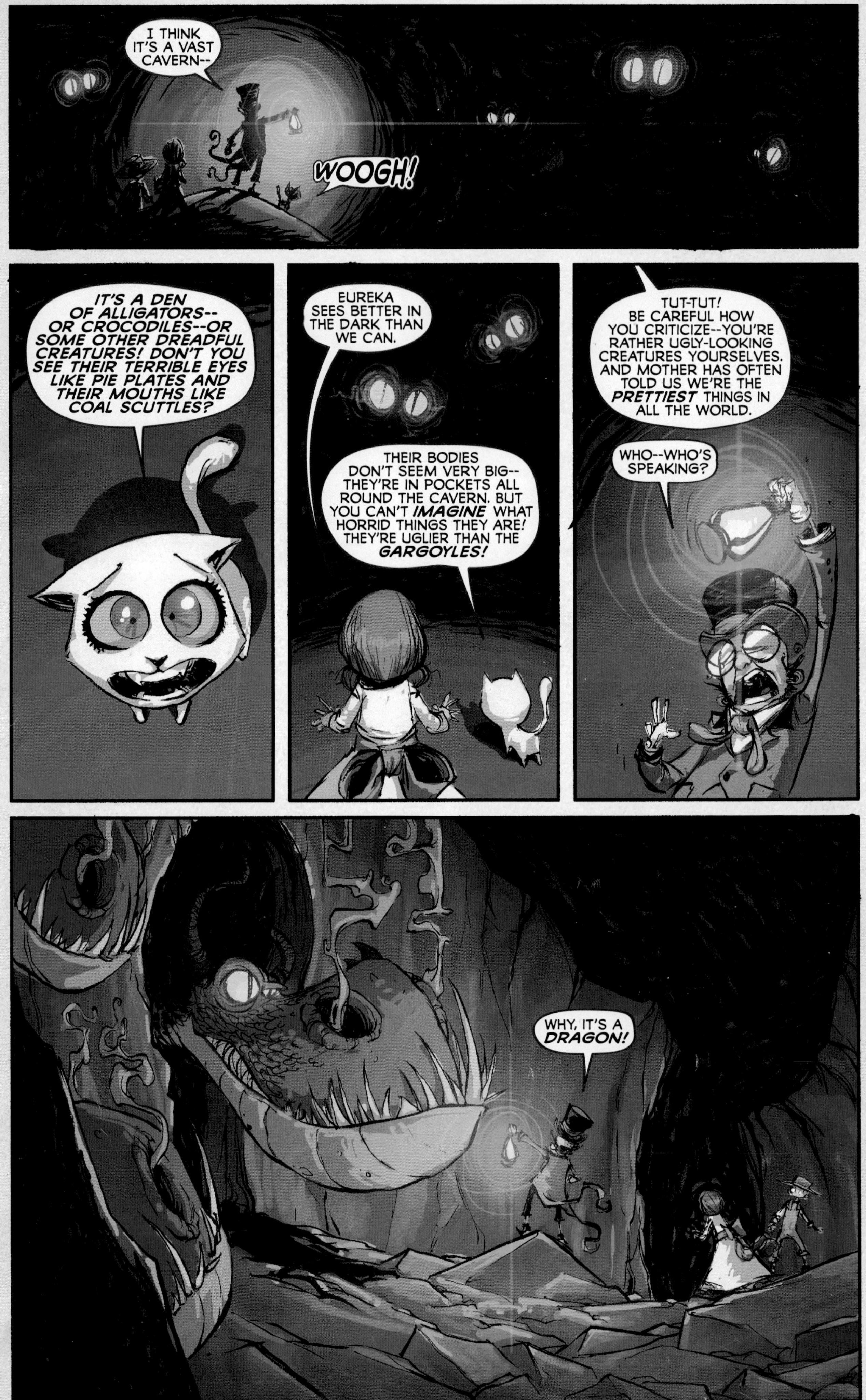
I THINK IT'S A VAST CAVERN--
WOOGH!
IT'S A DEN OF ALLIGATORS-- OR CROCODILES--OR SOME OTHER DREADFUL CREATURES! DON'T YOU SEE THEIR TERRIBLE EYES LIKE PIE PLATES AND THEIR MOUTHS LIKE COAL SCUTTLES?
EUREKA SEES BETTER IN THE DARK THAN WE CAN.
THEIR BODIES DON'T SEEM VERY BIG-- THEY'RE IN POCKETS ALL ROUND THE CAVERN. BUT YOU CAN'T IMAGINE WHAT HORRID THINGS THEY ARE! THEY'RE UGLIER THAN THE GARGOYLES!
TUT-TUT! BE CAREFUL HOW YOU CRITICIZE--YOU'RE RATHER UGLY-LOOKING CREATURES YOURSELVES. AND MOTHER HAS OFTEN TOLD US WE'RE THE PRETTIEST THINGS IN ALL THE WORLD.
WHO--WHO'S SPEAKING?
WHY, IT'S A DRAGON!

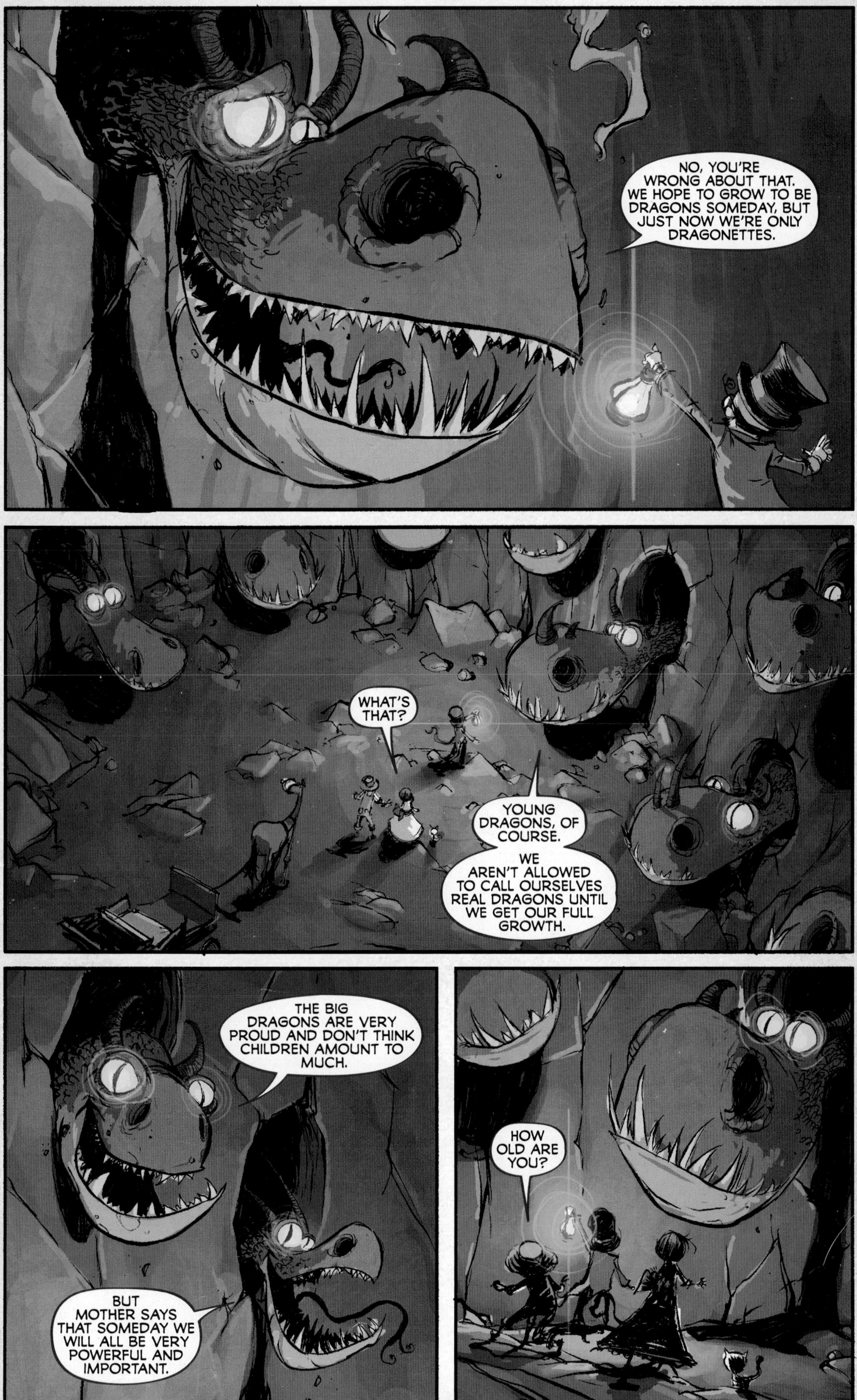
NO, YOU'RE WRONG ABOUT THAT. WE HOPE TO GROW TO BE DRAGONS SOMEDAY, BUT JUST NOW WE'RE ONLY DRAGONETTES.
WHAT'S THAT?
YOUNG DRAGONS, OF COURSE.
WE AREN'T ALLOWED TO CALL OURSELVES REAL DRAGONS UNTIL WE GET OUR FULL GROWTH.
THE BIG DRAGONS ARE VERY PROUD AND DON'T THINK CHILDREN AMOUNT TO MUCH.
BUT MOTHER SAYS THAT SOMEDAY WE WILL ALL BE VERY POWERFUL AND IMPORTANT.
HOW OLD ARE YOU?

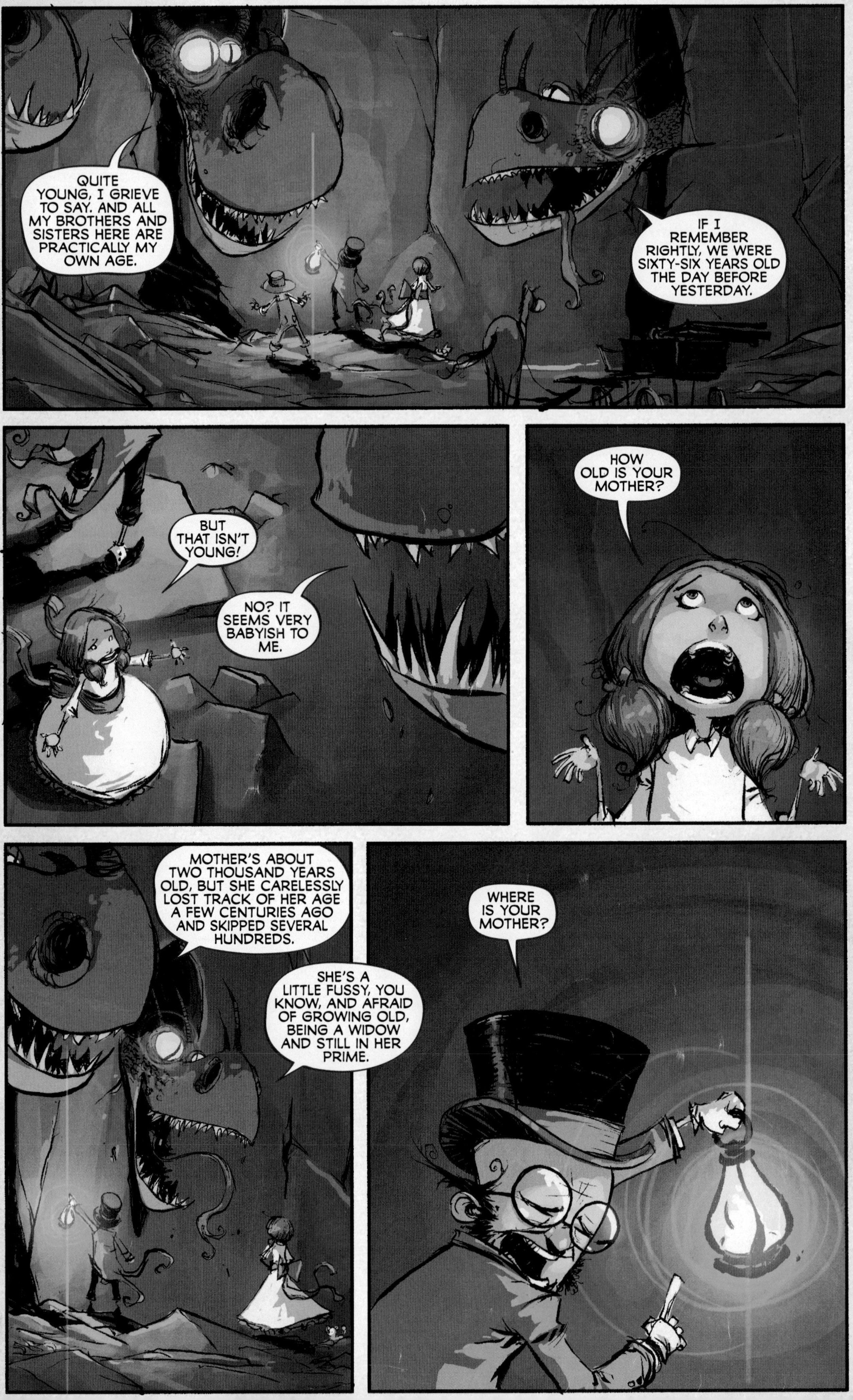
QUITE YOUNG, I GRIEVE TO SAY. AND ALL MY BROTHERS AND SISTERS HERE ARE PRACTICALLY MY OWN AGE.
IF I REMEMBER RIGHTLY, WE WERE SIXTY-SIX YEARS OLD THE DAY BEFORE YESTERDAY.
BUT THAT ISN'T YOUNG!
NO? IT SEEMS VERY BABYISH TO ME.
HOW OLD IS YOUR MOTHER?
MOTHER'S ABOUT TWO THOUSAND YEARS OLD, BUT SHE CARELESSLY LOST TRACK OF HER AGE A FEW CENTURIES AGO AND SKIPPED SEVERAL HUNDREDS.
SHE'S A LITTLE FUSSY, YOU KNOW, AND AFRAID OF GROWING OLD, BEING A WIDOW AND STILL IN HER PRIME.
WHERE IS YOUR MOTHER?

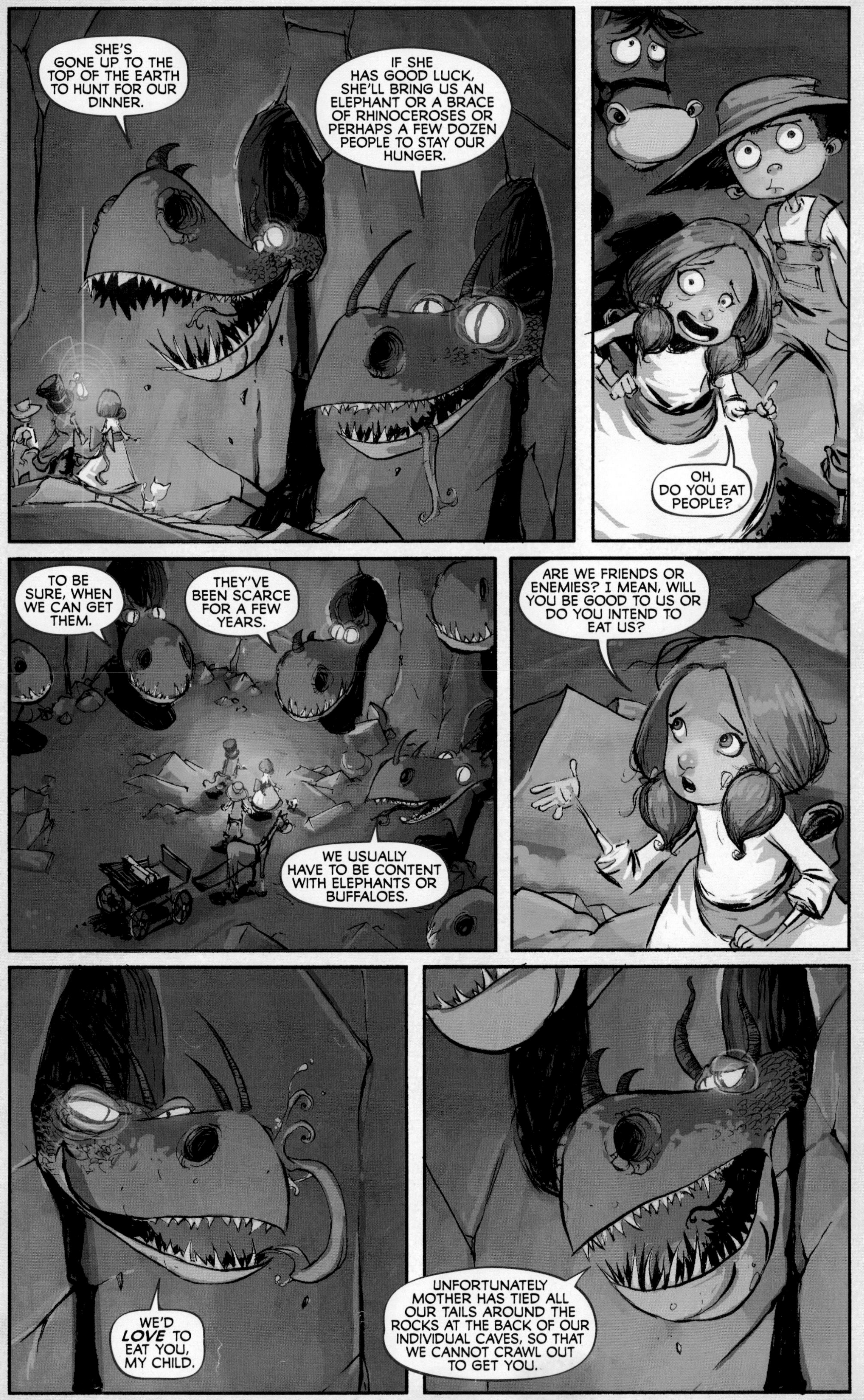
SHE'S GONE UP TO THE TOP OF THE EARTH TO HUNT FOR OUR DINNER.
IF SHE HAS GOOD LUCK, SHE'LL BRING US AN ELEPHANT OR A BRACE OF RHINOCEROSES OR PERHAPS A FEW DOZEN PEOPLE TO STAY OUR HUNGER.
OH, DO YOU EAT PEOPLE?
TO BE SURE, WHEN WE CAN GET THEM.
THEY'VE BEEN SCARCE FOR A FEW YEARS.
WE USUALLY HAVE TO BE CONTENT WITH ELEPHANTS OR BUFFALOES.
ARE WE FRIENDS OR ENEMIES? I MEAN, WILL YOU BE GOOD TO US OR DO YOU INTEND TO EAT US?
WE'D *LOVE* TO EAT YOU, MY CHILD.
UNFORTUNATELY MOTHER HAS TIED ALL OUR TAILS AROUND THE ROCKS AT THE BACK OF OUR INDIVIDUAL CAVES, SO THAT WE CANNOT CRAWL OUT TO GET YOU.

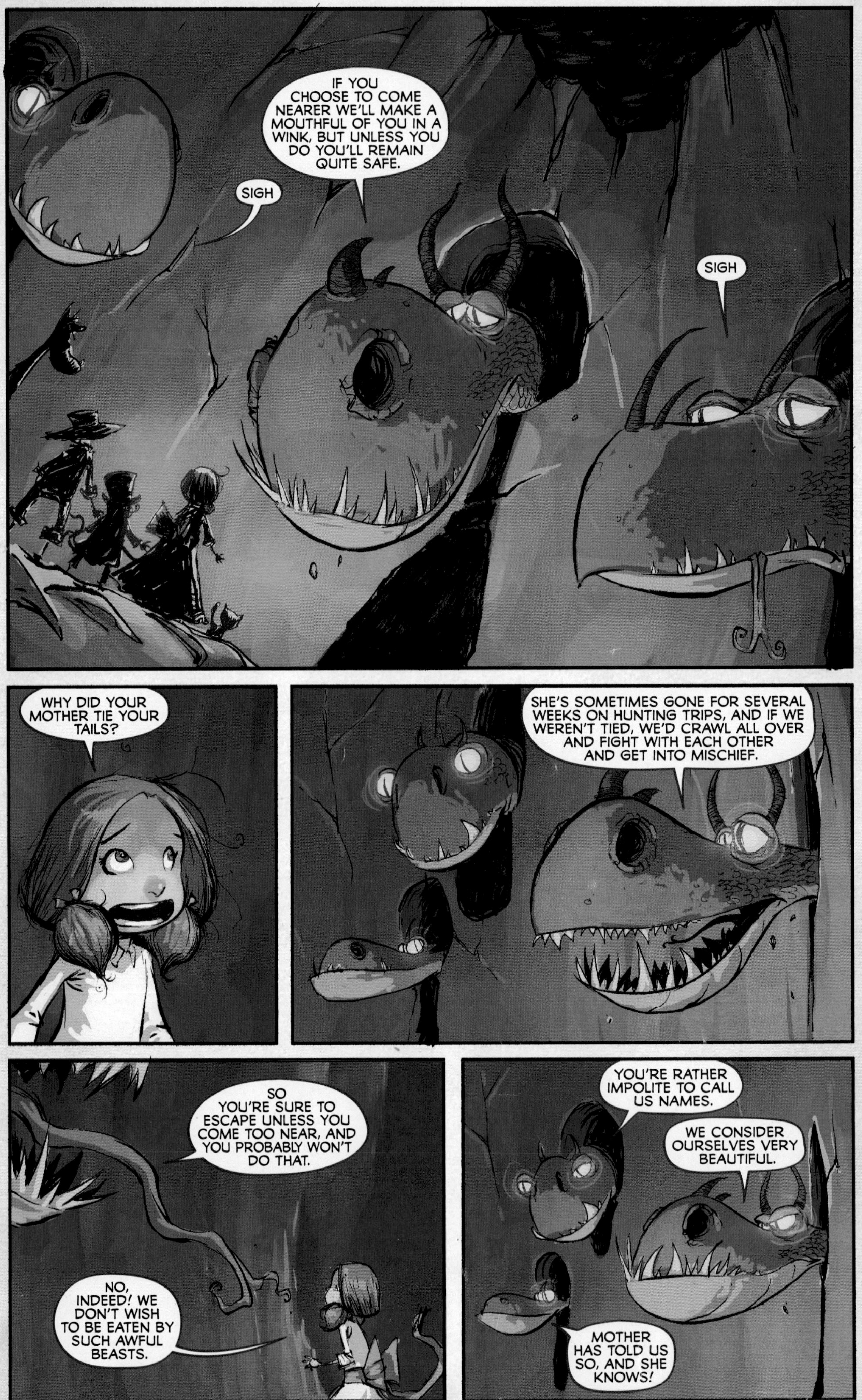
IF YOU CHOOSE TO COME NEARER WE'LL MAKE A MOUTHFUL OF YOU IN A WINK, BUT UNLESS YOU DO YOU'LL REMAIN QUITE SAFE.
SIGH
SIGH
WHY DID YOUR MOTHER TIE YOUR TAILS?
SHE'S SOMETIMES GONE FOR SEVERAL WEEKS ON HUNTING TRIPS, AND IF WE WEREN'T TIED, WE'D CRAWL ALL OVER AND FIGHT WITH EACH OTHER AND GET INTO MISCHIEF.
SO YOU'RE SURE TO ESCAPE UNLESS YOU COME TOO NEAR, AND YOU PROBABLY WON'T DO THAT.
NO, INDEED! WE DON'T WISH TO BE EATEN BY SUCH AWFUL BEASTS.
YOU'RE RATHER IMPOLITE TO CALL US NAMES.
WE CONSIDER OURSELVES VERY BEAUTIFUL.
MOTHER HAS TOLD US SO, AND SHE KNOWS!

WE'RE OF AN *EXCELLENT* FAMILY. OUR PEDIGREE EXTENDS BACK TWENTY THOUSAND YEARS TO THE GREEN DRAGON OF ATLANTIS, WHO LIVED WHEN HUMANS HADN'T YET BEEN CREATED.

CAN YOU MATCH THAT PEDIGREE, LITTLE GIRL?

WELL, I WAS BORN ON A FARM IN KANSAS--I GUESS THAT'S JUST AS RESPECTABLE AND HAUGHTY AS LIVING IN A CAVE WITH YOUR TAIL TIED TO A ROCK.

TASTES DIFFER.

WE OUGHT TO GET OUT OF THIS PLACE BEFORE THE MOTHER DRAGON COMES BACK.

DON'T HURRY--MOTHER WILL BE GLAD TO MEET YOU, I'M SURE.

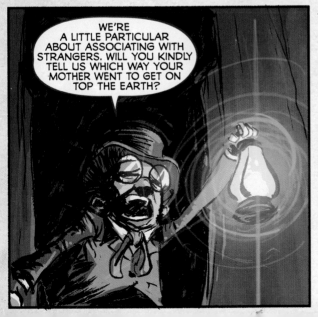

WE'RE A LITTLE PARTICULAR ABOUT ASSOCIATING WITH STRANGERS. WILL YOU KINDLY TELL US WHICH WAY YOUR MOTHER WENT TO GET ON TOP THE EARTH?

THAT'S NOT A FAIR QUESTION--IF WE TOLD YOU TRULY, YOU MIGHT ESCAPE--AND IF WE TOLD YOU AN UNTRUTH WE'D BE NAUGHTY AND DESERVE TO BE PUNISHED.

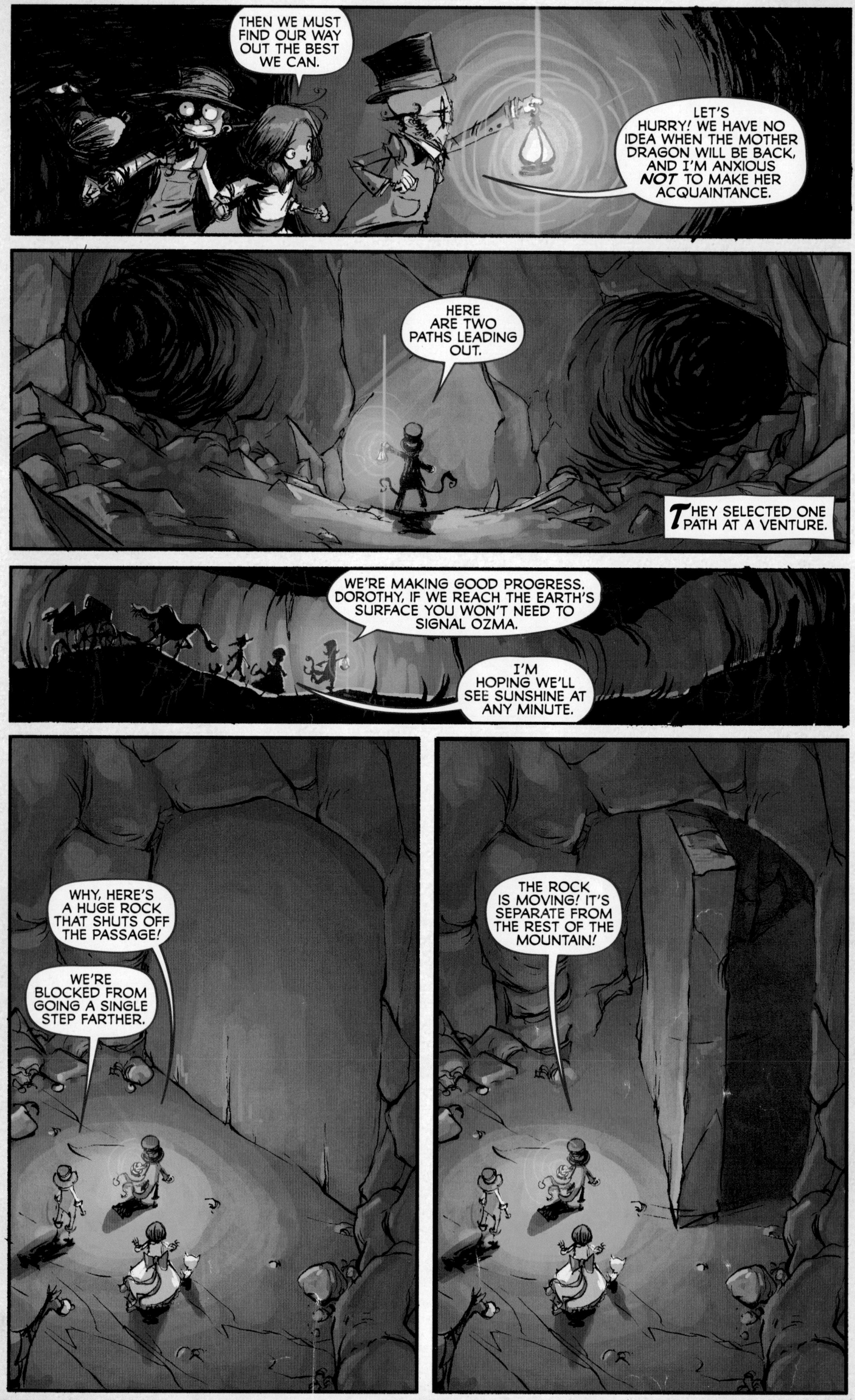
THEN WE MUST FIND OUR WAY OUT THE BEST WE CAN.
LET'S HURRY! WE HAVE NO IDEA WHEN THE MOTHER DRAGON WILL BE BACK, AND I'M ANXIOUS NOT TO MAKE HER ACQUAINTANCE.
HERE ARE TWO PATHS LEADING OUT.
THEY SELECTED ONE PATH AT A VENTURE.
WE'RE MAKING GOOD PROGRESS. DOROTHY, IF WE REACH THE EARTH'S SURFACE YOU WON'T NEED TO SIGNAL OZMA.
I'M HOPING WE'LL SEE SUNSHINE AT ANY MINUTE.
WHY, HERE'S A HUGE ROCK THAT SHUTS OFF THE PASSAGE!
WE'RE BLOCKED FROM GOING A SINGLE STEP FARTHER.
THE ROCK IS MOVING! IT'S SEPARATE FROM THE REST OF THE MOUNTAIN!

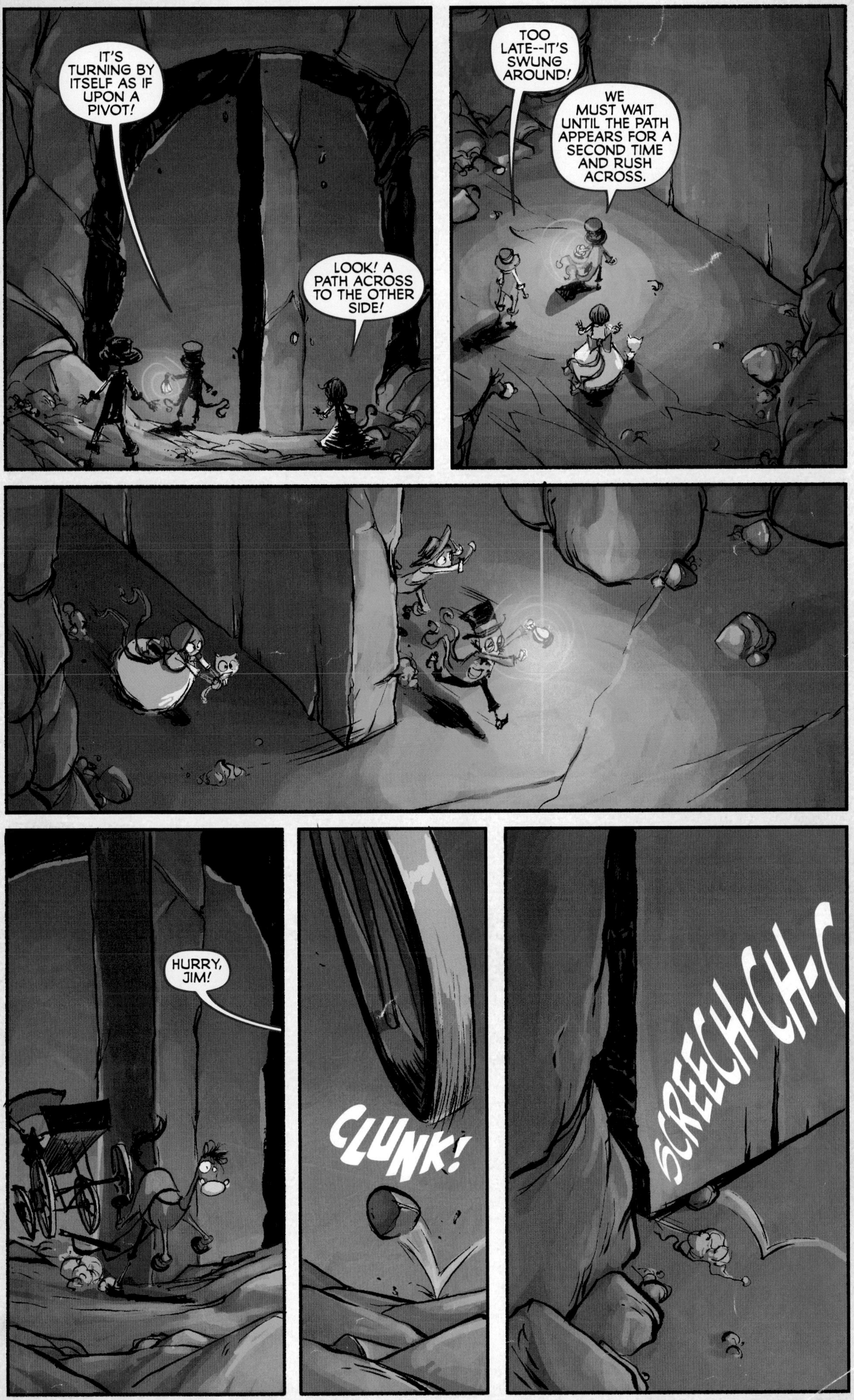
IT'S TURNING BY ITSELF AS IF UPON A PIVOT!
LOOK! A PATH ACROSS TO THE OTHER SIDE!
TOO LATE--IT'S SWUNG AROUND!
WE MUST WAIT UNTIL THE PATH APPEARS FOR A SECOND TIME AND RUSH ACROSS.
HURRY, JIM!
CLUNK!
SCREECH-CH-C

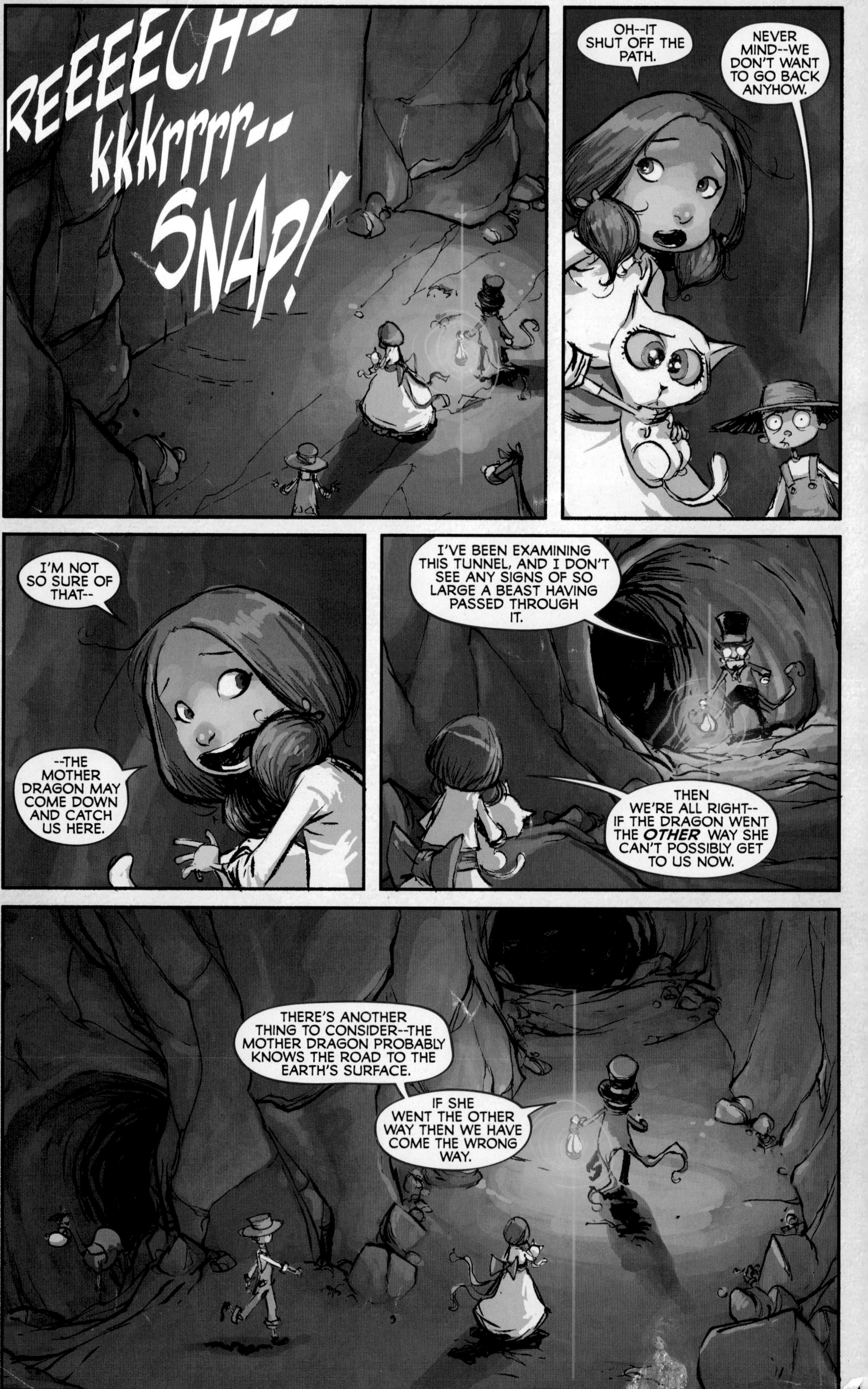
REEEECH--
kkkrrrr--
SNAP!
OH--IT SHUT OFF THE PATH.
NEVER MIND--WE DON'T WANT TO GO BACK ANYHOW.
I'M NOT SO SURE OF THAT--
--THE MOTHER DRAGON MAY COME DOWN AND CATCH US HERE.
I'VE BEEN EXAMINING THIS TUNNEL, AND I DON'T SEE ANY SIGNS OF SO LARGE A BEAST HAVING PASSED THROUGH IT.
THEN WE'RE ALL RIGHT--IF THE DRAGON WENT THE *OTHER* WAY SHE CAN'T POSSIBLY GET TO US NOW.
THERE'S ANOTHER THING TO CONSIDER--THE MOTHER DRAGON PROBABLY KNOWS THE ROAD TO THE EARTH'S SURFACE.
IF SHE WENT THE OTHER WAY THEN WE HAVE COME THE WRONG WAY.

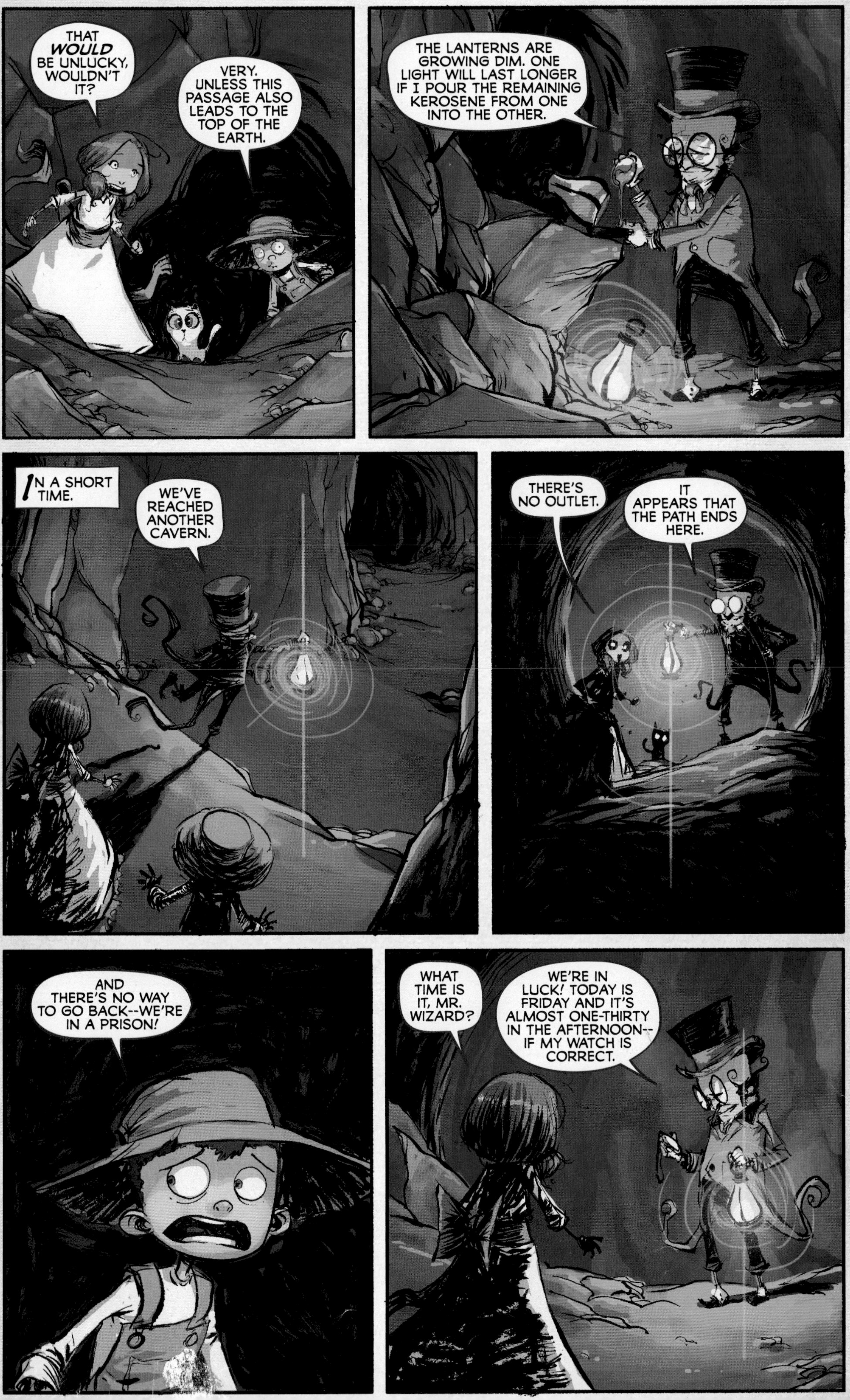
THAT WOULD BE UNLUCKY, WOULDN'T IT?
VERY. UNLESS THIS PASSAGE ALSO LEADS TO THE TOP OF THE EARTH.
THE LANTERNS ARE GROWING DIM. ONE LIGHT WILL LAST LONGER IF I POUR THE REMAINING KEROSENE FROM ONE INTO THE OTHER.
IN A SHORT TIME.
WE'VE REACHED ANOTHER CAVERN.
THERE'S NO OUTLET.
IT APPEARS THAT THE PATH ENDS HERE.
AND THERE'S NO WAY TO GO BACK--WE'RE IN A PRISON!
WHAT TIME IS IT, MR. WIZARD?
WE'RE IN LUCK! TODAY IS FRIDAY AND IT'S ALMOST ONE-THIRTY IN THE AFTERNOON-- IF MY WATCH IS CORRECT.

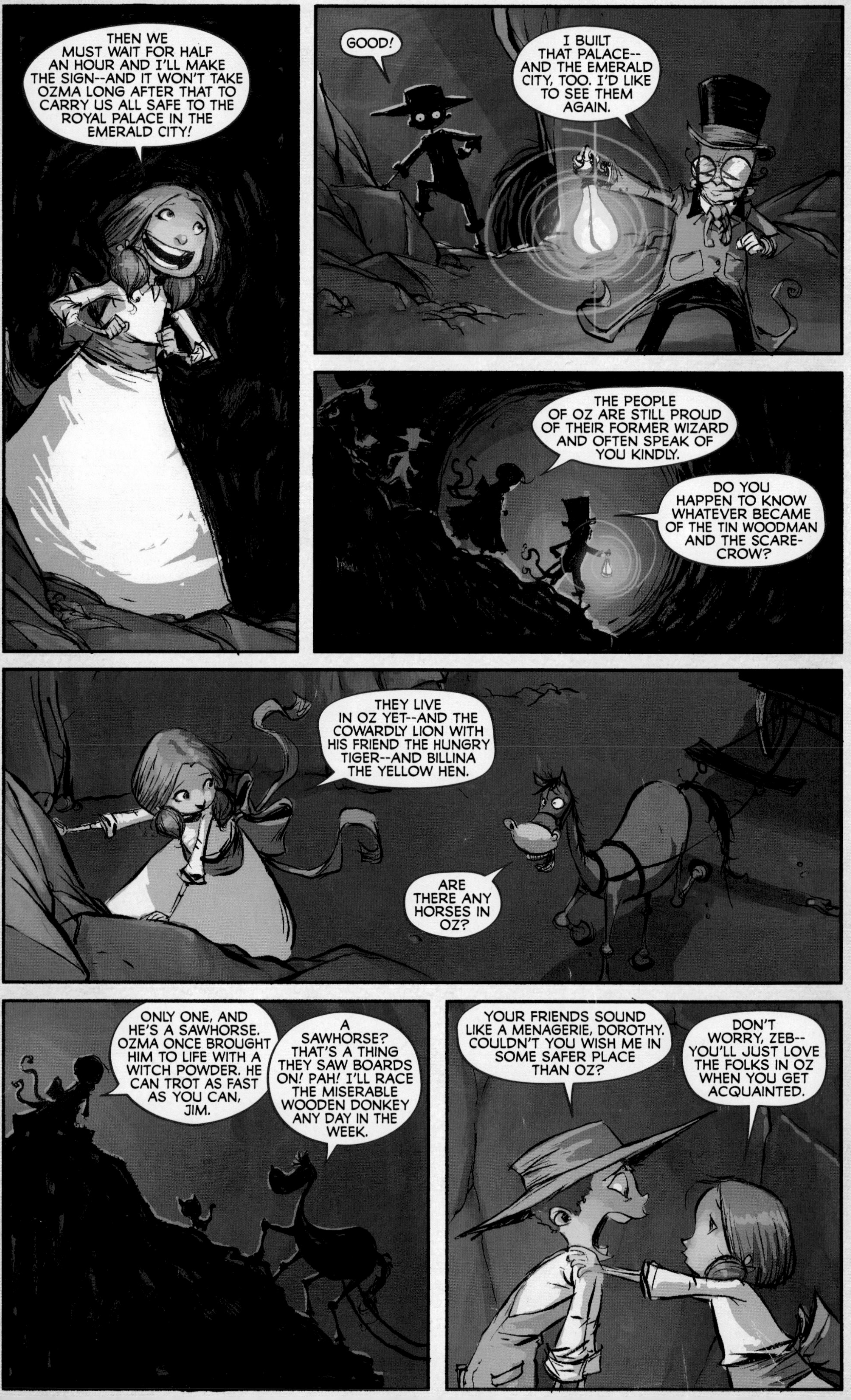
THEN WE MUST WAIT FOR HALF AN HOUR AND I'LL MAKE THE SIGN--AND IT WON'T TAKE OZMA LONG AFTER THAT TO CARRY US ALL SAFE TO THE ROYAL PALACE IN THE EMERALD CITY!
GOOD!
I BUILT THAT PALACE--AND THE EMERALD CITY, TOO. I'D LIKE TO SEE THEM AGAIN.
THE PEOPLE OF OZ ARE STILL PROUD OF THEIR FORMER WIZARD AND OFTEN SPEAK OF YOU KINDLY.
DO YOU HAPPEN TO KNOW WHATEVER BECAME OF THE TIN WOODMAN AND THE SCARE-CROW?
THEY LIVE IN OZ YET--AND THE COWARDLY LION WITH HIS FRIEND THE HUNGRY TIGER--AND BILLINA THE YELLOW HEN.
ARE THERE ANY HORSES IN OZ?
ONLY ONE, AND HE'S A SAWHORSE. OZMA ONCE BROUGHT HIM TO LIFE WITH A WITCH POWDER. HE CAN TROT AS FAST AS YOU CAN, JIM.
A SAWHORSE? THAT'S A THING THEY SAW BOARDS ON! PAH! I'LL RACE THE MISERABLE WOODEN DONKEY ANY DAY IN THE WEEK.
YOUR FRIENDS SOUND LIKE A MENAGERIE, DOROTHY. COULDN'T YOU WISH ME IN SOME SAFER PLACE THAN OZ?
DON'T WORRY, ZEB--YOU'LL JUST LOVE THE FOLKS IN OZ WHEN YOU GET ACQUAINTED.

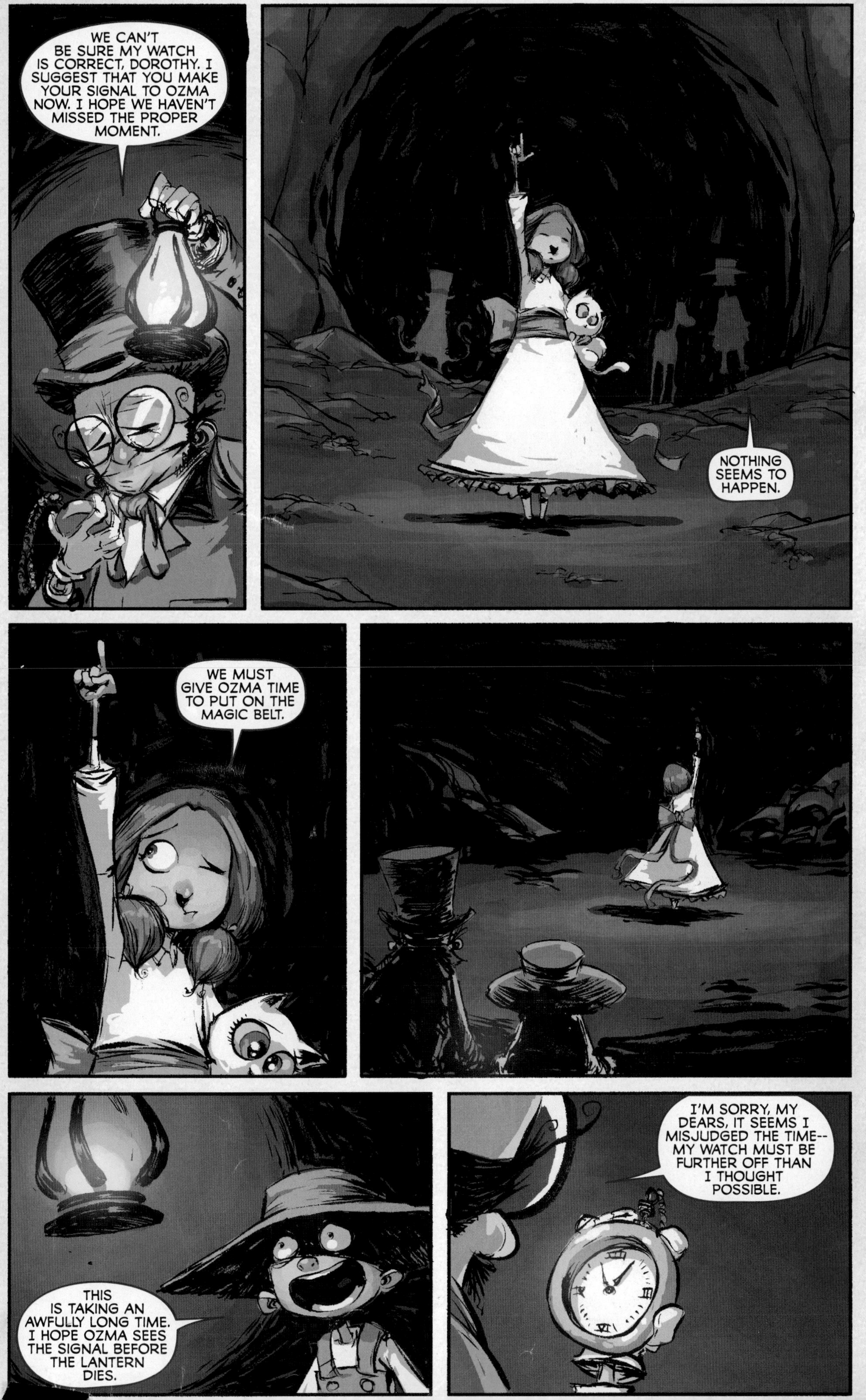
WE CAN'T BE SURE MY WATCH IS CORRECT, DOROTHY. I SUGGEST THAT YOU MAKE YOUR SIGNAL TO OZMA NOW. I HOPE WE HAVEN'T MISSED THE PROPER MOMENT.
NOTHING SEEMS TO HAPPEN.
WE MUST GIVE OZMA TIME TO PUT ON THE MAGIC BELT.
THIS IS TAKING AN AWFULLY LONG TIME. I HOPE OZMA SEES THE SIGNAL BEFORE THE LANTERN DIES.
I'M SORRY, MY DEARS, IT SEEMS I MISJUDGED THE TIME-- MY WATCH MUST BE FURTHER OFF THAN I THOUGHT POSSIBLE.

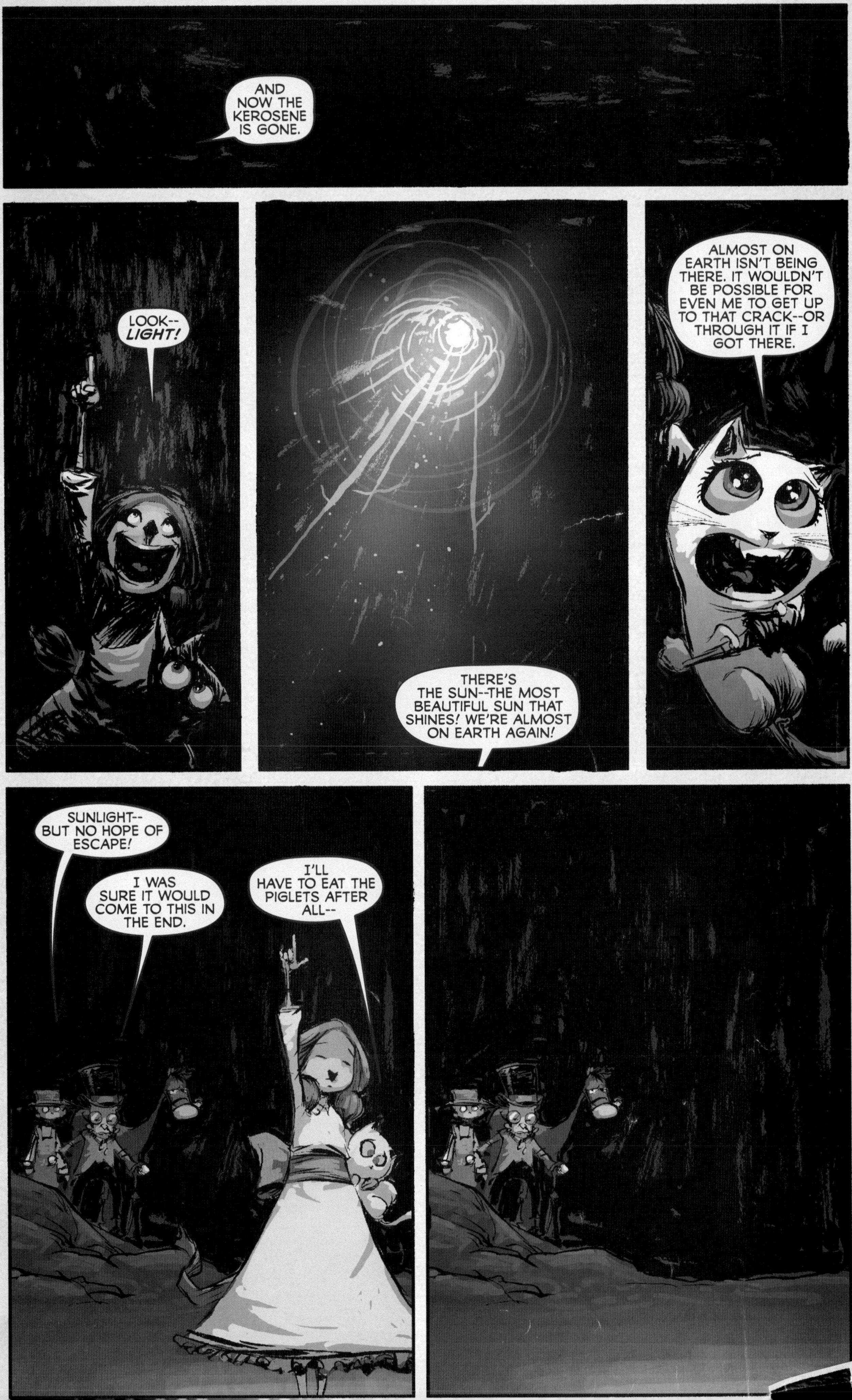
AND NOW THE KEROSENE IS GONE.
LOOK-- *LIGHT!*
THERE'S THE SUN--THE MOST BEAUTIFUL SUN THAT SHINES! WE'RE ALMOST ON EARTH AGAIN!
ALMOST ON EARTH ISN'T BEING THERE. IT WOULDN'T BE POSSIBLE FOR EVEN ME TO GET UP TO THAT CRACK--OR THROUGH IT IF I GOT THERE.
SUNLIGHT-- BUT NO HOPE OF ESCAPE!
I WAS SURE IT WOULD COME TO THIS IN THE END.
I'LL HAVE TO EAT THE PIGLETS AFTER ALL--

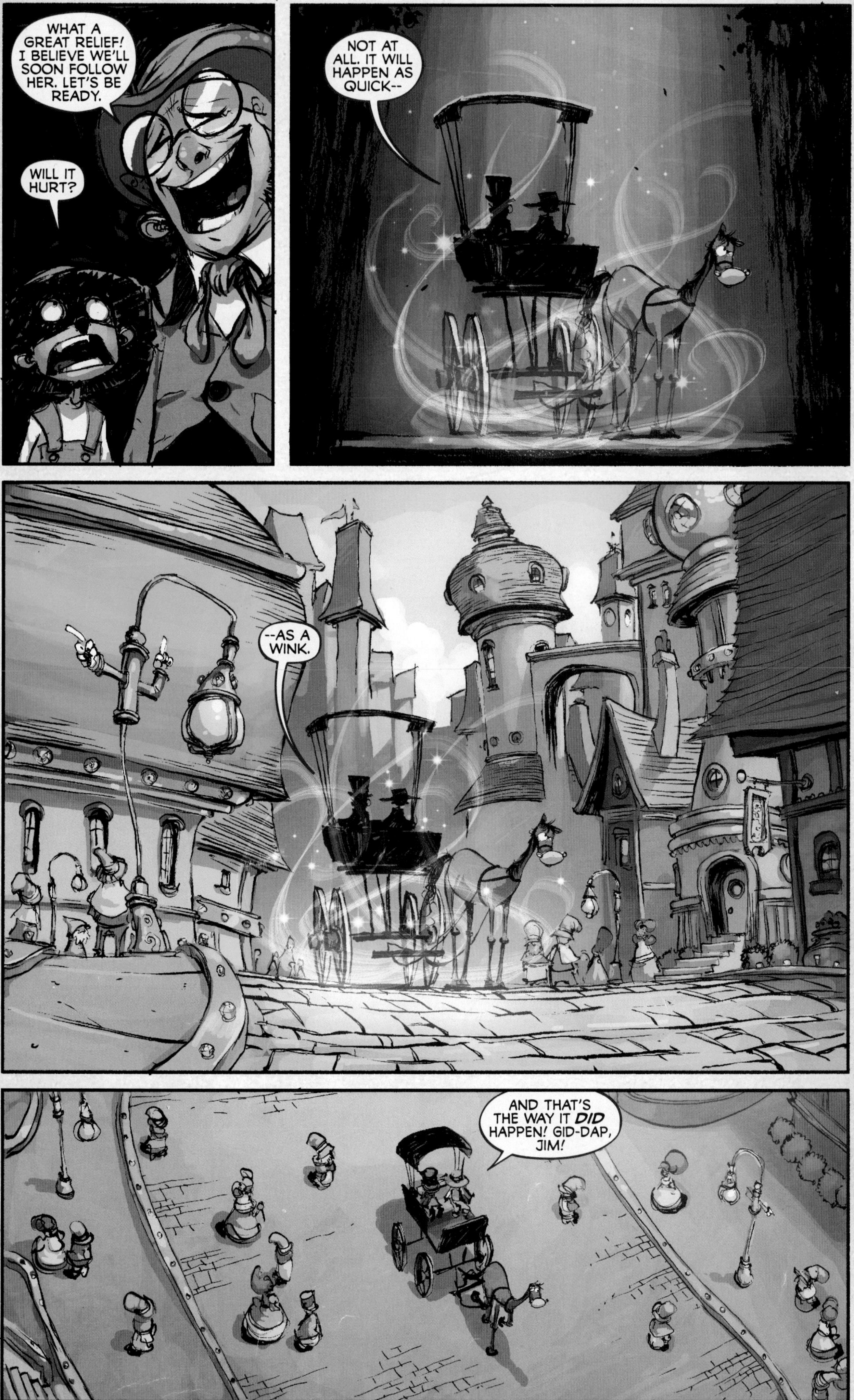
WHAT A GREAT RELIEF! I BELIEVE WE'LL SOON FOLLOW HER. LET'S BE READY.
WILL IT HURT?
NOT AT ALL. IT WILL HAPPEN AS QUICK--
--AS A WINK.
AND THAT'S THE WAY IT *DID* HAPPEN! GID-DAP, JIM!

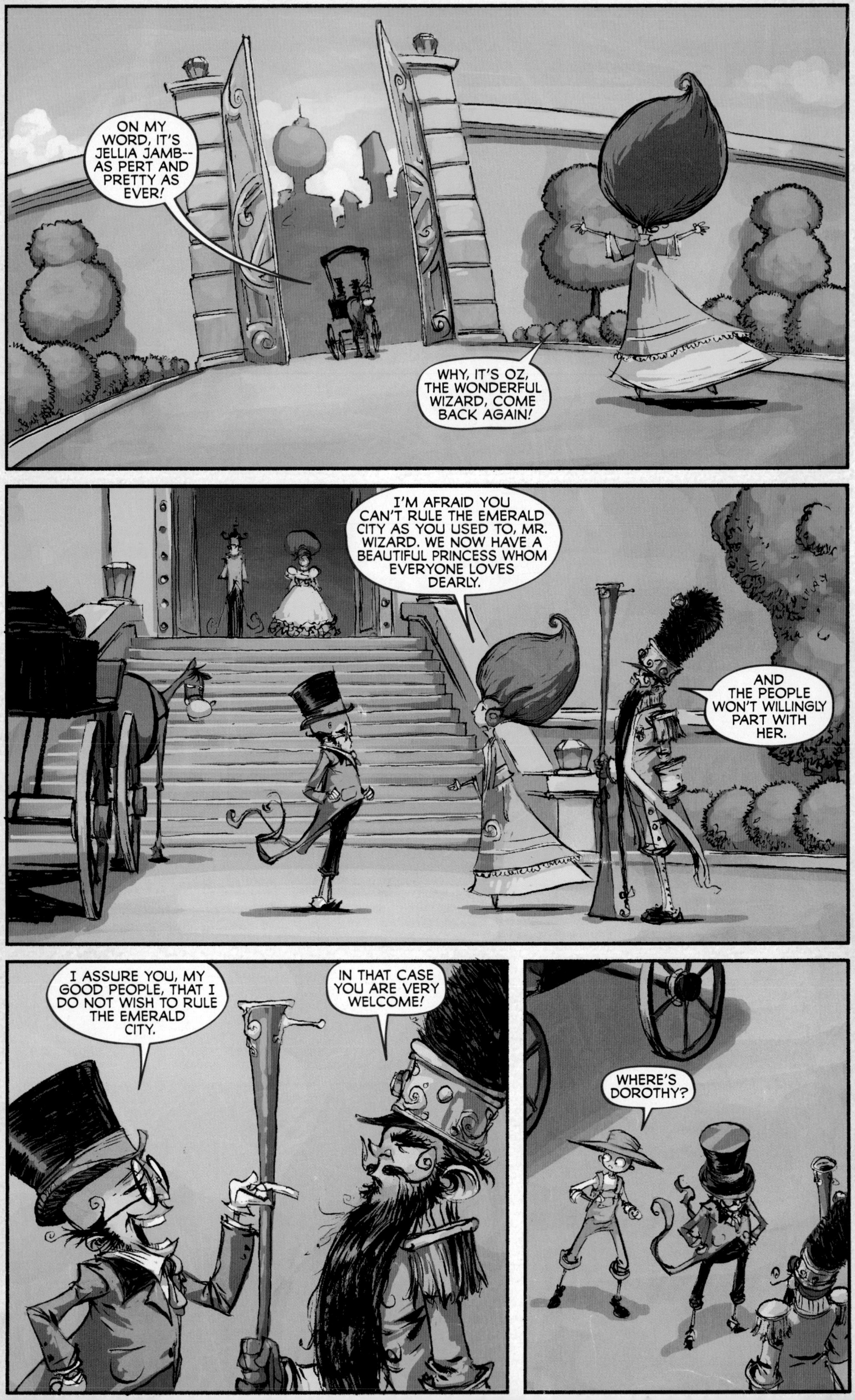
ON MY WORD, IT'S JELLIA JAMB-- AS PERT AND PRETTY AS EVER!
WHY, IT'S OZ, THE WONDERFUL WIZARD, COME BACK AGAIN!
I'M AFRAID YOU CAN'T RULE THE EMERALD CITY AS YOU USED TO, MR. WIZARD. WE NOW HAVE A BEAUTIFUL PRINCESS WHOM EVERYONE LOVES DEARLY.
AND THE PEOPLE WON'T WILLINGLY PART WITH HER.
I ASSURE YOU, MY GOOD PEOPLE, THAT I DO NOT WISH TO RULE THE EMERALD CITY.
IN THAT CASE YOU ARE VERY WELCOME!
WHERE'S DOROTHY?

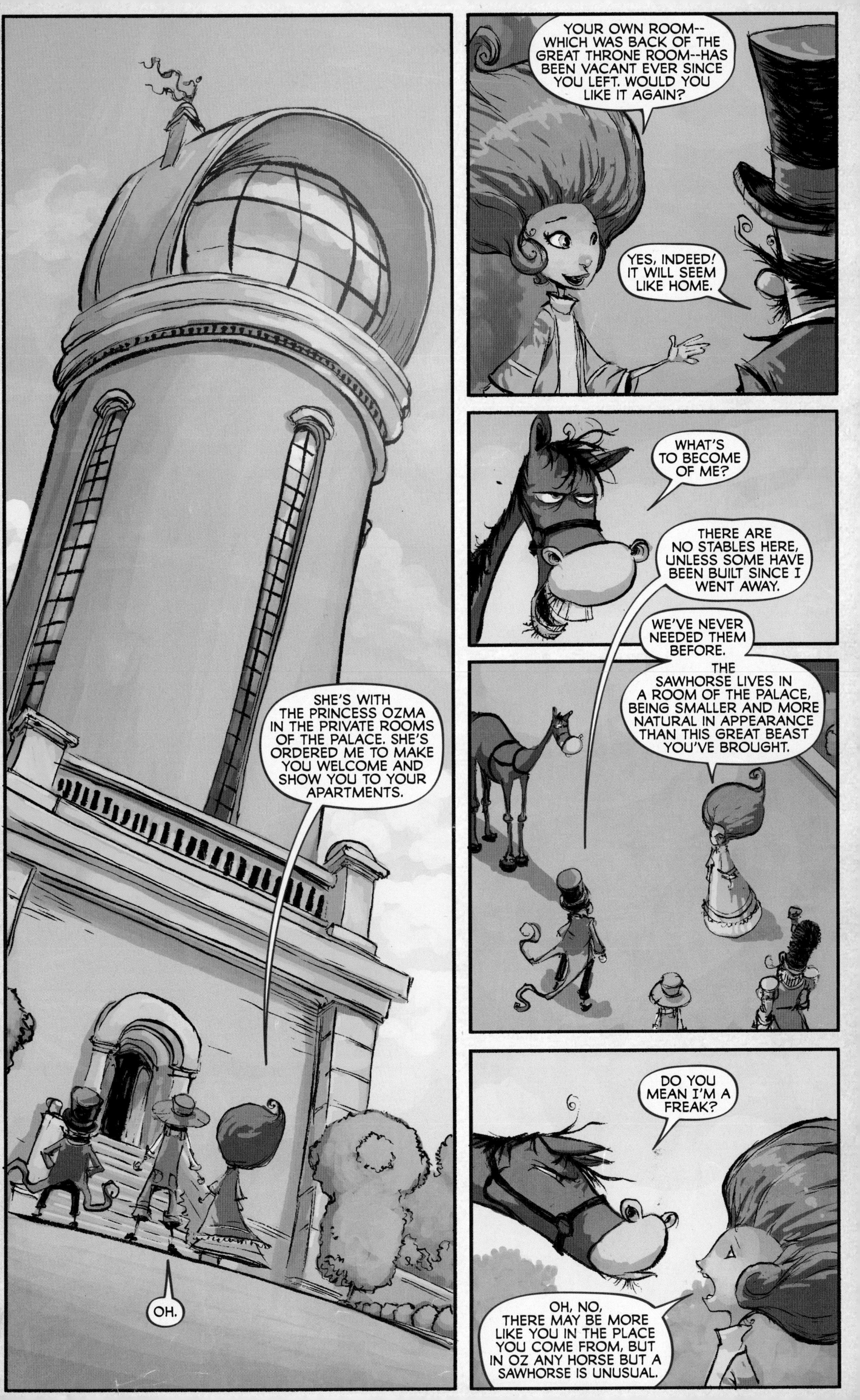
SHE'S WITH THE PRINCESS OZMA IN THE PRIVATE ROOMS OF THE PALACE. SHE'S ORDERED ME TO MAKE YOU WELCOME AND SHOW YOU TO YOUR APARTMENTS.
OH.
YOUR OWN ROOM-- WHICH WAS BACK OF THE GREAT THRONE ROOM--HAS BEEN VACANT EVER SINCE YOU LEFT. WOULD YOU LIKE IT AGAIN?
YES, INDEED! IT WILL SEEM LIKE HOME.
WHAT'S TO BECOME OF ME?
THERE ARE NO STABLES HERE, UNLESS SOME HAVE BEEN BUILT SINCE I WENT AWAY.
WE'VE NEVER NEEDED THEM BEFORE.
THE SAWHORSE LIVES IN A ROOM OF THE PALACE, BEING SMALLER AND MORE NATURAL IN APPEARANCE THAN THIS GREAT BEAST YOU'VE BROUGHT.
DO YOU MEAN I'M A FREAK?
OH, NO, THERE MAY BE MORE LIKE YOU IN THE PLACE YOU COME FROM, BUT IN OZ ANY HORSE BUT A SAWHORSE IS UNUSUAL.

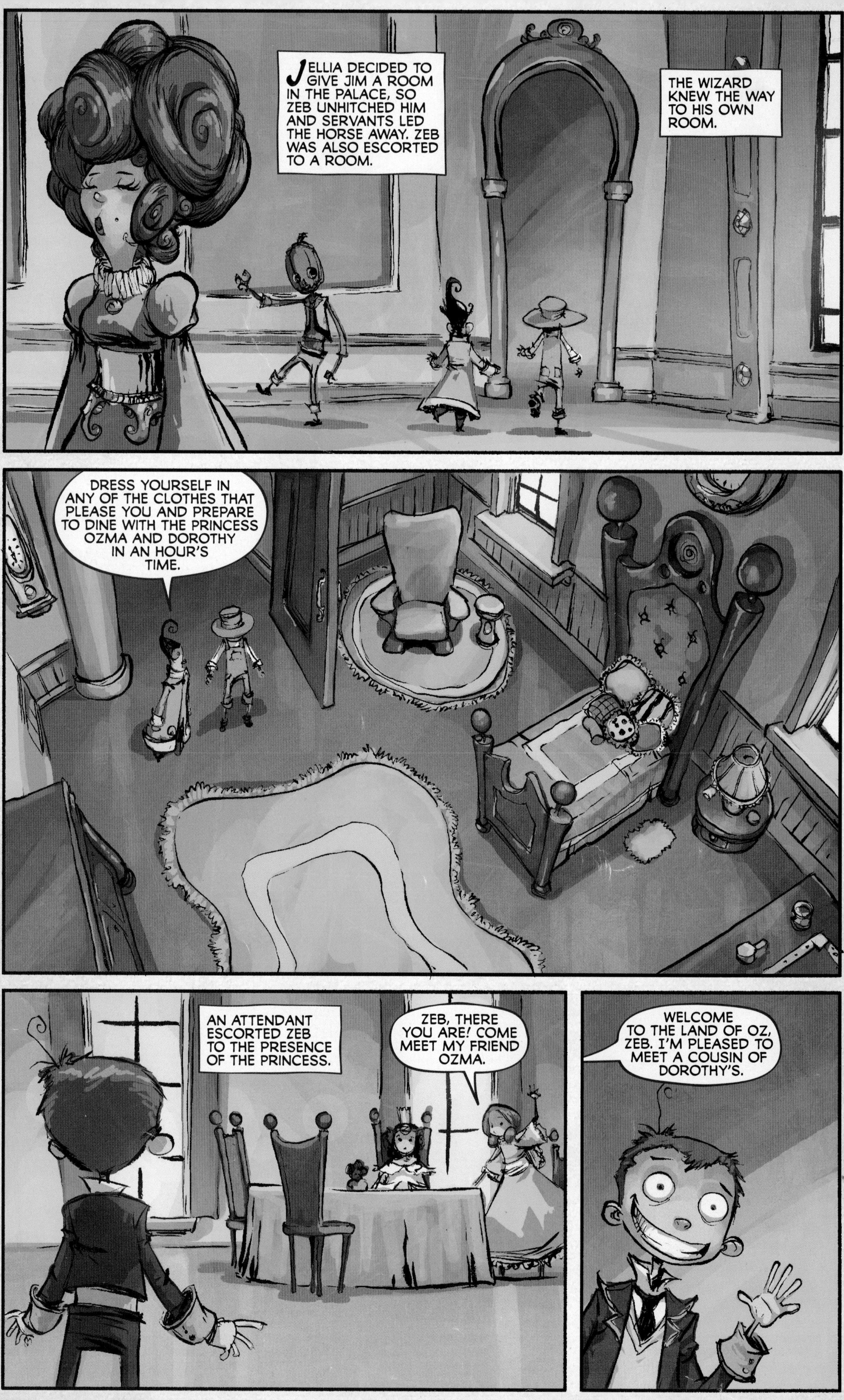
JELLIA DECIDED TO GIVE JIM A ROOM IN THE PALACE, SO ZEB UNHITCHED HIM AND SERVANTS LED THE HORSE AWAY. ZEB WAS ALSO ESCORTED TO A ROOM.
THE WIZARD KNEW THE WAY TO HIS OWN ROOM.
DRESS YOURSELF IN ANY OF THE CLOTHES THAT PLEASE YOU AND PREPARE TO DINE WITH THE PRINCESS OZMA AND DOROTHY IN AN HOUR'S TIME.
AN ATTENDANT ESCORTED ZEB TO THE PRESENCE OF THE PRINCESS.
ZEB, THERE YOU ARE! COME MEET MY FRIEND OZMA.
WELCOME TO THE LAND OF OZ, ZEB. I'M PLEASED TO MEET A COUSIN OF DOROTHY'S.

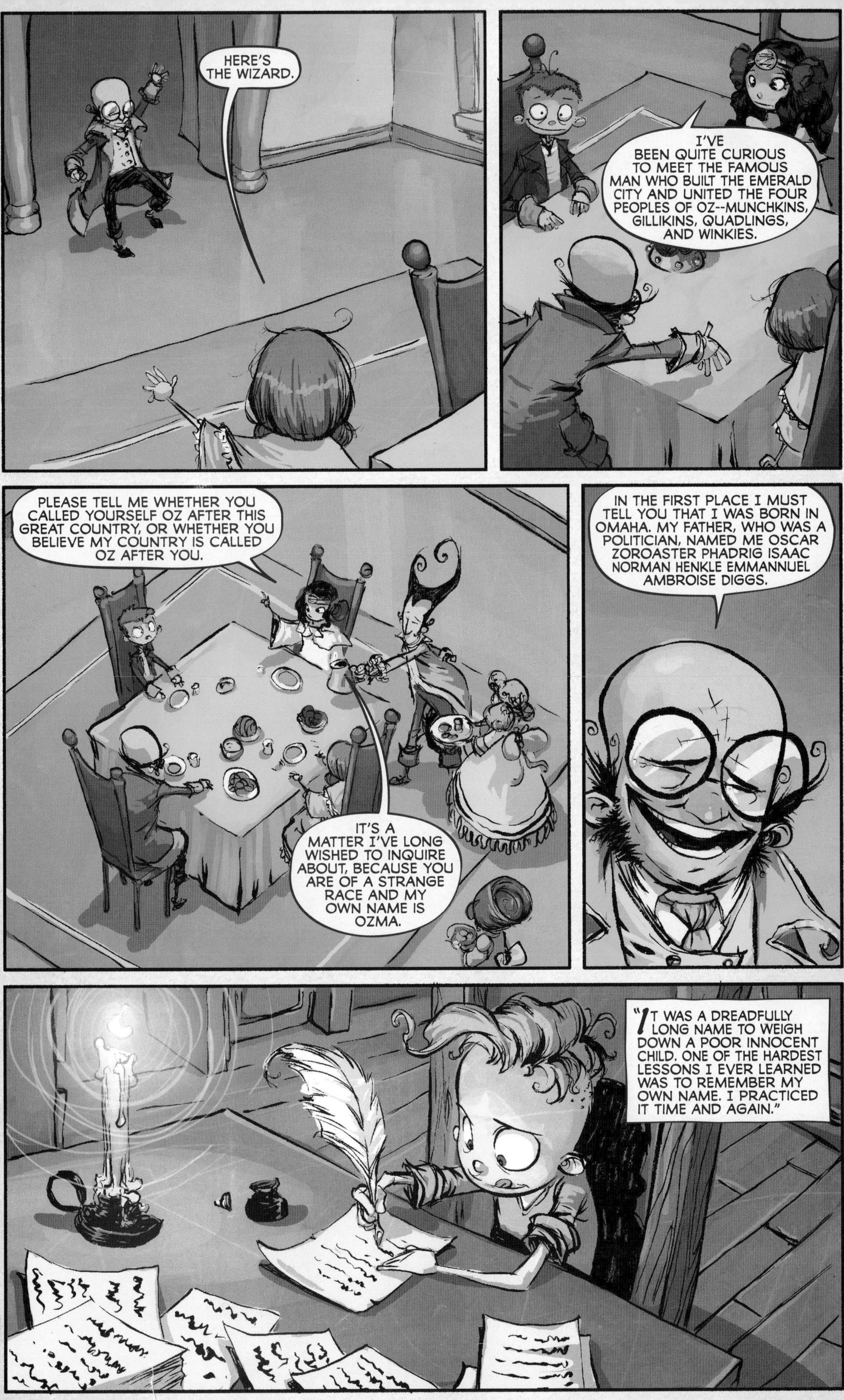
HERE'S THE WIZARD.
I'VE BEEN QUITE CURIOUS TO MEET THE FAMOUS MAN WHO BUILT THE EMERALD CITY AND UNITED THE FOUR PEOPLES OF OZ--MUNCHKINS, GILLIKINS, QUADLINGS, AND WINKIES.
PLEASE TELL ME WHETHER YOU CALLED YOURSELF OZ AFTER THIS GREAT COUNTRY, OR WHETHER YOU BELIEVE MY COUNTRY IS CALLED OZ AFTER YOU.
IT'S A MATTER I'VE LONG WISHED TO INQUIRE ABOUT, BECAUSE YOU ARE OF A STRANGE RACE AND MY OWN NAME IS OZMA.
IN THE FIRST PLACE I MUST TELL YOU THAT I WAS BORN IN OMAHA. MY FATHER, WHO WAS A POLITICIAN, NAMED ME OSCAR ZOROASTER PHADRIG ISAAC NORMAN HENKLE EMMANNUEL AMBROISE DIGGS.
"IT WAS A DREADFULLY LONG NAME TO WEIGH DOWN A POOR INNOCENT CHILD. ONE OF THE HARDEST LESSONS I EVER LEARNED WAS TO REMEMBER MY OWN NAME. I PRACTICED IT TIME AND AGAIN."

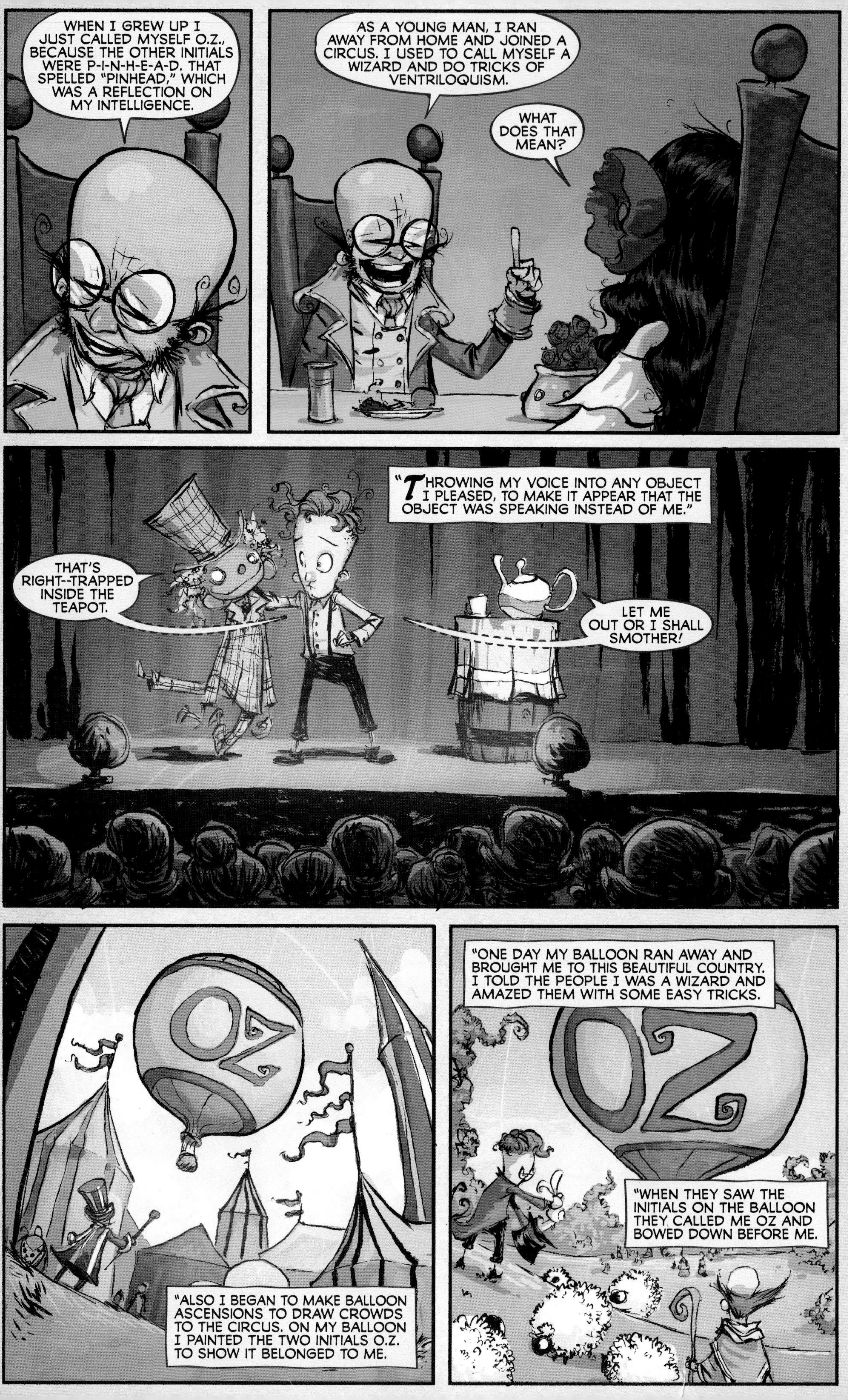
WHEN I GREW UP I JUST CALLED MYSELF O.Z., BECAUSE THE OTHER INITIALS WERE P-I-N-H-E-A-D. THAT SPELLED "PINHEAD," WHICH WAS A REFLECTION ON MY INTELLIGENCE.
AS A YOUNG MAN, I RAN AWAY FROM HOME AND JOINED A CIRCUS. I USED TO CALL MYSELF A WIZARD AND DO TRICKS OF VENTRILOQUISM.
WHAT DOES THAT MEAN?
"THROWING MY VOICE INTO ANY OBJECT I PLEASED, TO MAKE IT APPEAR THAT THE OBJECT WAS SPEAKING INSTEAD OF ME."
THAT'S RIGHT--TRAPPED INSIDE THE TEAPOT.
LET ME OUT OR I SHALL SMOTHER!
OZ
"ALSO I BEGAN TO MAKE BALLOON ASCENSIONS TO DRAW CROWDS TO THE CIRCUS. ON MY BALLOON I PAINTED THE TWO INITIALS O.Z. TO SHOW IT BELONGED TO ME.
"ONE DAY MY BALLOON RAN AWAY AND BROUGHT ME TO THIS BEAUTIFUL COUNTRY. I TOLD THE PEOPLE I WAS A WIZARD AND AMAZED THEM WITH SOME EASY TRICKS.
OZ
"WHEN THEY SAW THE INITIALS ON THE BALLOON THEY CALLED ME OZ AND BOWED DOWN BEFORE ME.

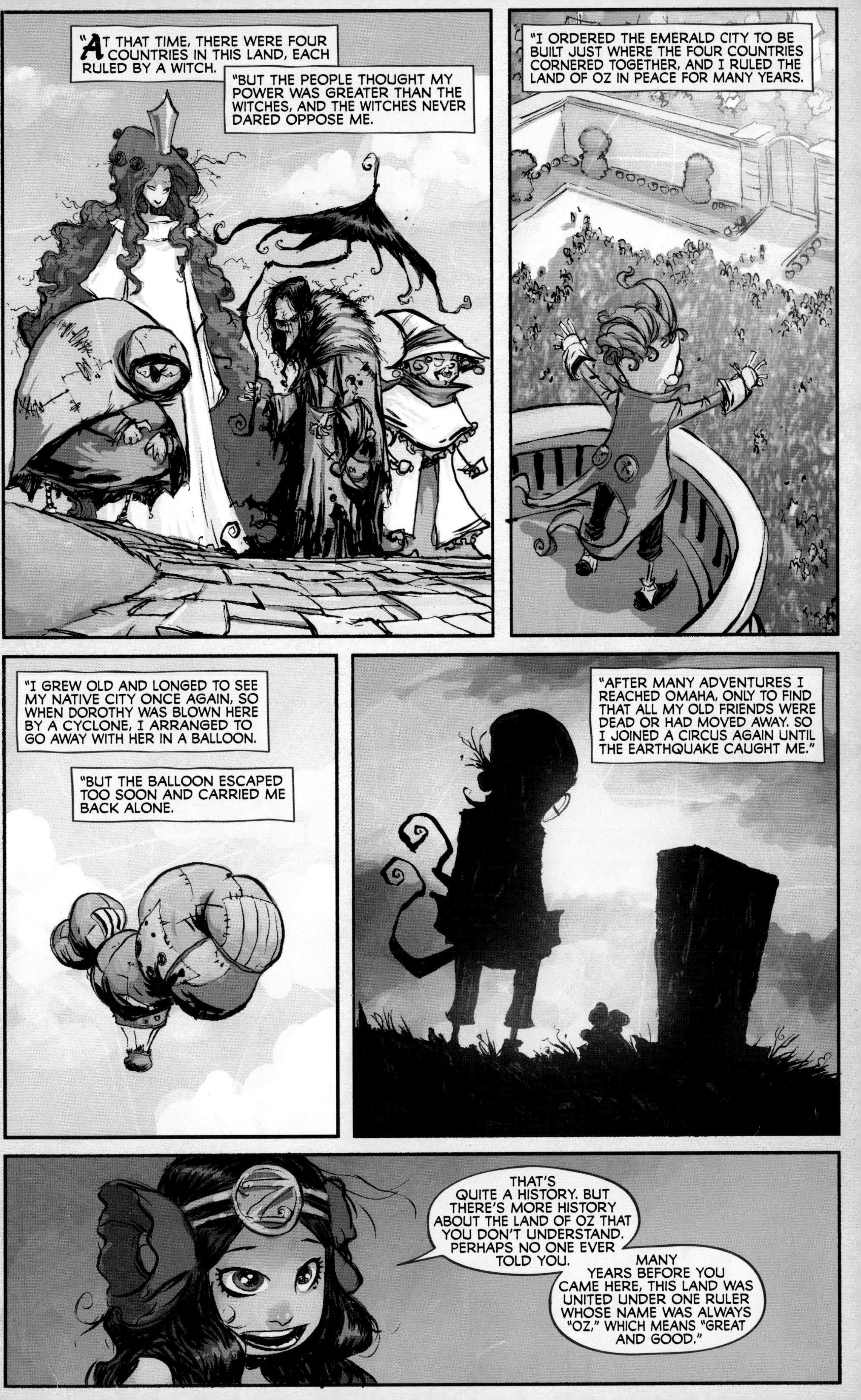
"AT THAT TIME, THERE WERE FOUR COUNTRIES IN THIS LAND, EACH RULED BY A WITCH.
"BUT THE PEOPLE THOUGHT MY POWER WAS GREATER THAN THE WITCHES, AND THE WITCHES NEVER DARED OPPOSE ME.
"I ORDERED THE EMERALD CITY TO BE BUILT JUST WHERE THE FOUR COUNTRIES CORNERED TOGETHER, AND I RULED THE LAND OF OZ IN PEACE FOR MANY YEARS.
"I GREW OLD AND LONGED TO SEE MY NATIVE CITY ONCE AGAIN, SO WHEN DOROTHY WAS BLOWN HERE BY A CYCLONE, I ARRANGED TO GO AWAY WITH HER IN A BALLOON.
"BUT THE BALLOON ESCAPED TOO SOON AND CARRIED ME BACK ALONE.
"AFTER MANY ADVENTURES I REACHED OMAHA, ONLY TO FIND THAT ALL MY OLD FRIENDS WERE DEAD OR HAD MOVED AWAY. SO I JOINED A CIRCUS AGAIN UNTIL THE EARTHQUAKE CAUGHT ME."
THAT'S QUITE A HISTORY. BUT THERE'S MORE HISTORY ABOUT THE LAND OF OZ THAT YOU DON'T UNDERSTAND. PERHAPS NO ONE EVER TOLD YOU.
MANY YEARS BEFORE YOU CAME HERE, THIS LAND WAS UNITED UNDER ONE RULER WHOSE NAME WAS ALWAYS "OZ," WHICH MEANS "GREAT AND GOOD."

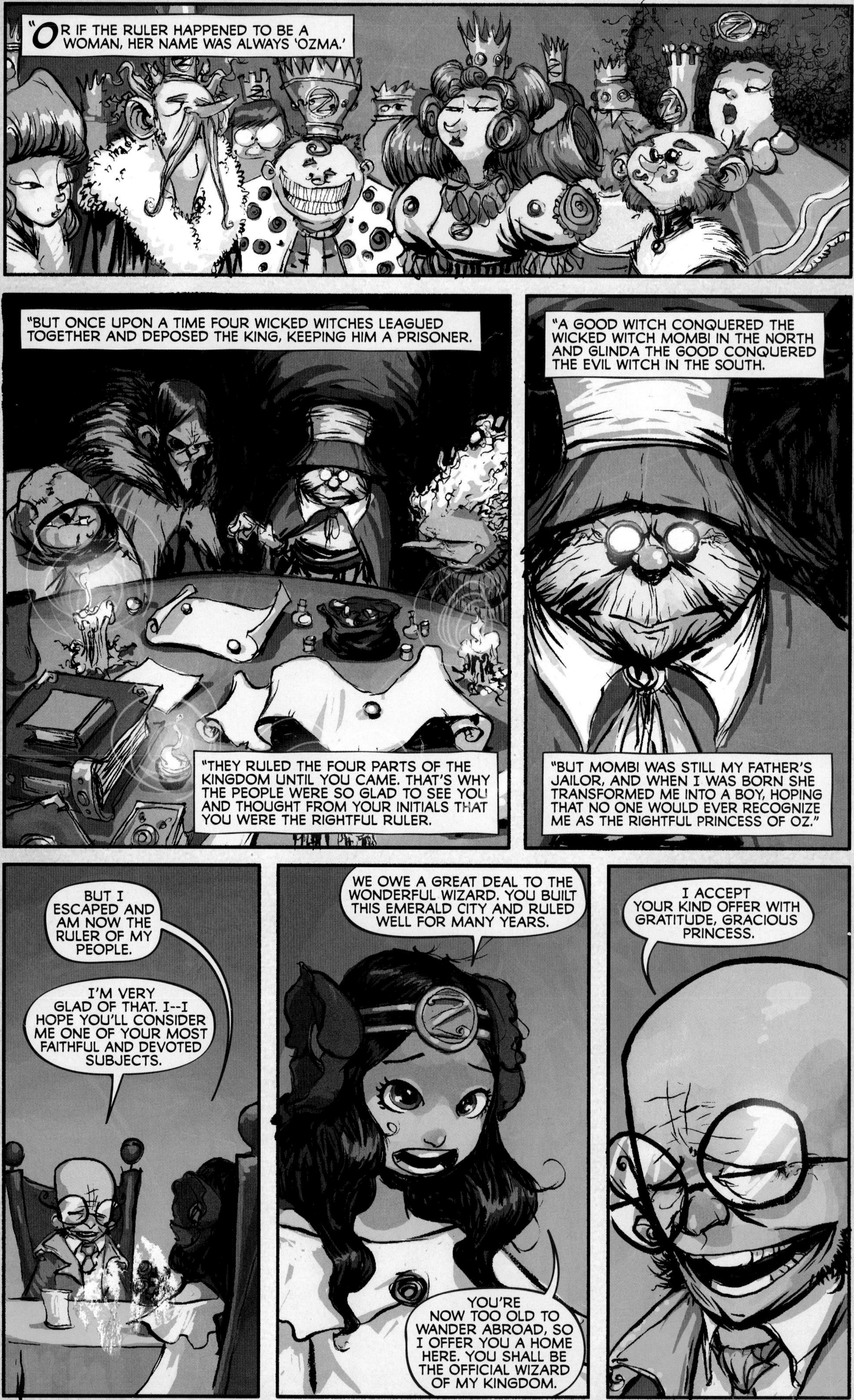
"OR IF THE RULER HAPPENED TO BE A WOMAN, HER NAME WAS ALWAYS 'OZMA.'
"BUT ONCE UPON A TIME FOUR WICKED WITCHES LEAGUED TOGETHER AND DEPOSED THE KING, KEEPING HIM A PRISONER.
"THEY RULED THE FOUR PARTS OF THE KINGDOM UNTIL YOU CAME. THAT'S WHY THE PEOPLE WERE SO GLAD TO SEE YOU AND THOUGHT FROM YOUR INITIALS THAT YOU WERE THE RIGHTFUL RULER.
"A GOOD WITCH CONQUERED THE WICKED WITCH MOMBI IN THE NORTH AND GLINDA THE GOOD CONQUERED THE EVIL WITCH IN THE SOUTH.
"BUT MOMBI WAS STILL MY FATHER'S JAILOR, AND WHEN I WAS BORN SHE TRANSFORMED ME INTO A BOY, HOPING THAT NO ONE WOULD EVER RECOGNIZE ME AS THE RIGHTFUL PRINCESS OF OZ."
BUT I ESCAPED AND AM NOW THE RULER OF MY PEOPLE.
I'M VERY GLAD OF THAT. I--I HOPE YOU'LL CONSIDER ME ONE OF YOUR MOST FAITHFUL AND DEVOTED SUBJECTS.
WE OWE A GREAT DEAL TO THE WONDERFUL WIZARD. YOU BUILT THIS EMERALD CITY AND RULED WELL FOR MANY YEARS.
YOU'RE NOW TOO OLD TO WANDER ABROAD, SO I OFFER YOU A HOME HERE. YOU SHALL BE THE OFFICIAL WIZARD OF MY KINGDOM.
I ACCEPT YOUR KIND OFFER WITH GRATITUDE, GRACIOUS PRINCESS.

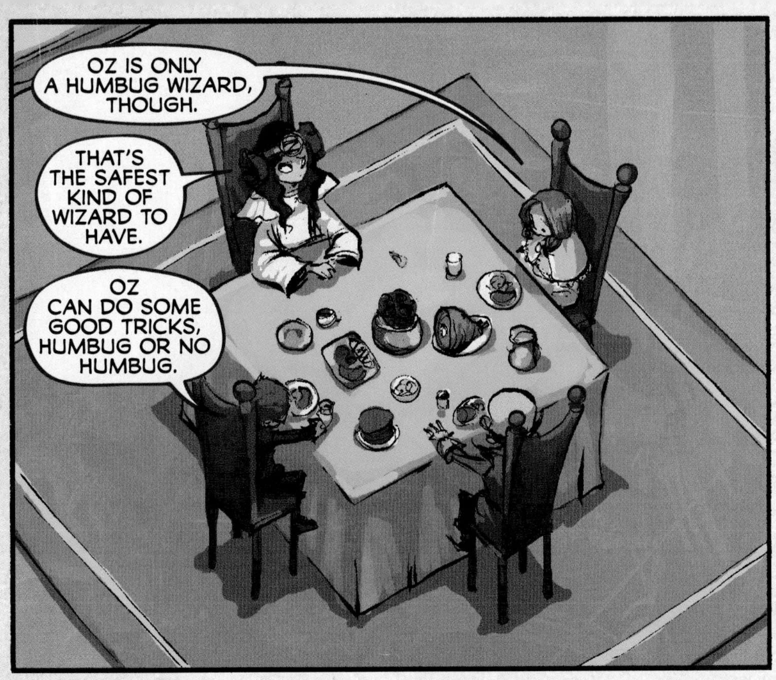
OZ IS ONLY A HUMBUG WIZARD, THOUGH.
THAT'S THE SAFEST KIND OF WIZARD TO HAVE.
OZ CAN DO SOME GOOD TRICKS, HUMBUG OR NO HUMBUG.

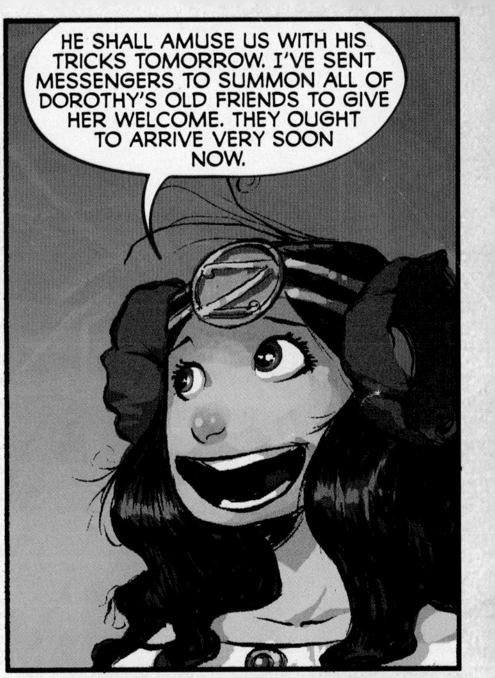
HE SHALL AMUSE US WITH HIS TRICKS TOMORROW. I'VE SENT MESSENGERS TO SUMMON ALL OF DOROTHY'S OLD FRIENDS TO GIVE HER WELCOME. THEY OUGHT TO ARRIVE VERY SOON NOW.

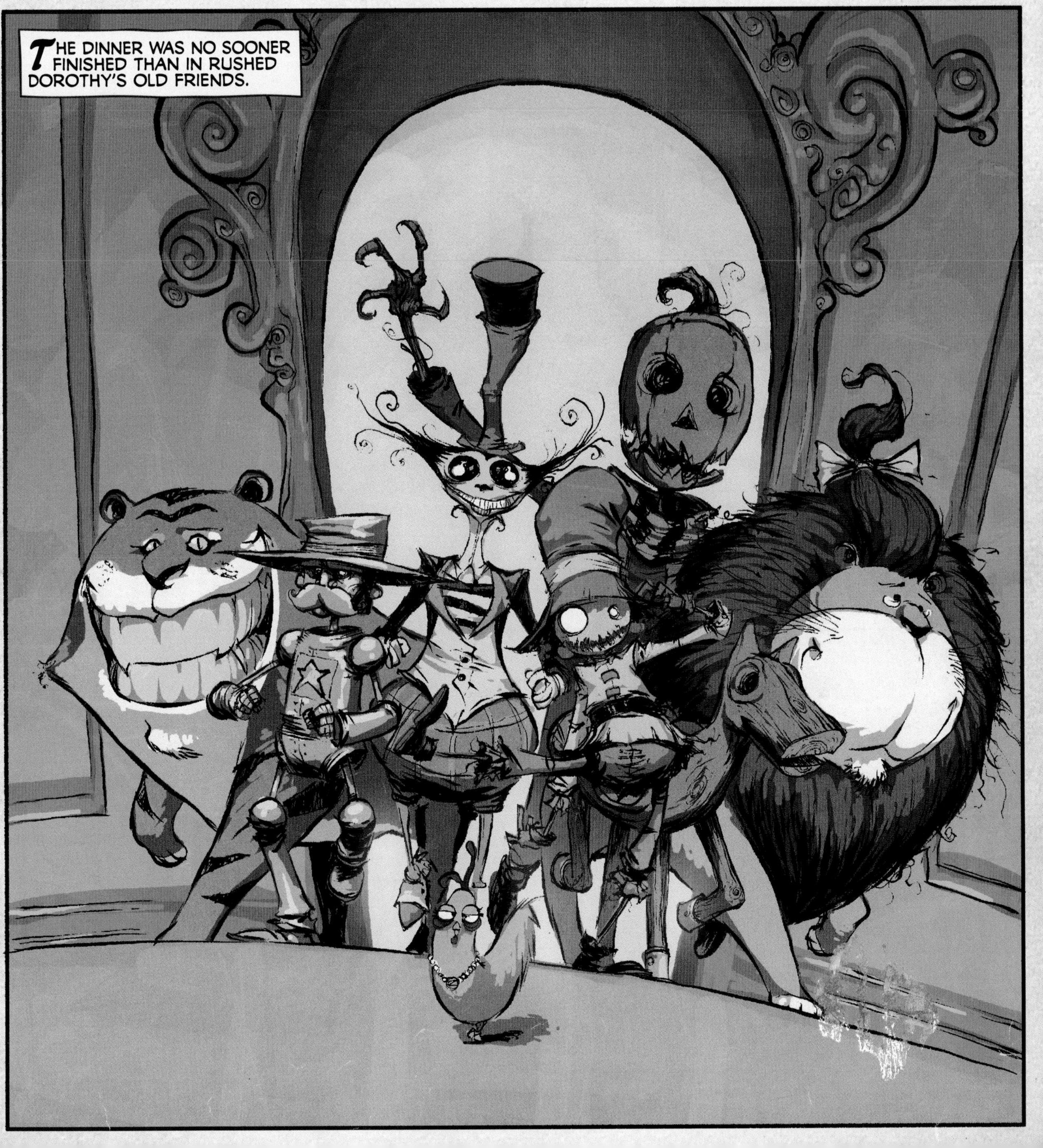
THE DINNER WAS NO SOONER FINISHED THAN IN RUSHED DOROTHY'S OLD FRIENDS.

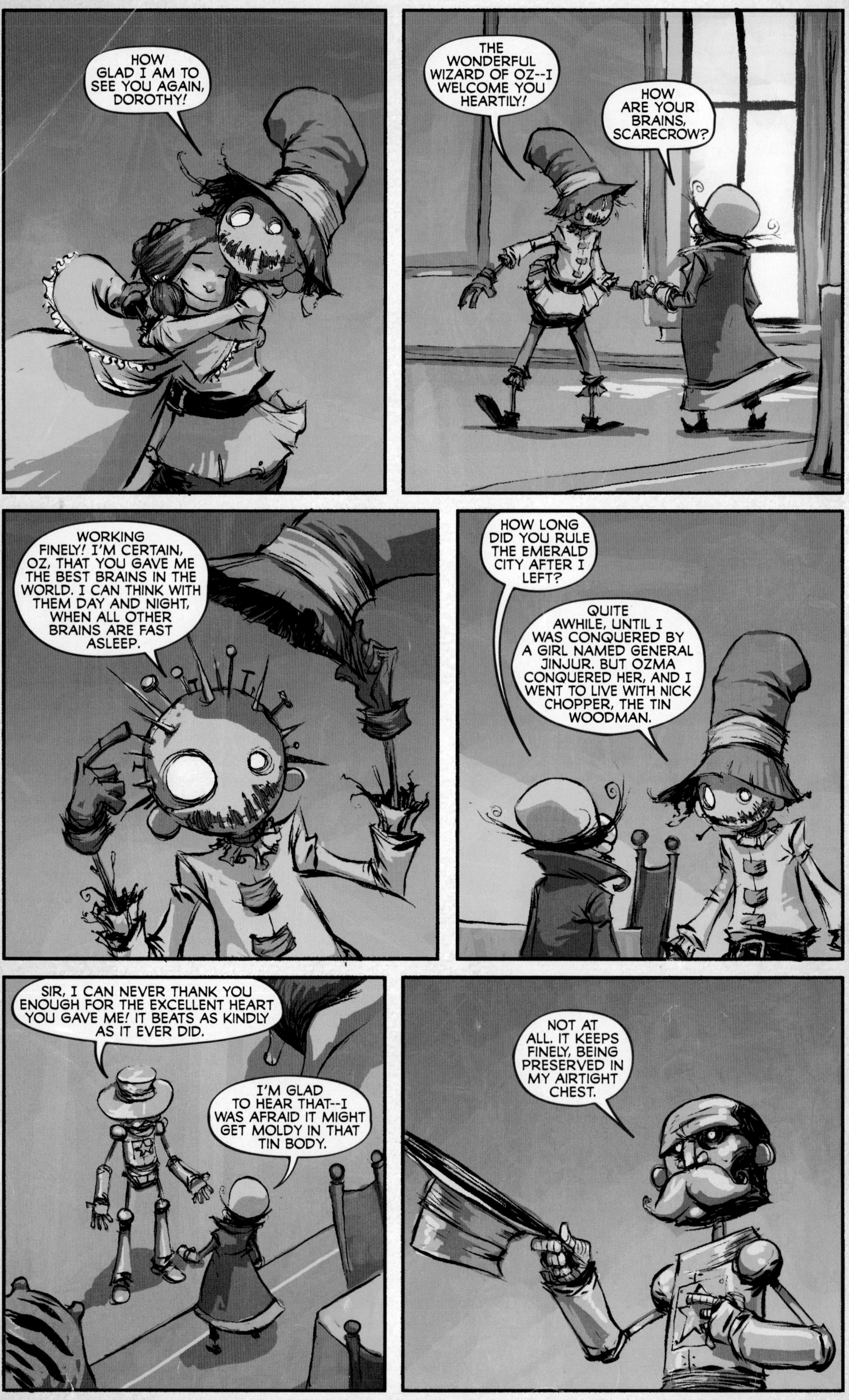
HOW GLAD I AM TO SEE YOU AGAIN, DOROTHY!
THE WONDERFUL WIZARD OF OZ--I WELCOME YOU HEARTILY!
HOW ARE YOUR BRAINS, SCARECROW?
WORKING FINELY! I'M CERTAIN, OZ, THAT YOU GAVE ME THE BEST BRAINS IN THE WORLD. I CAN THINK WITH THEM DAY AND NIGHT, WHEN ALL OTHER BRAINS ARE FAST ASLEEP.
HOW LONG DID YOU RULE THE EMERALD CITY AFTER I LEFT?
QUITE AWHILE, UNTIL I WAS CONQUERED BY A GIRL NAMED GENERAL JINJUR. BUT OZMA CONQUERED HER, AND I WENT TO LIVE WITH NICK CHOPPER, THE TIN WOODMAN.
SIR, I CAN NEVER THANK YOU ENOUGH FOR THE EXCELLENT HEART YOU GAVE ME! IT BEATS AS KINDLY AS IT EVER DID.
I'M GLAD TO HEAR THAT--I WAS AFRAID IT MIGHT GET MOLDY IN THAT TIN BODY.
NOT AT ALL. IT KEEPS FINELY, BEING PRESERVED IN MY AIRTIGHT CHEST.

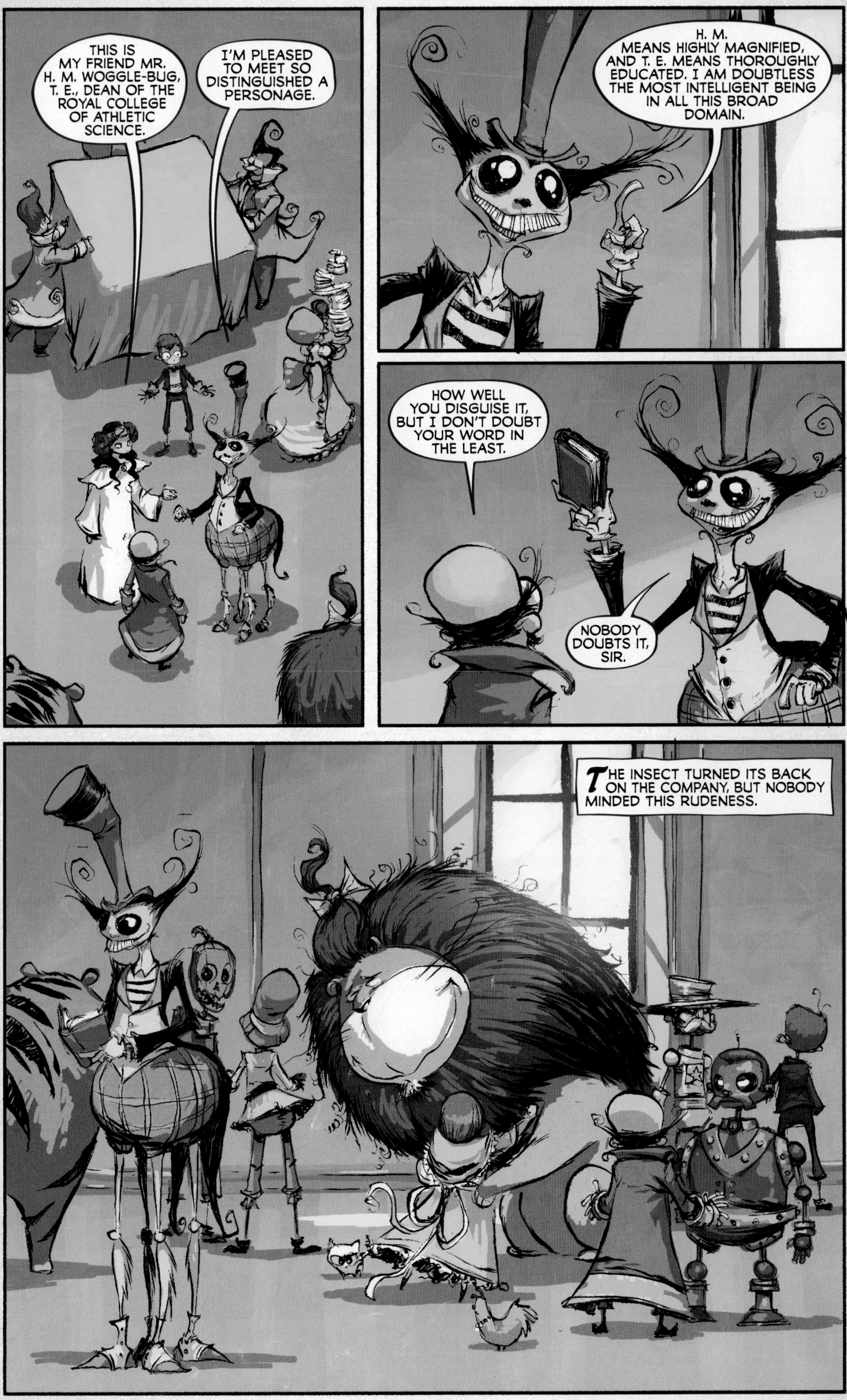
THIS IS MY FRIEND MR. H. M. WOGGLE-BUG, T. E., DEAN OF THE ROYAL COLLEGE OF ATHLETIC SCIENCE.
I'M PLEASED TO MEET SO DISTINGUISHED A PERSONAGE.
H. M. MEANS HIGHLY MAGNIFIED, AND T. E. MEANS THOROUGHLY EDUCATED. I AM DOUBTLESS THE MOST INTELLIGENT BEING IN ALL THIS BROAD DOMAIN.
HOW WELL YOU DISGUISE IT, BUT I DON'T DOUBT YOUR WORD IN THE LEAST.
NOBODY DOUBTS IT, SIR.
THE INSECT TURNED ITS BACK ON THE COMPANY, BUT NOBODY MINDED THIS RUDENESS.

OH, BILLINA--HOW FAT AND SLEEK YOU'VE GROWN!

WHY SHOULDN'T I? I LIVE ON THE FAT OF THE LAND.

REEEOWW!

HOW HORRID OF YOU, EUREKA!

IS THAT THE WAY TO TREAT MY FRIENDS?

YOU HAVE STRANGE FRIENDS, SEEMS TO ME.

SEEMS TO ME THE SAME WAY IF THAT BEASTLY CAT IS ONE OF THEM.

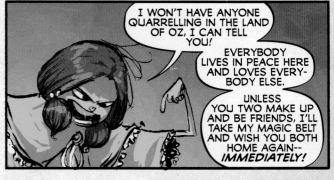

I WON'T HAVE ANYONE QUARRELLING IN THE LAND OF OZ, I CAN TELL YOU!

EVERYBODY LIVES IN PEACE HERE AND LOVES EVERY-BODY ELSE.

UNLESS YOU TWO MAKE UP AND BE FRIENDS, I'LL TAKE MY MAGIC BELT AND WISH YOU BOTH HOME AGAIN-- *IMMEDIATELY!*

I PROMISE TO BE GOOD.

I PROMISE TOO.

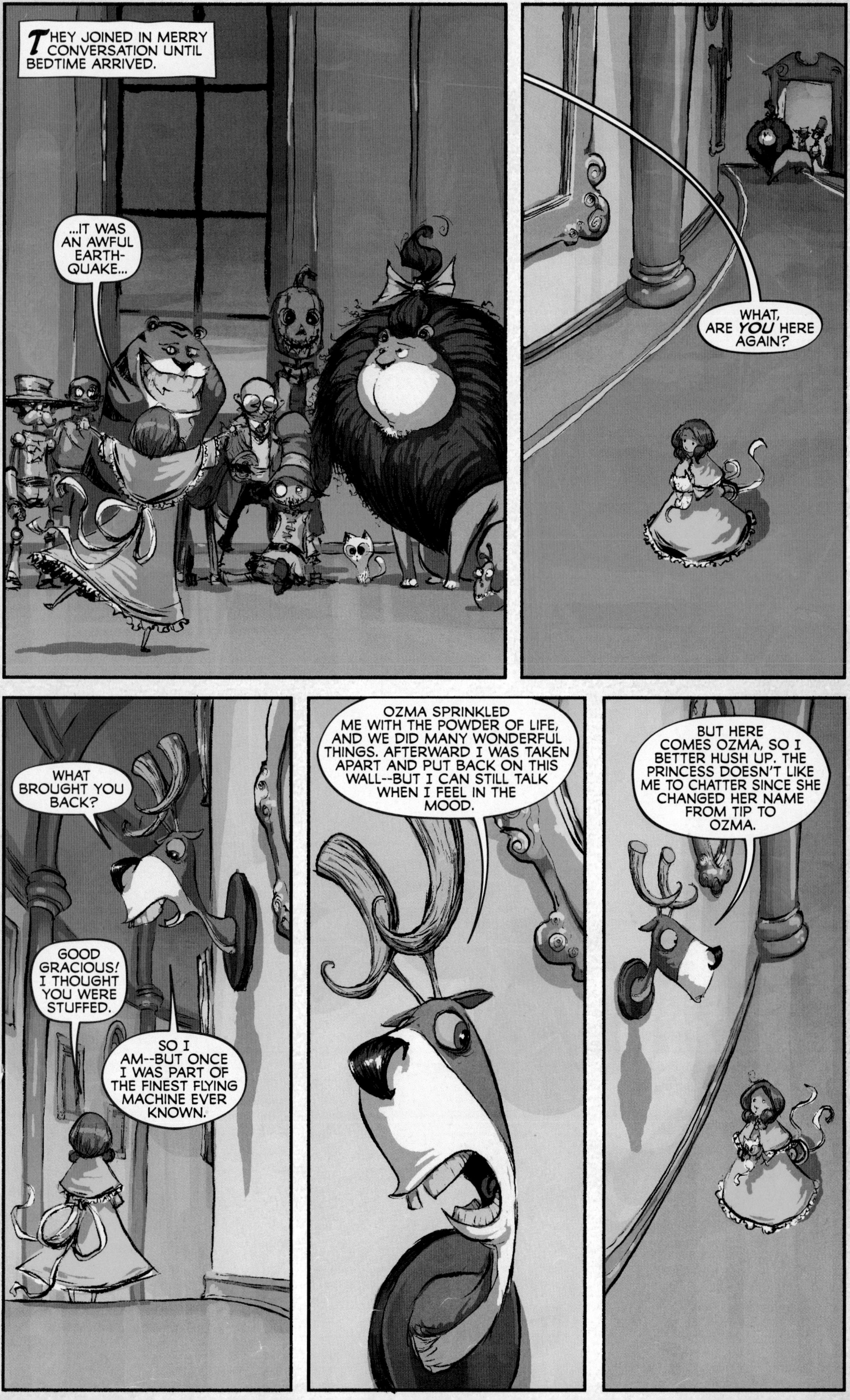
THEY JOINED IN MERRY CONVERSATION UNTIL BEDTIME ARRIVED.
...IT WAS AN AWFUL EARTH-QUAKE...
WHAT, ARE *YOU* HERE AGAIN?
WHAT BROUGHT YOU BACK?
GOOD GRACIOUS! I THOUGHT YOU WERE STUFFED.
SO I AM--BUT ONCE I WAS PART OF THE FINEST FLYING MACHINE EVER KNOWN.
OZMA SPRINKLED ME WITH THE POWDER OF LIFE, AND WE DID MANY WONDERFUL THINGS. AFTERWARD I WAS TAKEN APART AND PUT BACK ON THIS WALL--BUT I CAN STILL TALK WHEN I FEEL IN THE MOOD.
BUT HERE COMES OZMA, SO I BETTER HUSH UP. THE PRINCESS DOESN'T LIKE ME TO CHATTER SINCE SHE CHANGED HER NAME FROM TIP TO OZMA.

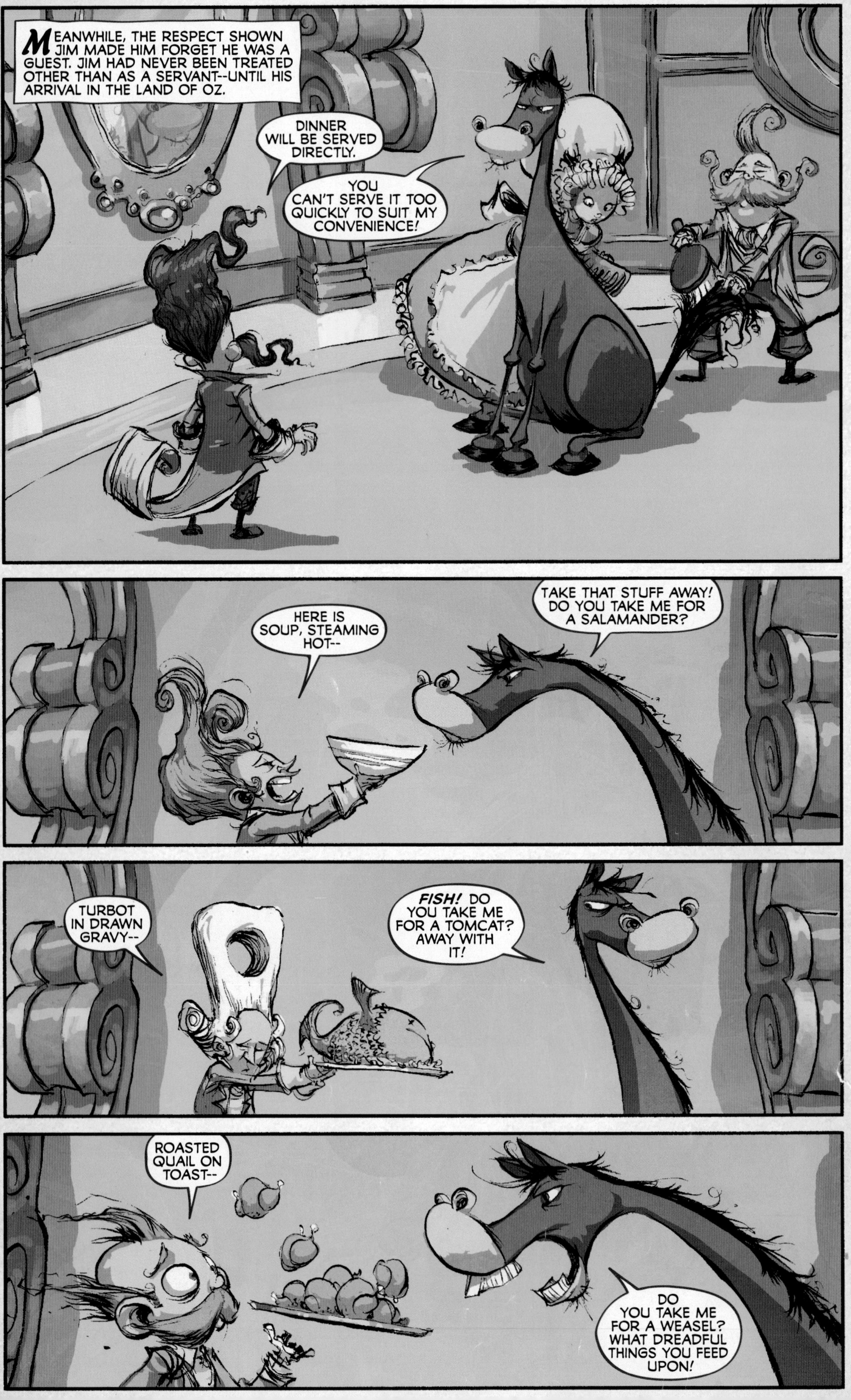
MEANWHILE, THE RESPECT SHOWN JIM MADE HIM FORGET HE WAS A GUEST. JIM HAD NEVER BEEN TREATED OTHER THAN AS A SERVANT--UNTIL HIS ARRIVAL IN THE LAND OF OZ.
DINNER WILL BE SERVED DIRECTLY.
YOU CAN'T SERVE IT TOO QUICKLY TO SUIT MY CONVENIENCE!
HERE IS SOUP, STEAMING HOT--
TAKE THAT STUFF AWAY! DO YOU TAKE ME FOR A SALAMANDER?
TURBOT IN DRAWN GRAVY--
FISH! DO YOU TAKE ME FOR A TOMCAT? AWAY WITH IT!
ROASTED QUAIL ON TOAST--
DO YOU TAKE ME FOR A WEASEL? WHAT DREADFUL THINGS YOU FEED UPON!

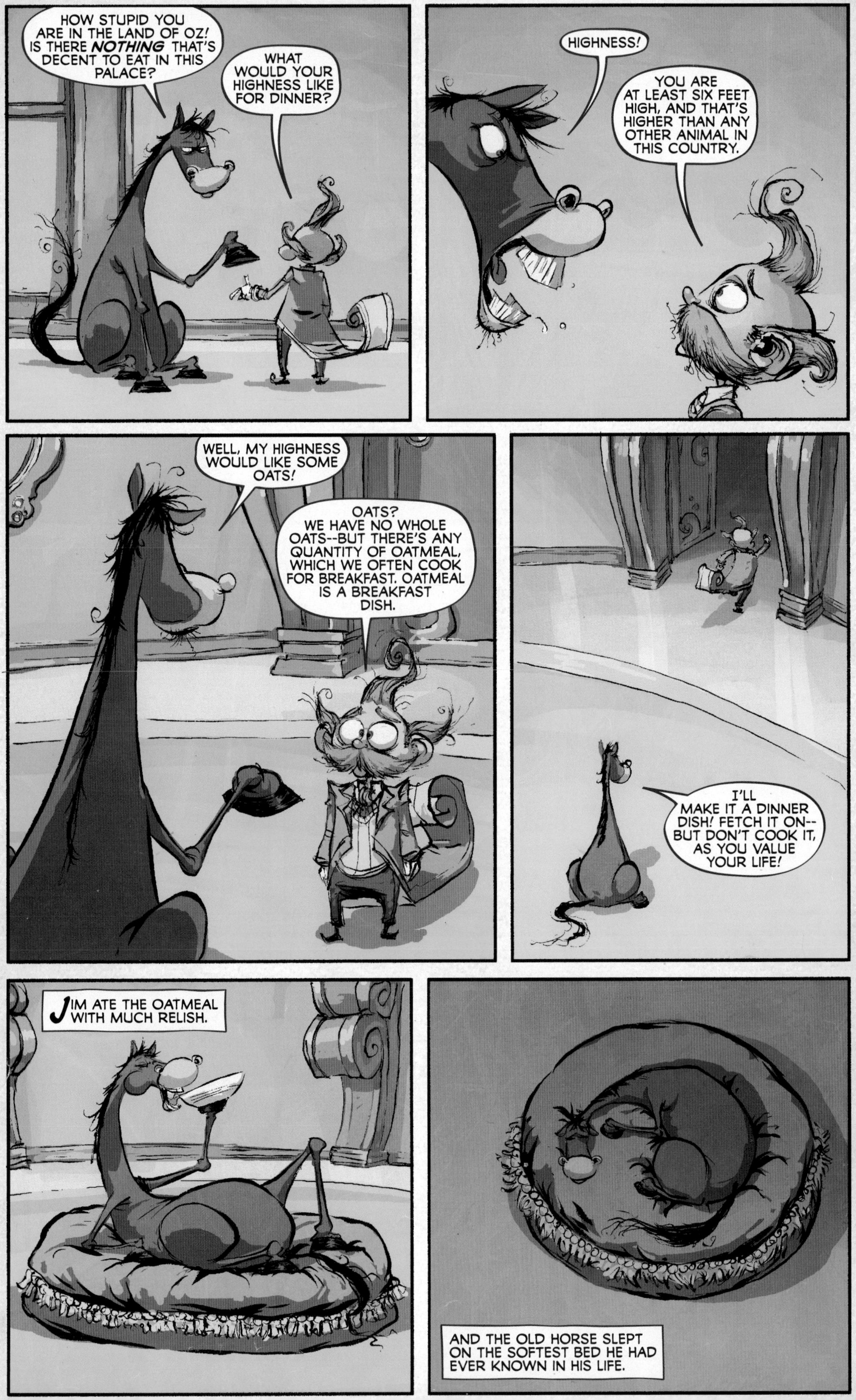
HOW STUPID YOU ARE IN THE LAND OF OZ! IS THERE *NOTHING* THAT'S DECENT TO EAT IN THIS PALACE?
WHAT WOULD YOUR HIGHNESS LIKE FOR DINNER?
HIGHNESS!
YOU ARE AT LEAST SIX FEET HIGH, AND THAT'S HIGHER THAN ANY OTHER ANIMAL IN THIS COUNTRY.
WELL, MY HIGHNESS WOULD LIKE SOME OATS!
OATS? WE HAVE NO WHOLE OATS--BUT THERE'S ANY QUANTITY OF OATMEAL, WHICH WE OFTEN COOK FOR BREAKFAST. OATMEAL IS A BREAKFAST DISH.
I'LL MAKE IT A DINNER DISH! FETCH IT ON--BUT DON'T COOK IT, AS YOU VALUE YOUR LIFE!
JIM ATE THE OATMEAL WITH MUCH RELISH.
AND THE OLD HORSE SLEPT ON THE SOFTEST BED HE HAD EVER KNOWN IN HIS LIFE.

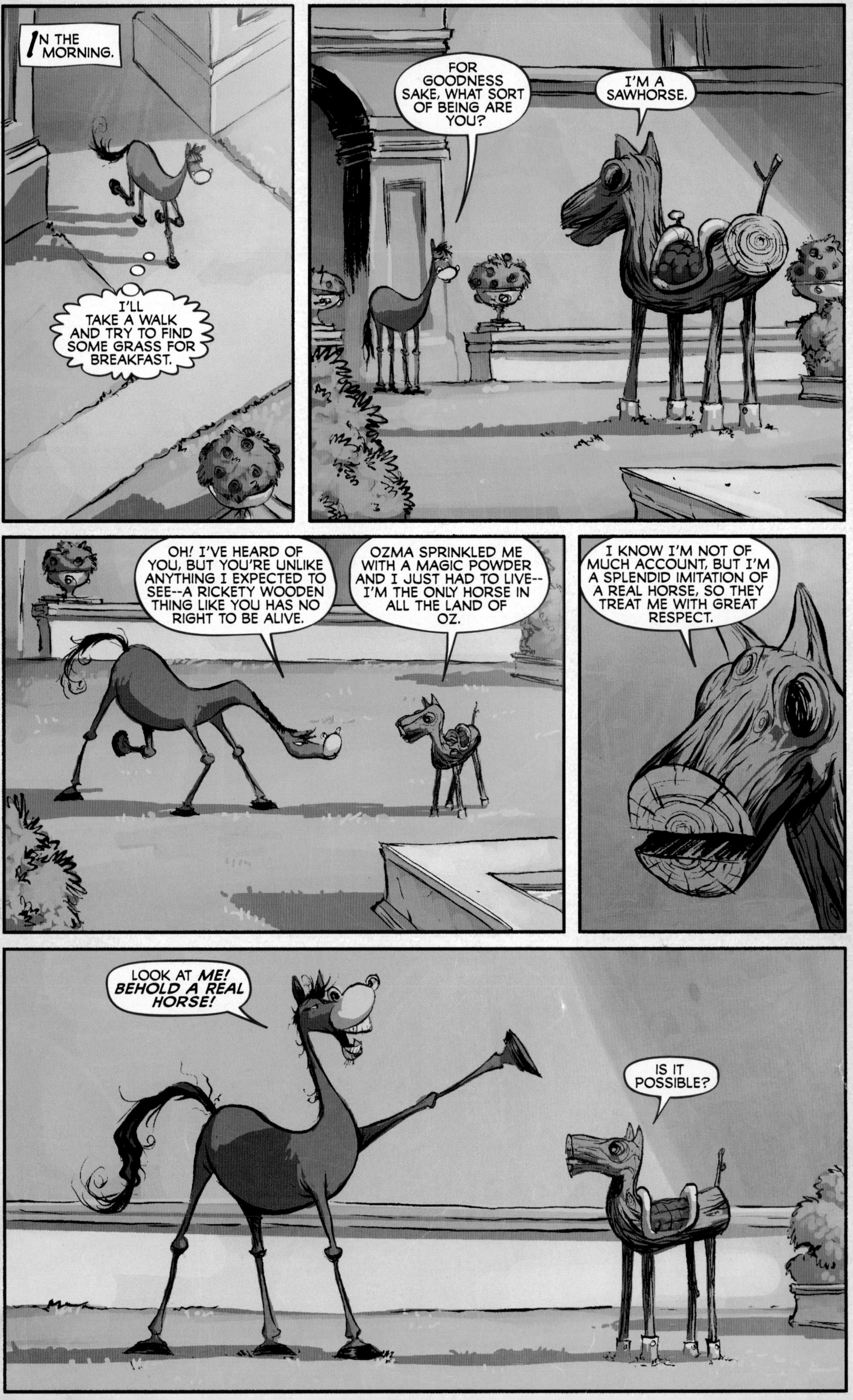
IN THE MORNING.
I'LL TAKE A WALK AND TRY TO FIND SOME GRASS FOR BREAKFAST.
FOR GOODNESS SAKE, WHAT SORT OF BEING ARE YOU?
I'M A SAWHORSE.
OH! I'VE HEARD OF YOU, BUT YOU'RE UNLIKE ANYTHING I EXPECTED TO SEE--A RICKETY WOODEN THING LIKE YOU HAS NO RIGHT TO BE ALIVE.
OZMA SPRINKLED ME WITH A MAGIC POWDER AND I JUST HAD TO LIVE--I'M THE ONLY HORSE IN ALL THE LAND OF OZ.
I KNOW I'M NOT OF MUCH ACCOUNT, BUT I'M A SPLENDID IMITATION OF A REAL HORSE, SO THEY TREAT ME WITH GREAT RESPECT.
LOOK AT ME! BEHOLD A REAL HORSE!
IS IT POSSIBLE?

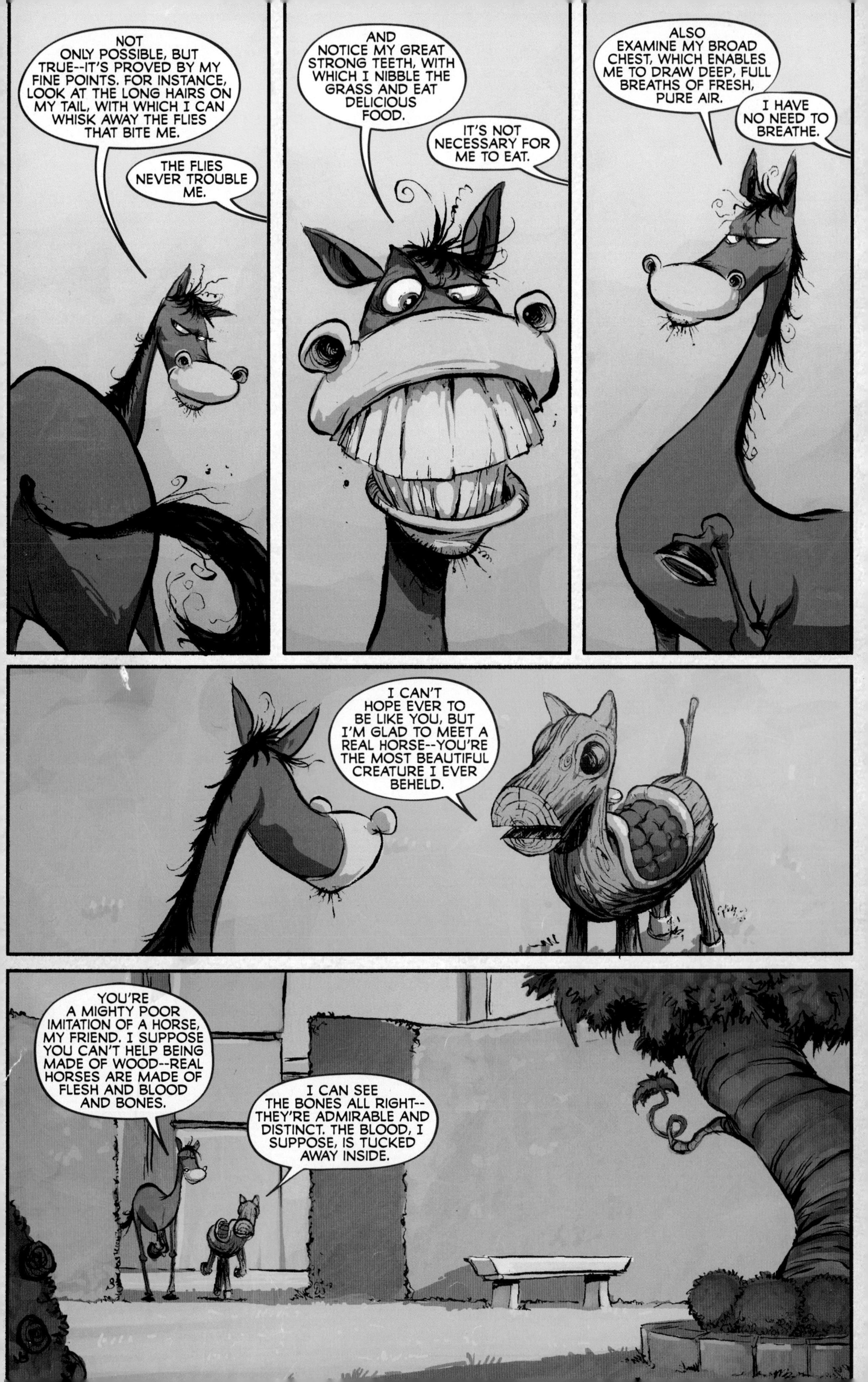
NOT ONLY POSSIBLE, BUT TRUE--IT'S PROVED BY MY FINE POINTS. FOR INSTANCE, LOOK AT THE LONG HAIRS ON MY TAIL, WITH WHICH I CAN WHISK AWAY THE FLIES THAT BITE ME.
THE FLIES NEVER TROUBLE ME.
AND NOTICE MY GREAT STRONG TEETH, WITH WHICH I NIBBLE THE GRASS AND EAT DELICIOUS FOOD.
IT'S NOT NECESSARY FOR ME TO EAT.
ALSO EXAMINE MY BROAD CHEST, WHICH ENABLES ME TO DRAW DEEP, FULL BREATHS OF FRESH, PURE AIR.
I HAVE NO NEED TO BREATHE.
I CAN'T HOPE EVER TO BE LIKE YOU, BUT I'M GLAD TO MEET A REAL HORSE--YOU'RE THE MOST BEAUTIFUL CREATURE I EVER BEHELD.
YOU'RE A MIGHTY POOR IMITATION OF A HORSE, MY FRIEND. I SUPPOSE YOU CAN'T HELP BEING MADE OF WOOD--REAL HORSES ARE MADE OF FLESH AND BLOOD AND BONES.
I CAN SEE THE BONES ALL RIGHT--THEY'RE ADMIRABLE AND DISTINCT. THE BLOOD, I SUPPOSE, IS TUCKED AWAY INSIDE.

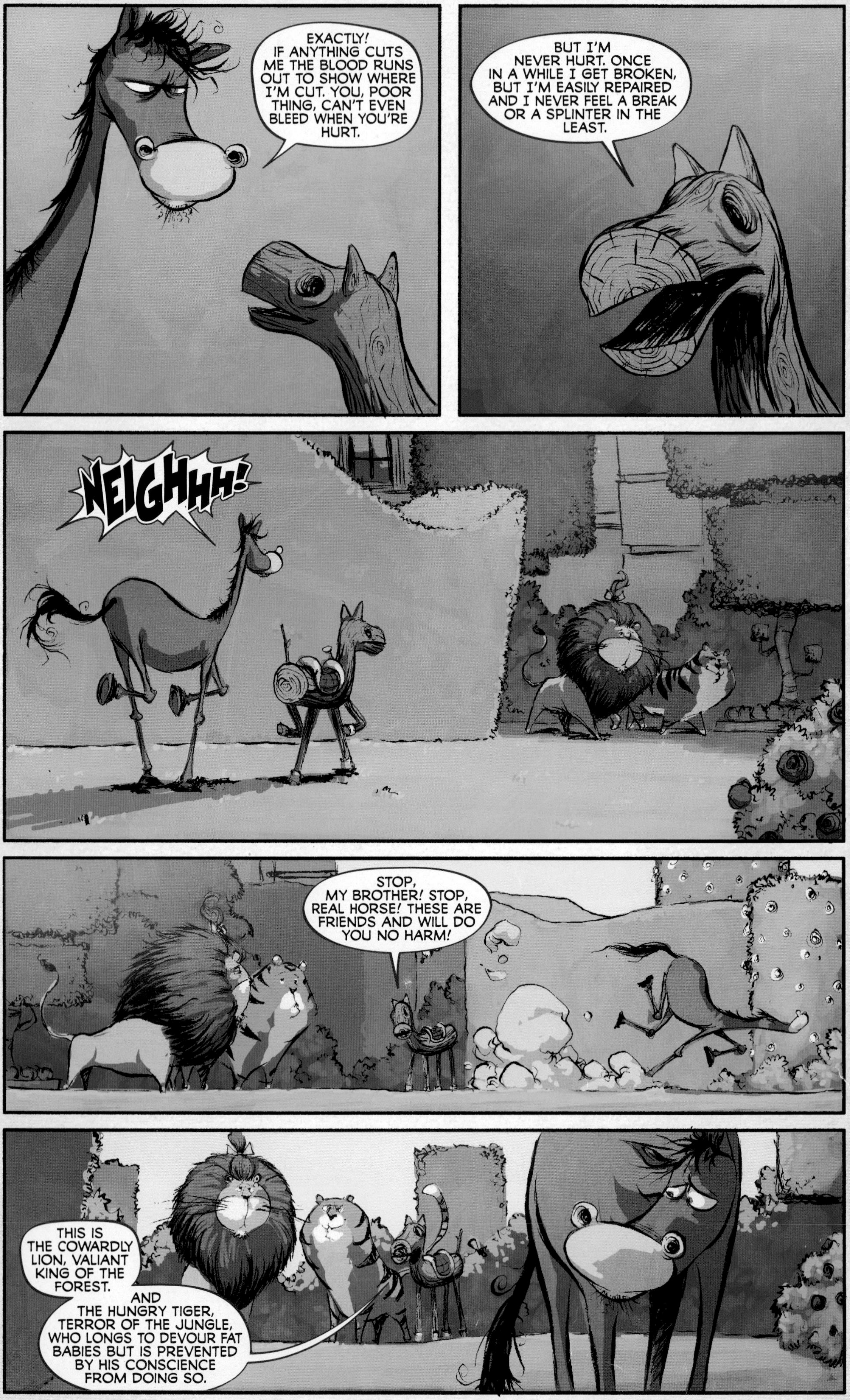
EXACTLY! IF ANYTHING CUTS ME THE BLOOD RUNS OUT TO SHOW WHERE I'M CUT. YOU, POOR THING, CAN'T EVEN BLEED WHEN YOU'RE HURT.
BUT I'M NEVER HURT. ONCE IN A WHILE I GET BROKEN, BUT I'M EASILY REPAIRED AND I NEVER FEEL A BREAK OR A SPLINTER IN THE LEAST.
NEIGHHH!
STOP, MY BROTHER! STOP, REAL HORSE! THESE ARE FRIENDS AND WILL DO YOU NO HARM!
THIS IS THE COWARDLY LION, VALIANT KING OF THE FOREST.
AND THE HUNGRY TIGER, TERROR OF THE JUNGLE, WHO LONGS TO DEVOUR FAT BABIES BUT IS PREVENTED BY HIS CONSCIENCE FROM DOING SO.

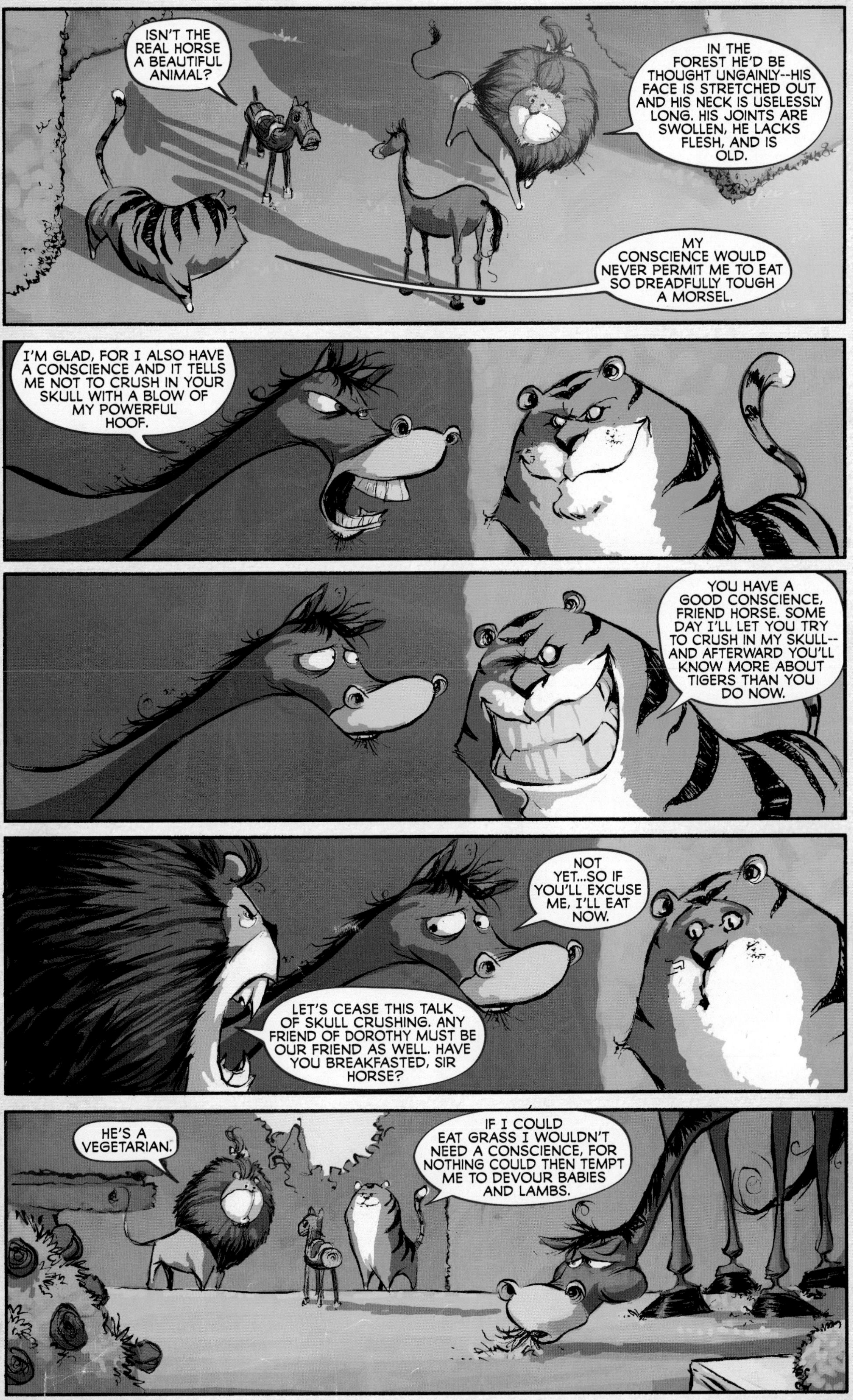
ISN'T THE REAL HORSE A BEAUTIFUL ANIMAL?
IN THE FOREST HE'D BE THOUGHT UNGAINLY--HIS FACE IS STRETCHED OUT AND HIS NECK IS USELESSLY LONG. HIS JOINTS ARE SWOLLEN, HE LACKS FLESH, AND IS OLD.
MY CONSCIENCE WOULD NEVER PERMIT ME TO EAT SO DREADFULLY TOUGH A MORSEL.
I'M GLAD, FOR I ALSO HAVE A CONSCIENCE AND IT TELLS ME NOT TO CRUSH IN YOUR SKULL WITH A BLOW OF MY POWERFUL HOOF.
YOU HAVE A GOOD CONSCIENCE, FRIEND HORSE. SOME DAY I'LL LET YOU TRY TO CRUSH IN MY SKULL-- AND AFTERWARD YOU'LL KNOW MORE ABOUT TIGERS THAN YOU DO NOW.
LET'S CEASE THIS TALK OF SKULL CRUSHING. ANY FRIEND OF DOROTHY MUST BE OUR FRIEND AS WELL. HAVE YOU BREAKFASTED, SIR HORSE?
NOT YET...SO IF YOU'LL EXCUSE ME, I'LL EAT NOW.
HE'S A VEGETARIAN.
IF I COULD EAT GRASS I WOULDN'T NEED A CONSCIENCE, FOR NOTHING COULD THEN TEMPT ME TO DEVOUR BABIES AND LAMBS.

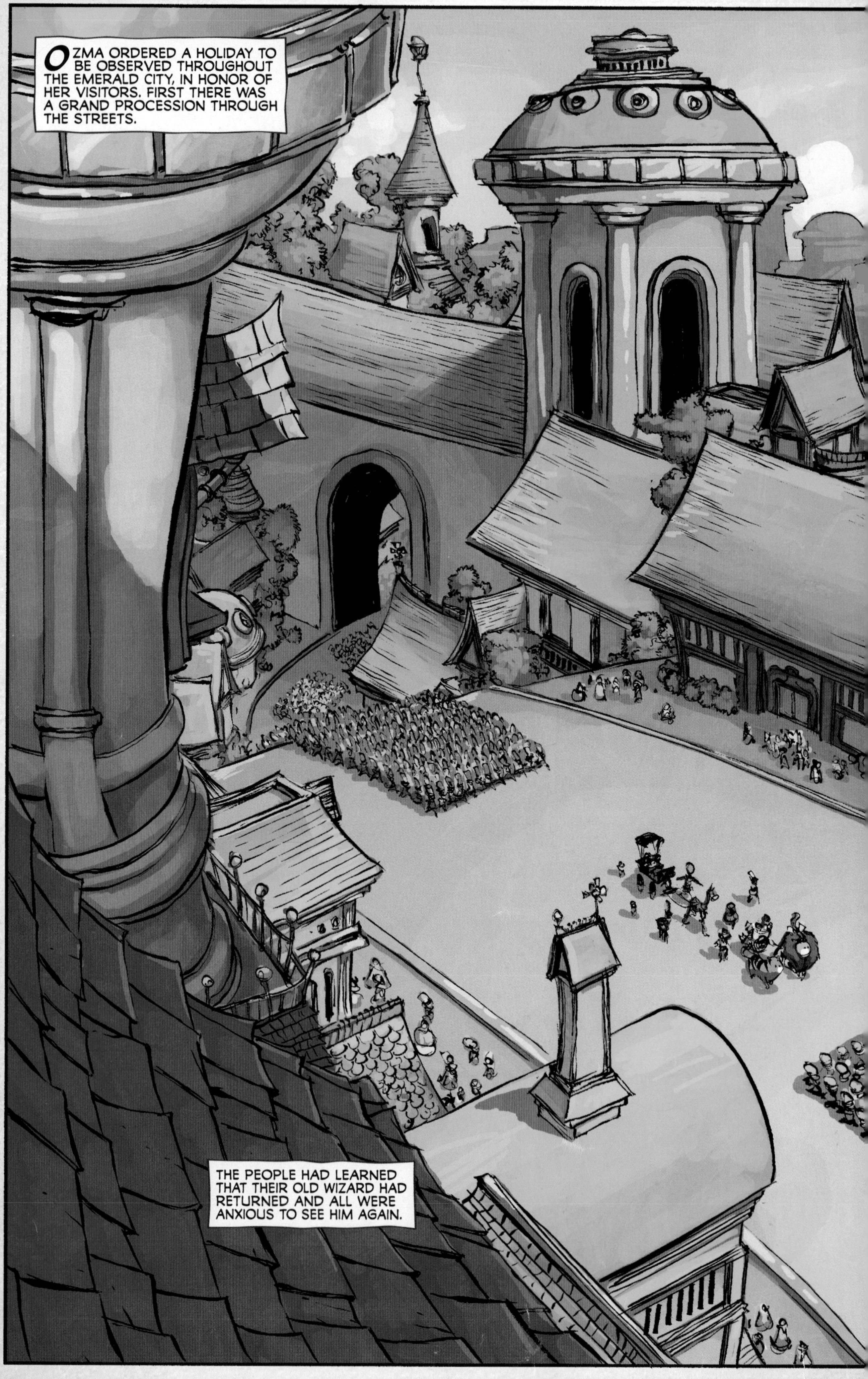
OZMA ORDERED A HOLIDAY TO BE OBSERVED THROUGHOUT THE EMERALD CITY, IN HONOR OF HER VISITORS. FIRST THERE WAS A GRAND PROCESSION THROUGH THE STREETS.
THE PEOPLE HAD LEARNED THAT THEIR OLD WIZARD HAD RETURNED AND ALL WERE ANXIOUS TO SEE HIM AGAIN.

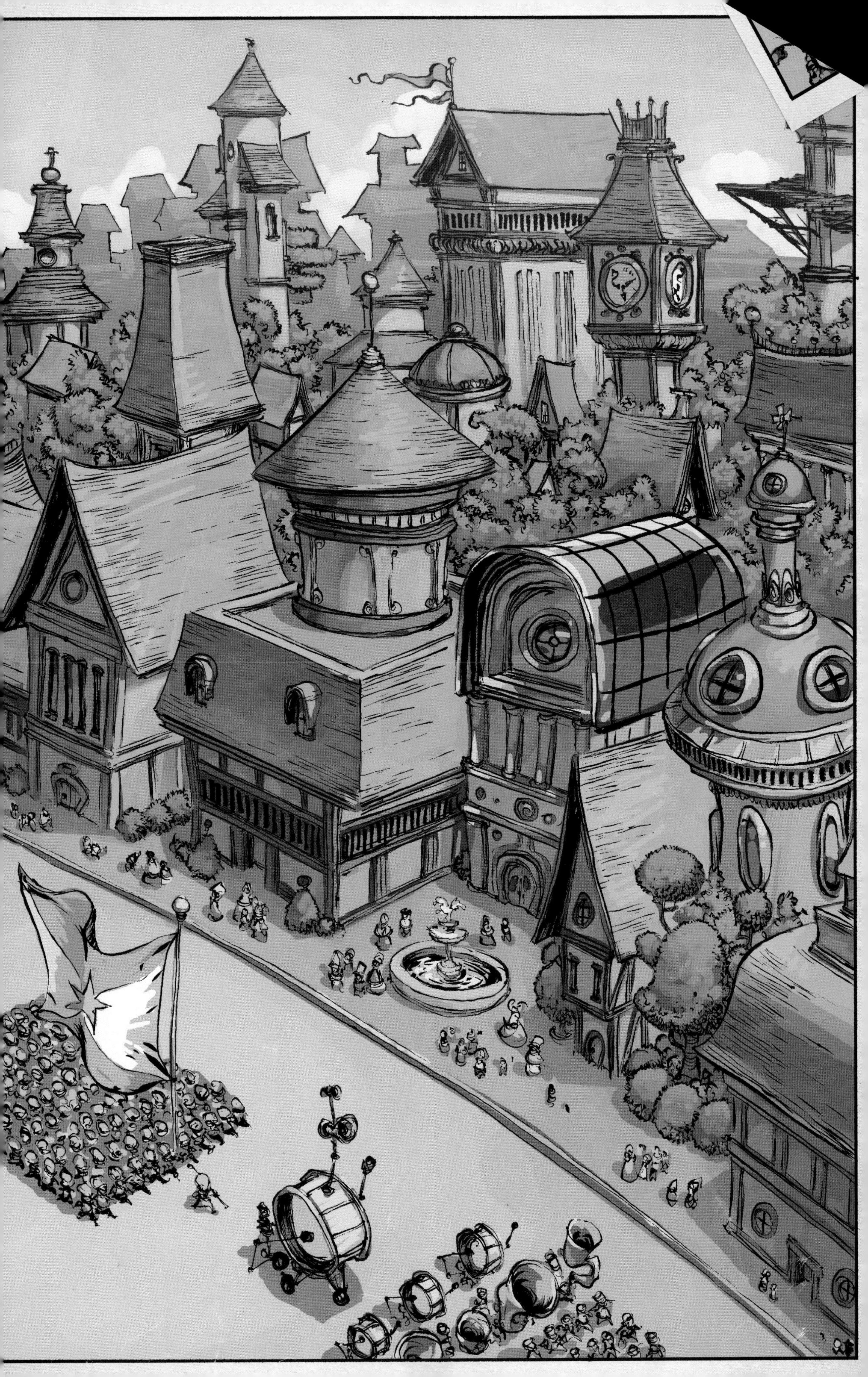

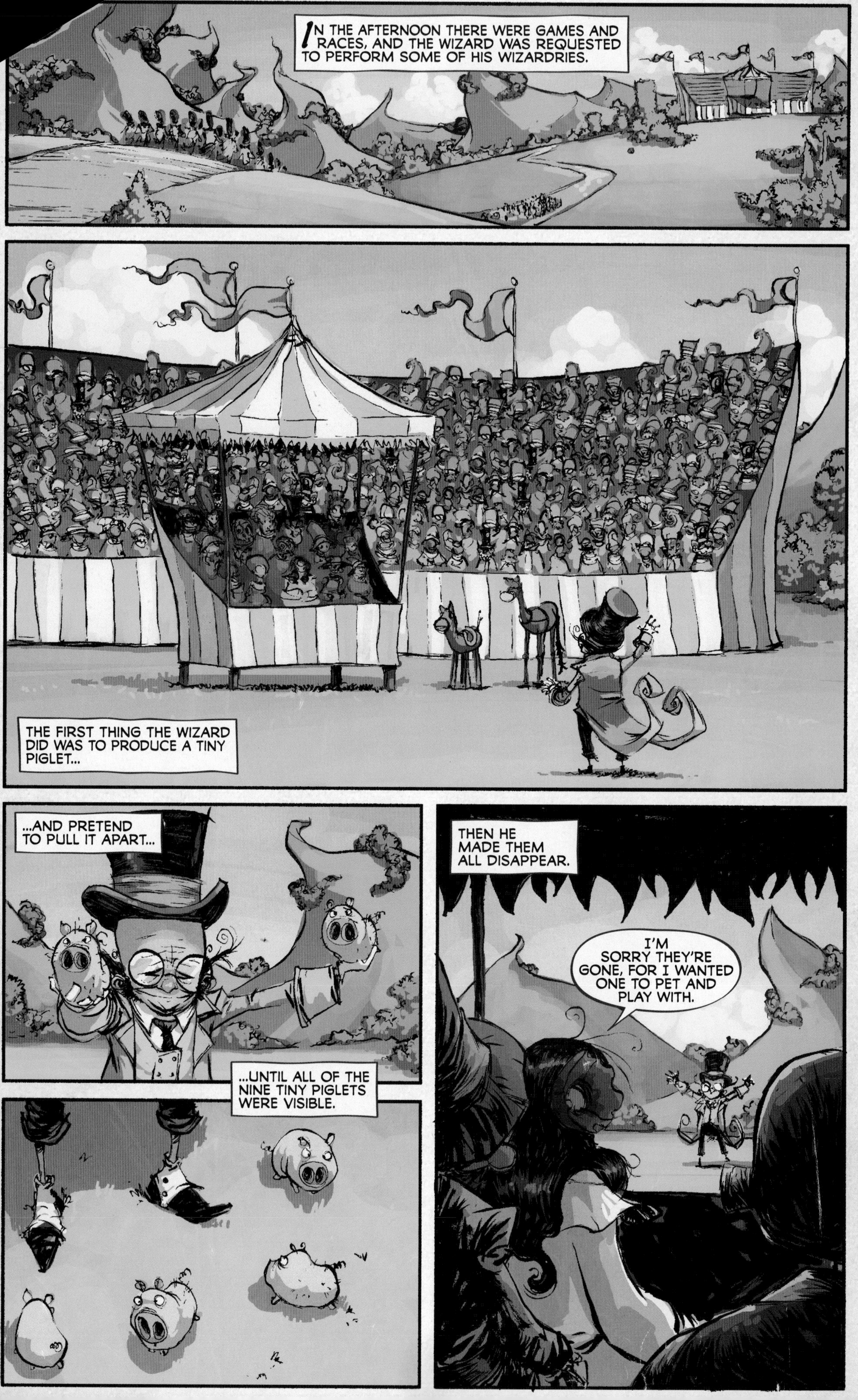
IN THE AFTERNOON THERE WERE GAMES AND RACES, AND THE WIZARD WAS REQUESTED TO PERFORM SOME OF HIS WIZARDRIES.
THE FIRST THING THE WIZARD DID WAS TO PRODUCE A TINY PIGLET...
...AND PRETEND TO PULL IT APART...
...UNTIL ALL OF THE NINE TINY PIGLETS WERE VISIBLE.
THEN HE MADE THEM ALL DISAPPEAR.
I'M SORRY THEY'RE GONE, FOR I WANTED ONE TO PET AND PLAY WITH.

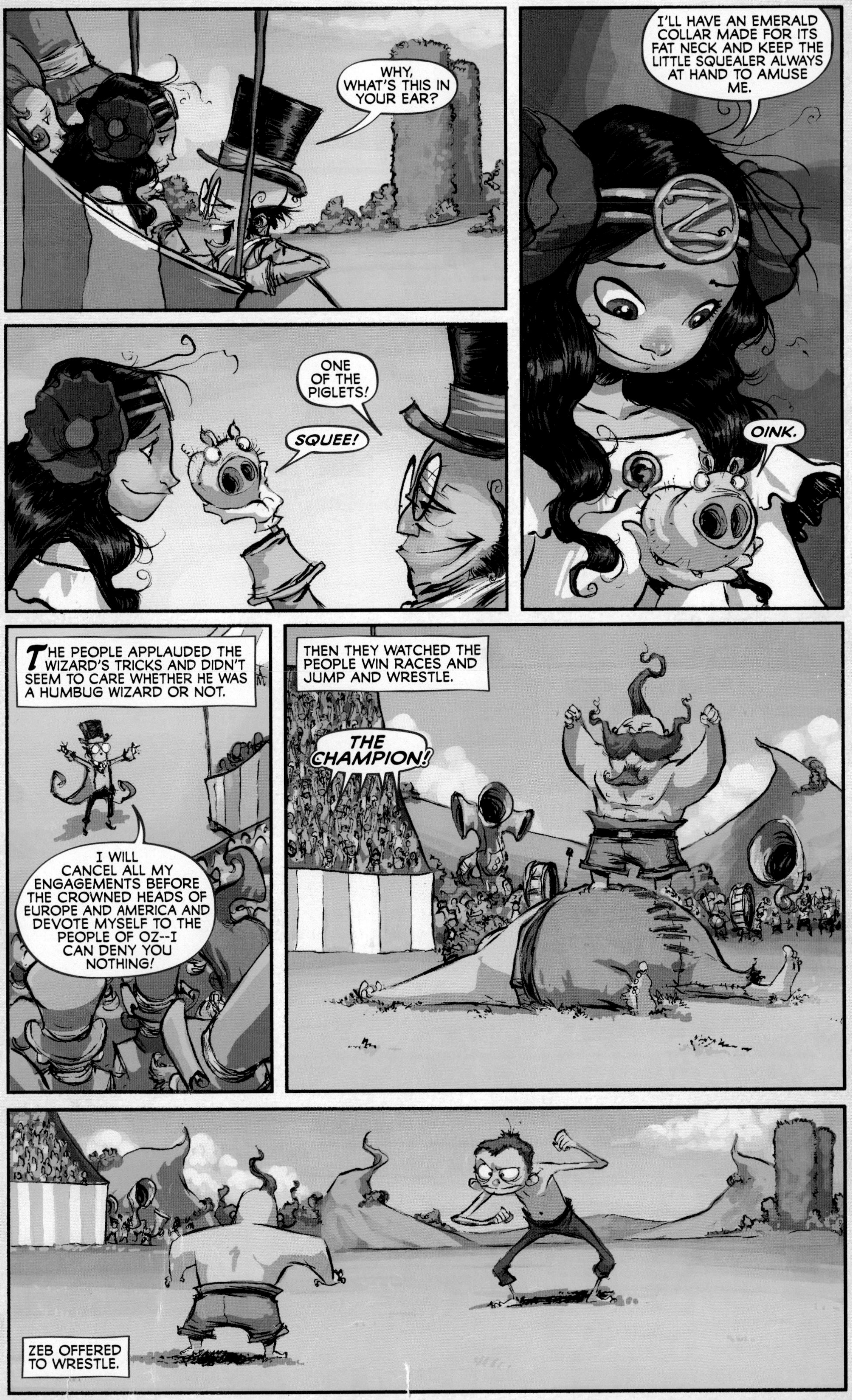
WHY, WHAT'S THIS IN YOUR EAR?
I'LL HAVE AN EMERALD COLLAR MADE FOR ITS FAT NECK AND KEEP THE LITTLE SQUEALER ALWAYS AT HAND TO AMUSE ME.
ONE OF THE PIGLETS!
SQUEE!
OINK.
THE PEOPLE APPLAUDED THE WIZARD'S TRICKS AND DIDN'T SEEM TO CARE WHETHER HE WAS A HUMBUG WIZARD OR NOT.
I WILL CANCEL ALL MY ENGAGEMENTS BEFORE THE CROWNED HEADS OF EUROPE AND AMERICA AND DEVOTE MYSELF TO THE PEOPLE OF OZ--I CAN DENY YOU NOTHING!
THEN THEY WATCHED THE PEOPLE WIN RACES AND JUMP AND WRESTLE.
THE CHAMPION!
ZEB OFFERED TO WRESTLE.

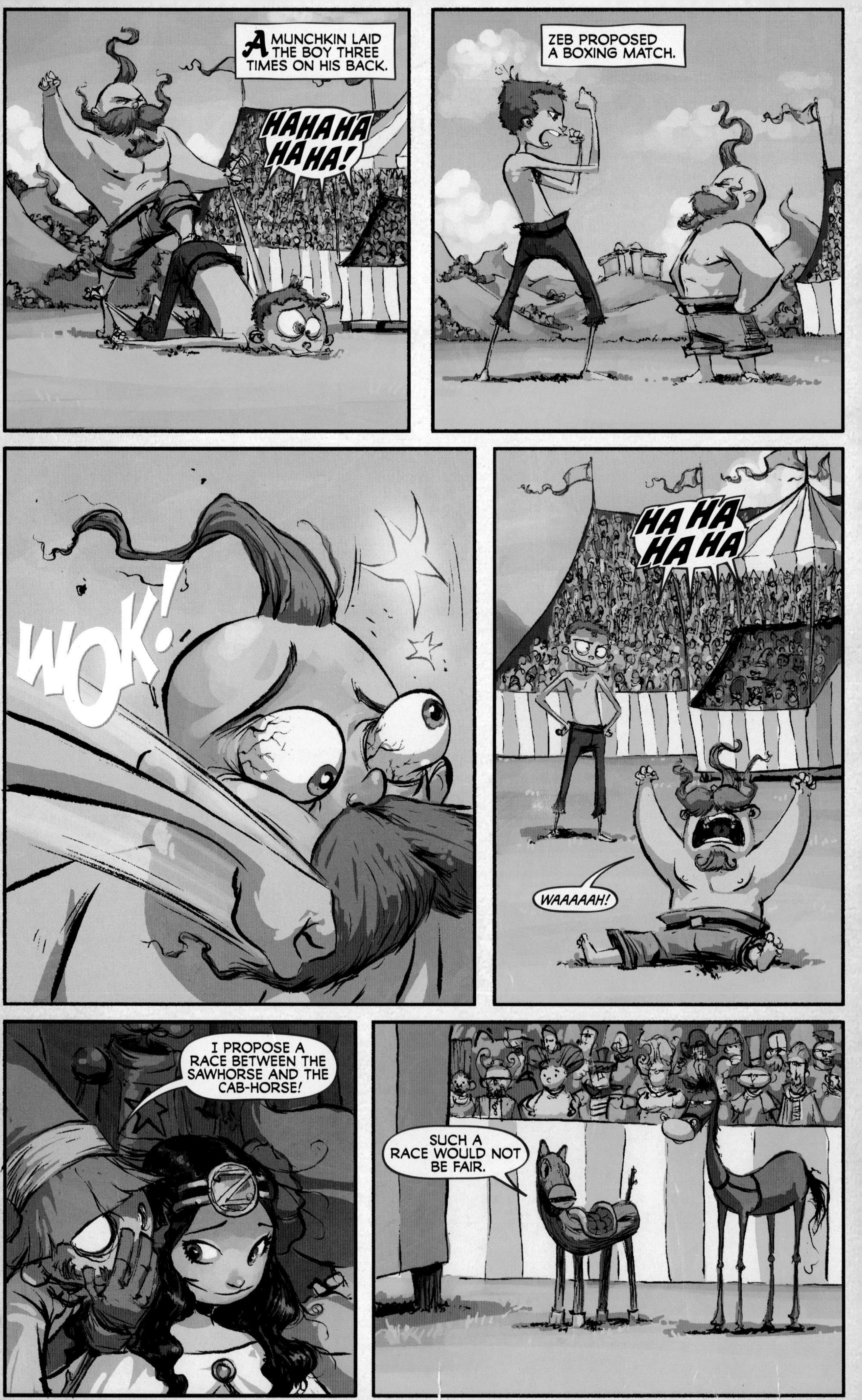
A MUNCHKIN LAID THE BOY THREE TIMES ON HIS BACK.
HAHAHA HAHA!
ZEB PROPOSED A BOXING MATCH.
WOK!
HA HA HA HA
WAAAAAH!
I PROPOSE A RACE BETWEEN THE SAWHORSE AND THE CAB-HORSE!
SUCH A RACE WOULD NOT BE FAIR.

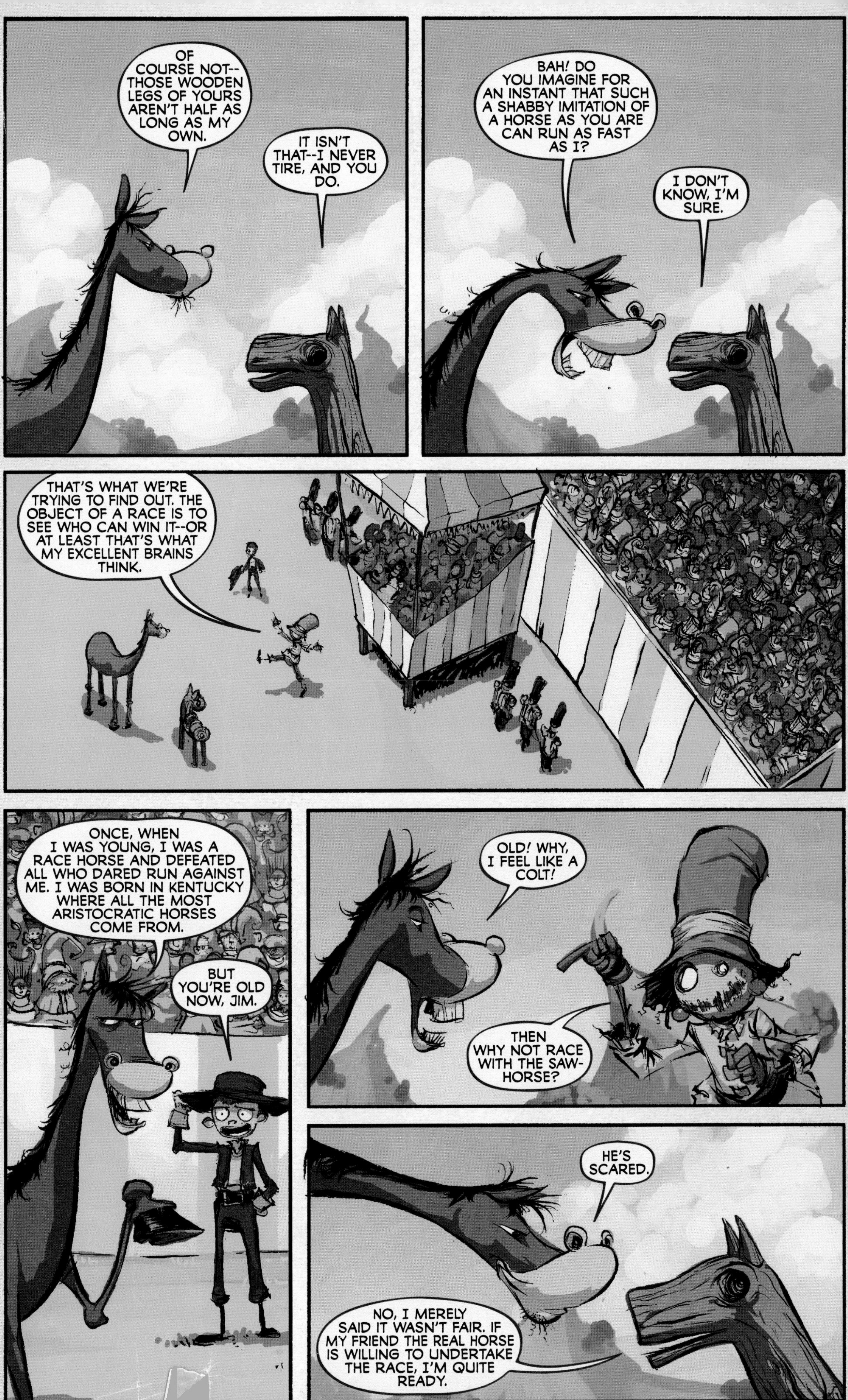
OF COURSE NOT--THOSE WOODEN LEGS OF YOURS AREN'T HALF AS LONG AS MY OWN.
IT ISN'T THAT--I NEVER TIRE, AND YOU DO.
BAH! DO YOU IMAGINE FOR AN INSTANT THAT SUCH A SHABBY IMITATION OF A HORSE AS YOU ARE CAN RUN AS FAST AS I?
I DON'T KNOW, I'M SURE.
THAT'S WHAT WE'RE TRYING TO FIND OUT. THE OBJECT OF A RACE IS TO SEE WHO CAN WIN IT--OR AT LEAST THAT'S WHAT MY EXCELLENT BRAINS THINK.
ONCE, WHEN I WAS YOUNG, I WAS A RACE HORSE AND DEFEATED ALL WHO DARED RUN AGAINST ME. I WAS BORN IN KENTUCKY WHERE ALL THE MOST ARISTOCRATIC HORSES COME FROM.
BUT YOU'RE OLD NOW, JIM.
OLD! WHY, I FEEL LIKE A COLT!
THEN WHY NOT RACE WITH THE SAW-HORSE?
HE'S SCARED.
NO, I MERELY SAID IT WASN'T FAIR. IF MY FRIEND THE REAL HORSE IS WILLING TO UNDERTAKE THE RACE, I'M QUITE READY.

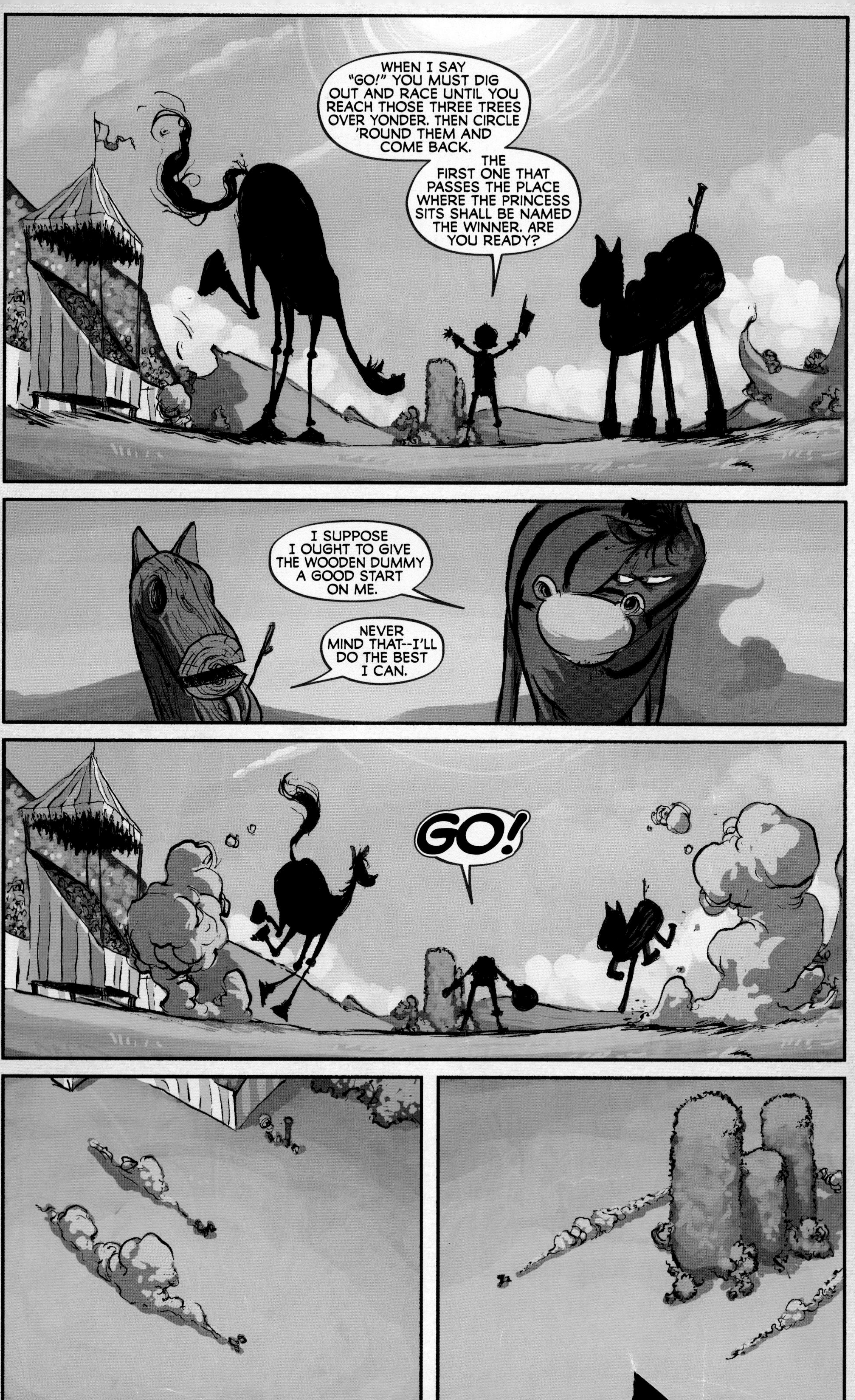
WHEN I SAY "GO!" YOU MUST DIG OUT AND RACE UNTIL YOU REACH THOSE THREE TREES OVER YONDER. THEN CIRCLE 'ROUND THEM AND COME BACK.
THE FIRST ONE THAT PASSES THE PLACE WHERE THE PRINCESS SITS SHALL BE NAMED THE WINNER. ARE YOU READY?
I SUPPOSE I OUGHT TO GIVE THE WOODEN DUMMY A GOOD START ON ME.
NEVER MIND THAT--I'LL DO THE BEST I CAN.
GO!

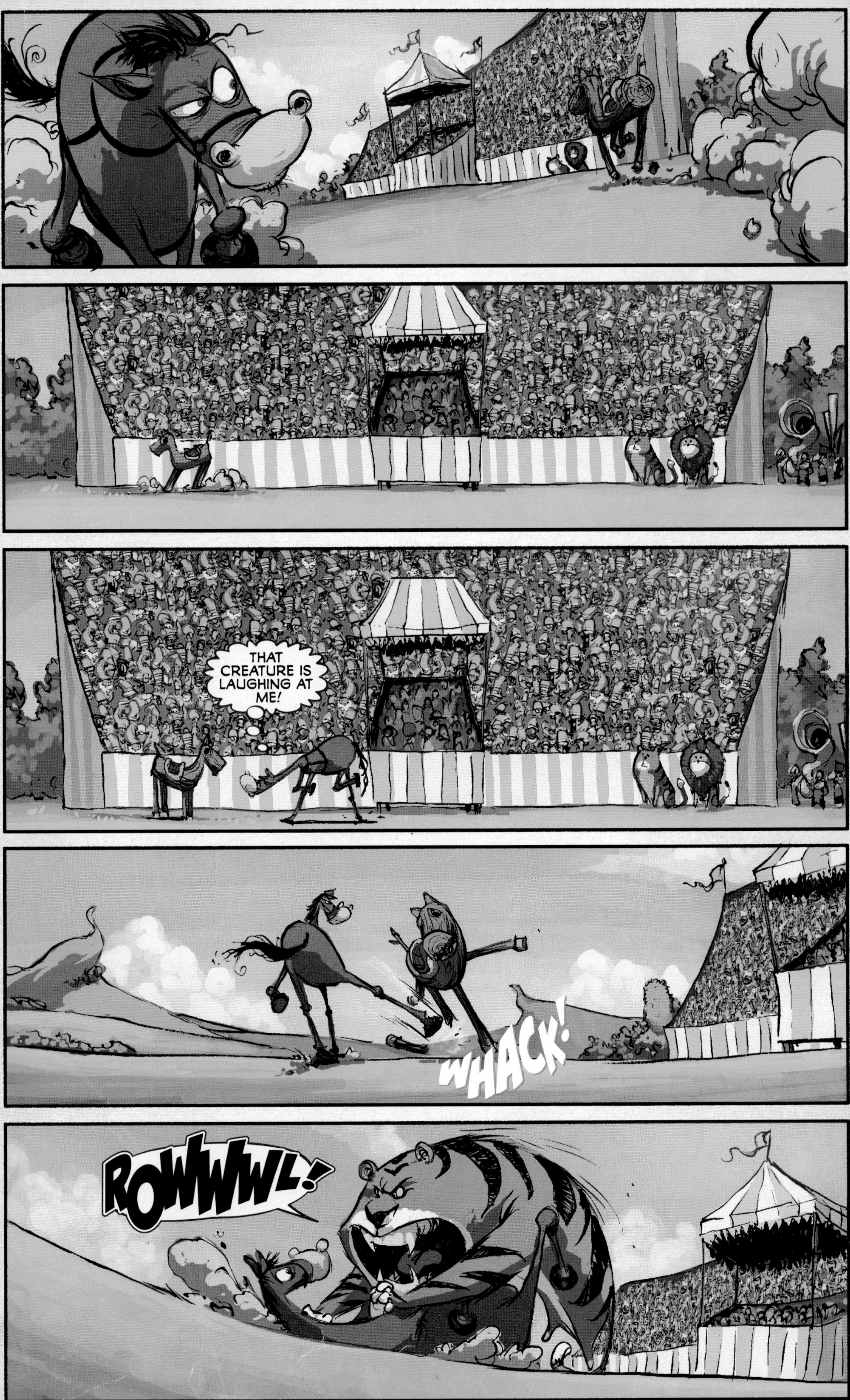
THAT CREATURE IS LAUGHING AT ME!
WHACK!
ROWWWL!

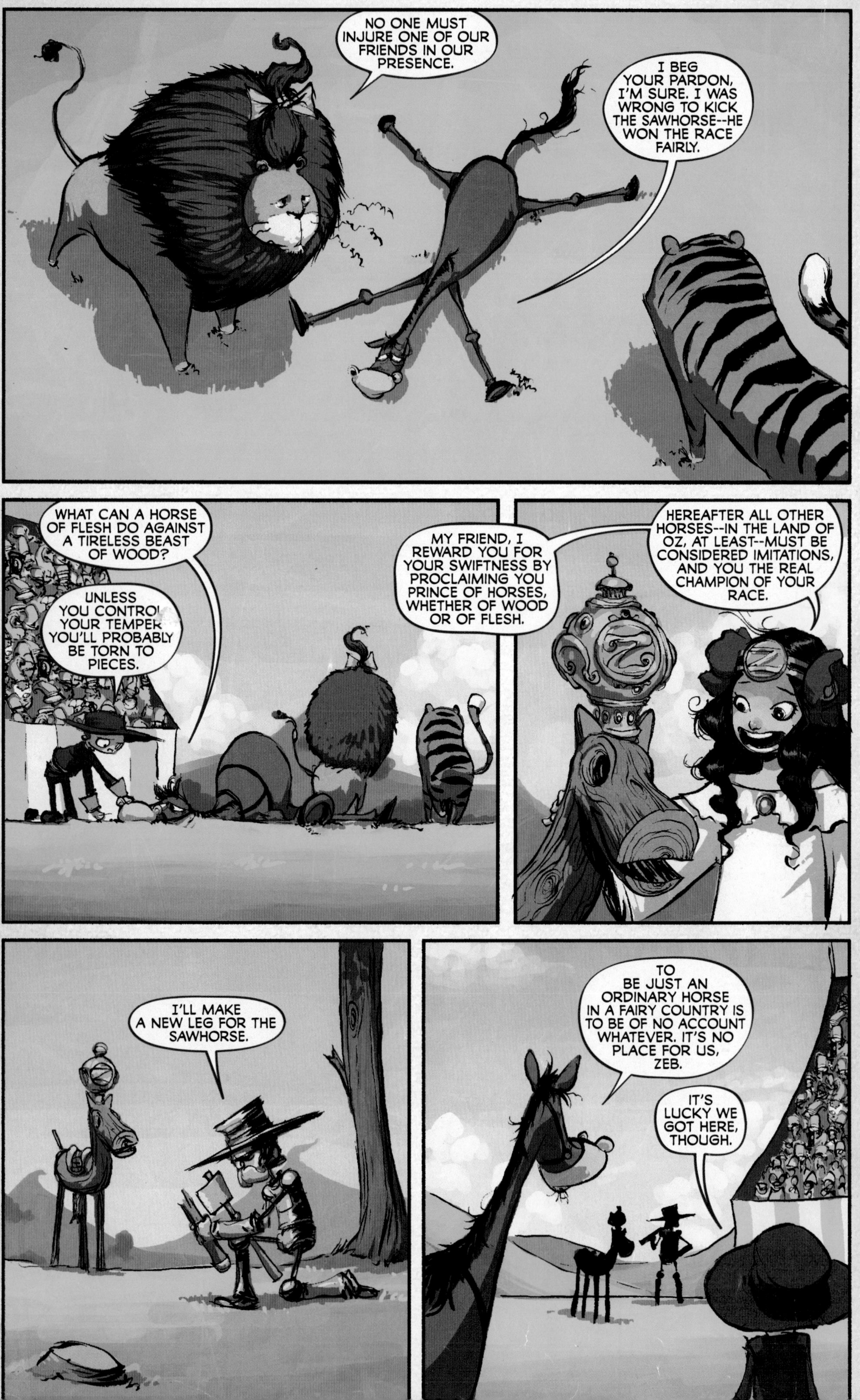
NO ONE MUST INJURE ONE OF OUR FRIENDS IN OUR PRESENCE.
I BEG YOUR PARDON, I'M SURE. I WAS WRONG TO KICK THE SAWHORSE--HE WON THE RACE FAIRLY.
WHAT CAN A HORSE OF FLESH DO AGAINST A TIRELESS BEAST OF WOOD?
UNLESS YOU CONTROL YOUR TEMPER YOU'LL PROBABLY BE TORN TO PIECES.
MY FRIEND, I REWARD YOU FOR YOUR SWIFTNESS BY PROCLAIMING YOU PRINCE OF HORSES, WHETHER OF WOOD OR OF FLESH.
HEREAFTER ALL OTHER HORSES--IN THE LAND OF OZ, AT LEAST--MUST BE CONSIDERED IMITATIONS, AND YOU THE REAL CHAMPION OF YOUR RACE.
I'LL MAKE A NEW LEG FOR THE SAWHORSE.
TO BE JUST AN ORDINARY HORSE IN A FAIRY COUNTRY IS TO BE OF NO ACCOUNT WHATEVER. IT'S NO PLACE FOR US, ZEB.
IT'S LUCKY WE GOT HERE, THOUGH.

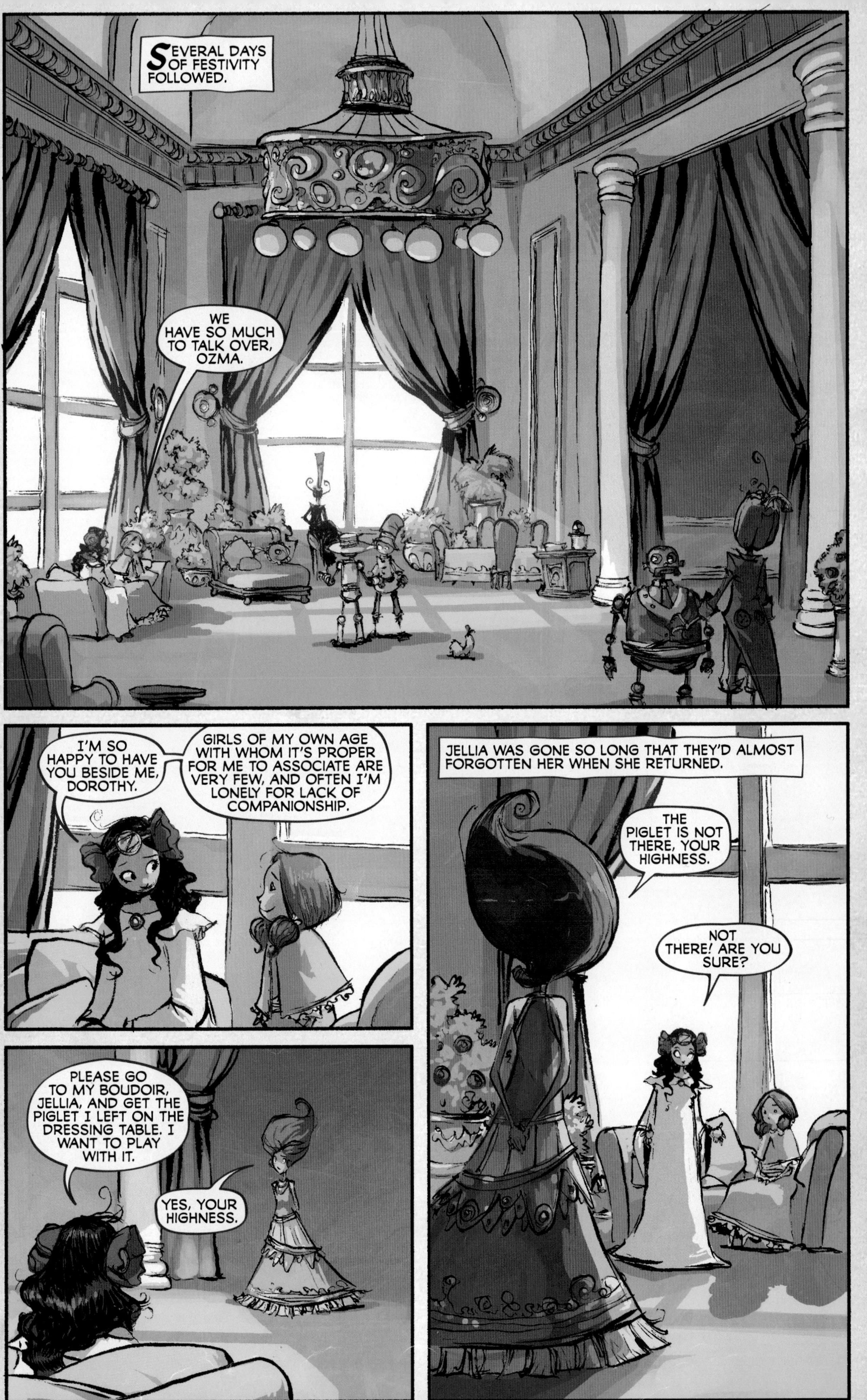
SEVERAL DAYS OF FESTIVITY FOLLOWED.
WE HAVE SO MUCH TO TALK OVER, OZMA.
I'M SO HAPPY TO HAVE YOU BESIDE ME, DOROTHY.
GIRLS OF MY OWN AGE WITH WHOM IT'S PROPER FOR ME TO ASSOCIATE ARE VERY FEW, AND OFTEN I'M LONELY FOR LACK OF COMPANIONSHIP.
PLEASE GO TO MY BOUDOIR, JELLIA, AND GET THE PIGLET I LEFT ON THE DRESSING TABLE. I WANT TO PLAY WITH IT.
YES, YOUR HIGHNESS.
JELLIA WAS GONE SO LONG THAT THEY'D ALMOST FORGOTTEN HER WHEN SHE RETURNED.
THE PIGLET IS NOT THERE, YOUR HIGHNESS.
NOT THERE! ARE YOU SURE?

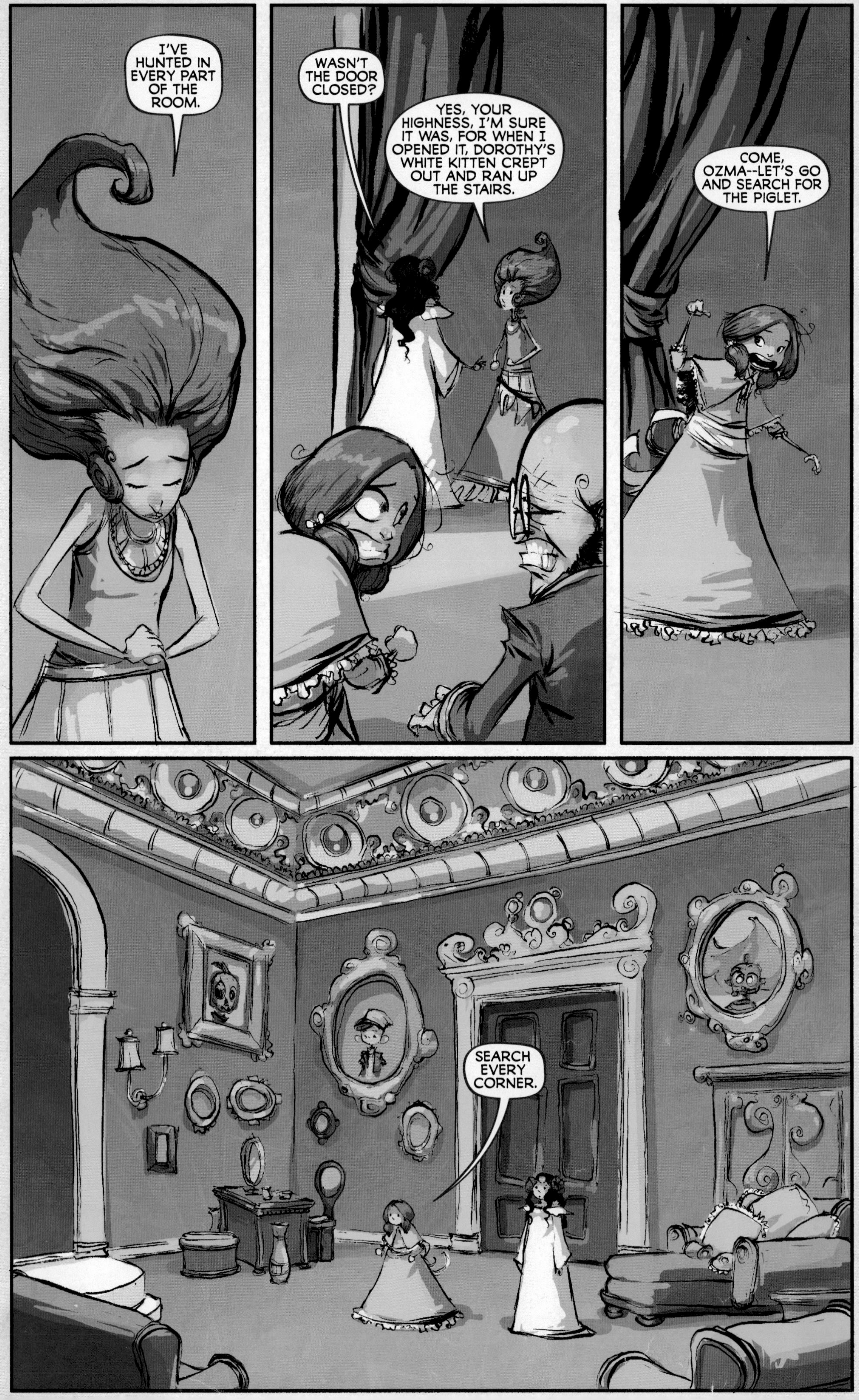
I'VE HUNTED IN EVERY PART OF THE ROOM.
WASN'T THE DOOR CLOSED?
YES, YOUR HIGHNESS, I'M SURE IT WAS, FOR WHEN I OPENED IT, DOROTHY'S WHITE KITTEN CREPT OUT AND RAN UP THE STAIRS.
COME, OZMA--LET'S GO AND SEARCH FOR THE PIGLET.
SEARCH EVERY CORNER.

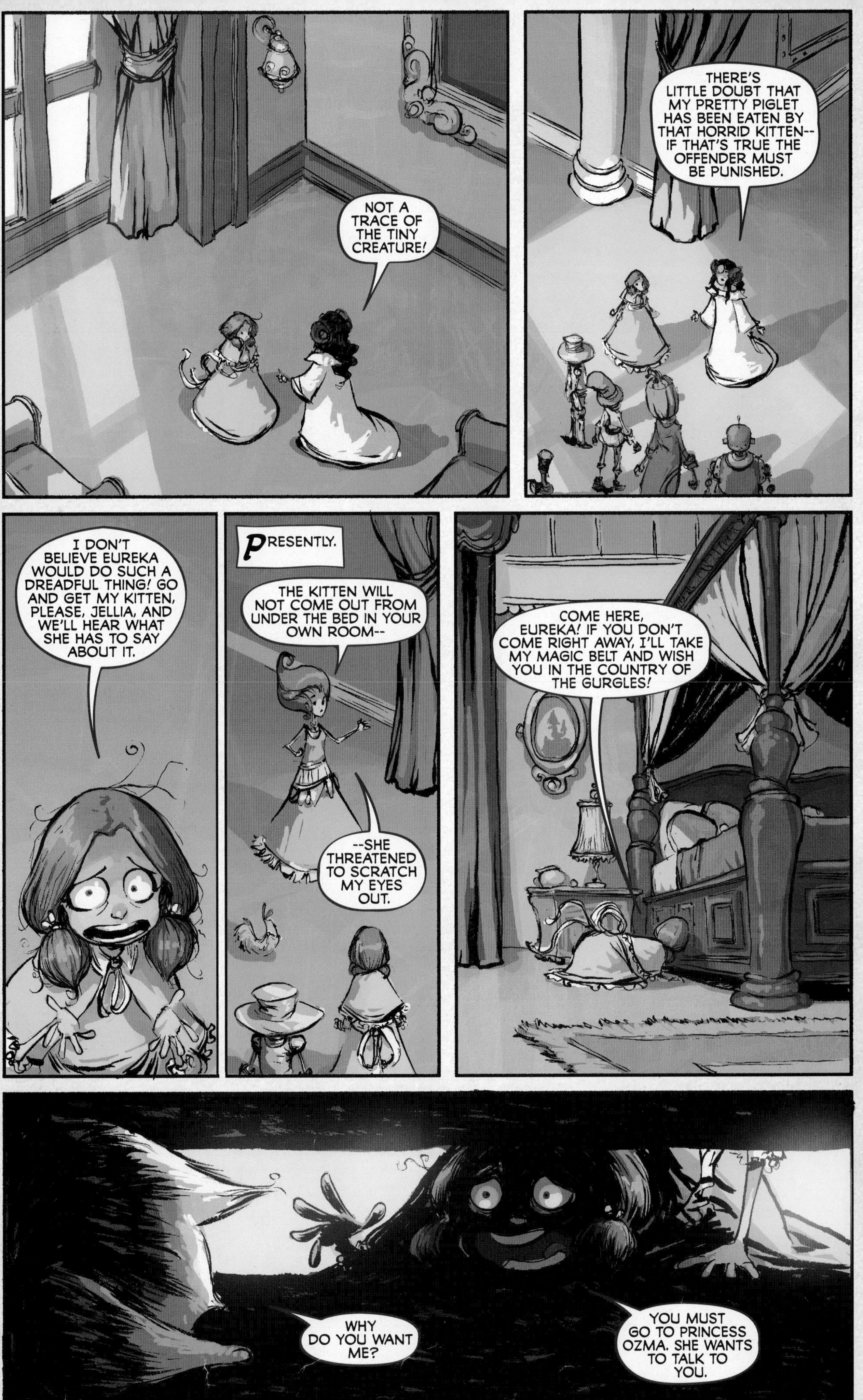
NOT A TRACE OF THE TINY CREATURE!
THERE'S LITTLE DOUBT THAT MY PRETTY PIGLET HAS BEEN EATEN BY THAT HORRID KITTEN-- IF THAT'S TRUE THE OFFENDER MUST BE PUNISHED.
I DON'T BELIEVE EUREKA WOULD DO SUCH A DREADFUL THING! GO AND GET MY KITTEN, PLEASE, JELLIA, AND WE'LL HEAR WHAT SHE HAS TO SAY ABOUT IT.
PRESENTLY.
THE KITTEN WILL NOT COME OUT FROM UNDER THE BED IN YOUR OWN ROOM--
--SHE THREATENED TO SCRATCH MY EYES OUT.
COME HERE, EUREKA! IF YOU DON'T COME RIGHT AWAY, I'LL TAKE MY MAGIC BELT AND WISH YOU IN THE COUNTRY OF THE GURGLES!
WHY DO YOU WANT ME?
YOU MUST GO TO PRINCESS OZMA. SHE WANTS TO TALK TO YOU.

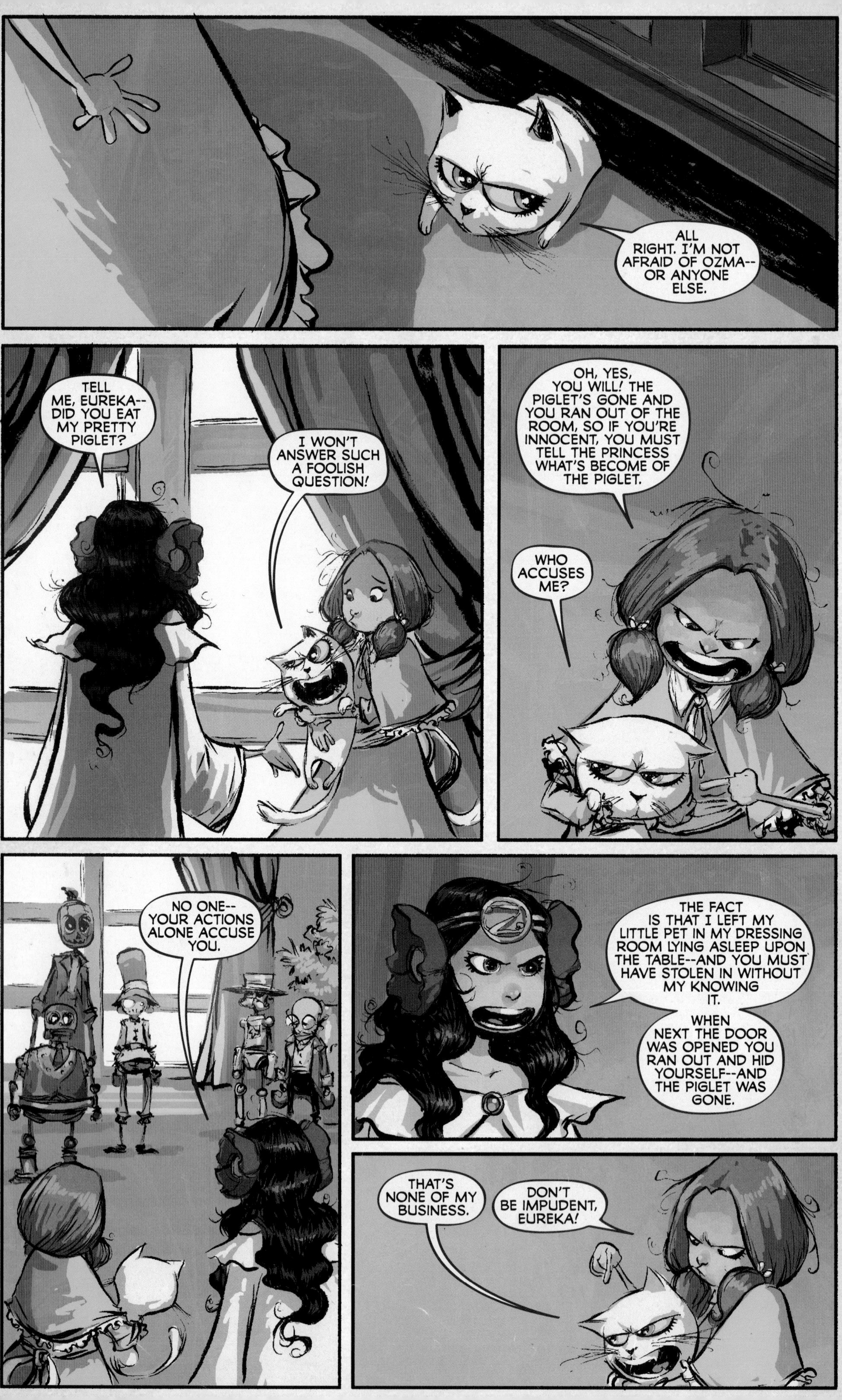
ALL RIGHT. I'M NOT AFRAID OF OZMA-- OR ANYONE ELSE.
TELL ME, EUREKA-- DID YOU EAT MY PRETTY PIGLET?
I WON'T ANSWER SUCH A FOOLISH QUESTION!
OH, YES, YOU WILL! THE PIGLET'S GONE AND YOU RAN OUT OF THE ROOM, SO IF YOU'RE INNOCENT, YOU MUST TELL THE PRINCESS WHAT'S BECOME OF THE PIGLET.
WHO ACCUSES ME?
NO ONE-- YOUR ACTIONS ALONE ACCUSE YOU.
THE FACT IS THAT I LEFT MY LITTLE PET IN MY DRESSING ROOM LYING ASLEEP UPON THE TABLE--AND YOU MUST HAVE STOLEN IN WITHOUT MY KNOWING IT.
WHEN NEXT THE DOOR WAS OPENED YOU RAN OUT AND HID YOURSELF--AND THE PIGLET WAS GONE.
THAT'S NONE OF MY BUSINESS.
DON'T BE IMPUDENT, EUREKA!

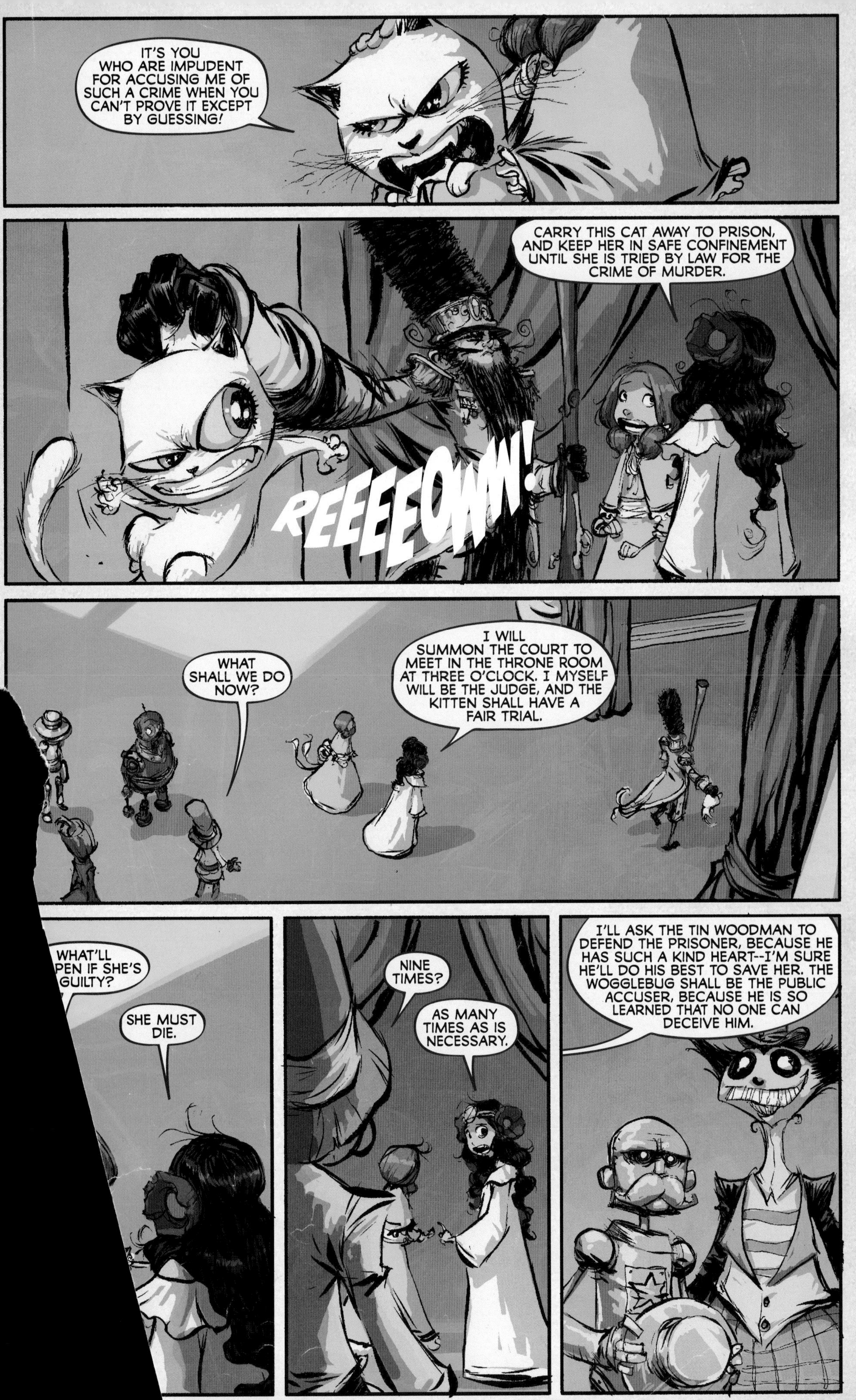
IT'S YOU WHO ARE IMPUDENT FOR ACCUSING ME OF SUCH A CRIME WHEN YOU CAN'T PROVE IT EXCEPT BY GUESSING!
CARRY THIS CAT AWAY TO PRISON, AND KEEP HER IN SAFE CONFINEMENT UNTIL SHE IS TRIED BY LAW FOR THE CRIME OF MURDER.
REEEEEOWW!
WHAT SHALL WE DO NOW?
I WILL SUMMON THE COURT TO MEET IN THE THRONE ROOM AT THREE O'CLOCK. I MYSELF WILL BE THE JUDGE, AND THE KITTEN SHALL HAVE A FAIR TRIAL.
WHAT'LL
PEN IF SHE'S
GUILTY?
SHE MUST DIE.
NINE TIMES?
AS MANY TIMES AS IS NECESSARY.
I'LL ASK THE TIN WOODMAN TO DEFEND THE PRISONER, BECAUSE HE HAS SUCH A KIND HEART--I'M SURE HE'LL DO HIS BEST TO SAVE HER. THE WOGGLEBUG SHALL BE THE PUBLIC ACCUSER, BECAUSE HE IS SO LEARNED THAT NO ONE CAN DECEIVE HIM.

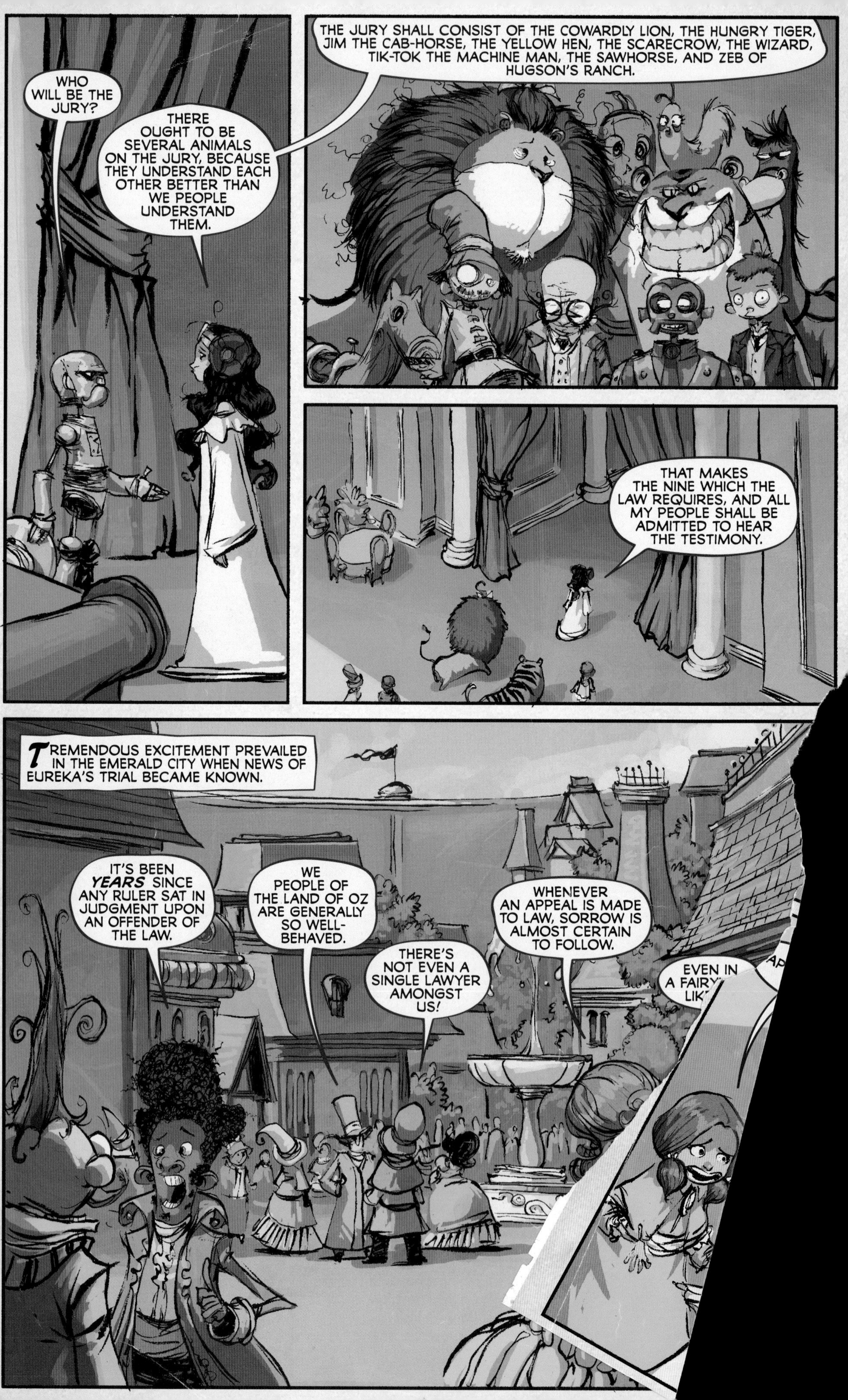

WHO WILL BE THE JURY?
THERE OUGHT TO BE SEVERAL ANIMALS ON THE JURY, BECAUSE THEY UNDERSTAND EACH OTHER BETTER THAN WE PEOPLE UNDERSTAND THEM.
THE JURY SHALL CONSIST OF THE COWARDLY LION, THE HUNGRY TIGER, JIM THE CAB-HORSE, THE YELLOW HEN, THE SCARECROW, THE WIZARD, TIK-TOK THE MACHINE MAN, THE SAWHORSE, AND ZEB OF HUGSON'S RANCH.
THAT MAKES THE NINE WHICH THE LAW REQUIRES, AND ALL MY PEOPLE SHALL BE ADMITTED TO HEAR THE TESTIMONY.
TREMENDOUS EXCITEMENT PREVAILED IN THE EMERALD CITY WHEN NEWS OF EUREKA'S TRIAL BECAME KNOWN.
IT'S BEEN YEARS SINCE ANY RULER SAT IN JUDGMENT UPON AN OFFENDER OF THE LAW.
WE PEOPLE OF THE LAND OF OZ ARE GENERALLY SO WELL-BEHAVED.
THERE'S NOT EVEN A SINGLE LAWYER AMONGST US!
WHENEVER AN APPEAL IS MADE TO LAW, SORROW IS ALMOST CERTAIN TO FOLLOW.
EVEN IN

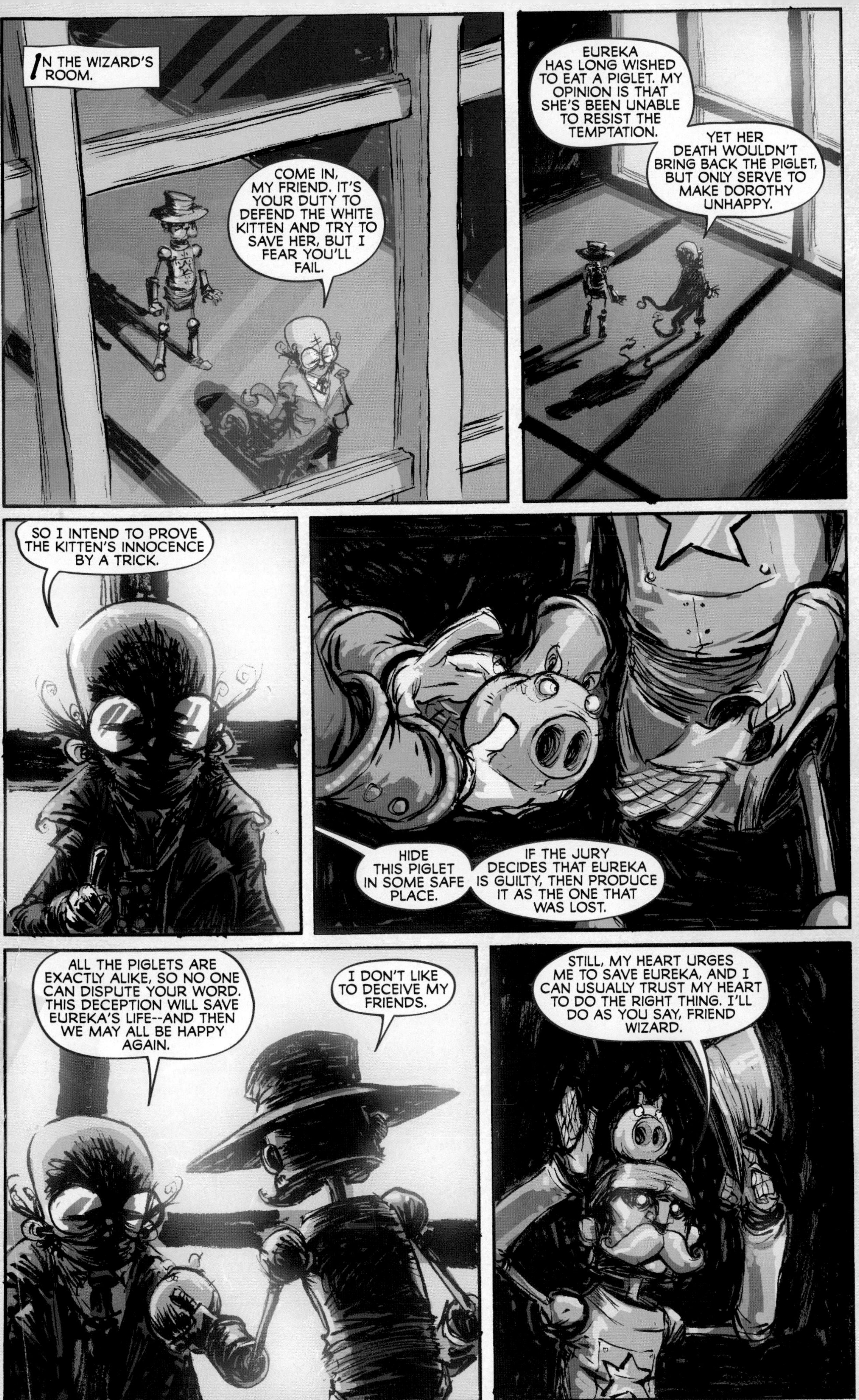
IN THE WIZARD'S ROOM.
COME IN, MY FRIEND. IT'S YOUR DUTY TO DEFEND THE WHITE KITTEN AND TRY TO SAVE HER, BUT I FEAR YOU'LL FAIL.
EUREKA HAS LONG WISHED TO EAT A PIGLET. MY OPINION IS THAT SHE'S BEEN UNABLE TO RESIST THE TEMPTATION.
YET HER DEATH WOULDN'T BRING BACK THE PIGLET, BUT ONLY SERVE TO MAKE DOROTHY UNHAPPY.
SO I INTEND TO PROVE THE KITTEN'S INNOCENCE BY A TRICK.
HIDE THIS PIGLET IN SOME SAFE PLACE.
IF THE JURY DECIDES THAT EUREKA IS GUILTY, THEN PRODUCE IT AS THE ONE THAT WAS LOST.
ALL THE PIGLETS ARE EXACTLY ALIKE, SO NO ONE CAN DISPUTE YOUR WORD. THIS DECEPTION WILL SAVE EUREKA'S LIFE--AND THEN WE MAY ALL BE HAPPY AGAIN.
I DON'T LIKE TO DECEIVE MY FRIENDS.
STILL, MY HEART URGES ME TO SAVE EUREKA, AND I CAN USUALLY TRUST MY HEART TO DO THE RIGHT THING. I'LL DO AS YOU SAY, FRIEND WIZARD.

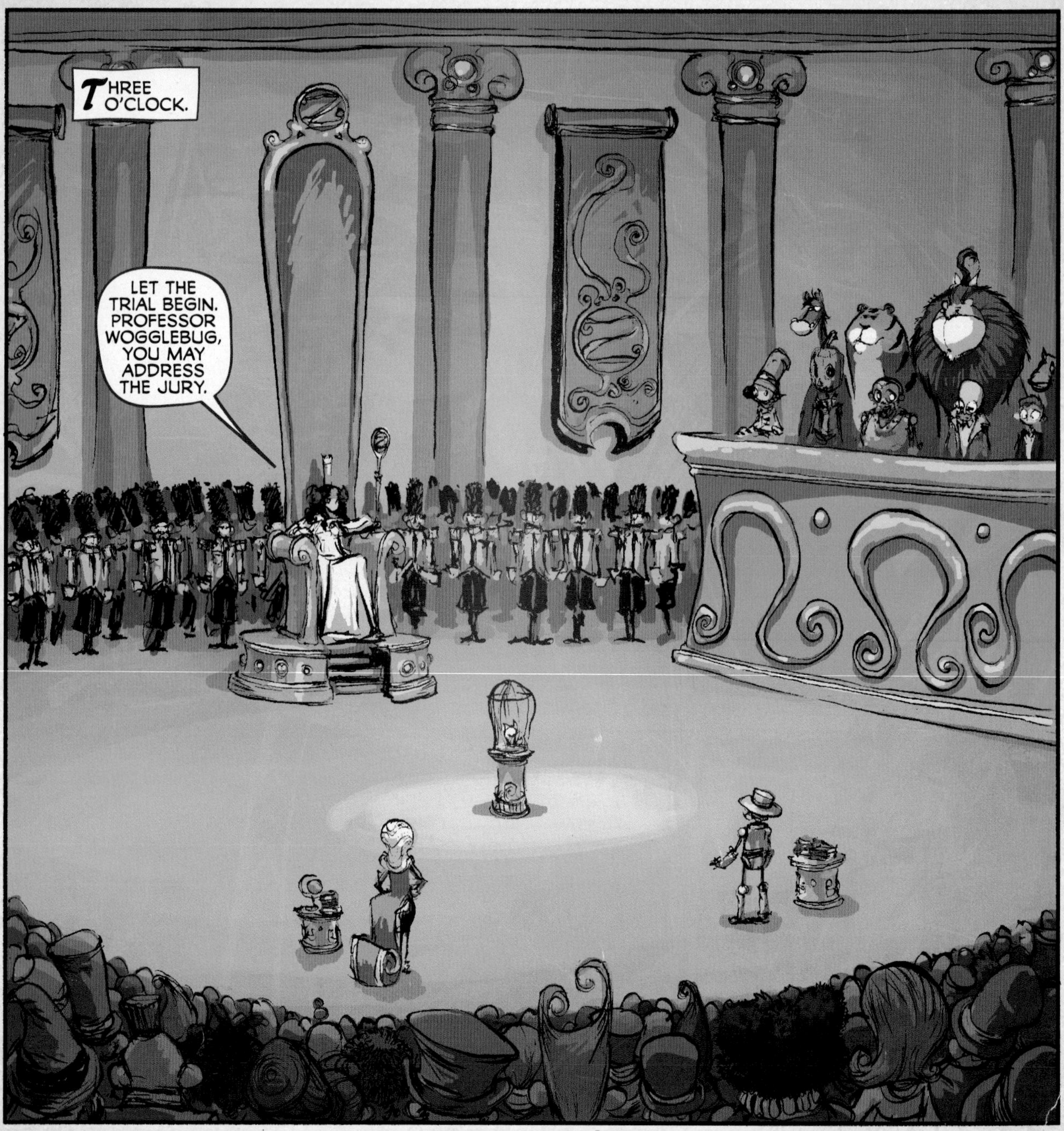
THREE O'CLOCK.
LET THE TRIAL BEGIN. PROFESSOR WOGGLEBUG, YOU MAY ADDRESS THE JURY.

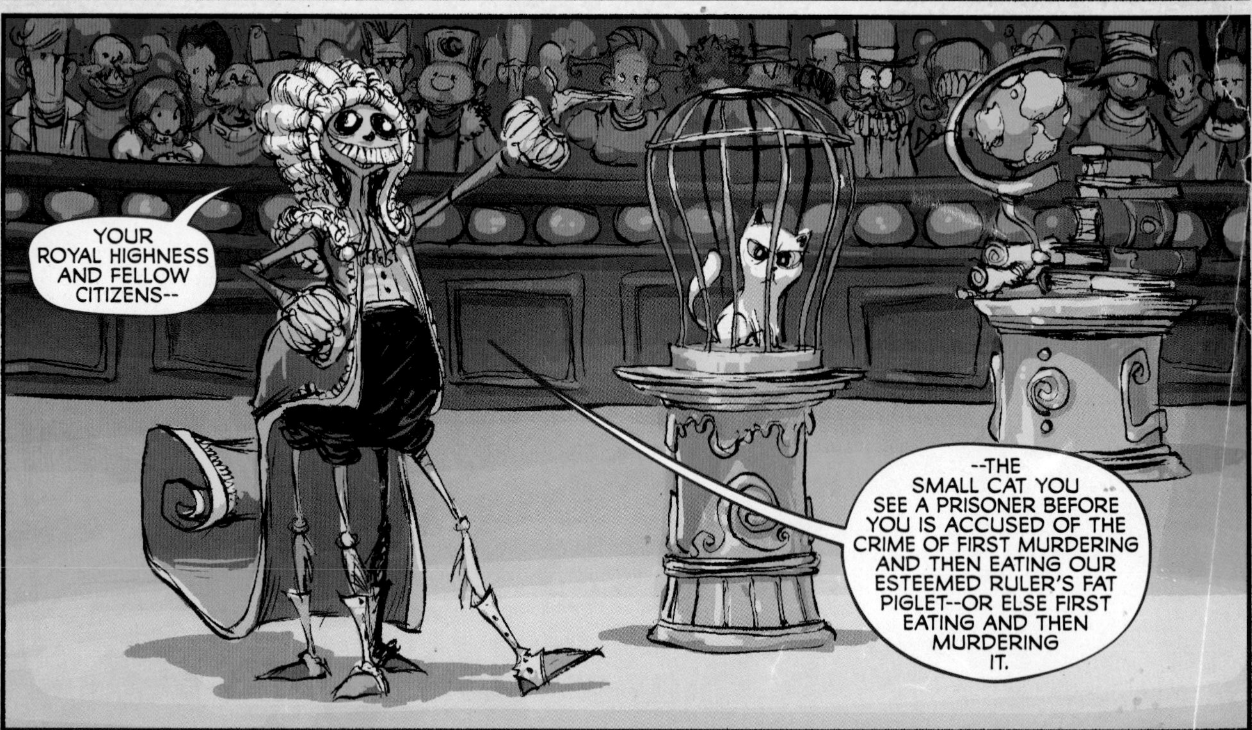
YOUR ROYAL HIGHNESS AND FELLOW CITIZENS--
--THE SMALL CAT YOU SEE A PRISONER BEFORE YOU IS ACCUSED OF THE CRIME OF FIRST MURDERING AND THEN EATING OUR ESTEEMED RULER'S FAT PIGLET--OR ELSE FIRST EATING AND THEN MURDERING IT.

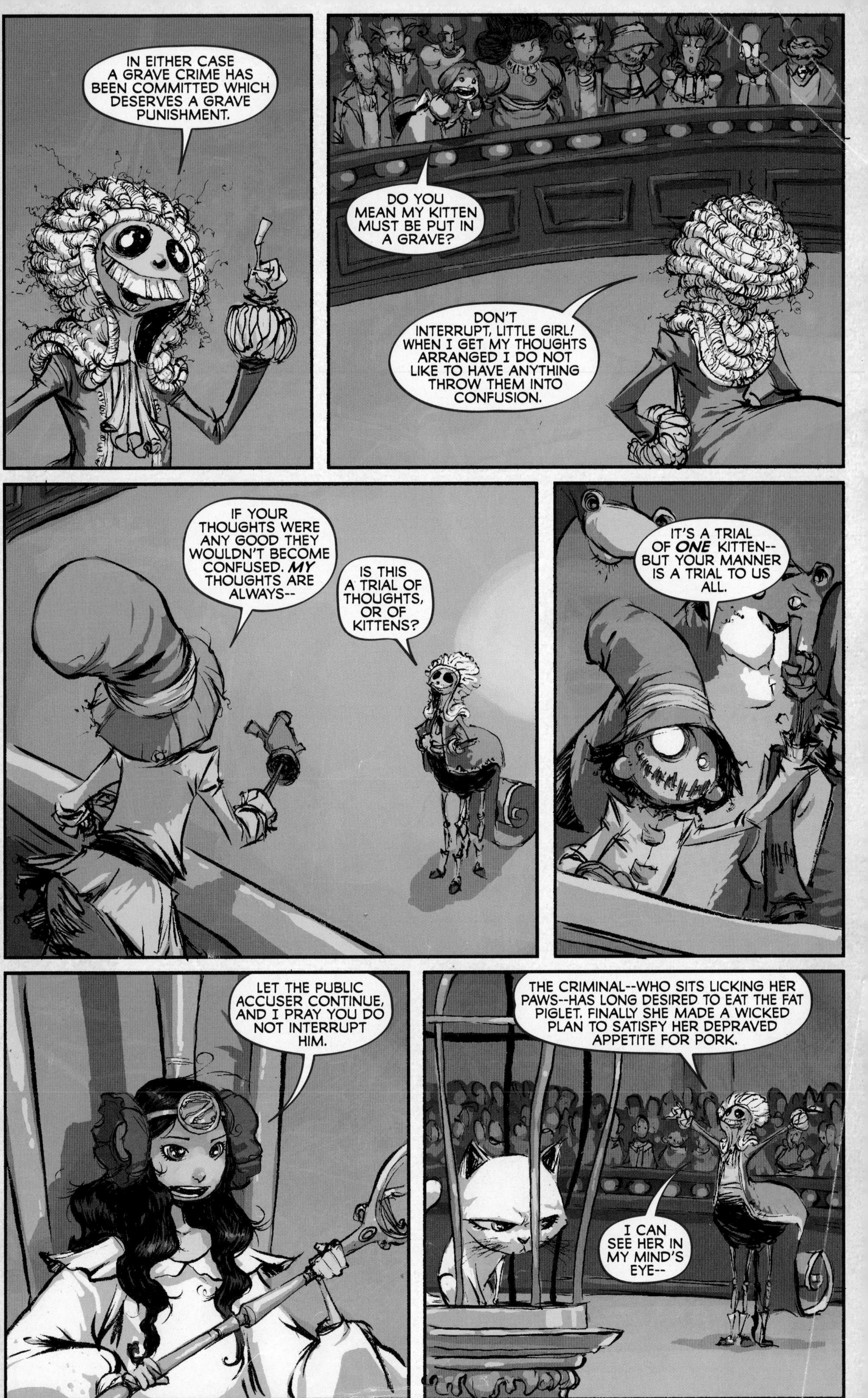
IN EITHER CASE A GRAVE CRIME HAS BEEN COMMITTED WHICH DESERVES A GRAVE PUNISHMENT.
DO YOU MEAN MY KITTEN MUST BE PUT IN A GRAVE?
DON'T INTERRUPT, LITTLE GIRL! WHEN I GET MY THOUGHTS ARRANGED I DO NOT LIKE TO HAVE ANYTHING THROW THEM INTO CONFUSION.
IF YOUR THOUGHTS WERE ANY GOOD THEY WOULDN'T BECOME CONFUSED. *MY* THOUGHTS ARE ALWAYS--
IS THIS A TRIAL OF THOUGHTS, OR OF KITTENS?
IT'S A TRIAL OF *ONE* KITTEN-- BUT YOUR MANNER IS A TRIAL TO US ALL.
LET THE PUBLIC ACCUSER CONTINUE, AND I PRAY YOU DO NOT INTERRUPT HIM.
THE CRIMINAL--WHO SITS LICKING HER PAWS--HAS LONG DESIRED TO EAT THE FAT PIGLET. FINALLY SHE MADE A WICKED PLAN TO SATISFY HER DEPRAVED APPETITE FOR PORK.
I CAN SEE HER IN MY MIND'S EYE--

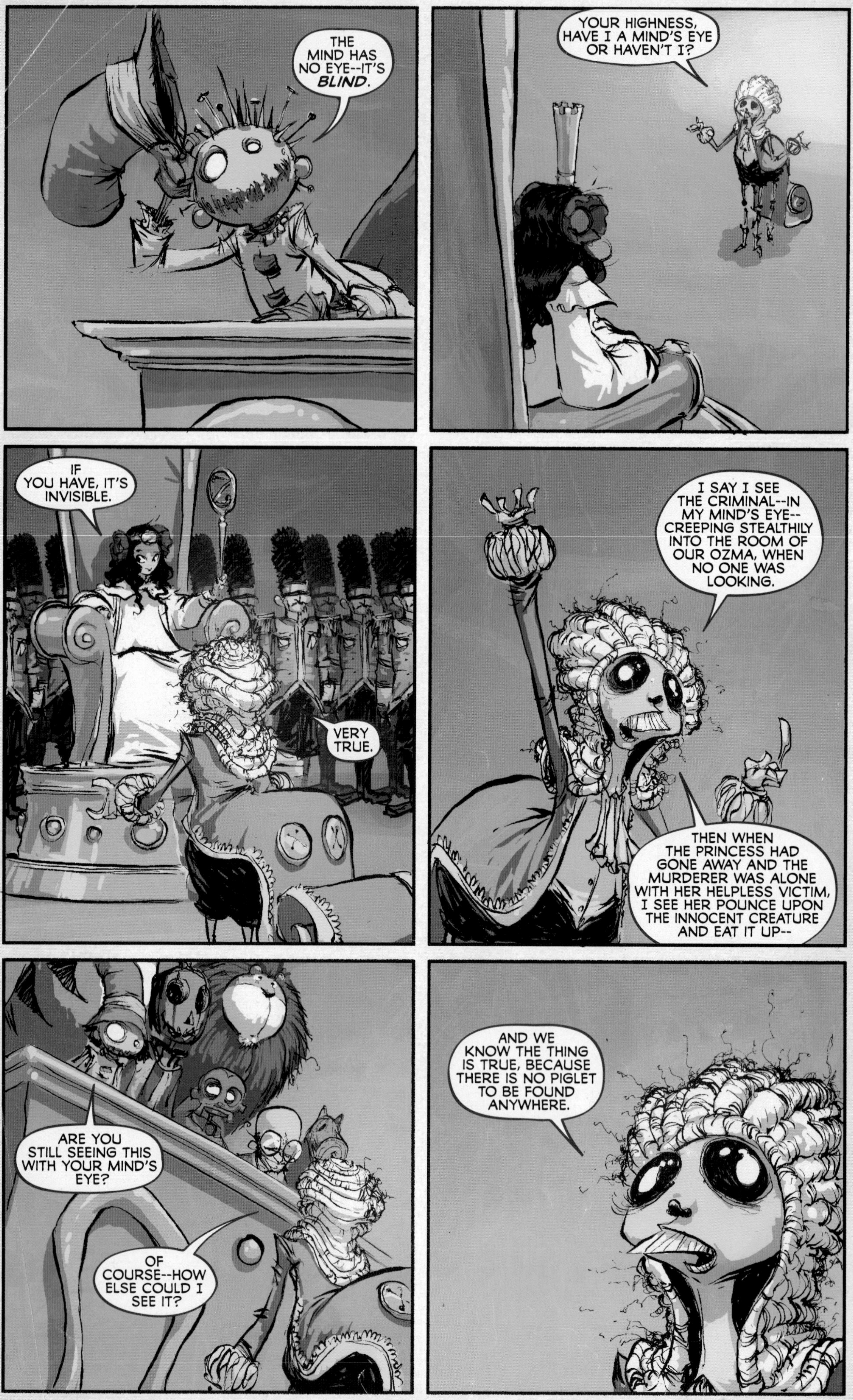
THE MIND HAS NO EYE--IT'S *BLIND*.
YOUR HIGHNESS, HAVE I A MIND'S EYE OR HAVEN'T I?
IF YOU HAVE, IT'S INVISIBLE.
VERY TRUE.
I SAY I SEE THE CRIMINAL--IN MY MIND'S EYE--CREEPING STEALTHILY INTO THE ROOM OF OUR OZMA, WHEN NO ONE WAS LOOKING.
THEN WHEN THE PRINCESS HAD GONE AWAY AND THE MURDERER WAS ALONE WITH HER HELPLESS VICTIM, I SEE HER POUNCE UPON THE INNOCENT CREATURE AND EAT IT UP--
ARE YOU STILL SEEING THIS WITH YOUR MIND'S EYE?
OF COURSE--HOW ELSE COULD I SEE IT?
AND WE KNOW THE THING IS TRUE, BECAUSE THERE IS NO PIGLET TO BE FOUND ANYWHERE.

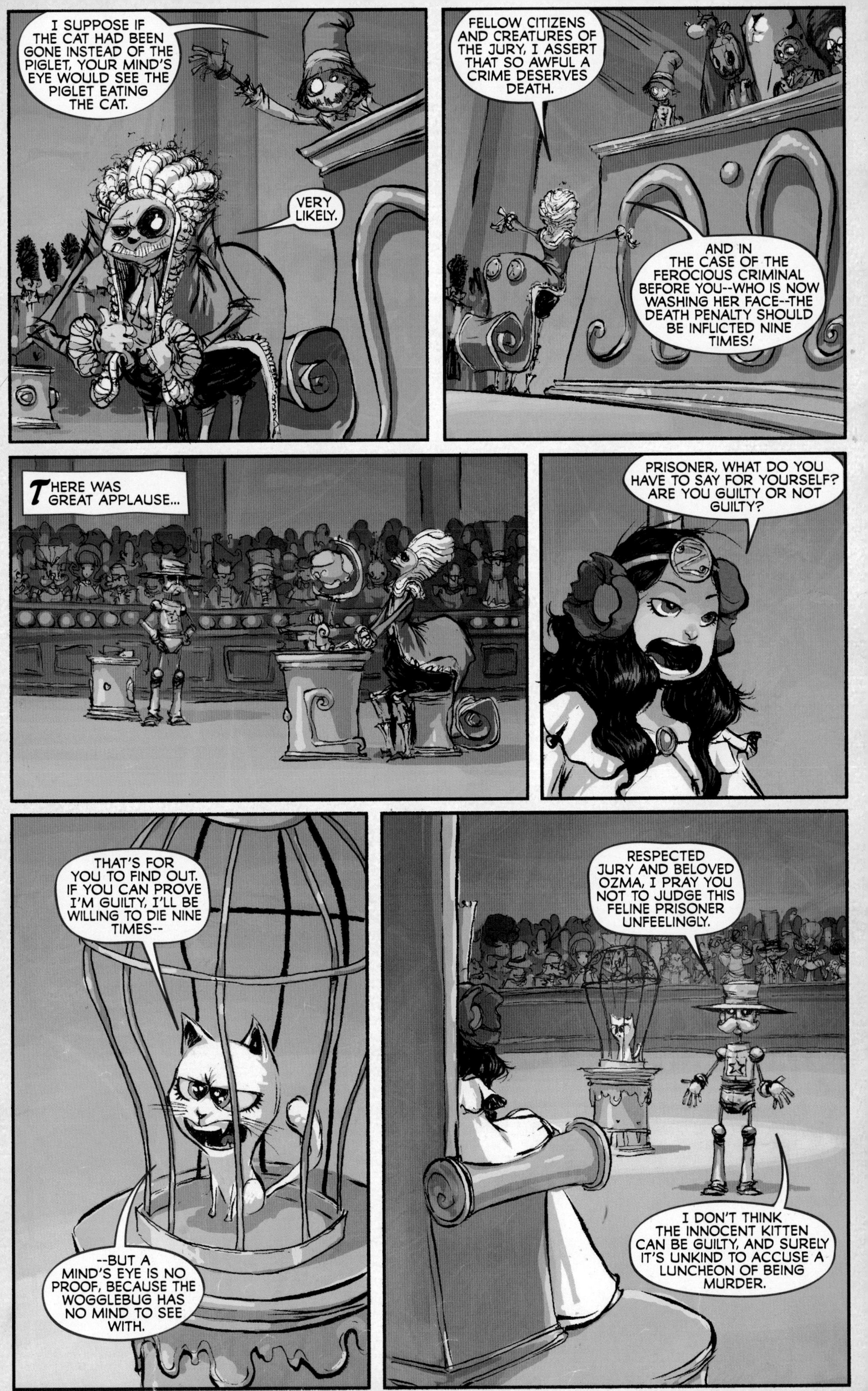
I SUPPOSE IF THE CAT HAD BEEN GONE INSTEAD OF THE PIGLET, YOUR MIND'S EYE WOULD SEE THE PIGLET EATING THE CAT.
VERY LIKELY.
FELLOW CITIZENS AND CREATURES OF THE JURY, I ASSERT THAT SO AWFUL A CRIME DESERVES DEATH.
AND IN THE CASE OF THE FEROCIOUS CRIMINAL BEFORE YOU--WHO IS NOW WASHING HER FACE--THE DEATH PENALTY SHOULD BE INFLICTED NINE TIMES!
THERE WAS GREAT APPLAUSE...
PRISONER, WHAT DO YOU HAVE TO SAY FOR YOURSELF? ARE YOU GUILTY OR NOT GUILTY?
THAT'S FOR YOU TO FIND OUT. IF YOU CAN PROVE I'M GUILTY, I'LL BE WILLING TO DIE NINE TIMES--
--BUT A MIND'S EYE IS NO PROOF, BECAUSE THE WOGGLEBUG HAS NO MIND TO SEE WITH.
RESPECTED JURY AND BELOVED OZMA, I PRAY YOU NOT TO JUDGE THIS FELINE PRISONER UNFEELINGLY.
I DON'T THINK THE INNOCENT KITTEN CAN BE GUILTY, AND SURELY IT'S UNKIND TO ACCUSE A LUNCHEON OF BEING MURDER.

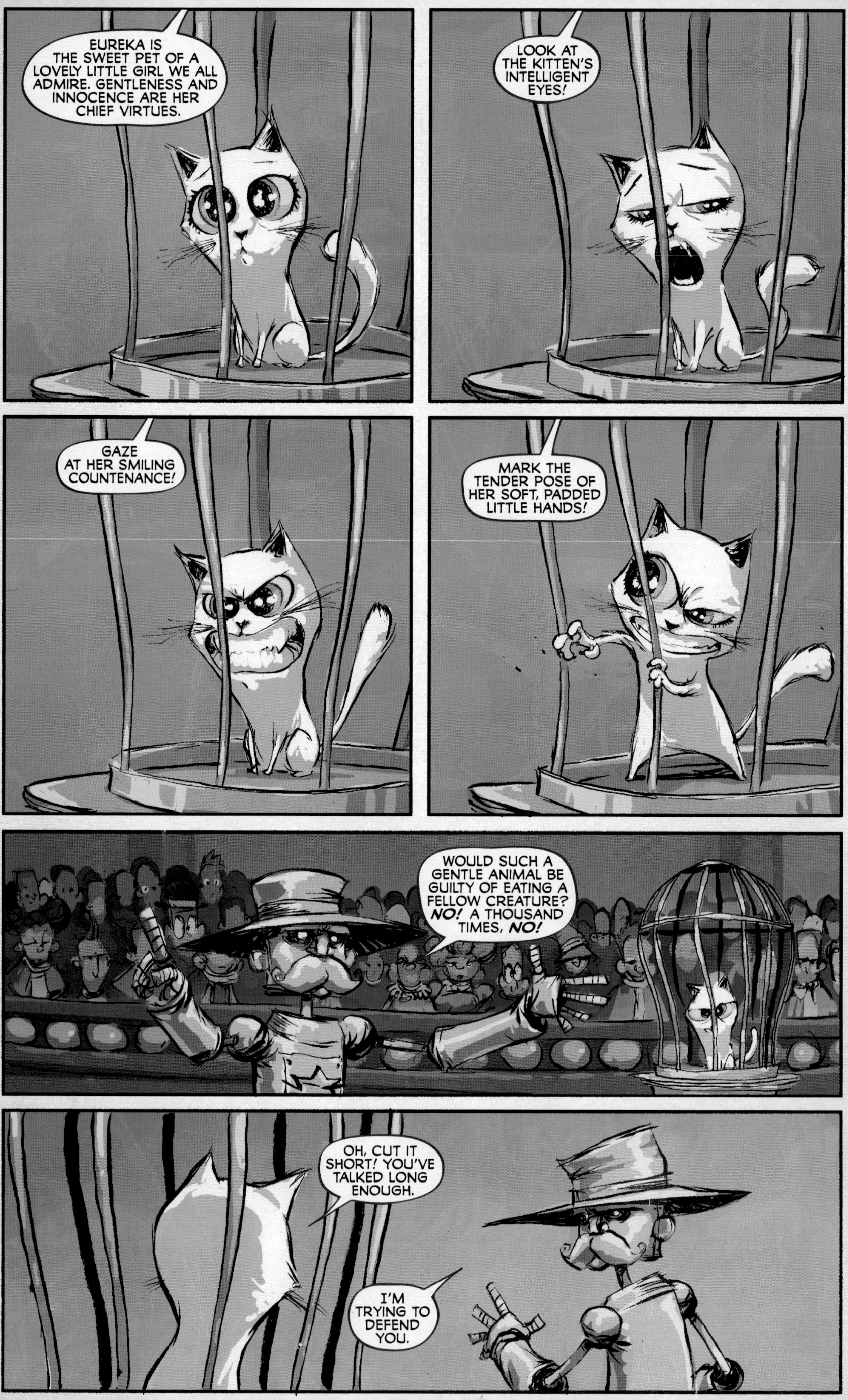
EUREKA IS THE SWEET PET OF A LOVELY LITTLE GIRL WE ALL ADMIRE. GENTLENESS AND INNOCENCE ARE HER CHIEF VIRTUES.
LOOK AT THE KITTEN'S INTELLIGENT EYES!
GAZE AT HER SMILING COUNTENANCE!
MARK THE TENDER POSE OF HER SOFT, PADDED LITTLE HANDS!
WOULD SUCH A GENTLE ANIMAL BE GUILTY OF EATING A FELLOW CREATURE? **NO!** A THOUSAND TIMES, **NO!**
OH, CUT IT SHORT! YOU'VE TALKED LONG ENOUGH.
I'M TRYING TO DEFEND YOU.

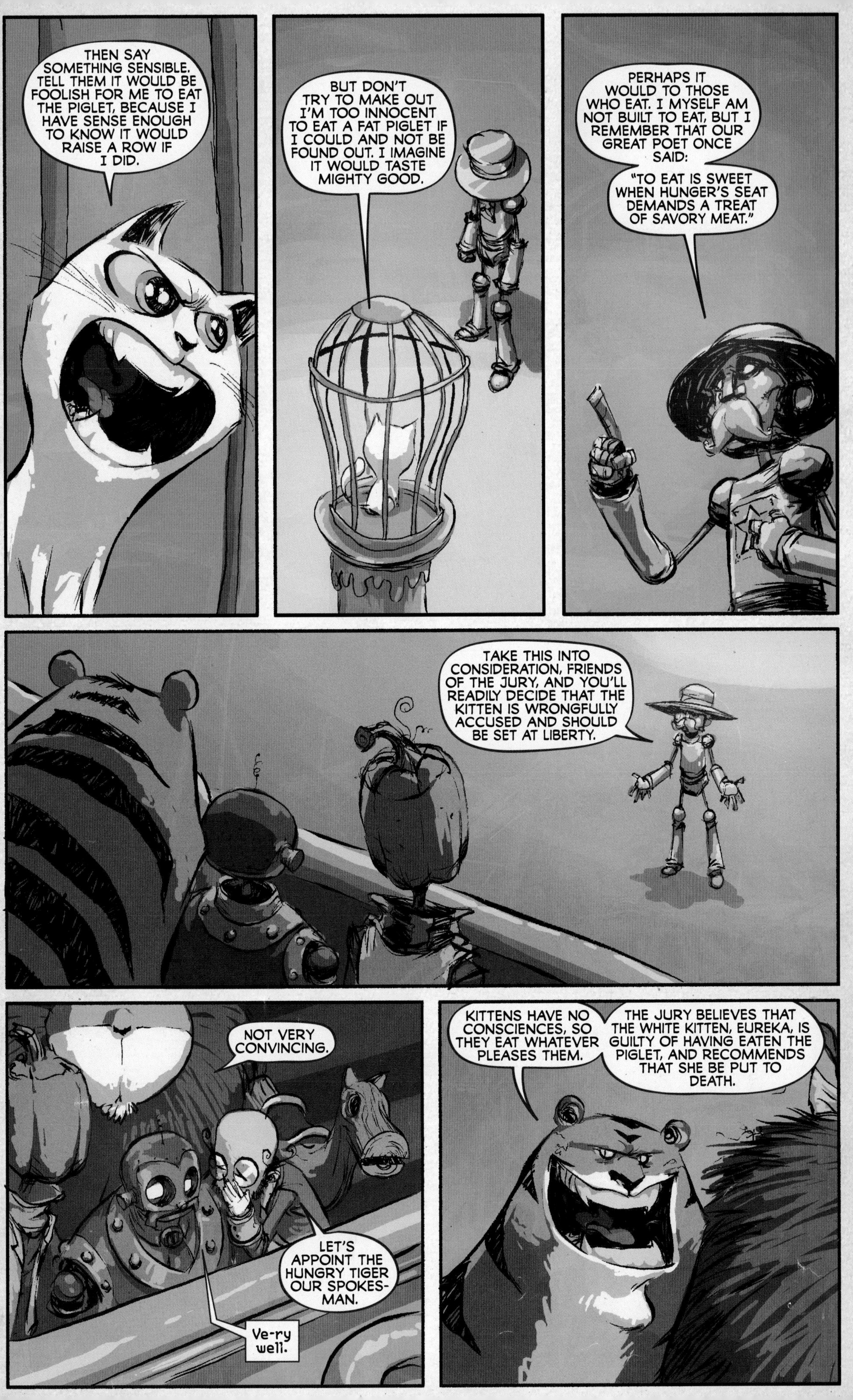
THEN SAY SOMETHING SENSIBLE. TELL THEM IT WOULD BE FOOLISH FOR ME TO EAT THE PIGLET, BECAUSE I HAVE SENSE ENOUGH TO KNOW IT WOULD RAISE A ROW IF I DID.
BUT DON'T TRY TO MAKE OUT I'M TOO INNOCENT TO EAT A FAT PIGLET IF I COULD AND NOT BE FOUND OUT. I IMAGINE IT WOULD TASTE MIGHTY GOOD.
PERHAPS IT WOULD TO THOSE WHO EAT. I MYSELF AM NOT BUILT TO EAT, BUT I REMEMBER THAT OUR GREAT POET ONCE SAID:
"TO EAT IS SWEET WHEN HUNGER'S SEAT DEMANDS A TREAT OF SAVORY MEAT."
TAKE THIS INTO CONSIDERATION, FRIENDS OF THE JURY, AND YOU'LL READILY DECIDE THAT THE KITTEN IS WRONGFULLY ACCUSED AND SHOULD BE SET AT LIBERTY.
NOT VERY CONVINCING.
LET'S APPOINT THE HUNGRY TIGER OUR SPOKES-MAN.
Ve-ry well.
KITTENS HAVE NO CONSCIENCES, SO THEY EAT WHATEVER PLEASES THEM.
THE JURY BELIEVES THAT THE WHITE KITTEN, EUREKA, IS GUILTY OF HAVING EATEN THE PIGLET, AND RECOMMENDS THAT SHE BE PUT TO DEATH.

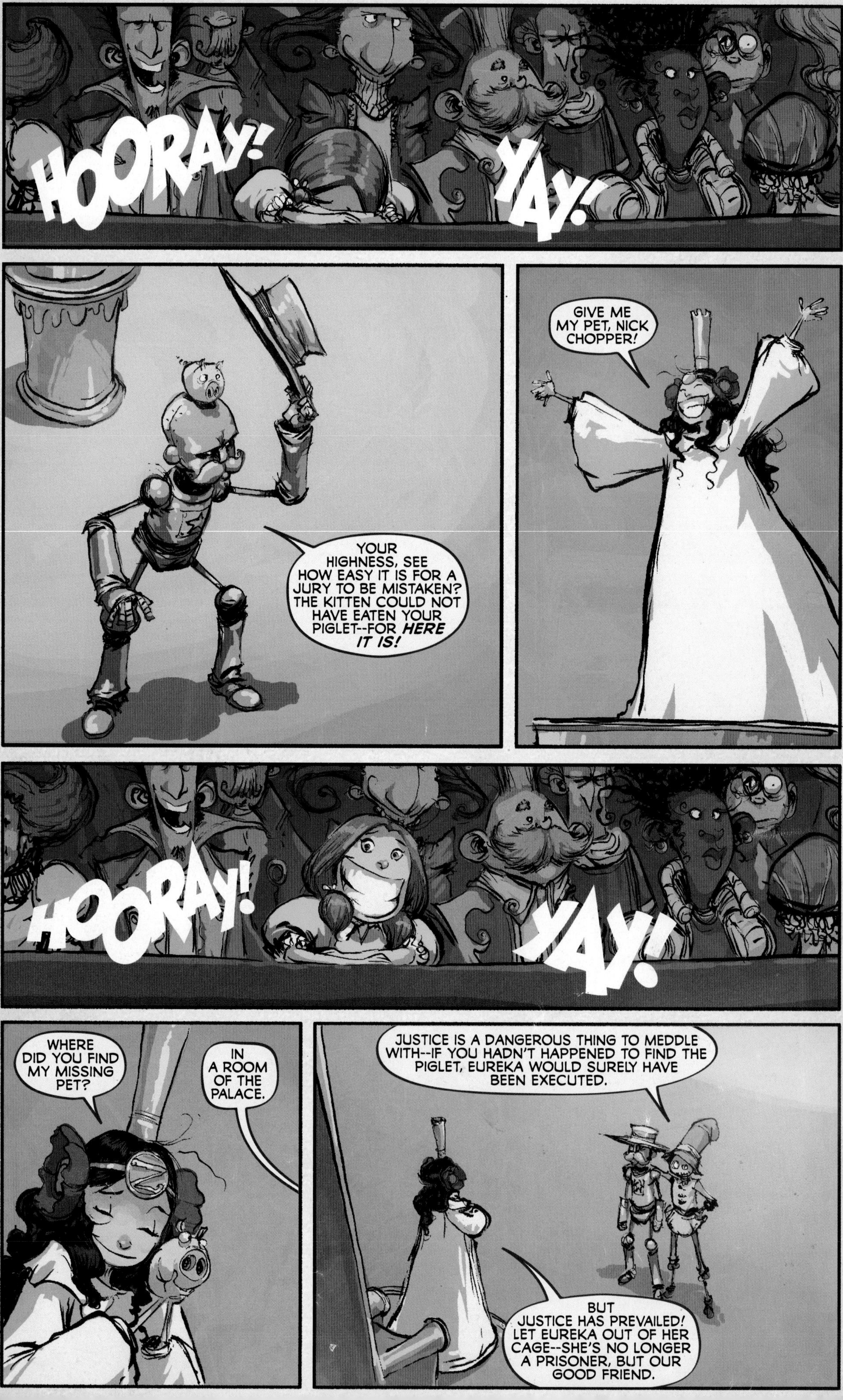

HOORAY!
YAY!
YOUR HIGHNESS, SEE HOW EASY IT IS FOR A JURY TO BE MISTAKEN? THE KITTEN COULD NOT HAVE EATEN YOUR PIGLET--FOR *HERE IT IS!*
GIVE ME MY PET, NICK CHOPPER!
HOORAY!
YAY!
WHERE DID YOU FIND MY MISSING PET?
IN A ROOM OF THE PALACE.
JUSTICE IS A DANGEROUS THING TO MEDDLE WITH--IF YOU HADN'T HAPPENED TO FIND THE PIGLET, EUREKA WOULD SURELY HAVE BEEN EXECUTED.
BUT JUSTICE HAS PREVAILED! LET EUREKA OUT OF HER CAGE--SHE'S NO LONGER A PRISONER, BUT OUR GOOD FRIEND.

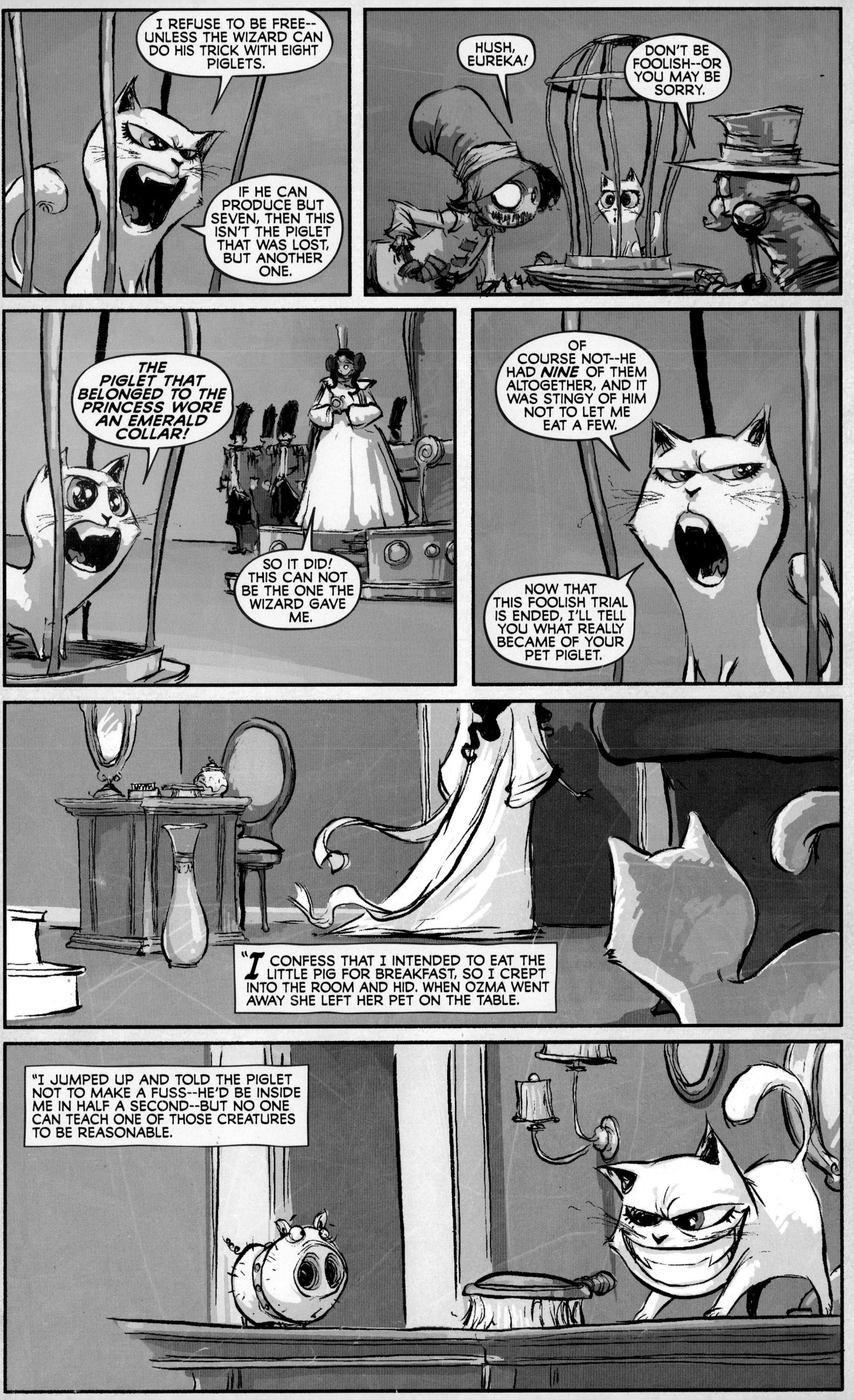
I REFUSE TO BE FREE--UNLESS THE WIZARD CAN DO HIS TRICK WITH EIGHT PIGLETS.
IF HE CAN PRODUCE BUT SEVEN, THEN THIS ISN'T THE PIGLET THAT WAS LOST, BUT ANOTHER ONE.
HUSH, EUREKA!
DON'T BE FOOLISH--OR YOU MAY BE SORRY.
THE PIGLET THAT BELONGED TO THE PRINCESS WORE AN EMERALD COLLAR!
SO IT DID! THIS CAN NOT BE THE ONE THE WIZARD GAVE ME.
OF COURSE NOT--HE HAD NINE OF THEM ALTOGETHER, AND IT WAS STINGY OF HIM NOT TO LET ME EAT A FEW.
NOW THAT THIS FOOLISH TRIAL IS ENDED, I'LL TELL YOU WHAT REALLY BECAME OF YOUR PET PIGLET.
"I CONFESS THAT I INTENDED TO EAT THE LITTLE PIG FOR BREAKFAST, SO I CREPT INTO THE ROOM AND HID. WHEN OZMA WENT AWAY SHE LEFT HER PET ON THE TABLE.
"I JUMPED UP AND TOLD THE PIGLET NOT TO MAKE A FUSS--HE'D BE INSIDE ME IN HALF A SECOND--BUT NO ONE CAN TEACH ONE OF THOSE CREATURES TO BE REASONABLE.

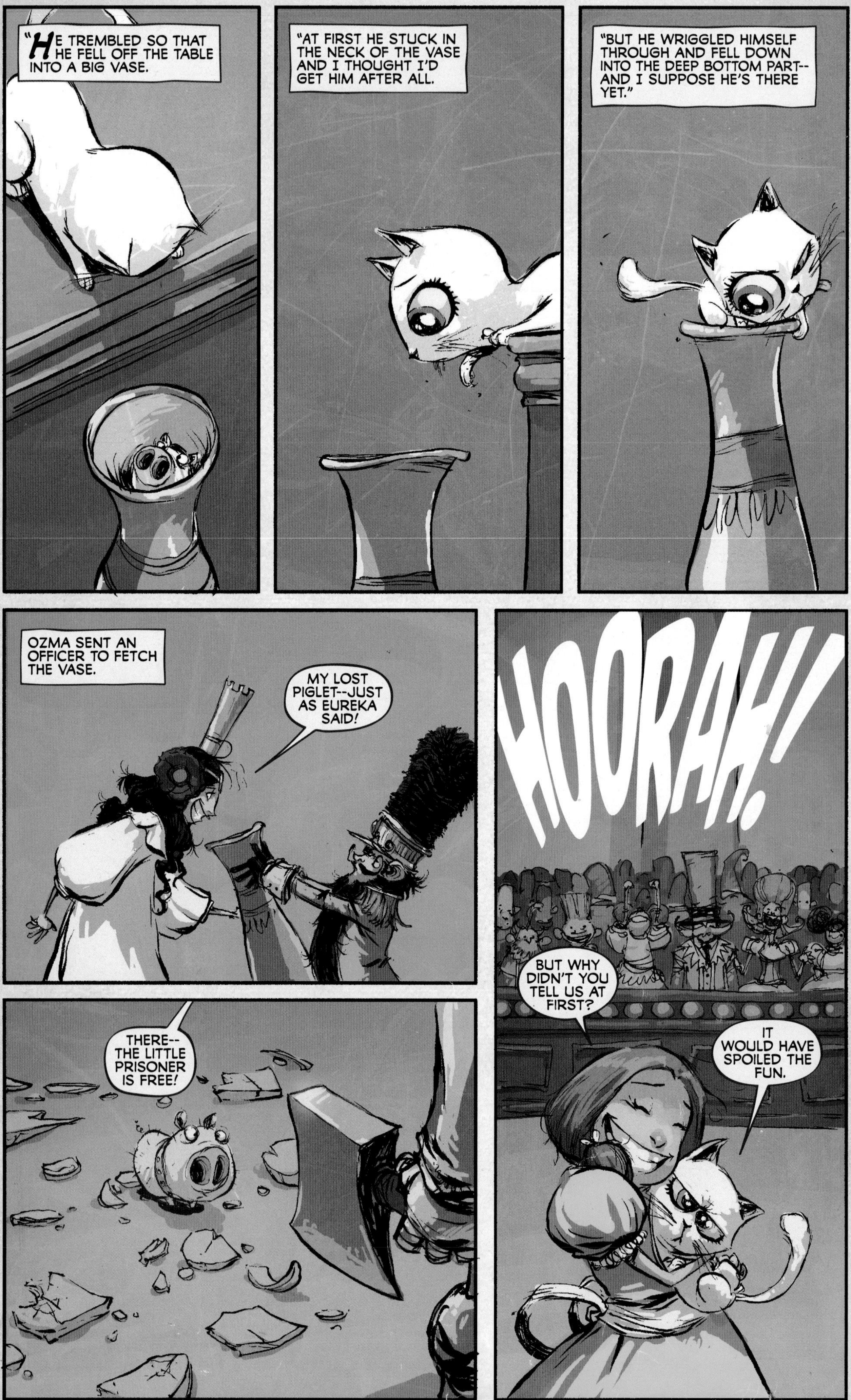
"HE TREMBLED SO THAT HE FELL OFF THE TABLE INTO A BIG VASE.
"AT FIRST HE STUCK IN THE NECK OF THE VASE AND I THOUGHT I'D GET HIM AFTER ALL.
"BUT HE WRIGGLED HIMSELF THROUGH AND FELL DOWN INTO THE DEEP BOTTOM PART--AND I SUPPOSE HE'S THERE YET."
OZMA SENT AN OFFICER TO FETCH THE VASE.
MY LOST PIGLET--JUST AS EUREKA SAID!
THERE--THE LITTLE PRISONER IS FREE!
HOORAH!
BUT WHY DIDN'T YOU TELL US AT FIRST?
IT WOULD HAVE SPOILED THE FUN.

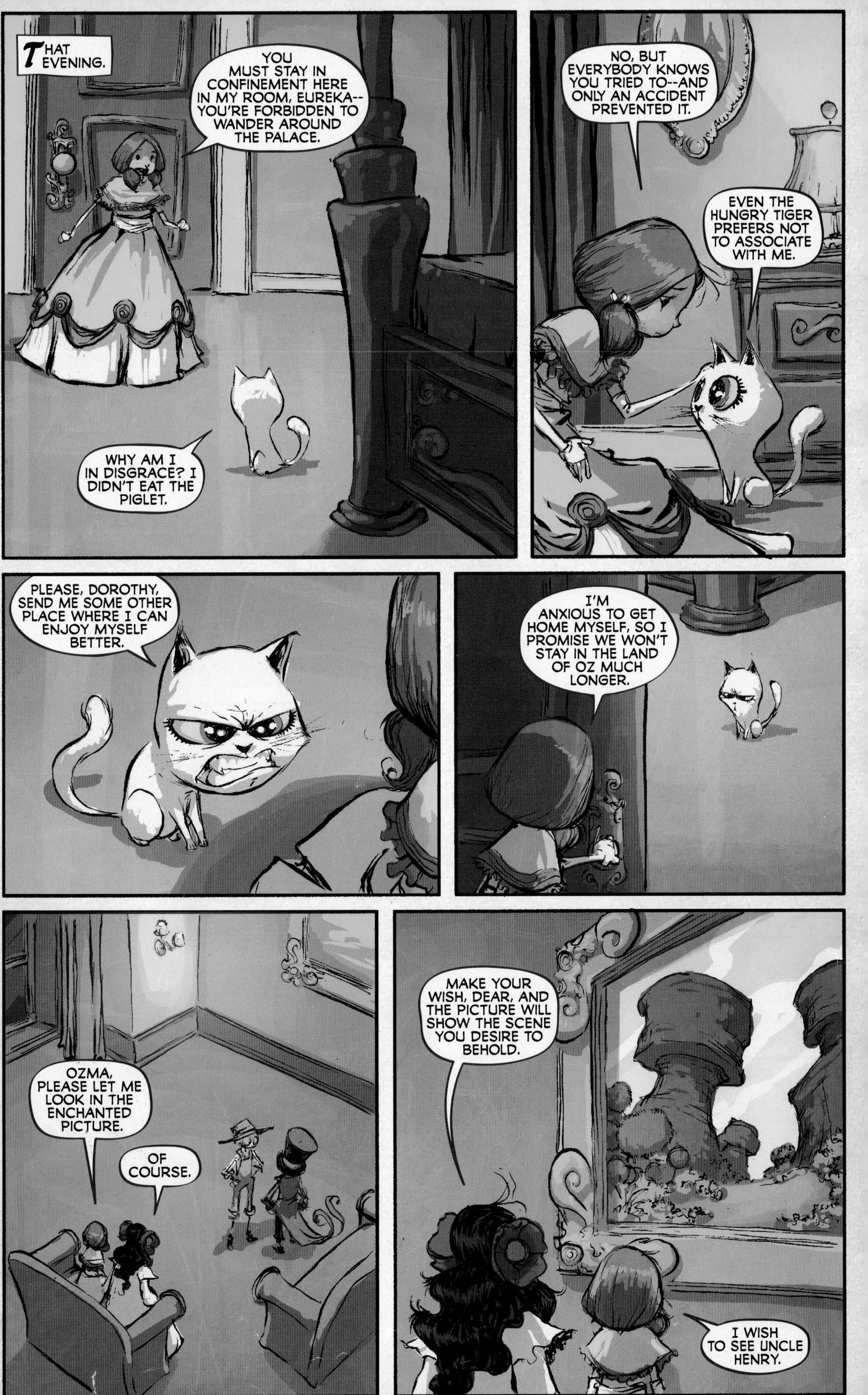
THAT EVENING.
YOU MUST STAY IN CONFINEMENT HERE IN MY ROOM, EUREKA-- YOU'RE FORBIDDEN TO WANDER AROUND THE PALACE.
WHY AM I IN DISGRACE? I DIDN'T EAT THE PIGLET.
NO, BUT EVERYBODY KNOWS YOU TRIED TO--AND ONLY AN ACCIDENT PREVENTED IT.
EVEN THE HUNGRY TIGER PREFERS NOT TO ASSOCIATE WITH ME.
PLEASE, DOROTHY, SEND ME SOME OTHER PLACE WHERE I CAN ENJOY MYSELF BETTER.
I'M ANXIOUS TO GET HOME MYSELF, SO I PROMISE WE WON'T STAY IN THE LAND OF OZ MUCH LONGER.
OZMA, PLEASE LET ME LOOK IN THE ENCHANTED PICTURE.
OF COURSE.
MAKE YOUR WISH, DEAR, AND THE PICTURE WILL SHOW THE SCENE YOU DESIRE TO BEHOLD.
I WISH TO SEE UNCLE HENRY.

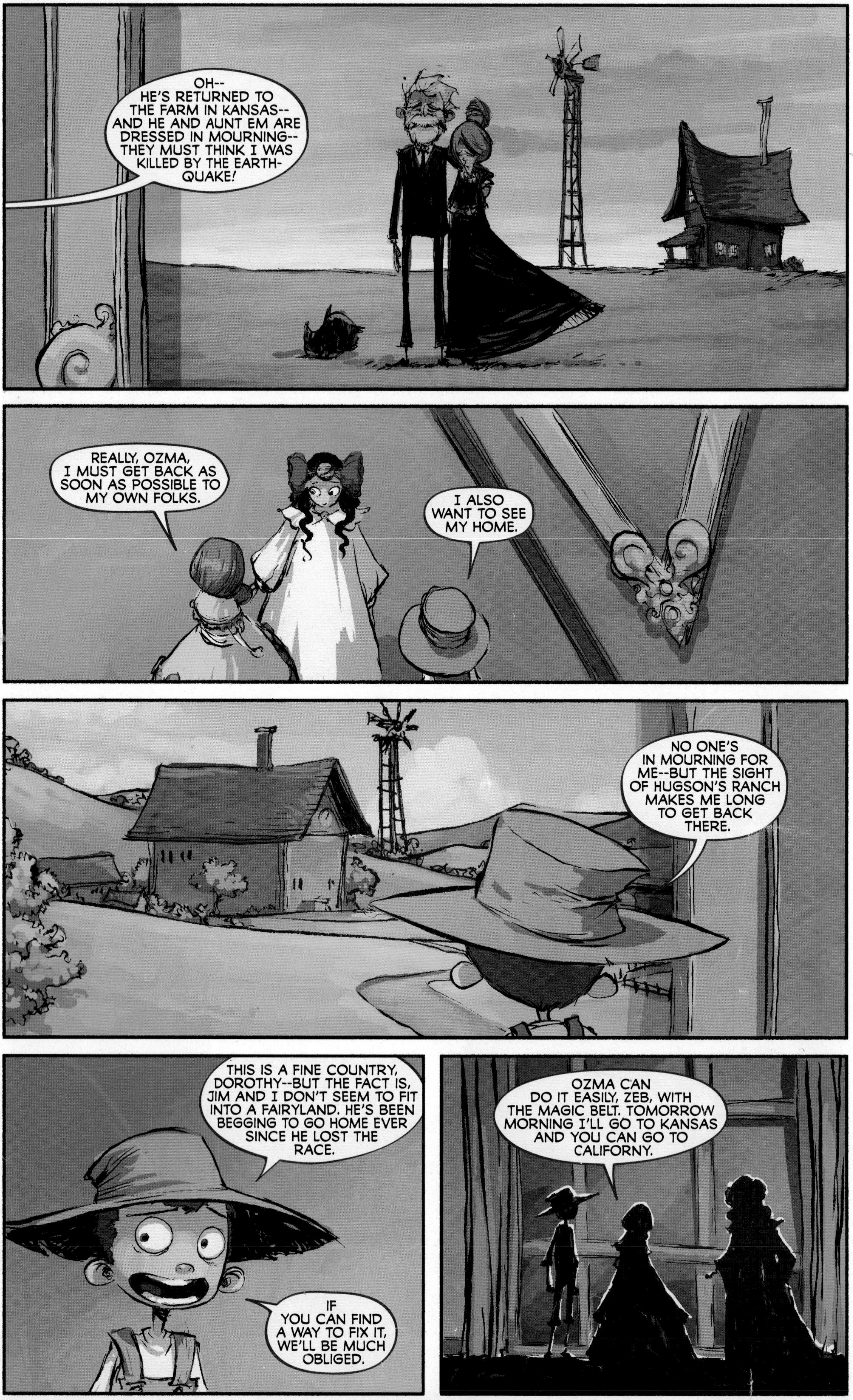
OH-- HE'S RETURNED TO THE FARM IN KANSAS-- AND HE AND AUNT EM ARE DRESSED IN MOURNING-- THEY MUST THINK I WAS KILLED BY THE EARTH-QUAKE!
REALLY, OZMA, I MUST GET BACK AS SOON AS POSSIBLE TO MY OWN FOLKS.
I ALSO WANT TO SEE MY HOME.
NO ONE'S IN MOURNING FOR ME--BUT THE SIGHT OF HUGSON'S RANCH MAKES ME LONG TO GET BACK THERE.
THIS IS A FINE COUNTRY, DOROTHY--BUT THE FACT IS, JIM AND I DON'T SEEM TO FIT INTO A FAIRYLAND. HE'S BEEN BEGGING TO GO HOME EVER SINCE HE LOST THE RACE.
IF YOU CAN FIND A WAY TO FIX IT, WE'LL BE MUCH OBLIGED.
OZMA CAN DO IT EASILY, ZEB, WITH THE MAGIC BELT. TOMORROW MORNING I'LL GO TO KANSAS AND YOU CAN GO TO CALIFORNY.

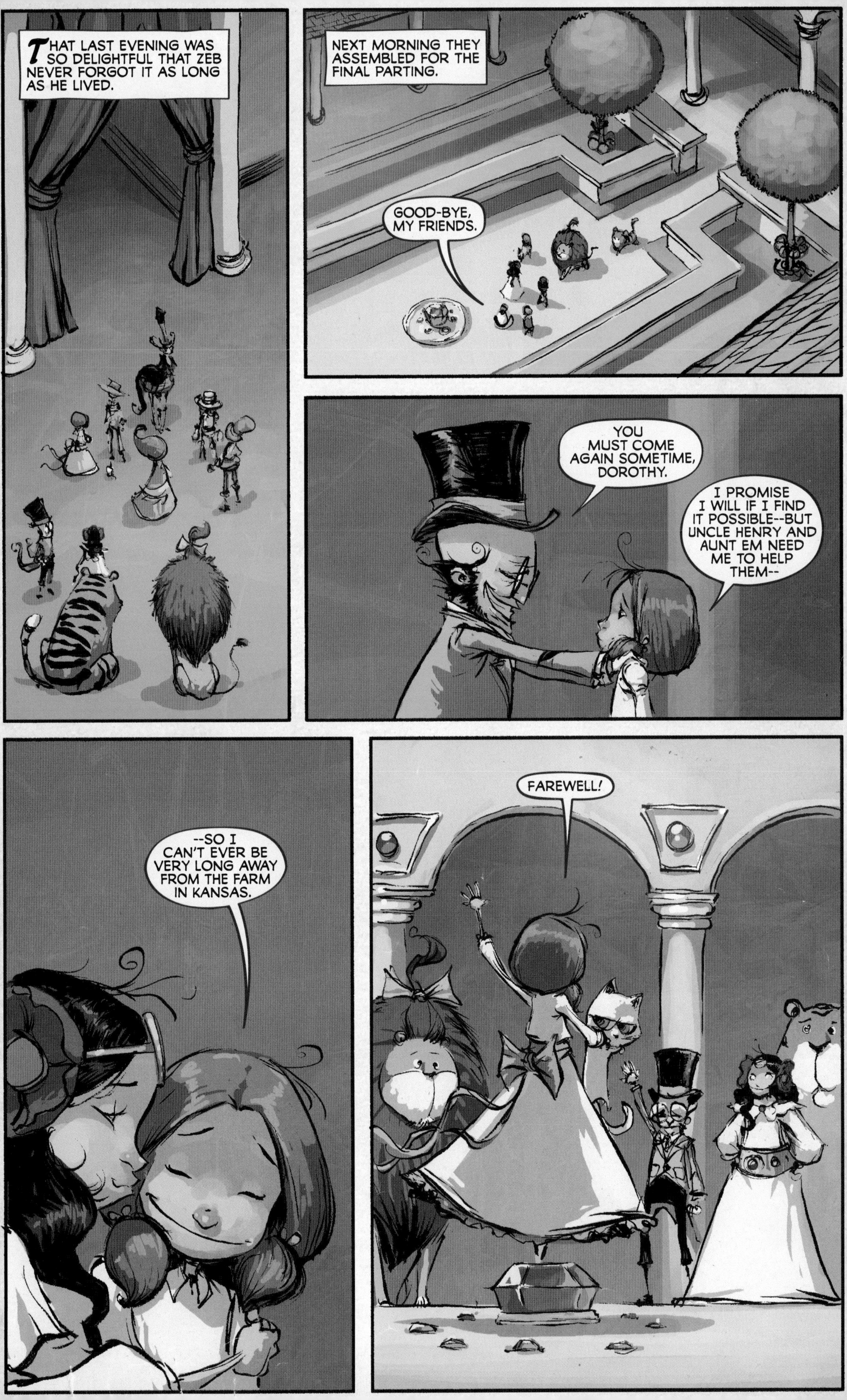
THAT LAST EVENING WAS SO DELIGHTFUL THAT ZEB NEVER FORGOT IT AS LONG AS HE LIVED.
NEXT MORNING THEY ASSEMBLED FOR THE FINAL PARTING.
GOOD-BYE, MY FRIENDS.
YOU MUST COME AGAIN SOMETIME, DOROTHY.
I PROMISE I WILL IF I FIND IT POSSIBLE--BUT UNCLE HENRY AND AUNT EM NEED ME TO HELP THEM--
--SO I CAN'T EVER BE VERY LONG AWAY FROM THE FARM IN KANSAS.
FAREWELL!

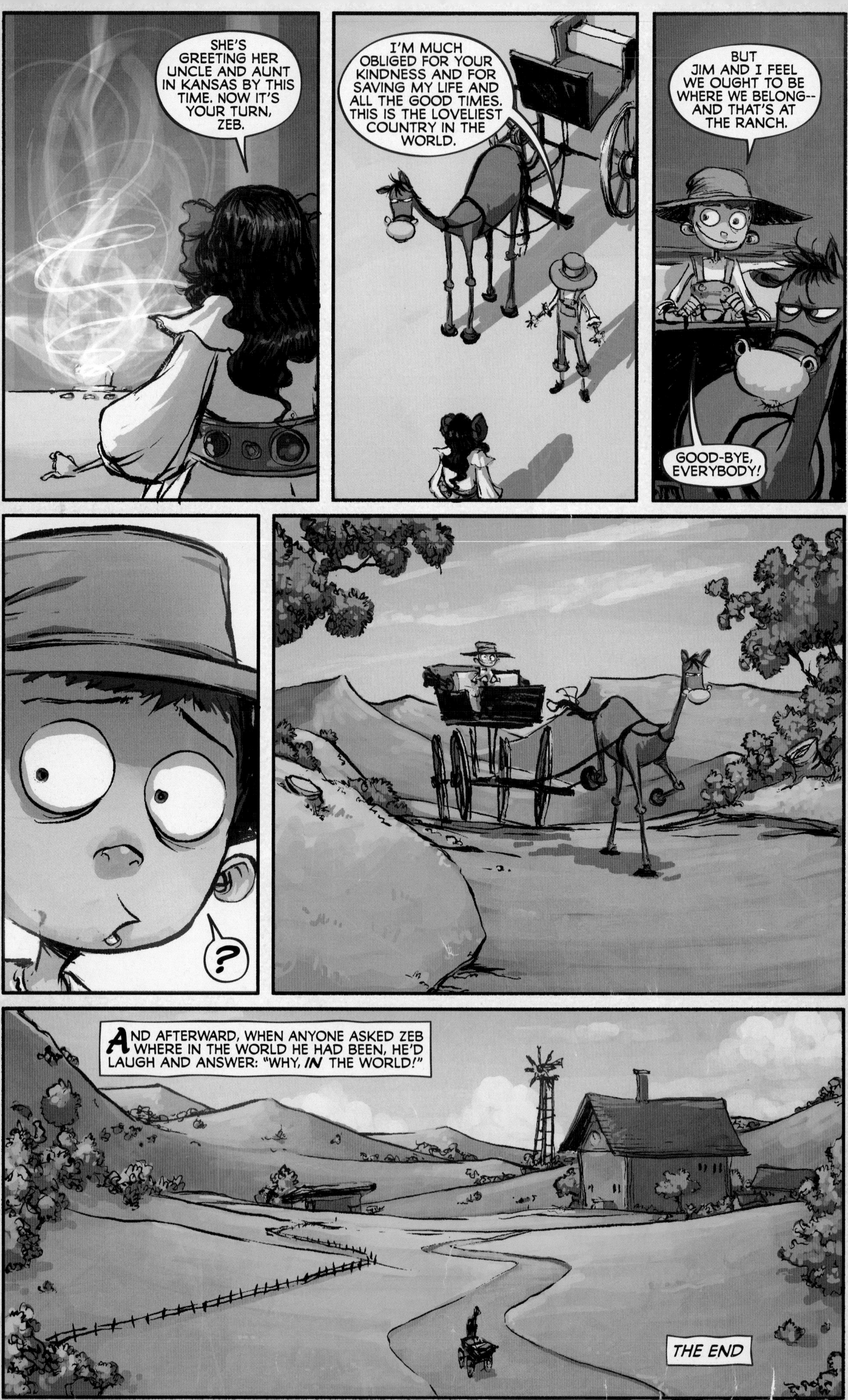
SHE'S GREETING HER UNCLE AND AUNT IN KANSAS BY THIS TIME. NOW IT'S YOUR TURN, ZEB.
I'M MUCH OBLIGED FOR YOUR KINDNESS AND FOR SAVING MY LIFE AND ALL THE GOOD TIMES. THIS IS THE LOVELIEST COUNTRY IN THE WORLD.
BUT JIM AND I FEEL WE OUGHT TO BE WHERE WE BELONG-- AND THAT'S AT THE RANCH.
GOOD-BYE, EVERYBODY!
?
AND AFTERWARD, WHEN ANYONE ASKED ZEB WHERE IN THE WORLD HE HAD BEEN, HE'D LAUGH AND ANSWER: "WHY, *IN* THE WORLD!"
THE END

THE STORY CONTINUES IN...

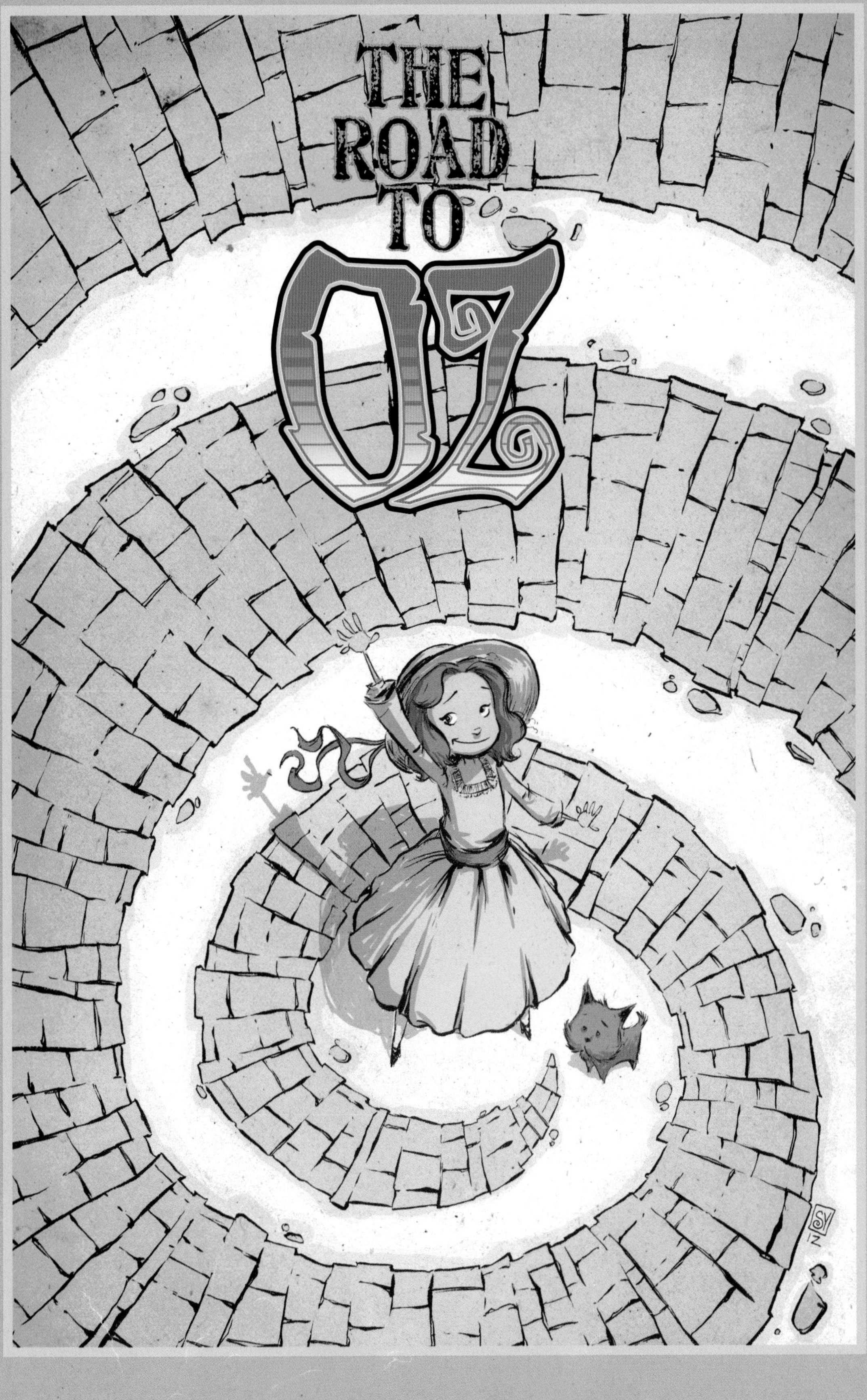
THE ROAD TO OZ

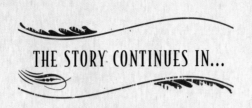

ONE

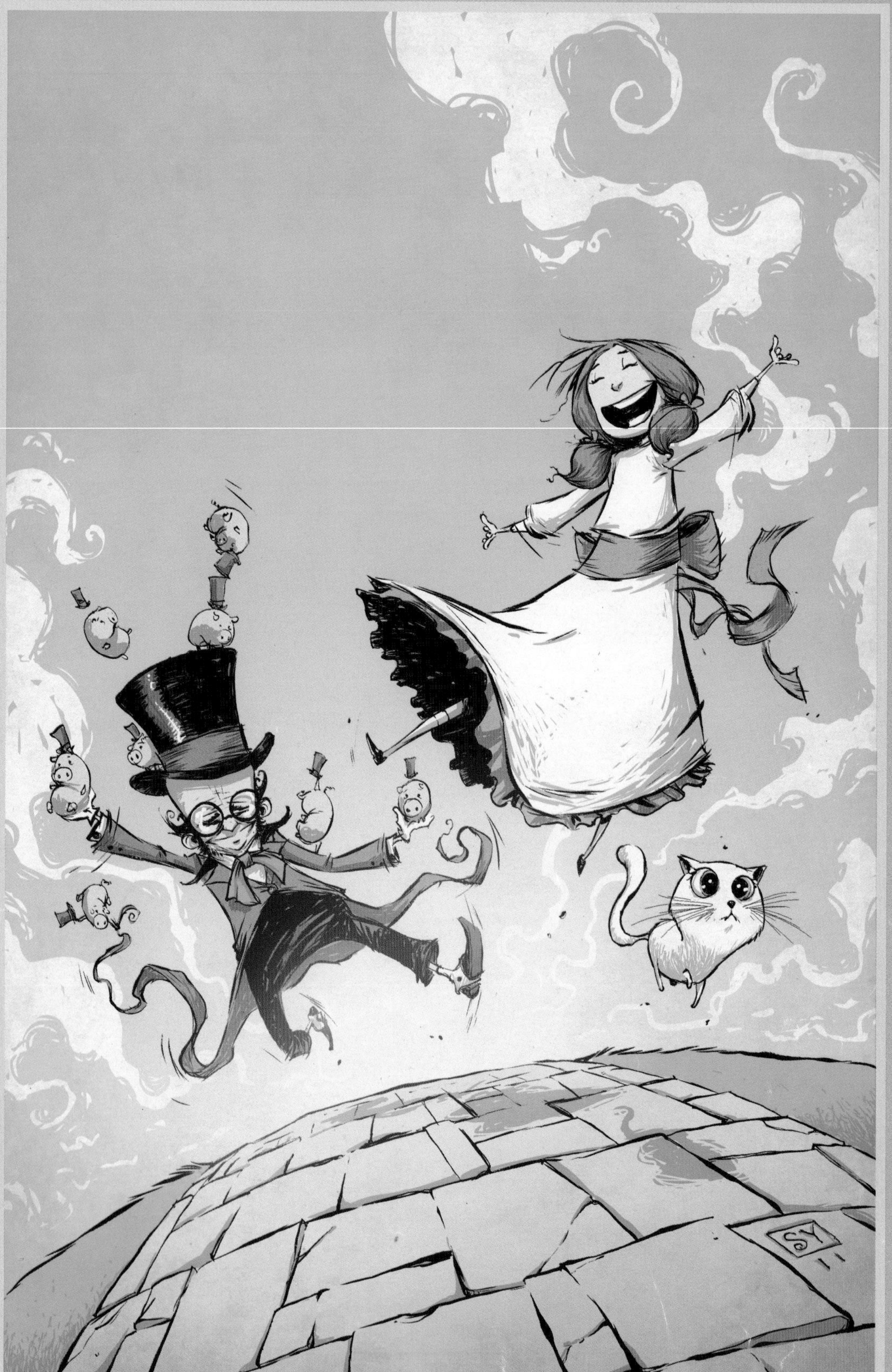
SY

ONE

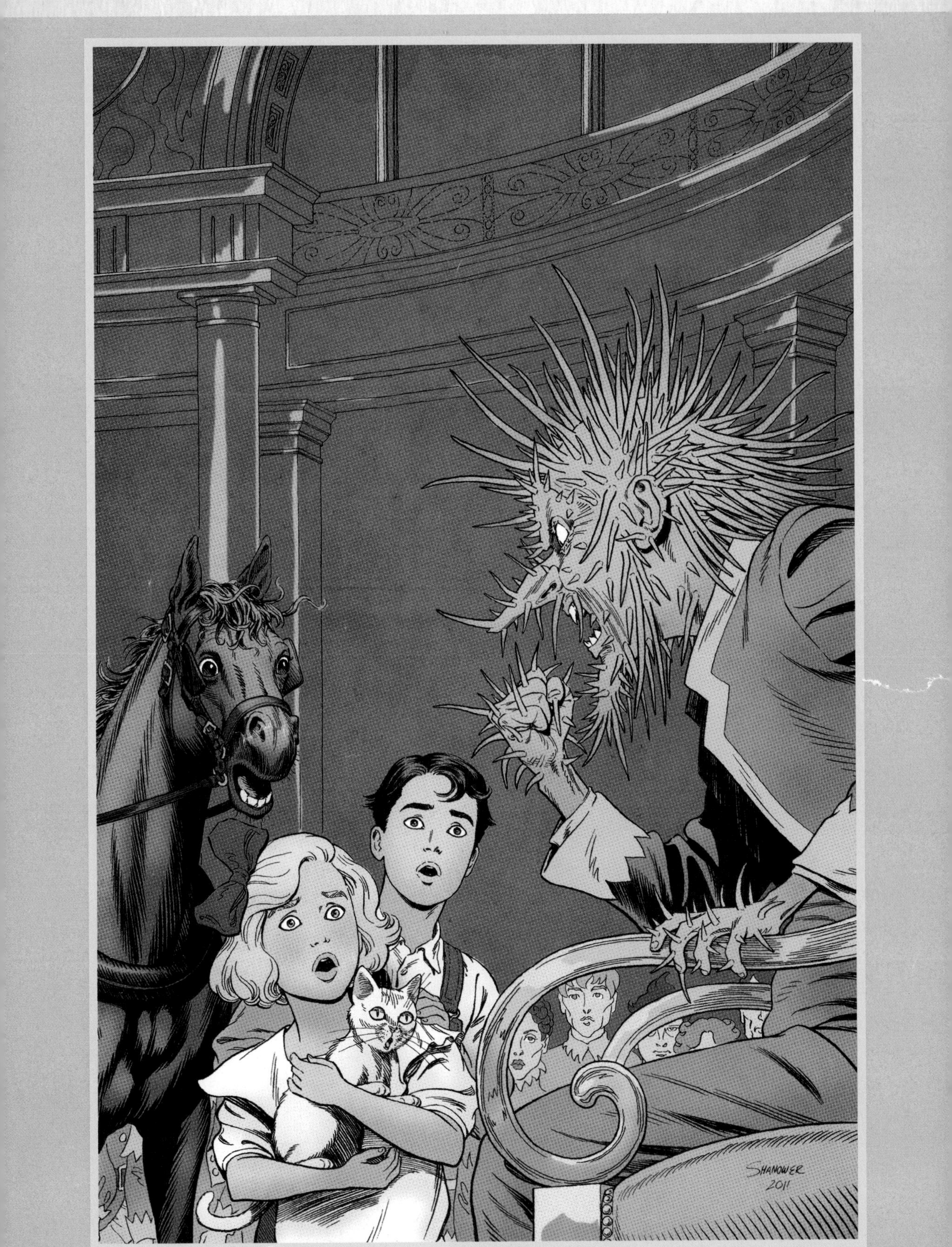
SHANOWER
2011

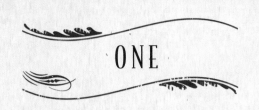

VARIANT COVER BY ERIC SHANOWER

ONE

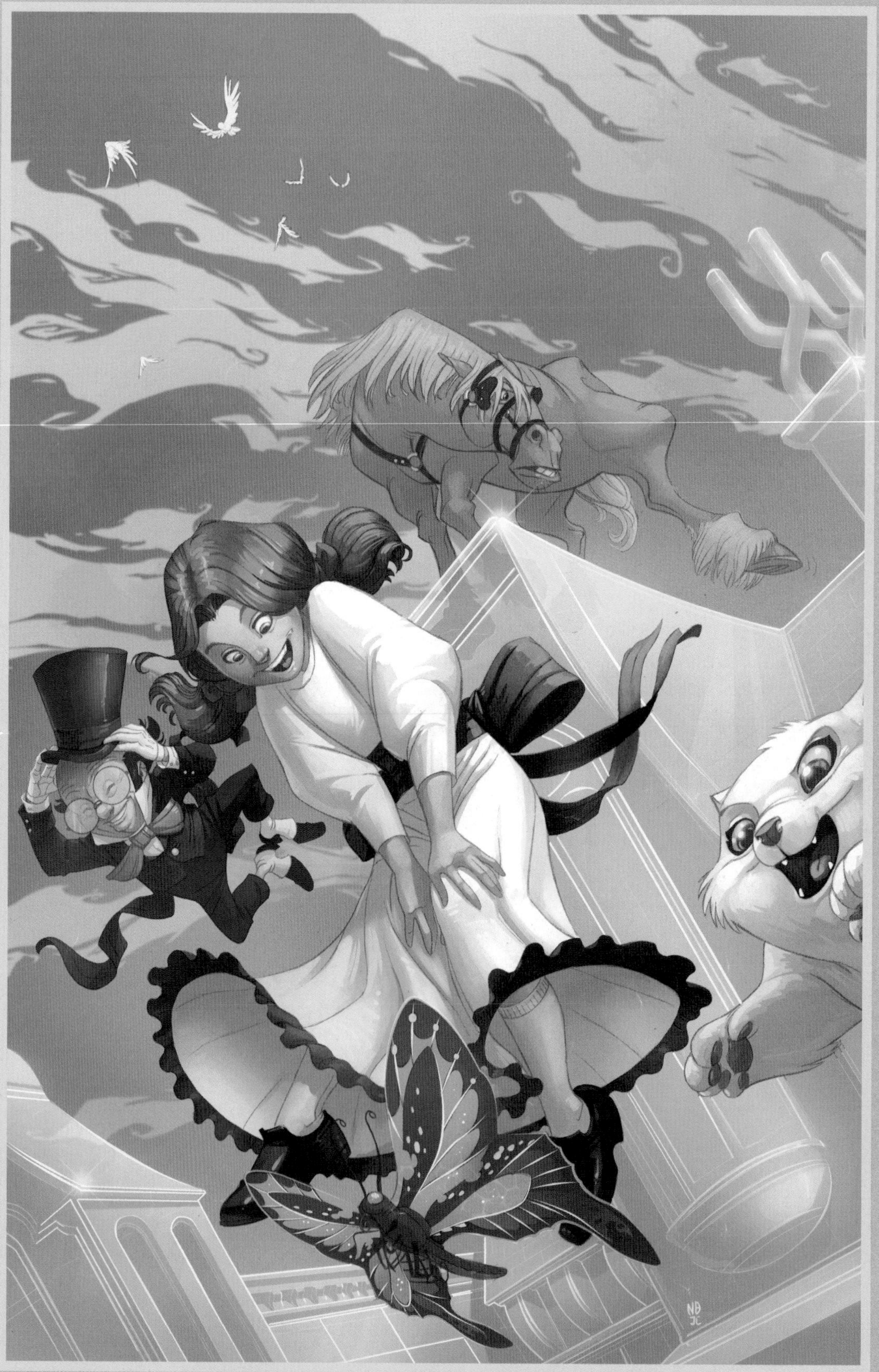

Variant Cover by Nick Bradshaw

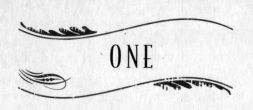

TWO

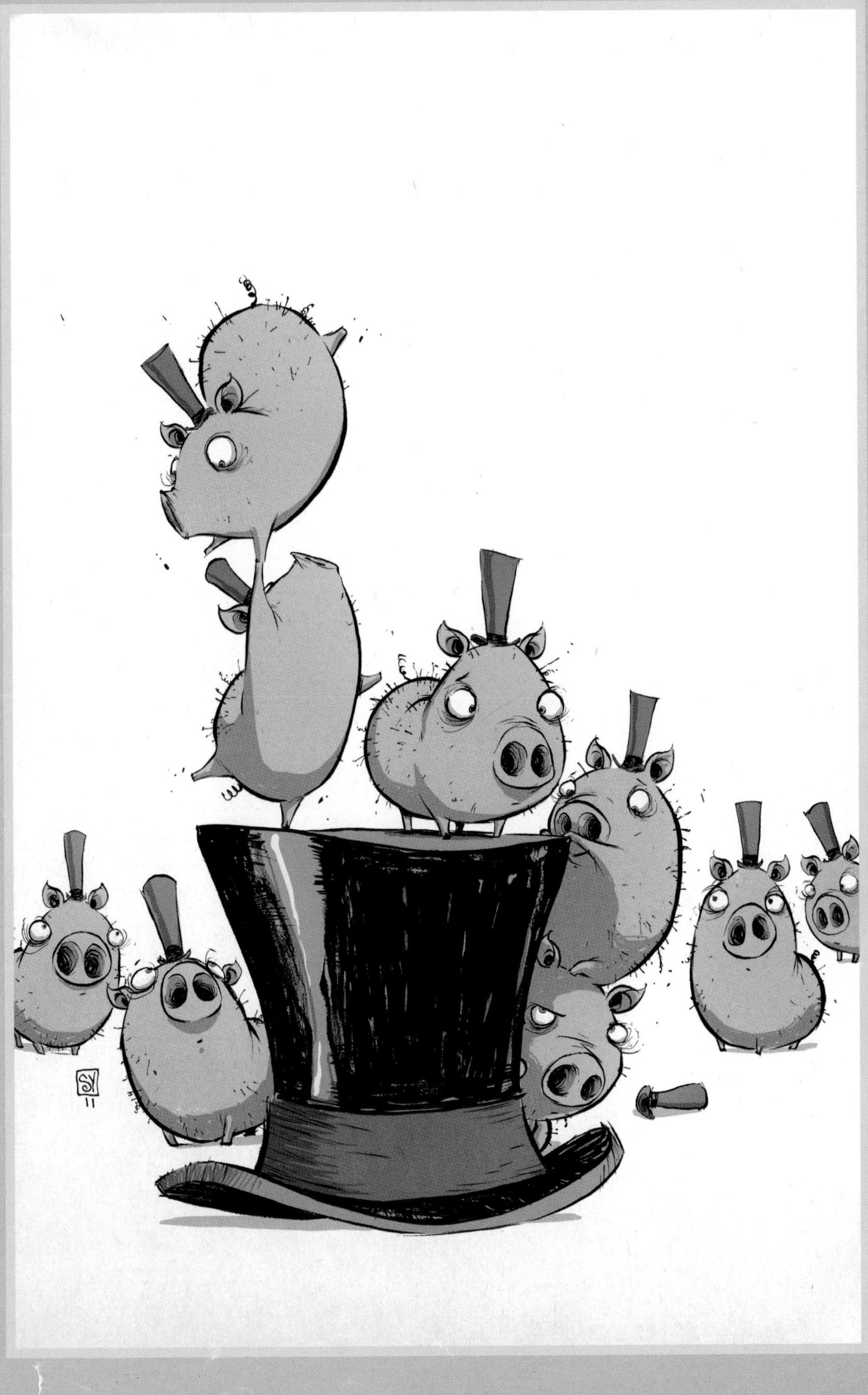

THREE

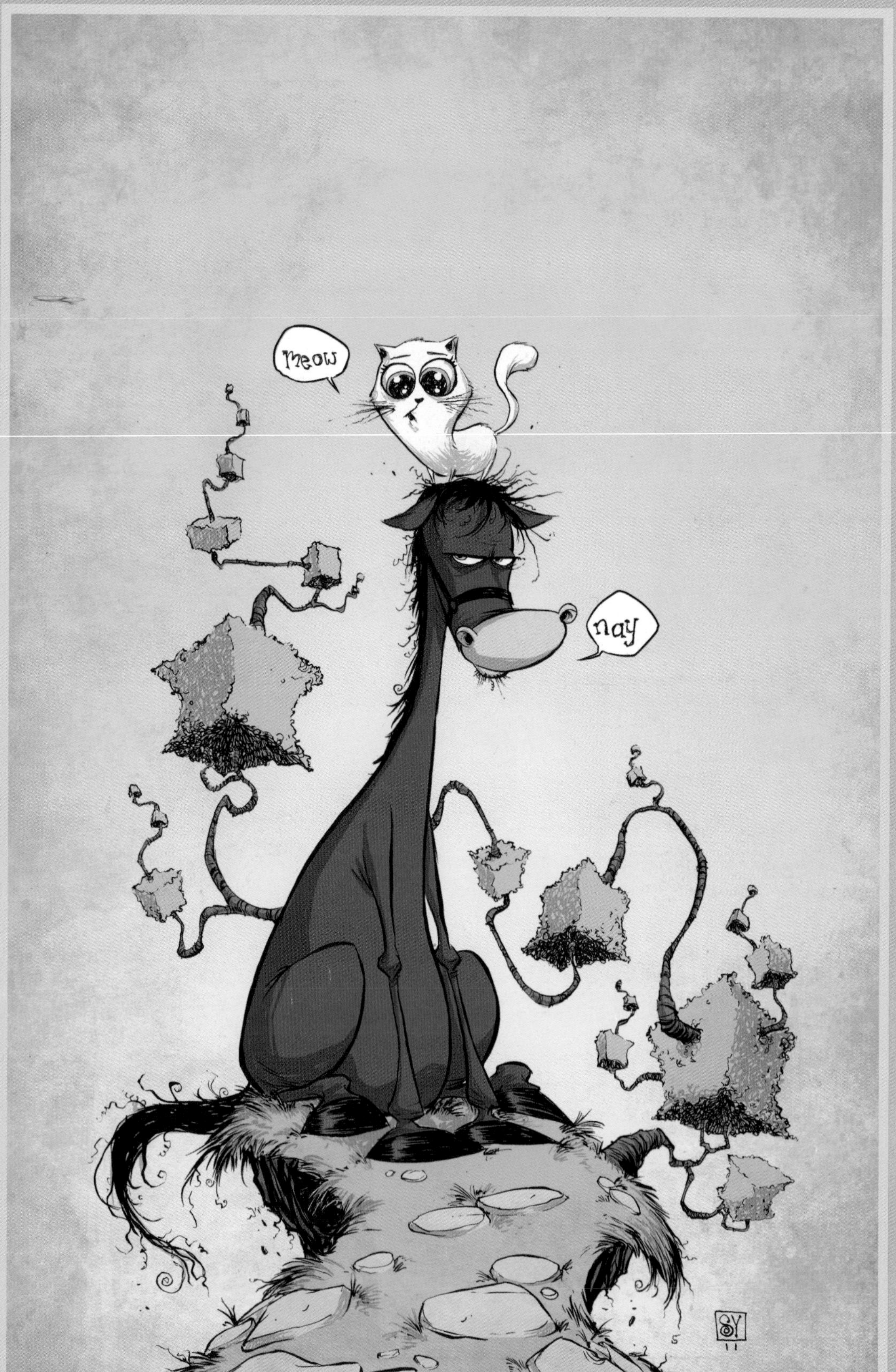
meow
nay

FOUR

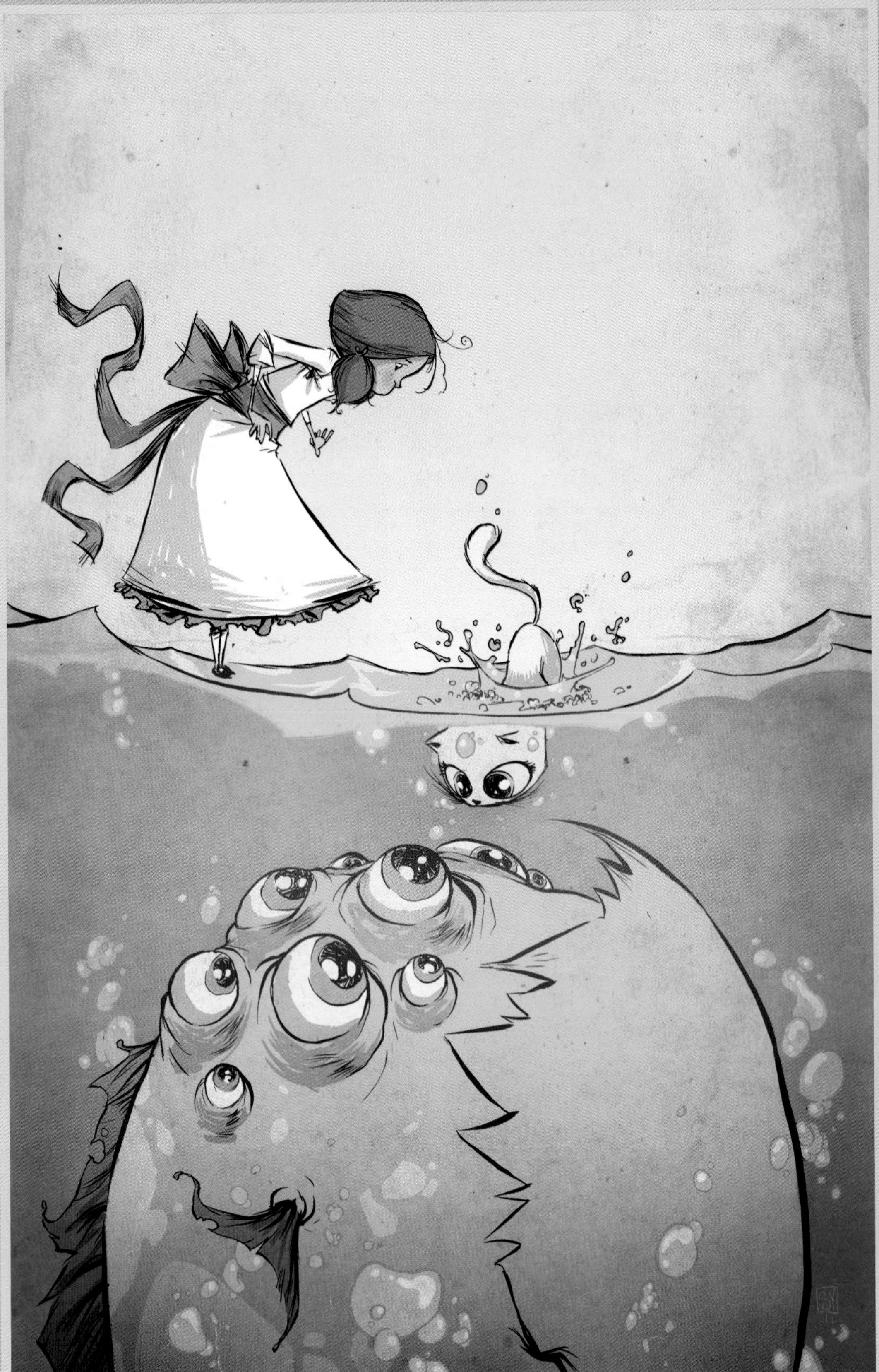

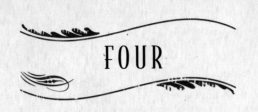

FIVE

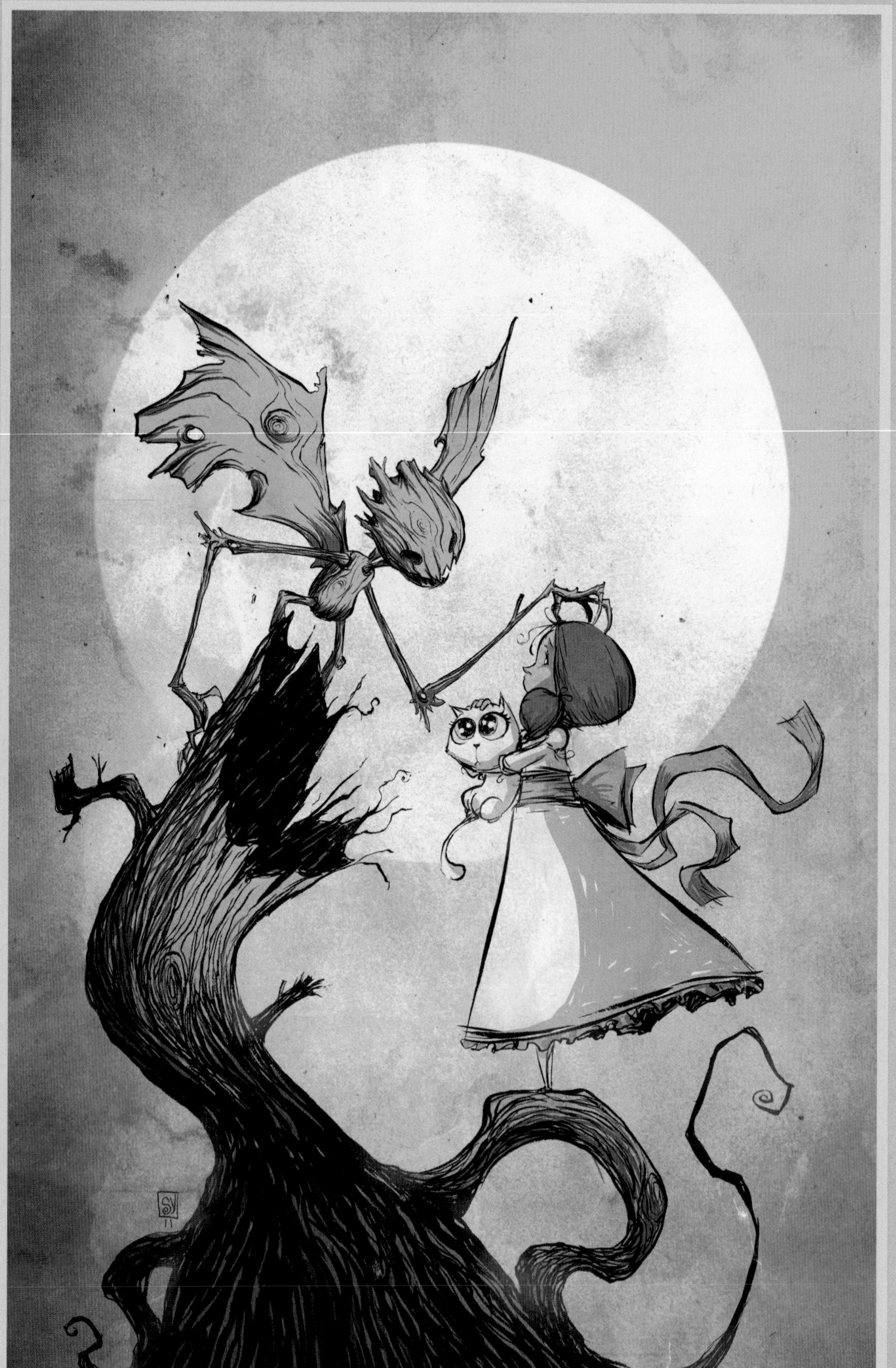

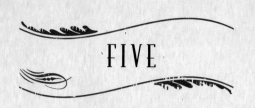

SIX

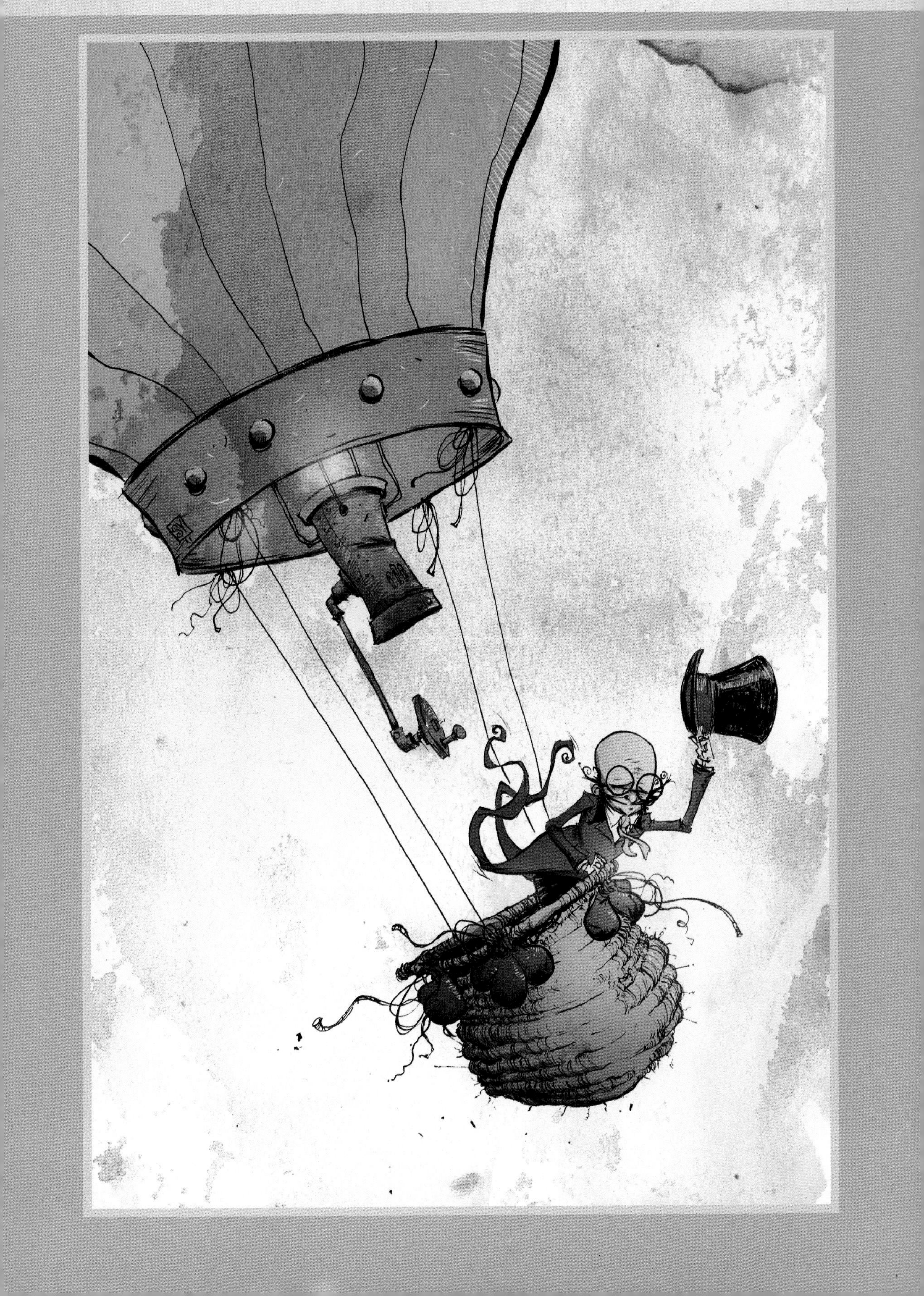

SEVEN

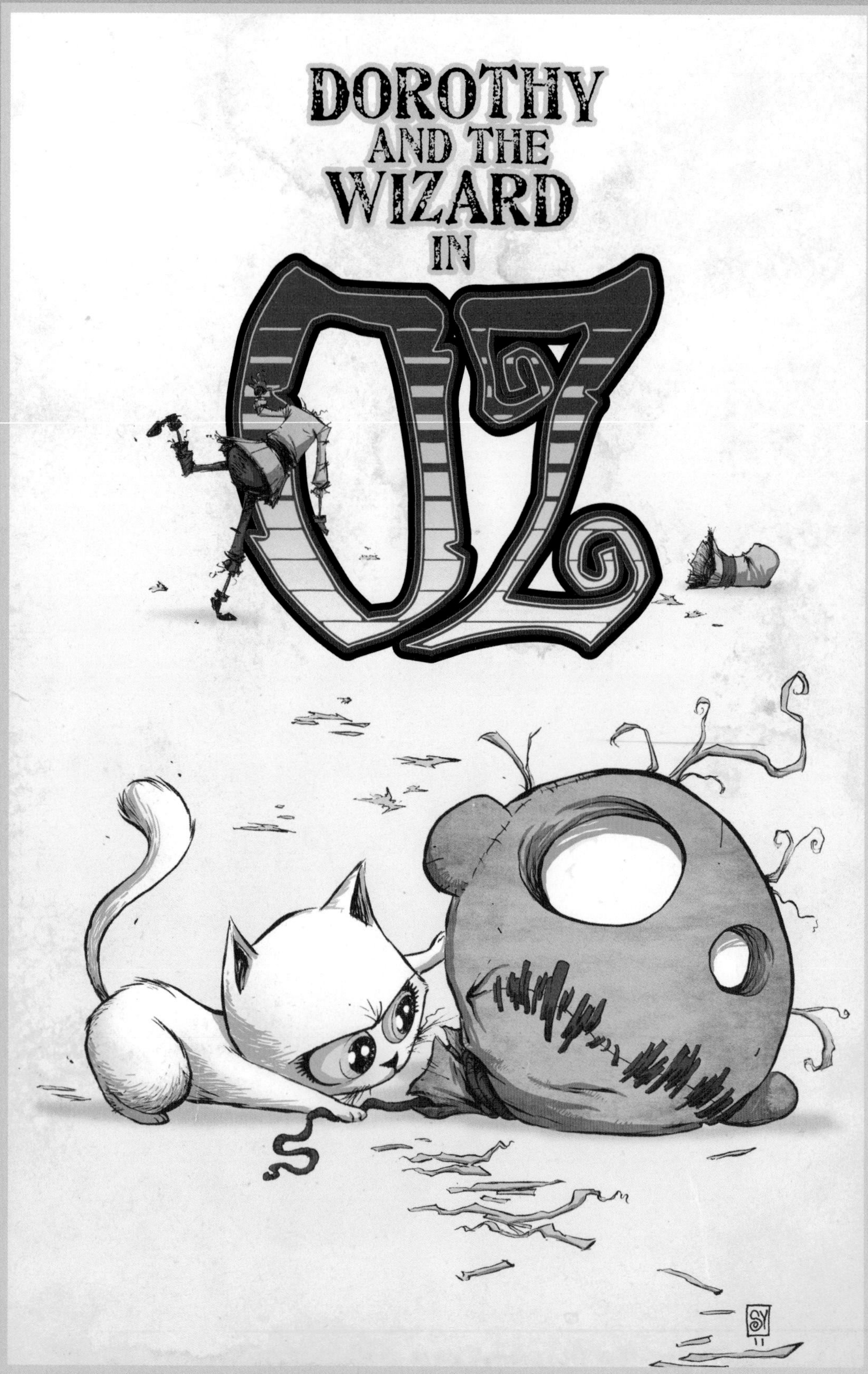
DOROTHY
AND THE
WIZARD
IN
OZ

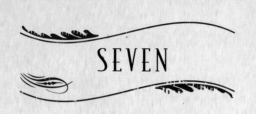

EIGHT

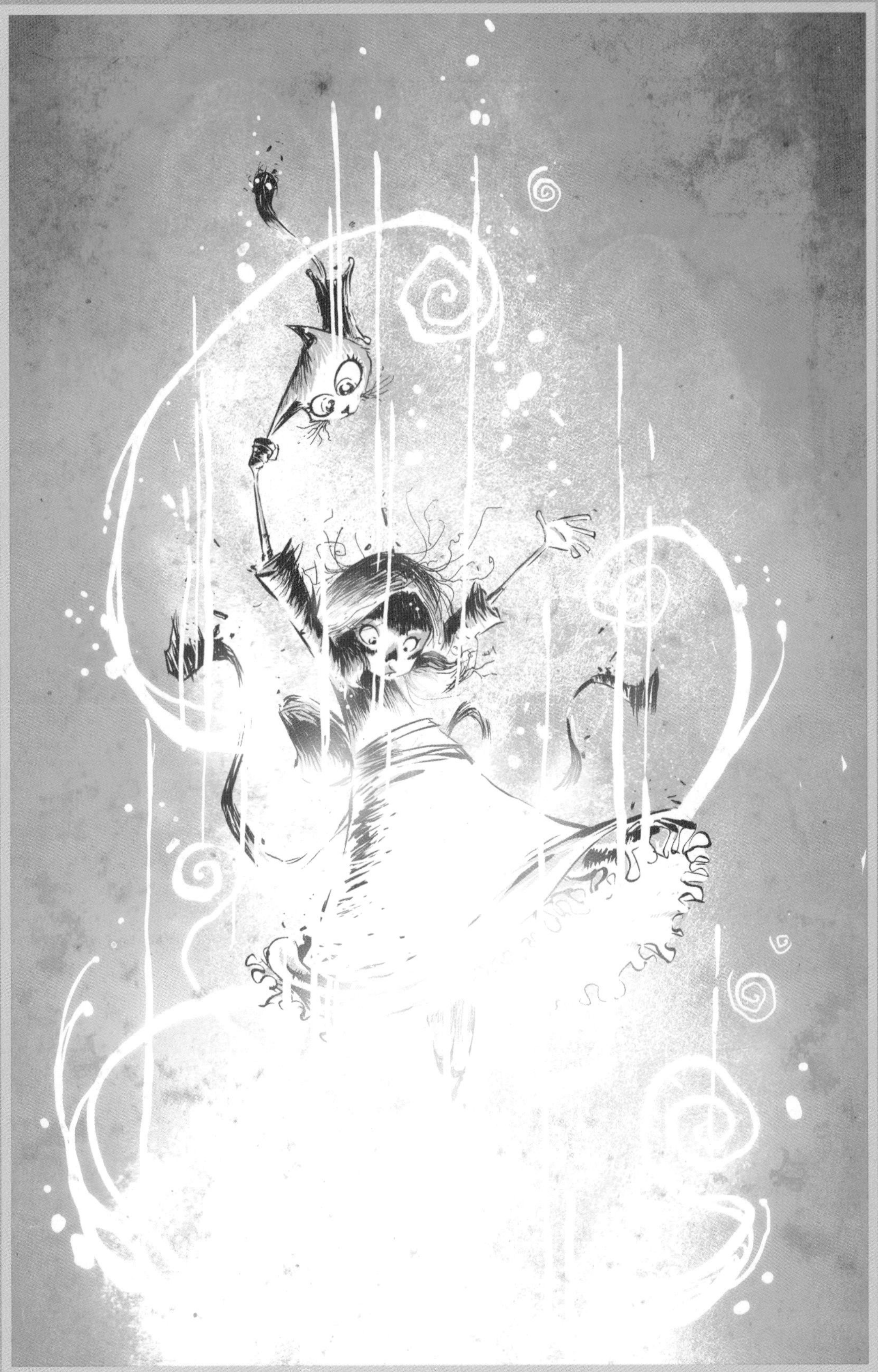

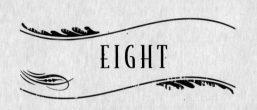

DOROTHY AND ZEB

Gargoyle and Braided Man

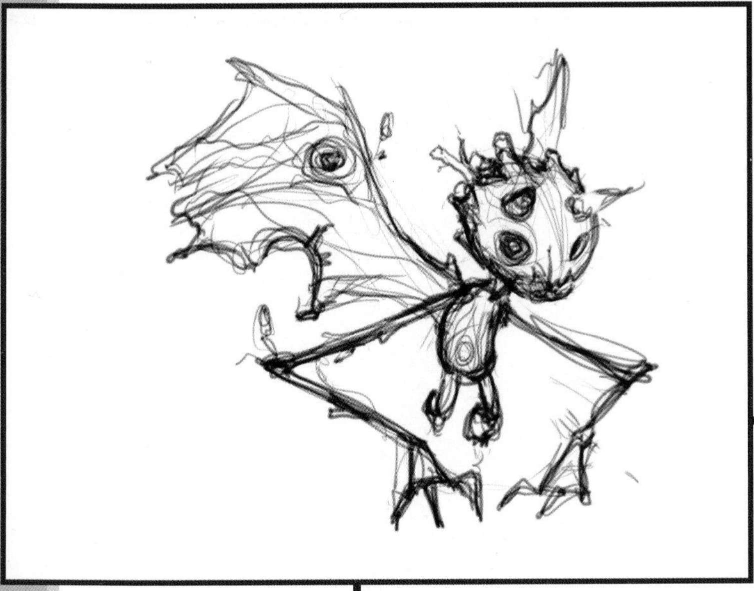

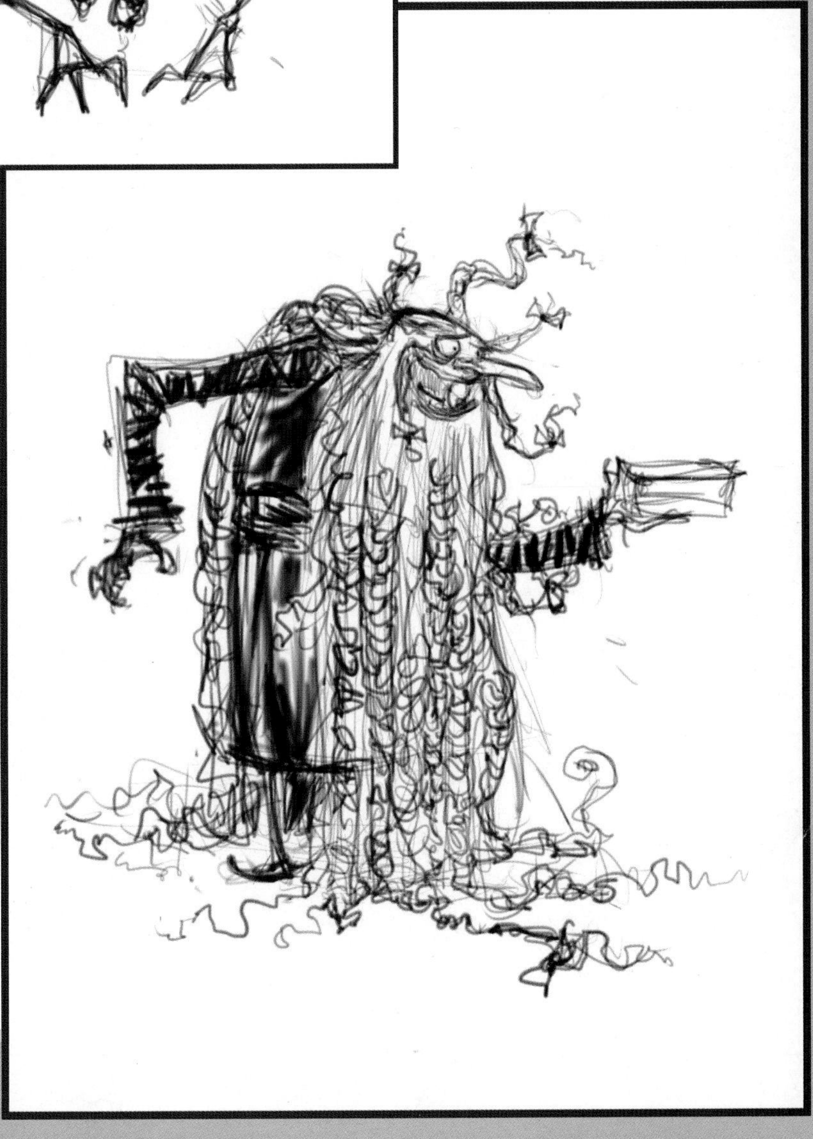